CURRENT CONTROVERSIES ON FAMILY VIOLENCE

CURRENT
CONTROVERSIES
ON
FAMILY
VIOLENCE

RICHARD J. GELLES
DONILEEN R. LOSEKE

editors

HQ
809.3
.U5
C87
1993

SAGE Publications
International Educational and Professional Publisher
Newbury Park   London   New Delhi

For information address:

SAGE Publications, Inc.
2455 Teller Road
Newbury Park, California 91320

SAGE Publications Ltd.
6 Bonhill Street
London EC2A 4PU
United Kingdom

SAGE Publications India Pvt. Ltd.
M-32 Market
Greater Kailash I
New Delhi 110 048 India

Printed in the United States of America

Library of Congress Cataloging-in-Publication Data

Main entry under title:

Current controversies on family violence / edited by Richard J.
Gelles, Donileen R. Loseke.
    p. cm.
Includes bibliographical references and index.
ISBN 0-8039-4673-2. — ISBN 0-8039-4674-0 (pbk.)
    1. Family violence—United States. 2. Victims of family violence—
United States. 3. Family violence—United States—Prevention.
I. Gelles, Richard J. II. Loseke, Donileen R., 1947–
HQ809.3.U5C87 1993
362.82′92—dc20   93-28925

        95 96 97 10 9 8 7 6 5 4

Sage Production Editor: Astrid Virding

Contents

Introduction
Examining and Evaluating Controversies on Family Violence

A traditional American cautionary saying advises against "hanging out your dirty laundry for all the neighbors to see." In use, such a folk saying promotes the value of secrecy in maintaining a public image of respectability—don't show or tell others anything that would be detrimental to the image you want to advance. In the not-so-distant past, family violence, in its many forms, was considered dirty laundry, best kept out of sight in order to maintain the idealized image of happy family life. From the 1960s to the 1990s, however, there has been much social change. The various forms of violence we now call child abuse, wife abuse, spouse abuse, elder abuse, and so on have been publicly redefined. Although such behaviors still are forms of dirty laundry, secrets to be kept in all too many American homes, at least they are publicly defined as behaviors that need to be brought into the bright light of public scrutiny.

Thirty years ago there was not enough research to generate controversies on family violence. Indeed, in those days the public did not believe that such behaviors existed in a magnitude to warrant attention, or believed that such behaviors were found only in already stigmatized segments of the population (such as in poor and/or minority families or among the mentally ill), or believed that such behaviors were perhaps unfortunate but nonetheless a "normal" and "legitimate" part of family life. Persons who were victims of family violence in the past had no choice but to keep their experiences to themselves. They could not call for help because there was little help available.

Predictably, social change has been uneven. Shelters for battered women are called "lifesaving resources" by some Americans and "homes for runaway wives" by others. Child abuse intervention is applauded by some even as it is criticized by others as an interference in parental power. Some victims now seek help and find sensitive social service providers and specific services, whereas other victims and social service providers believe experiences with family violence are best "swept under the carpet," because they are "private family matters." Complexity and confusion surround this topic and the public response to it. This ambivalence is predictable, because family violence challenges deeply held cultural ideals. In a society such as ours, where homes and families are often idealized as havens and people protecting us from the heartless world of dangerous strangers, how can it be that more people are injured by loved ones than by strangers? How can we make sense of the fact that for women and children their homes are more dangerous than public places?

The controversies discussed in this volume represent a mere sampling of unresolved issues surrounding the meanings, definitions, measurement, causes, consequences, and social interventions of this form of dirty laundry called *family violence*. What kind of a problem is this violence? What causes it? What are its consequences? Should the public intervene at all? If the public should intervene, how should this be done?

"Issues in Conceptualization" is Part I of this volume because these theoretical disagreements lead to other controversies about causes and social intervention. In defining the types of problems we face, theoretical frameworks define where we should look if we want to make sense of violence, and hence where we should intervene if we want to stop it. The psychological, sociological, and feminist frameworks are competing ways to conceptualize the behaviors involved in family violence; each viewpoint provides a way to place the phenomenon of violence in a larger frame of meaning.

Part II, "Issues in Definition and Measurement," examines the importance of how we define and measure our topic of interest. Answers to questions about whether or not physical assaults by women are a serious social problem, whether or not date rape is an exaggerated social problem, and whether or not abused women suffer from a "battered woman's syndrome" depend on conceptualization, definition, and measurement.

Questions about theoretical and methodological frameworks are critical because conceptualization and measurement influence everything else. Yet such questions might seem academic—if not downright esoteric—to members of the general public, who are often concerned with more practical issues. Part III, "Issues in Causes," turns to practical issues. These chapters illustrate how subtle differences in arguments can yield major differences in conclusions, and how common-sense logic can often support very different conclusions.

The final section of this volume, "Issues in Social Intervention," asks, What should the public *do* about family violence? Of course, what we should do to stop violence, to help victims, to punish or change offenders depends on how we conceptualize and define the problem, and on how we understand the causes. Yet the social world cannot wait until controversies are resolved and agreement is reached. Regardless of unresolved debates, social interventions have been designed and implemented and, not surprisingly, these interventions themselves are surrounded by controversy.

This volume is about some of the most important and most hotly debated issues surrounding family violence. Clearly, its organization differs from that of most mass-media treatments of social problems. In this world of 30-second sound bites and television talk shows, the expert of the moment often seems to hold the "simple truths." Such mass-media images of simple truths are calming, because they allow audiences to believe that there are simple solutions to complex moral, practical, and political problems. But that is the made-for-television world. When taken as a whole, the chapters in this volume reflect real life—the arguments are complex, and they contain no "simple truths."

By highlighting controversies, the chapters in this volume also challenge popularly held beliefs that a group of experts, such as experts in family violence, hold a *united vision* of "the truth." Just as idealized images of home and loved ones often stand in stark contrast to lived realities, public images of professional groups of experts as holders of singular and agreed-upon objective truths most often stand in contrast to the realities. Indeed, professional groups of any type in modern-day America are much like families, in that such groups often seek to project united images to their publics. As in the phenomena of family violence, disagreements among professionals often occur behind closed doors or in the pages of journals read only by professionals who are "family insiders." Like families in a more traditional sense, professional groups often sweep disagreements under the carpet before the public arrives. By asking contributors to focus their comments on controversies rather than on agreements, we are airing a type of professional dirty laundry shared by *all* professional groups yet rarely made publicly visible: We do not all agree.

The chapters in this volume have all been written by persons who are members of a professional group, the family of family violence experts. These chapters are the work of only a few representatives of this family, which is composed of persons who in one way or another

have taken on the tasks of thinking about, writing about, and ultimately doing something about various facets of family violence. We
are a family in the sense that we all share common values—we do not
promote the use of violence. We are a family in the sense that we share
common goals—in one way or another, we all want to change some
aspect of how the public evaluates and responds to violence. We also
are a family in the sense that we are engaged in a joint enterprise, in
which the efforts of each of us can and often do influence the work of
the others.

Yet, as with families in general, and professional groups in particular, there is much that members of this family of family violence experts
do not share or agree upon. Indeed, in this case, we do not even agree
on the parameters of this thing we try to study or change. This book,
for example, has *family* in its title, but some persons argue that drawing
attention to the scene of the family is misleading, and that our correct
focus should be larger—violence among *intimates*. Still others argue
that attention to all intimate violence is wrongheaded and that we
should narrow our attention to the typical *victims* of violence—
battered women, abused children, and abused elderly. These are major
differences among us—do we focus on the scene of the family, on
intimate relationships in general, or on the victims of violence in
particular? We do not agree. We do not agree on how to define this
thing, how to measure it, how to think about the causes; we do not
agree on what should be done about it.

Regardless of the public image, professional groups of all kinds are
characterized by controversy. Indeed, controversy is *necessary*, because
knowledge is advanced through controversy: Controversy leads to
debate, debate stirs reflection, reflection leads to research, and research
leads to refinement of ideas. If internal controversy is a characteristic
of a productive professional family, then the family of family violence
experts is healthy indeed. Such controversy is a part of all professional
groups and, in this case, it is particularly to be expected, for two
reasons. First and most simply, the public history of family violence—
or whatever it is to be called—is short. Only three decades have passed
since child abuse first received particular attention; it has been only
during the past two decades that wife abuse has been a specific topic
of concern; the phenomenon of date rape has only recently entered
public consciousness; and so on. To conceptualize and make sense of
any human social phenomenon is difficult; something as complex as
family violence cannot be understood, much less resolved, in the short
span of a few decades. Regrettably, it is only in fiction that complex
human troubles are easily and quickly fixed.

Second, the complexity of this violence lends itself to myriad and deeply competing conceptualizations, so, not surprisingly, it has drawn the attention of persons who approach our work from very different perspectives with different goals. Hence the family of violence experts is a family of adoptees: Persons in this field might focus on the same—or similar—topics, but we come from many distinct and often competing lineages. Some of the authors of these chapters are lawyers; others are physicians, sociologists, psychologists, and social welfare practitioners. Some of the authors identify themselves primarily as basic researchers, whereas others identify as clinicians and still others see themselves primarily as social advocates. Thus we do not share a theoretical perspective, a common vocabulary of discourse, or one specific social agenda.

The short history of family violence as a public problem, coupled with the multiple perspectives of family violence experts, at least partially accounts for the presence of controversies. Yet in the case of controversies surrounding family violence, four additional characteristics of the topic lead to disagreements that are heated, long-lasting, and resistant to resolution. First, family violence—however it is defined—is first and foremost a topic of *practical* interest. Debates among violence experts do not, cannot, and should not disguise the fact that the topic at hand is immediate and critical; it is about real people who experience violence and it is about people who do violence to others. Because the consequences of violence are devastating, our internal debates—our "family bickering"—are not about issues of interest only to professional insiders. Debates about immediate and practical concerns are more heated than controversies over obscure issues having little relevance in the real world. Because our topic is immediate, practical, and urgent, so too are our debates and disagreements.

Second, and related to the practical nature of our concern, family violence is of *political* concern. Members of the family of family violence experts are powerful in various ways because each can influence what should be done; practical consequences are associated with "winning" debates. Individually, money for research and/or social service jobs might become available, social prestige can follow. But there are far larger issues than the shaping of individual careers. When one side of a controversy "wins," even if only momentarily, social policies can be designed, public attitudes can be shaped, and these influence the real world. Although this volume contains a special section on "social intervention," all controversies on family violence have implications for practical action: Will interventions focus on changing persons or on changing social situations? What particular social conditions should be targeted for change? What type of change is needed? Where will social service providers look in the lives of their individual clients for causes and hence resolutions of violence? When controversies are political they are about how the social world will be organized and changed. Controversies and disagreements increase in intensity as the practical—and, hence, political—stakes become higher.

Third, controversies become passionate when the issues at hand cannot be resolved solely by reason and logic. Although only sometimes explicit, views on *morality* underlie all definitions and measurements of family violence. Whether explicit or implicit, each definition and argument involves moral evaluations: What behaviors are acceptable or at least tolerable? What behaviors are wrong? What values should be preserved? Whether a person is an expert or not, how he or she "thinks" about this violence is related to how he or she evaluates it morally. When controversies have moral dimensions, they are emotionally charged.

Finally, but nonetheless critical, controversies in this field can be volatile because of the strong *feelings* associated with this topic. Although the public image of professionals is one of persons who are immune to human feeling, this does not describe the lived realities of professional work in general, and it certainly does not adequately describe the work of family violence experts in particular. Many persons in the family of family violence experts have been exposed repeatedly to the graphic details of cases of physical, sexual, and emotional abuse; many have witnessed the unintended negative consequences of well-intentioned social policies. Such practical experiences are associated with human feelings such as sadness, rage, anger, and frustration. How we examine "intellectual" issues can be highly charged and energized by our emotional responses.

In the case of the family of family violence experts, the newness and complexity of our topic, our divergent perspectives and agendas, the high practical and political consequences of what we say, the moral dimension of our work, and the inextricable combination of rationality and passion associated with our concerns have combined to yield extreme controversy. At times, debates about theories, logic, methods, and conclusions have been transformed into questions about the basic moral character of those holding opposing views; there have been recurring allegations that various sets of family members consciously have attempted to stop others from advancing opposing views by maliciously blocking research opportunities, by threats of career destruction, or even by threats of death. Although professional conferences are a form of "family reunion," uniting members who live far apart and encouraging conversation, conference organizers in this professional group often restrict invitations to a subset of family members known to share perspectives. But exclusion is not only imposed from without—even if invited, some members of this group refuse to be in the same rooms with or even to attend the same conferences as others. Indeed, in the process of putting together this volume we found that not all persons in the family would allow their writing to be contained in the same book; we found that some persons believe that any effort to create a turf for debate is condemned to failure, and that debate in and of itself is contaminating, dangerous, and thus should be avoided. Hence, although we have conjured the image of the professional group of family violence experts as similar to a family, it is clear that some members of this family would be quick to disavow their membership. As in the families we study, practical experiences and perceptions have led us to define others in the family as threatening, if not downright dangerous.

Just as too much controversy among members in traditional families leads to problems, too much controversy in a professional family leads to divisions and divisiveness. Too much controversy in the family of family violence experts has, at times, led to professional family dysfunction, with enemies rather than colleagues, opposition rather than cooperation, sabotage rather than assistance, silence rather than communication.

To be absolutely clear, this dysfunctional family analogy aptly describes the internal workings of many (if not all) professional groups. Much like the public's idealized image of families as places of solidarity and goodwill, the image of professional groups as united can often stand in stark contrast with the realities of those groups. The family of family violence experts is not unique in this regard. That is, it is common for a book on *any* complex topic to advance only one theory and simply dismiss or ignore rival views; it is common for experts of *all* types to focus their reading on articles written only or primarily by like-minded others; it is common for experts of *all* types to interact solely or primarily with others who share their basic beliefs. This common tendency for intellectual insulation is beneficial for the individuals involved because it can lead them to the comforting conclusion that there are no controversies or that other views are obviously mistaken. Yet it remains that persons who cling tenaciously to their beliefs and refuse to practice critical reasoning do not advance knowledge; rather, they merely reproduce their own beliefs.

It is important to understand why there are controversies, and why controversy is good in any professional family. In the case of the professional family of family violence experts, it is important to understand why controversies can be somewhat more than simple failures to agree on the facts. The issues at hand are immediate, practical, political, emotionally charged, and ultimately moral. At the same time, for controversies to have beneficial consequences they must be swept out from the musty pages of academic journals and from behind the closed doors of professional debate into the bright light of public scrutiny. Although we do not naively believe that these controversies can be resolved, or that those of us in this line of work can become "one big happy family," we do believe that closing off debate by choosing sides and by clinging tenaciously to belief is counterproductive when there is so little known about such important issues. There is reason, then, for this particular volume. Taken as a whole, the chapters presented here do not answer questions; rather, they encourage debate and reflection about complex theoretical, practical, political, and moral questions.

The organization of this volume is inherently risky in a society where information most often comes to us through one clear, authoritative voice, such as in a textbook or newspaper article written by one person, or a television talk show featuring one expert. By presenting opposing views side by side, we run the risk that readers will simply dismiss all the experts' views because the experts do not agree. That, of course, is not our intention. Although the experts certainly do not agree, it also is clear that these spokespersons are offering readers much more than "common sense." Our hope is that readers will weigh the evidence presented in their arguments.

Asking readers to make their own judgments about the validity of the arguments contained in these chapters raises a practical question: What criteria should be used for evaluation? Surely, readers might ask the usual questions associated with critical reasoning: Is the argument logical? What is the evidence offered in its support? Even in a topic area as volatile as family violence, "logical" and "objective" standards should be used to assess arguments. Yet we offer a word of warning about the difficulty of actually applying such seemingly objective standards to these articles: How we tend to evaluate an argument cognitively is inextricably tied to how we feel about it. Readers should be cautious and should examine how it is that their feelings about the way the world "should be" might be influencing their cognitive evaluations of arguments about how the world "is."

Hence we hope that our readers will use scientific criteria in evaluating the power of the arguments contained in these chapters. At the same time, we also believe that these complex arguments should not be judged *solely* in terms of usual scientific standards. First, although family violence is most importantly a *practical* and *political* problem, scientific standards of evaluation are *academic* standards. The sole use of such "scientific" criteria would give unfair advantage to persons with academic training, skills, and agendas; the sole use of these criteria implicitly discounts the skills and priorities of persons most concerned with family violence as a practical or political problem. Second, scientific criteria value the impartiality and generalizability of the kinds of evidence associated with academic studies; such guidelines often ignore or discount the value of data generated by and of relevance to social service or political agendas and needs. Third, whereas family violence is associated with strong *feelings* and *moral* evaluations, scientific concerns are limited to examining logic and objective evidence. Much that might reasonably pertain to understanding family violence escapes empirical conceptualization and measurement.

In brief, although it is important to examine these opposing viewpoints in terms of their logic and empirical support, it also is important to remember that the arguments made by some of the authors are new, and hence "scientific" evidence supporting or refuting them is not yet available; it is important to remember that the authors write from many different perspectives with differing agendas and that what does and does not constitute "evidence" can vary; it is important to remember that the evidence for arguments made by some authors could *never* be found in statistics; it is important to remember that academic, scientific research is only one way of knowing about the social world. Family violence—however it is defined—is a new topic of study, with practical, emotional, political, and moral dimensions. The messiness of our subject matter therefore leads to complexities in evaluation.

We are grateful to all of the contributors to this volume, who have demonstrated that the best spokespersons for the various sides of issues can and will engage in debate. Although this volume does not yield a simple truth about the myriad questions of family violence, the high quality of the chapters presented here repeatedly demonstrates how equally intelligent and dedicated people can come to quite different conclusions.

Donileen R. Loseke
Richard J. Gelles

PART I

Issues in Conceptualization

This book is about controversies, and many disagreements about specific issues have a common beginning: failure to agree on conceptual or theoretical frameworks. In this volume, we introduce three such frameworks for family violence: K. Daniel O'Leary presents the *psychological* perspective, Richard Gelles argues for the *sociological* approach, and Kersti Yllö offers the *feminist* view. Such conceptual frameworks are of crucial importance because they answer the most fundamental questions about social problems such as family violence: What *type* of a problem are we dealing with? What *behaviors* are of concern? *Who* is involved? What is the *relationship* between victims and offenders? At first glance, questions about theoretical perspectives might seem esoteric and of interest only to persons who first and foremost are interested in family violence as a problem to be studied rather than to persons who define this as a practical and hence political problem to be resolved. But such a relegation of theory to scholarly interests ignores the importance of conceptual frameworks to practical action.

Conceptual frameworks first define violence as a particular type of problem. O'Leary's chapter illustrates that the psychological perspective centers on examining how the personality traits and psychological disorders of individuals can lead to violence. The psychological perspective is presented first in this section because this framework is the oldest, and because it is the commonsense perspective of everyday life in modern-day U.S. society, where we tend to think that problematic behaviors of all sorts are created by individual pathology. In the second chapter, Gelles presents the sociological challenge to the psychological perspective. Because the core assumption of this framework is that "social structures affect people and their behaviors," the sociological perspective leads to questions about the social environment rather than to questions about people in it: How is our social world, particularly the institution of the family, set up in ways that allow and even

1

encourage violence among family members? In the third chapter, Yllö presents a feminist challenge to both the psychological and sociological perspectives. By directing our attention to the gendered nature of our world and how it encourages violence by men against women, the feminist perspective conceptualizes such violence as somewhat more than an individual problem and more than a vague and amorphous social problem. Within the feminist perspective, "violence is about gender and power."

These authors also differ in how they define the specific topic matter of interest: *What*, specifically, is the behavior to be examined and understood? O'Leary argues that violence is of two types, "mild forms of physical aggression" and acts of "brutal aggression done by truly violent men." According to him, the greater the level of physical aggression, the greater the likelihood that the offender has some sort of psychological pathology. With such a definition, O'Leary's psychological framework applies only to those forms of aggression that all but the most barbaric of Americans would morally evaluate as intolerable. Gelles, in turn, never specifically defines terms such as *wife abuse, family violence*, or *child maltreatment*. But because he does discuss some negative consequences of focusing on only the "most sensational cases" of violence, it seems his definition of our topic would include what O'Leary calls "mild forms of physical aggression." Thus Gelles's sociological definition of violence includes the forms of violence that many Americans are willing to tolerate—even if they do not personally agree with their use. Finally, Yllö also never specifically defines what constitutes "violence against women," yet she criticizes definitions of violence that include only *physical* aggression. Her feminist definition of violence against women would include "economic deprivation, sexual abuse, intimidation, isolation, stalking, and terrorizing." In brief, while none of these authors maintains that violence of any type is acceptable, each does make distinctions among different types of violence; each directs our attention to different kinds of behavior.

Next, these authors disagree on *who* they define as involved in family violence and who they define as typical victims and offenders. Gelles uses the widest definition; he does not invariably distinguish victims and offenders either by gender or by generational relationship. Within his definition, family violence could involve persons within one generation (sibling abuse) or across generations (child abuse, elder abuse); violence between adults in one generation could involve women as the a priori victims (wife abuse) or not (violence by women, spouse abuse). In comparison, Yllö's feminist framework explicitly defines women as the a priori victims of violence and men as the a priori offenders.

Because this framework focuses solely on gender, it has "produced relatively less insight into child abuse or elder abuse." O'Leary's definition of who is involved in family violence rests somewhere between those of Gelles and Yllö. O'Leary is like Yllö in that he does not apply his perspective to elder abuse or sibling abuse, but, like Gelles, O'Leary is concerned with the between-generation violence of parents toward children. He also is similar to Gelles in his definition of victims and offenders of violence between adults: Sometimes O'Leary's focus is on the gendered violence of "wife abuse"; at other times his focus is on the nongendered violence of "spouse abuse." Again, while none of these spokespersons claims that violence by some people is acceptable, each defines particular types of people as those involved in violence; their perspectives sometimes do, and sometimes do not, contain a priori assumptions about who is the victim and who is the offender.

Finally, each of these conceptual frameworks defines the relationship between victims and offenders of violence. Gelles offers the narrowest definition. Because he believes that the site of family has "special and unique features" that create a fertile turf for violence, his focus is on violence occurring between the members of the same family. In comparison, O'Leary includes violence in dating relationships, so he broadens his concern to include violence in intimate relationships, whether or not intimates are in families. Yllö, in turn, argues that relationships between victims and offenders should not be of concern, so she maintains that the word *family* in the title of this volume misdirects our attention to family relationships. According to her, relationships between victims and offenders should not matter—we should be looking at all "violence against women," whether this violence occurs inside or outside marital relationships, whether it occurs inside or outside intimate relationships. Thus these authors do not agree on their definitions of the typical relationships between victims and offenders.

Theoretical perspectives such as those presented in this section are like the lenses of a camera. Each conceptual framework yields a picture of violence as a particular type of problem caused by particular types of behaviors done by particular types of people in particular types of relationships. Again, it is not that these spokespersons are arguing that other forms of violence by other people in other places are somehow acceptable. Yet, each makes distinctions, and these reflect moral considerations: What, specifically, should be defined as morally intolerable and in need of change? Which persons, specifically, deserve and need public attention?

Certainly, the authors of these chapters all share the view that the question is how to make sense of violence. Furthermore, none of these authors denies the relevance of competing perspectives. O'Leary agrees with Gelles that "economic and social stressors must be addressed in any full account of child abuse"; he agrees with Yllö that "patriarchal society is a critical risk factor" for wife abuse. Likewise, Gelles believes that the sociological perspective does not "diminish the contributions of psychological or social psychological variables"; he agrees with Yllö that the feminist framework has "significant strengths." Finally, Yllö agrees with Gelles that "the family is undeniably a unique context" shaping abuse; she agrees with O'Leary that "efforts to understand the psychology of violence are important."

Multiple perspectives are sensible given the complexity of the subject matter, yet conceptual frameworks cannot simply be merged into one grand theory of violence, because there are sharp disagreements about the proper *focus*. Indeed, each of these authors sees negative consequences from relying too heavily on pictures produced by other theoretical lenses. O'Leary, for example, disagrees with Gelles that social characteristics and processes are sufficient to understand the behaviors of "truly violent men"; he disagrees with Yllö that "patriarchal society is a sufficient risk factor" for wife abuse. According to O'Leary, controversies such as those discussed in this volume will remain until we more fully examine the pictures taken with his psychological lens. Gelles, in turn, argues that O'Leary's focus on brutal victimization and the ensuing portrait of abusers as "psychotic aliens" or "horrible and bizarre people" allows Americans to deny that violence can be done by and to "people like us." Gelles also believes that the feminist focus on patriarchy, dominance, and control "excludes from vision other salient and important aspects of social structures and social institutions." In her discussion, Yllö maintains that a psychological explanation for battering often is transformed into mere "excuses" for intolerable behavior; she criticizes the gender-neutral sociological frameworks for being "not as fruitful as they might be if a feminist lens sharpened their focus." In brief, these perspectives cannot simply be merged into one all-encompassing theory of family violence. As when we focus through a camera lens, we must choose a foreground for our picture, and by choosing to focus on some types of problems, on some events, and on some people in some relationships, we relegate others to the background.

How, then, can readers evaluate the worth of these arguments? For at least two reasons, this is a complex task. First, evaluation involves multiple decisions: Is family violence first and foremost a matter of individual pathology or an outcome of the characteristics of family or the arrangements of gender? In a world of limited attention and resources, what "type" of violence deserves attention? Which victims and which offenders deserve attention? Answering such questions requires a basis for making determinations. Some grounds for evaluating the value of different perspectives clearly are moral, because when we focus on some events and people we ignore others. Other grounds involve practicality: Where is the best place to invest our attention and resources? So, appraisal is difficult because it involves multiple determinations with varying bases for evaluation. Second, evaluation is not easy because our logical and cognitive evaluations often are influenced by our feelings and beliefs. Consider, for example, how O'Leary's psychological perspective does not deeply challenge typical American beliefs: He focuses on the extreme violence most Americans already evaluate as intolerable, and his route to problem resolution would be through "individual therapy," a social intervention with widespread acceptance. In comparison, both the sociological and feminist frameworks challenge typical cultural beliefs. Gelles asks us to take seriously some types of violence (so-called mild violence) and violence by some types of people (such as siblings and women) that typically are ignored; a sociological route to eliminating violence requires nothing less than changing the structure of the American family. Yllö's feminist framework also is deeply challenging. She would extend the definition of abuse to include a wide range of behaviors; a feminist agenda for change requires a complete transformation of the structure and practices of gender. In brief, evaluating frameworks requires that we examine how our vaguely articulated but deeply held feelings and beliefs about gender and family influence our cognitive appraisals. What might seem to be the easiest route to change might—or might not—be the most effective.

Should we concentrate our attention and resources on examining and eliminating all violence, or only extreme violence? Which specific persons should be the center of our concern? Should we focus our research and social services on understanding and perhaps changing the characteristics of individuals, family structure, or gender? In a world of limited resources, what is *most* important? Such are the decisions influenced by competing conceptual frameworks.

CHAPTER 1

Through a Psychological Lens
Personality Traits, Personality Disorders, and Levels of Violence

K. Daniel O'Leary

Family violence is an emerging field, and like most developing fields, it faces many controversial issues. The issue I have been asked to address is the value of psychological explanations for family violence. That task is a pleasant challenge, for I am a clinical psychologist, and I feel that psychological explanations have a great deal to offer to both the understanding and the treatment of family violence. In my opinion, even the most well-developed sociological, feminist, historical, and biological theories do not by themselves provide adequate bases for an understanding of family violence. Thus I will document the critical value of a psychological analysis of family violence, using both conceptual and empirical findings to buttress this position.

In addressing the value of one type of analysis—in this case, a psychological analysis—one is often inclined to relegate other analyses to a lesser position. That is not my goal. The field of family violence is fraught with many problems and should not develop unnecessary divisions among the professional ranks. One important problem involves the so-called violence initiative by the federal government, an initiative that was to be the basis of a major new effort in the prevention

AUTHOR'S NOTE: Support during the writing of this chapter was provided in part by NIMH grants MH 19107 and MH 35340. Special thanks are due Drs. Richard Gelles and Donileen Loseke for their comments on an earlier version of this chapter. Special thanks also are due Michael and Susan O'Leary for their editorial and substantive suggestions.

and treatment of violence by organizations such as the National Institute of Mental Health. Unfortunately, as stated in a recent National Institutes of Health editorial, that violence initiative was "murdered" (Barnes, 1992); the initiative was placed in abeyance because of political problems associated with racial and bureaucratic differences. I still hope that federal organizations will resolve these differences and provide new monies for research aimed at furthering the understanding, treatment, and prevention of family violence. In the meantime, however, it is important that the value of varied theoretical points of view be considered with as little acrimony as possible.

The very title of this book, *Current Controversies on Family Violence*, could be used as a rallying point to sharpen differences and to reinforce theoretical "camps." Although I have been asked to address the value of a psychological analysis of family violence, I see the value of other analyses as well, such as sociological, feminist, and biological analyses. The sociological and feminist views are well explicated in this volume by Gelles and Yllö, respectively, and we can all learn from them. It is time for a certain maturity and understanding in the field if family violence is to develop as an area with respect across disciplines. I am in total accord with Yllö, who urges in Chapter 3 that we welcome challenges and other viewpoints and give them respectful consideration. As I will document in the next few paragraphs, family violence is receiving a great deal of national attention. It is time for professionals to consider the differences and controversial issues in the family violence area as important questions to address, both conceptually and empirically.

The Rapidly Emerging Area of Family Violence

Both the professional and the lay press are now devoting some long overdue attention to family violence. Through the auspices of the American Medical Association, *Time* magazine ran a full-page advertisement devoted to issues of physical abuse of women in March 1992. On November 2, 1992, *Newsweek* carried a two-page announcement about newly published AMA guidelines to help identify wife abuse in the emergency room. The AMA also devoted one of its 1992 issues of the *Archives of Internal Medicine* to problems of physical abuse in intimate relationships. Similarly, the *Journal of Behavioral Assessment* had a 1992 issue devoted to spouse abuse. The most publicized events regarding wife abuse in 1990 and 1991 were grants of clemency to women who were serving time in prison for murdering their husbands. Governor Celeste of Ohio spearheaded the movement to grant clemency to women who had been found guilty of murdering their partners. With the help of mental health professionals, he was able to educate the legal profession on the subject of the "battered woman syndrome." Stated most simply, the use of the battered woman syndrome as part of a defense plea is based on the premise that the abused woman repeatedly feared for her life and was unable to leave the relationship (Johann & Osanka, 1989; Walker, 1984). Following Governor Celeste's lead, governors in other states granted clemency to women in similar situations, and these stories were carried in the press across the nation (see Blum, 1991). At the time I was completing this chapter, *Time* magazine (January 13, 1993) carried a cover story, "Fighting Back," about the clemency issue in cases of physical abuse of women who murdered their husbands.

Child abuse has received more attention than has abuse of adult intimate partners, and child abuse reporting laws were established in all states by 1970. In addition, a special federal institute, the National Center on Child Abuse and Neglect, was established in 1974 (Starr, 1988). Moreover, attention has focused on child physical and sexual abuse in almost every national magazine in the past few years, owing in part to the famous Joel Steinberg/Hedda Nussbaum case involving both child and wife abuse (see Johnson, 1989).

My own research involves risk factors for wife abuse and treatment evaluation of individuals and/or couples in relationships characterized by physical abuse. Therefore, this summary of controversial issues in family violence has a greater focus on wife abuse than on child abuse. Nonetheless, there are many common correlates of child abuse and wife abuse, and this chapter will cover some important controversies that have special relevance for both wife/partner abuse and child abuse. Despite the common correlates of child and spouse abuse, important differences should be noted. Most important, two predictors of wife abuse are psychological aggression against a partner and approval of physical aggression against a partner. Neither of these variables has been evaluated as having special relevance for child abuse. Moreover, in cross-cultural analyses, Levinson (1988), an anthropologist, found only a .48 correlation between child abuse and spouse abuse. Alternatively stated, cross-culturally, child abuse and spouse abuse certainly do not covary in any one-to-one fashion. In the United States, the repeated observation that spouse abusers report being the victims of child abuse has led to the conclusion that child abuse causes spouse abuse. This intergenerational effect is certainly significant (see Kalmuss, 1984; Widom, 1989), but the strength of the association is not always high (Malone, O'Leary, & Tyree, 1989). More specifically, Malone et al. (1989) found that the correlation between parental use of physical punishment and a man's engaging in physical aggression against a spouse was .18 at premarriage and .14 at 6 months. Using the same data set, Arias and O'Leary (1984) found that only 12% of the women and 13% of the men who physically aggressed against their partners had been exposed to violence in their families of origin. On the other hand, when one goes to a clinical population, the likelihood of observing violence in the family of origin increases. For example, 60% of a sample of physically abusive men reported that they were the victims of child abuse, and 44% witnessed violence between parents; these percentages were higher than those for men who were maritally discordant but not physically abusive (Rosenbaum & O'Leary, 1981). When the joint occurrence of child abuse and observing spouse (wife) abuse was controlled for, it was found that 70% of the husbands had been exposed to some form of family violence. In brief, across diverse samples, there is no consistently high correlation of child and spouse abuse, but as the level of violence in the family of origin increases, spouse abuse is much more likely.

In addition to the lack of a consistently strong empirical association of child and spouse abuse, with some notable exceptions, research, conceptual writing, and clinical practice have been conducted by different individuals or groups in the wife/spouse abuse and child abuse areas. For example, Yllö (Chapter 3, this volume) notes straightforwardly that feminists' analyses in the violence area have largely been limited to spouse abuse. One finds the names of different writers and researchers, with very little overlap, in the reference sections of recent chapters on wife/spouse abuse and child abuse (see, e.g., Margolin, Sibner, & Gleberman, 1988; O'Leary, 1988; Starr, 1988). Although significant relationships between child abuse and wife abuse certainly exist, these two phenomena are clearly independent enough to warrant being regarded as separate issues.

The attention given to family violence in psychology, psychiatry, sociology, and anthropology has clearly increased, as evidenced by the development of six new journals devoted to the topic, namely, the *Journal of Interpersonal Violence, Journal of Family Violence, Child Abuse and Neglect, Violence and Victims, Elder Abuse,* and *Sexual Abuse.* When specialized journals emerge, it is often a sign that mainstream professional journals would not carry articles in an area. Alternatively, it is possible that rapid developments in a field allow special journals to flourish. In my opinion, especially in the case of spouse abuse, both factors prompted the development of these specialized journals.

The problems of publishing research in any field usually relate to both conceptual and methodological differences between researchers who publish in, and review for, the mainstream journals and those in the emergent area. In the case of spouse abuse, some of the following conceptual and/or methodological issues prompted people to develop special journals: (a) conceptual or theoretical views of journal editors and reviewers that did not mesh with those of the authors, (b) the requirement by some journal reviewers that researchers provide observational measures of abuse, (c) the requirement that researchers employ a control group of men treated for various nonaggressive problems when assessing men treated in centers for physical abuse, and (d) the requirement of formal medical diagnoses of men and women in physically abusive relationships.

These issues will likely vanish as more research is published on wife abuse and as journal reviewers begin to understand some of the central theoretical and methodological problems in conducting research in the area. Control groups will be necessary for much of the research in this area, but the necessity to have particular control groups will probably end. In addition, it appears that the fourth revision of the *Diagnostic and Statistical Manual* of the American Psychiatric Association will contain diagnoses that will legitimately cover "partner relational problems with physical abuse," "partner relational problems with sexual abuse," and "parent-child problems involving child and sexual abuse" (see O'Leary & Jacobson, 1992, on partner relational problems with physical abuse).

The diagnoses regarding spouse abuse will cover problems of both the aggressor and the victim in physically and sexually abusive relationships. Fortunately, it also appears that these diagnoses will not be part of the diagnostic section of disorders "attributable to a mental condition." With formal diagnoses available for problems of child abuse, sexual abuse, and physical abuse of an adult intimate partner, there will be more acceptance of the problems of abuse in mental health and hospital facilities. In turn, individuals who are the victims or perpetrators of abuse will ultimately be able to be treated by private practitioners, because diagnostic manuals determine the problems for which treatment costs are reimbursed by insurers.

Other theoretical issues and/or controversies exist that are basic to the area and that have both clinical and research implications. I will address three of these issues: (a) the value of a psychological analysis of family violence, (b) the question of whether there is a continuum of physical aggression against partners and children, and (c) the question of whether men who physically abuse their partners or children have some psychopathological disorder.

What Is the Value of a
Psychological Analysis of Family Violence?

A Psychological Account of Wife/Spouse Abuse

Initial explanations of family violence had a clear focus on psychological and psychiatric factors. For example, early descriptions of spouse abuse used the wife's masochism as an explanatory mechanism of the phenomenon (Snell, Rosenwald, & Robey, 1964), and child abuse was seen as a by-product of personality disturbances and psychopathology (Gelles, Chapter 2, this volume). Across the past two decades, these depictions have fallen into disrepute for a number of reasons. First, the concept of masochism was used inappropriately as a means of blaming the victim (wife) for the abuse she received. Second, the evidence that abused wives generally were masochistic was nonexistent. Third, the invocation of personality disorders as an explanation for child abuse did little to ameliorate the problem and, in fact, again lessened the responsibility of the abusers, because they had "medical" conditions. Thus psychological/psychiatric explanations of family violence have been severely criticized, as perhaps they should.

Other accounts of a psychological nature have analyzed the interactions between spouses and have placed some clear emphasis on the dyadic patterns in relationships characterized by physical aggression and abuse (Margolin et al., 1988; O'Leary, 1988; O'Leary & Vivian, 1990; Rosenbaum & Maiuro, 1990). Few, if any, clinical psychologists have argued that all wife abuse should be treated with conjoint (couples) therapy, but the investigators cited above have argued that conjoint treatment is highly relevant in many cases.

Some of the concern about dyadic analyses in relationships in which there is physical aggression has been centered on the need to understand that men's aggression has more deleterious consequences than women's aggression. In explicit recognition of gender issues in spouse abuse, my colleagues and I have stressed, and indeed documented, the differential impacts of male and female aggression (Cantos, Neidig, & O'Leary, in press; Cascardi, Langhinrichsen, & Vivian, 1992), but a number of professionals are critical of any theoretical accounts of marital violence that are cast in any dyadic framework (e.g., Adams,

1988). Moreover, they are critical of therapeutic work of a marital nature in relationships where physical aggression occurs. Indeed, in certain states, such as Colorado, legislative standards sanction against couples treatment "utilizing traditional couples or family therapy techniques" (Estelle Ortiz, National Coalition Against Domestic Violence, Denver, Colorado, personal communication, January 21, 1993). In developing such guides or standards, dyadic accounts of physical aggression are criticized because, as noted in a recent letter from the executive director of a women's shelter to the editor of a weekly paper in Stony Brook, the *Three Village Herald* (October 21, 1992), "couple therapy is not only contra-indicated but potentially dangerous to the victim of such aggressive acts [pushing, slapping, or other more serious aggression]. Battering women is a *criminal* act, not marital or relationship 'problems,' and as such must be dealt with in the criminal justice system." Moreover, the shelter director argued that women in relationships characterized by abuse should receive individual support and that the husband's behavior should be treated as criminal.

In my opinion, attempts to explain and change various acts of physical and psychological aggression among family members through singular accounts, be they feminist, constructionist, sociological, biological, or psychological, are doomed. My colleagues and I have proffered a biopsychosocial account of a wide variety of abnormal behaviors, including attention deficit disorders, conduct disorders, eating disorders, depression, anxiety disorders, and personality disorders (Wilson, O'Leary, & Nathan, 1992). Indeed, most successful abnormal psychology books today provide some variant on this theme of a complex interaction of biological, sociological, and psychological factors in a wide variety of abnormal behaviors. The particular psychological account, however, may vary. It may be psychodynamic, cognitive-behavioral, or humanistic. Moreover, the biological and sociological accounts may take many forms. My own preference is to use the cognitive-behavioral account when providing a psychological explanation of family violence, and I will do so here as well.

The psychological model of wife abuse or partner abuse developed by my colleagues and me has received reasonable empirical documentation (O'Leary, Malone, & Tyree, 1992; see Figure 1.1). We certainly are not entirely happy with the predictive validity of the model. Although it accounts for 18% of variance in physical aggression of men toward their wives and 30% of the variance in physical aggressive of women toward their husbands, it could clearly do better. Of course, this model does not include prior physical aggression toward a partner in the prediction equation, as past physical aggression per se is the best

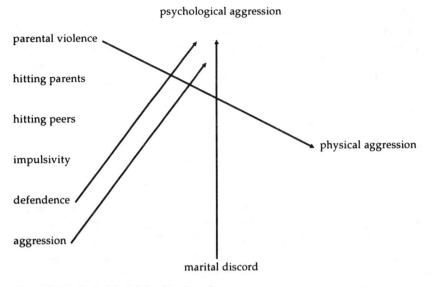

Figure 1.1. Path Model for Husbands

predictor of future physical aggression. Using past physical aggression toward a partner alone, we can account for approximately 50% of future physical aggression toward a partner (O'Leary et al., 1992).

With college students, our model has included more variables and has been somewhat more predictive of physical aggression against an intimate partner (Riggs & O'Leary, 1989, 1992). Basically, the factors that are most predictive of physical aggression toward an intimate partner are (a) acceptance of aggression, (b) past use of aggression, (c) relationship conflict, and (d) partner's aggression. Even these factors may not address the important issues of power and control raised by feminists (e.g., see Yllö, Chapter 3, this volume), and we are currently measuring both power and control in a wide variety of research endeavors. In addition, my colleague at Stony Brook, Dina Vivian, has been attempting to address the varied levels of psychological meaning that are depicted in problem-solving tasks of couples. Such analyses indicate that men and women place different meanings on the aggressive incidents in marriage (Cascardi, Vivian, & Meyer, 1991). Moreover, negative intentions are attributed to wives of physically aggressive men more than they are to wives of maritally discordant nonabusive men (see Holtzworth-Monroe & Hutchinson, in press). Finally, the work of Malamuth, Sockloskie, Koss, and Tanaka (1991) should receive critical attention, for it has also documented the value of a psychological model of coercive sexual and physically aggressive behavior against women. Delinquency, sexual promiscuity, attitudes supporting violence, and hostile masculinity were all supported in the model of aggression evaluated.

In summary, psychological accounts of physical aggression against a partner have been empirically documented in different laboratories, and we are beginning to develop an understanding of the relative values of different predictor variables through our theoretical models of intimate aggression.

A Psychological Account of Child Abuse

It appears to me that, irrespective of the theoretical account of child abuse, there is mention of impulse control, anger control, conditioned emotional arousal, weak personality development, or emotion-focused coping. These accounts all address an individual or psychological level of analysis. To buttress this point further, abuse researchers, whether dealing with children or adults, emphasize that the majority of individuals *do not abuse their children or partners,* even when highly stressed by economic problems or repression, racial discrimination, or highly aversive behavior of the children or partners (Straus, 1990). Such observations underscore the role of the individual or psychological analysis as one operates in a larger sociocultural context.

Psychological accounts of child abuse have not been evaluated empirically using a particular psychological theory, but a number of theoretical schemes have been used to organize psychological analyses of child abuse (e.g., Starr, 1988; Wolfe, 1987). At this point, the field has identified a set of risk factors for child abuse that have been replicated in a number of studies. Although there has been no empirical evaluation of the relative contribution of each of these factors, the following psychological factors are definitely important correlates of child abuse (Starr, 1988; Wolfe, 1987):

1. isolation from family and friends
2. high ratio of positive to negative interactions with various family members
3. high level of expressed anger and impulsivity
4. inappropriate expectations of the child
5. relatively high rates of both actual and perceived stress

In summary, psychological analyses have documented the role of a number of factors that repeatedly have been associated with child abuse. Although economic and social stressors must be addressed in any full account of child abuse, a psychological analysis of the problem seems inevitable, as the majority of the most economically and socially stressed parents do not physically abuse their children.

Is There a Continuum of Physical Aggression Against Partners and Children?

The answers to this question depend upon how the issue is conceptualized, and some of the debate about the issue results from a failure to make clear how the question is being cast. There are at least two major ways this question can be posed. First, are the more severe aggressive behaviors almost always preceded by a systematic progression from the milder forms of physical aggression? Second, do the more severe forms of aggressive behavior have different causes than the mild forms of physical aggression? It is my contention that the answer to the first question is yes, and the answer to the second question is also yes, though there is less convincing conceptual and empirical documentation to address the latter question.

Aggression Against Partners

Some researchers contend that low levels of physical aggression, such as slapping, escalate across time to more severe forms of physical aggression, such as beating and threatening with a knife or gun. For some, even murder may emerge at the end of the continuum of physically aggressive behaviors. Evidence in support of this continuum is the repeated finding that physically aggressive behaviors vary in their frequency, and behaviors such as slapping and pushing are almost always reported to occur if less frequent behaviors such as beating are also reported. Straus (1979) found a coefficient of reproducibility of approximately .80 for the behaviors on the Conflict Tactics Scales. My own research has found almost identical results, that is, on average, the more frequent aggressive behaviors such as slapping almost always occur if the less frequent but more severe behaviors such as beating occur.

An alternative view is that there are two distinct types of physical aggression against partners (Stark, 1992). The first includes highly coercive aggressive behaviors of men, such as periodic severe beatings, along with other psychological forms of coercive control. Such physical aggression and coercive control are seen as different in kind from other types of family fighting (Stark & Flitcraft, 1988). The second type of aggression against partners includes behaviors, such as pushing and slapping, that are seen as essentially normative in many married couples because of the high frequency of these behaviors in representative samples (Pan, Neidig, & O'Leary, 1992b; Straus, Gelles, & Steinmetz, 1980). Such behaviors also have been reported by 25-40% of both men and women in serious dating relationships (Riggs & O'Leary, 1992), bolstering the argument that slapping and pushing in anger are almost normative in intimate relationships. On the other hand, according to Stark (1992), some men engage in severe aggressive behaviors almost from the outset of their relationships, and these men are believed to be the batterers who physically injure their partners and who coercively control the total lives of their wives.

Another conceptualization of verbal and physical aggression is that the two are the results of two different phenomena, not simply levels of aggression with different thresholds. This issue was addressed by Stets (1990), who analyzed the data from the 1985 National Family Violence Survey. Using multivariate analyses to test models of similar or different causes, Stets found some support for the notion that different variables predict verbal and physical aggression. Physical aggression of men was predicted by two of the three variables that predicted verbal aggression—namely, age and using verbal aggression outside the family—but, in addition, approving of physical aggression and race (being black) uniquely predicted physical aggression. Stets compares two models statistically and argues that a two-step model best depicts the relationship between verbal and physical aggression. That is, she states that verbal and physical aggression are the results of different underlying phenomena.

Factor analyses of scores on the Conflict Tactics Scales obtained from 7,000 male military personnel clearly indicate that verbal aggression, mild physical aggression, and severe physical aggression of men are three distinct but correlated sets of behaviors (Pan, Neidig, & O'Leary, 1992a). Such data, along with information indicating that some of the predictors of severe physical aggression are different from the predictors of mild aggression, also argue for separate processes that may underlie the two phenomena. For example, Pan et al. (1992b) found that marital discord, the subject's use of psychological or verbal aggression, and the wife's threat to leave the relationship all predicted use of mild physical aggression by men. These variables also predicted severe aggression, but being black or Hispanic elevated the odds for the use of severe physical aggression, as did use of drugs. Moreover, these variables held as separate predictors even when pay grade and salary level were controlled. In many ways, these data are similar to those of Stets (1990), who found that men who are severely aggressive are more likely to be young, to be black, and to consume large amounts of alcohol compared with those who use mild levels of physical aggression. In addition, she did not find that income was significantly associated with race; she argues that the effects of cultural and structural variables account for the greater use of severe physical aggression by blacks. Specifically, she posits that "black men's aggressive behavior may be more instrumental, perhaps to maintain control over their partner. . . . Since black men grow up in an environment where aggression is accepted, they may use it more to possess power" (p. 512). If the main purpose of these large survey studies had been to assess racial effects, it would have been very important to include other measures that would be more likely to elucidate racial differences. Future research that examines racial issues either within or across groups should include measures that help explain possible racial differences in physical aggression (Williams, 1992). Such measures might include stress, perceived discrimination, attitudes toward use of aggression, educational level of parents, and use of physical aggression by parents.

As stated earlier, the answer to the question of the continuum versus category issue depends upon how the question is conceptualized. Evidence is reasonably strong that the more severe aggressive behaviors usually are preceded by the mild forms of physical aggression, and evidence is accumulating that different factors predict mild and severe aggression. The continuum versus continuity issue is basically one that has been addressed by diagnosticians for decades, and it is one that continues to the present in discussion of the revision of the *Diagnostic and Statistical Manual*. The dimensional or continuum view of psychological problems has been supported by Jung, Eysenck, Cattell, and Millon, to name a few. However, the categorical approach has been the pragmatic one taken by the authors of the diagnostic system used by the American Psychiatric Association.

Even those who conceptualize abnormalities of behavior as dimensional admit that some criteria will have to be used to differentiate pragmatically among those who receive a diagnosis or a categorical label. This dilemma is seen in the diagnoses of depression, learning disabilities, and attention deficit disorders. Often, the question that underlies the argument is whether a disorder, disease, or unusual behavior is triggered by some interaction of biological, psychological, and social stressors. In my opinion, most physically aggressive behavior in intimate relationships is not the result of a disease, but is the complex product of a number of factors. For research and clinical purposes in the study of aggression, as well as many other psychological problems, some arbitrary cut points on a continuum will have to be made to enhance our understanding of the phenomenon being studied.

Although some predictors of severe physical aggression are different from the predictors of mild physical aggression, I believe a continuum of aggressive behaviors toward a spouse can be seen to progress as follows: verbally aggressive behaviors, physically aggressive behaviors, severe physically aggressive behaviors, and murder of an intimate partner. The aggressive behaviors that make up the continuum and the causes thereof are listed in Table 1.1; they apply to both men and women, though many causal variables are more relevant for men than for women, as noted.

At the lower levels of physical aggression (pushing, slapping, and shoving), which occur very frequently in couples in early marriage, the behaviors would not be seen as disorders in the statistical sense. These self-reported physically aggressive behaviors were found to occur in more than one-third of the men and women in one study, and interviews with both the men and women involved indicated that such physical aggression generally was not abusive and not in self-defense (O'Leary et al., 1989). Similarly, in maritally discordant couples in which *mild* levels of physical aggression are reported, little or no physical aggression by the men or women is reported as being in self-defense (Cascardi et al., 1991). On the other hand, in highly discordant couples of older marriages, about 60% of the physically aggressive behavior of women is in self-defense (Cascardi et al., 1991). Moreover, women often murder in self-defense (Browne, 1987). In brief, in these marriages, cognitive variables such as attributions about control and self-defense, respectively, differentiate the women's reports about why their husbands engage in severe physically aggressive behaviors from those who engage in the mild levels of physical aggression. Finally, men who batter their wives and who attend domestic violence treatment programs can be clearly differentiated from men who are maritally discordant and who do not beat their wives. Men who batter are very disproportionally characterized by high scores on the Millon Clinical Multiaxial Inventory and score very high on a measure of emotional lability (Murphy, Meyer, & O'Leary, 1992).

At the extreme end of the violence continuum, spousal murder, different reasons appear to account for the murders committed by men and those by women. Women report having made repeated phone calls to police departments for protection prior to murdering their partners. In contrast, jealousy and need for control seem to be salient issues in

TABLE 1.1 The Continuum of Aggressive Behaviors in Intimate
Relationships

Verbal Aggression———▸	*Physical Aggression*———▸	*Severe Aggression*———▸ *Murder*
insults	pushing	beating
yelling	slapping	punching
name-calling	shoving	hitting with object

Causes
need to control[a]——▸
misuse of power[a]——▸
jealousy[a]——▸
marital discord——▸
           accept violence as a means of control ————————▸
           modeling of physical aggression————————————▸
           abused as a child————————————————————————▸
           aggressive personality styles————————————————▸
           alcohol abuse ————————————————————————————▸
                      personality disorders ————————▸
                      emotional lability————————————▸
                      poor self-esteem————————————▸

Contributing factors: job stressors and unemployment

NOTE: Need to control and variables on the left are associated with all forms of aggression; acceptance of violence and variables in the middle are associated with physical aggression, severe aggression, and murder. Personality disorders and the variables on the right are associated with severe aggression and murder.

a. More relevant for males than for females.

murders committed by men (Browne & Williams, in press; Cascardi & O'Leary, 1992). Finally, men who murder their partners and then commit suicide may also suffer from major depressive disorders.

If one conceptualizes aggression against a partner on a continuum as described herein, several implications follow: (a) Different causal variables predict aggression, depending upon where on the continuum the aggression in question lies. (b) Different treatments should be used depending upon the level of aggression. For example, marital therapy may be the most appropriate treatment for the lower levels of verbal and physical aggression that are commonly self-reported by both men and women and are not in self-defense. For women in relationships characterized by fear, severe physical aggression, and high levels of coercive control, gender-specific treatments may be most appropriate. (c) Preventive efforts are sorely needed to stop the escalation of physical aggression from mild to severe levels of physical aggression.

Aggression Against Children

A parallel argument regarding the continuum of physical aggression applies to child abuse. Wolfe (1987) presents the argument for a continuum of physical aggression or a "continuum model of parenting behavior" (Burgess, 1979) Using this concept, child abuse is seen as the "degree to which a parent uses negative, inappropriate control strategies with his or her child" (Wolfe, 1987). The concept is used to indicate that abusive parental behavior resembles "typical" parenting behavior but differs in terms of degree.

Gelles (1991) presents a number of arguments against the concept of a continuum of aggression. First, he argues that there are discontinuities in the data on violence, abuse, and homicide; that is, there were no differences in the rates of self-reported physical punishment between the years 1975 and 1985 in the survey he conducted, while in the same survey there was a 47% decrease in self-reported abuse of children (Straus & Gelles, 1986). Moreover, there was a 225% increase in the rates of reporting of child abuse to official agencies between the years 1976 and 1977. Clearly, the methods of data collection differed, and Gelles acknowledges that these method differences may account for the obtained differences. However, he also posits that the different methods may have tapped different types of violence. In my own state (New York), there have been dramatic changes in reports of all types of severe violence, and these increases can be attributed to major public media campaigns to encourage the reporting of such aggression, particularly for children. Thus any discontinuities across time must be placed in the social contexts in which they occur. In the case of child abuse, the reasons for the discontinuities seem too plausible to argue against in any cogent way.

A stronger argument for the discontinuity or categorical hypothesis is found in Gelles and Edfeldt's (1986) study comparing the United States and Sweden. They found that physical punishment occurs less frequently in Sweden than in the United States, yet rates of severe violence toward children in the two countries does not differ. Of course, it is possible that the law against physical punishment of children in Sweden may account for the lower reports of physical punishment there, and that more severe types of aggression may not have been amenable to change through such societal laws. Alternatively, as Gelles and Edfeldt argue, there may be different causes for the two types of aggressive behavior. Even so, this does not provide a strong argument that there is not a continuum of physical aggression against children in which parents escalate from one form of aggression to another.

A third argument against the continuum of aggression hypothesis noted by Gelles (1991) is that infant homicide and adult homicide rates are uncorrelated. Moreover, Gelles asserts that sociocultural factors explain adult homicide rates but not child homicide rates, thus it may be argued that factors that explain one form of physical aggression may not explain another. However, even with the different explanations for different types of physical aggression, it does not necessarily follow that individuals do not progress from one form of physical aggression to another, especially when the targets of the aggression are the same, that is, children or adults.

The evidence presented by Gelles (1991) raises questions about the commonly held assumption that there is a continuum of physical aggression toward children. As Gelles notes, homicide is not simply an "extreme form of interpersonal violence." He argues that it is a distinct form of behavior that requires a distinct explanation. I agree that such aggression requires different forms of explanation. However, as noted concerning spouse abuse, we have found that there are also important common predictors of the mild as well as the most severe forms of physical aggression. Finally, we do not yet know whether most child abusers systematically progress from the lower-level forms of physical punishment to the more severe forms of such aggression. At this point, the issue is unresolved.

Do Individuals Who
Physically Abuse Their Partners
Have Some Psychopathological Disorder?

Abuse of Partners

Whether there is a disorder of behavior in the arena of wife abuse has been debated for years. The nonpathological position regarding wife abuse receives support from several different vantage points. The most prominent of these is the feminist perspective, which holds that wife abuse is basically the result of attitudes held in a patriarchal society that supports the inequality of women through legal, social, and medical means (Dobash & Dobash, 1992; Yllö, Chapter 3, this volume). According to feminists, spouse abuse is essentially a "normal" result of the male socialization process, in which domination of women is covertly and overtly reinforced in our society (Dobash &

Dobash, 1979). A parallel perspective can be applied to eating disorders such as anorexia nervosa and bulimia nervosa. The male-dominated society, through movies, the advertising industry, and other mass media, portrays desirable women as thin sexual objects. The female is therefore motivated to engage in restrained eating, which later develops into a pattern of starvation, purging, and regurgitating. However, it must be recognized that only a small percentage of the population develops eating problems that are so severe they threaten the individuals' psychological and physical being. A society that supports the notion of a thin ideal female is seen as a critical risk factor but not a sufficient condition for the development of anorexia nervosa (Wilson et al., 1992). In my opinion, wife abuse can be similarly conceptualized. It develops out of a societal fabric in which women are treated in unequal ways and men's domination of women is normative. Anthropological studies across different cultures show that when men and women are treated more equally, men are much less likely to abuse women (Levinson, 1988). Similarly, societies in which women are not frequently depicted as thin sexual objects are less likely to have large numbers of women with anorexia or bulimia (Hsu, 1990).

My own analysis of the problem of wife abuse is that a patriarchal society is a critical but not a sufficient risk factor in the development of spouse abuse. That is, wife abuse will exist as a significant problem only in societies in which males learn that domination of females is appropriate. Where male and female inequality exists in salaries for the same jobs, where men are encouraged by the media to be sexually aggressive, and where men have more power in the home, physical abuse of women will be more likely. However, even with these conditions, many young married men never slap or hit their partners (O'Leary et al., 1989). Moreover, a number of studies suggest or directly indicate that physical aggression against women is seen as socially undesirable (e.g., Arias & Johnson, 1989; Riggs, Murphy, & O'Leary, 1989). For example, Arias and Johnson (1989) found that both male and female college students clearly evaluated physical aggression by men as negative. Using 12 seven-point scales (range 12-84), with low scores being negative and high scores being positive, men and women rated "ordinary" acts of physical aggression by men with mean scores of 22 or less. When rating severe acts of physical aggression by men, both men and women rated such aggression with mean scores of 15 or less. Both men and women rated men's physical aggression as more negative than physical aggression by a female, and physical aggression by men was certainly not seen as positive. Such data provide a challenge to the position that our society generally supports and approves physically aggressive behaviors of men toward women. Clearly, *most* college men and women do not generally approve of such behavior. Further, clinical experience indicates that if men learn that their daughters or sisters are physically abused, often the men will threaten and/or physically aggress against the perpetrators of the abuse. However, it appears that when attitudes of an individual are shaped that support the use of physical force against a woman, physical aggression is much more likely. Indeed, Riggs and O'Leary (1992) found that this attitudinal variable was one of the most salient predictors of physical aggression against a dating partner. In summary, our society does not appear to shape attitudes of *most* men and women to accept the use of violence by men toward women, but *some* individuals may learn that such behavior is acceptable. The challenge to understanding the use of violence then becomes a matter of individual prediction.

An alternative to the view that social institutions shape gender-specific attitudes is the view that men who physically abuse their partners have a certain psychopathology that plays a very important role in their abusive behavior. In a review of the diagnostic literature related to the topic of spouse abuse, we found that some abusive men may be legitimately diagnosed as having an intermittent explosive disorder or a sadistic personality disorder, but neither of these diagnoses would be applicable to most physically abusive men (O'Leary & Jacobson, 1992). Hamberger and Hastings (1986) found that physically abusive men attending a domestic violence abatement program had three personality profiles, as assessed with the Millon Clinical Multiaxial Inventory: schizoid/borderline, narcissistic/antisocial, and possessive/dependent/compulsive. In a review of the literature on male abusers, Hamberger and Hastings (1988) conclude that the preponderance of such men show evidence of personality disorders. Also using the Millon Multiaxial Clinical Inventory, Murphy et al. (1992) found that 75% of the physically abusive men attending a treatment facility for abuse had significantly elevated scores (>85) on the aggressive/sadistic personality disorder, and 62% of these men had elevated scores on the antisocial personality disorder subtest. The sum of standardized z scores on the scales for antisocial/narcissistic and aggressive/sadistic personality provided a measure of autonomous personality disturbance. The sum of standardized scores on the histrionic, passive aggressive, and borderline scales provided a measure of expressive personality disturbance. The physically abusive men evidenced more autonomous *and* more expressive personality disturbance than did the discordant nonabusive men. Patterns of affective dysregulation and antisocial tendencies were consistently prominent in the physically abusive men. When compared with controls, these abusive men had significantly different personality patterns from men who were (a) maritally discordant but not physically abusive or (b) maritally satisfied. There seems to be little question that physically abusive men who attend programs for containment of violence are significantly different from men who are maritally discordant but not physically abusive. These men are not *simply* products of a social system that fosters attitudes that promulgate the domination of women.

At the more moderate end of the continuum of physical aggression against a wife, my colleagues and I have found that personality traits or styles of aggression, impulsiveness, and "defendence" (readiness to defend oneself, suspicion of others, and a tendency to take offense easily), as assessed on the Jackson Personality Inventory, are associated with physical aggression (O'Leary et al., 1992). More specifically, these personality styles or traits are both correlated with and predictive of physical aggression against a wife. Similarly, such traits are associated with the use of physical aggression against a dating partner (Riggs & O'Leary, 1992).

In summary, it is clear that as the level of physical aggression increases, the greater the likelihood that some personality style, trait, or disorder will be associated with the physical aggression. In large community studies or in college student populations, the association of personality styles or traits and the use of physical aggression against a partner is small but statistically significant. In samples of men who engage in severe acts of physical aggression and coercive tactics against a partner, the likelihood of finding that an individual has a significantly elevated score on a scale that assesses personality disorders is very high.

As has been seen in controlled research assessing physically abusive men attending treatment programs for batterers, alcohol use and/ or alcoholism is higher than for various control groups (see, e.g., Rosenbaum & O'Leary, 1981). Further, in male alcoholic samples, 50% of the men report being physically violent against their partners during the past year (O'Farrell & Choquette, 1990). Paralleling the research on aggressive personality styles, the association of alcohol use and physical aggression against a partner is statistically significant but often small. Indeed, in young men, the results are not even consistent across measures of alcohol use/abuse. For young men, heavy episodic drinking rather than daily consumption of moderate amounts of alcohol is most associated with physical aggression (Leonard & Senchak, 1990).

The results on personality styles and/or disorders as well as the results on alcohol use/abuse indicate to me that the answer to the question about whether certain forms of psychopathology play a role in the use of physical aggression against a partner depends upon the level of physical aggression one is attempting to predict. At the lower, almost normative levels of physical aggression, the role of psychopathology or personality traits is small but often statistically significant. That is what should be expected, given that the level of physical aggression is very frequent in the population. As one goes to the severe end of the continuum of physical aggression, the percentage of men who have alcohol abuse problems and/or personality disorders is much higher than that found in general populations or in maritally discordant populations. Thus the way in which one answers the question about the role of psychopathology depends upon the level of aggression one wishes to explain.

Abuse of Children

The psychiatric or medical model of child abuse was popular in the 1970s. Basically, the premise was that abusive parents had personality disorders that reflected an inability to control aggressive impulses. The view that a personality disorder caused child abuse discouraged a focus on social and cultural factors, and it fit well with the opinion then held by psychologists and psychiatrists that personality traits are determinants of a great deal of human behavior.

Reviews of research on personality disorders have not found that child abusers and nonabusers differ in their personality characteristics (Gelles, 1973; Wolfe, 1985). The failure to find differences may be the result of the use of personality assessments, such as the MMPI, designed to measure major mental problems or disorders (Axis I disorders). Differences between child abusers and nonabusers may well be found with the new emphasis on assessment of personality disorders (Axis II disorders) with both interviews (e.g., the Diagnostic Interview Schedule) and self-report assessments (Millon Clinical Multiaxial Inventory II). Wolfe (1985) notes that there may be a resurgence of interest in the basic tenets of the psychopathological model to help explain which parents abuse their children under which circumstances (e.g., Lahey, Conger, Atkeson, & Treiber, 1984). In accord with Wolfe's prediction, it is my belief that a significant subgroup of parents who abuse their children will differ in terms of Axis II personality disorders or problems.

Summary

The value of a psychological analysis of child abuse and spouse abuse has been both empirically and conceptually validated. Clearly, there are psychological variables that consistently predict child abuse, and there is a related though somewhat different set of variables that predicts spouse abuse. The value of a psychological analysis has also been seen in analyzing whether there is a continuum of aggression that ranges from mild forms of aggression to severe forms of aggression. I believe that there is a continuum of physical aggression in that most individuals who engage in severe forms of physically aggressive behavior previously engaged in milder forms of physical aggression. However, separation of men who engage in physical aggression into groups—that is, separation of the truly violent men from those who engage in lesser forms of physical aggression, such as pushing and slapping—is necessary if the field is to progress. Most important, this separation is necessary because several studies indicate that different variables predict mild versus severe aggression. I believe that a number of the controversies about spouse abuse will largely vanish if these distinctions are made in the future. Finally, as new instruments are used in the assessment of personality disorders, I believe that child and spouse abusers will have significantly elevated scores on various personality disorder scales and on underlying measures of emotional lability.

References

Adams, D. (1988). Treatment models of men who batter: A profeminist analysis. In K. Ylló & M. Bograd (Eds.), *Feminist perspectives on wife abuse* (pp. 176-199). Newbury Park, CA: Sage.

Arias, I., & Johnson, P. (1989). Evaluation of physical aggression among intimate dyads. *Journal of Interpersonal Violence, 4,* 298-307.

Arias, I., & O'Leary, K. D. (1984, November). *Factors moderating the intergenerational transmission of marital aggression.* Paper presented at the 18th Annual Meeting of the Association for Advancement of Behavior Therapy, Philadelphia.

Barnes, D. M. (1992). Anatomy of an attempted murder: How to kill research on violent behavior. *Journal of NIH Research, 4,* 10.

Blum, J. (1991, March). Celeste's clemency for 25. *Columbus Monthly,* pp. 55-58.

Browne, A. (1987). *When battered women kill.* New York: Free Press.

Browne, A., & Williams, K. R. (in press). Gender, intimacy, and lethal violence: Trends from 1976 to 1987. *Gender & Society.*

Burgess, R. L. (1979). Child abuse: A social interactional analysis. In B. B. Lahey & A. E. Kazdin (Eds.), *Advances in clinical child psychology* (Vol. 2, pp. 142-172). New York: Plenum.

Cantos, A. L., Neidig, P. N., & O'Leary, K. D. (in press). Injuries of men and women in a treatment program for domestic violence. *Journal of Family Violence.*

Cascardi, M., Langhinrichsen, J., & Vivian, D. (1992). Marital aggression, impact, injury, and health correlates for husbands and wives. *Archives of Internal Medicine, 152,* 1178-1184.

Cascardi, M., & O'Leary, K. D. (1992). *Gender specific trends in spousal homicide across a decade.* Unpublished manuscript, State University of New York, Stony Brook.

Cascardi, M., Vivian, D., & Meyer, S. (1991). *Context and attributions for marital violence in discordant couples.* Paper presented at the 25th Annual Meeting of the Association for the Advancement of Behavior Therapy, New York.

Dobash, R. E., & Dobash, R. P. (1979). *Violence against wives: A case against the patriarchy.* New York: Free Press.

Dobash, R. P., & Dobash, R. E. (1992). *Women, violence, and social change.* New York: Routledge.

Gelles, R. J. (1973). Child abuse as psychopathology: A sociological critique and reformulation. *American Journal of Orthopsychiatry, 43,* 611-621.

Gelles, R. J. (1991). Physical violence, child abuse, and child homicide: A continuum of violence or distinct behaviors? *Human Nature, 2,* 59-72.

Gelles, R. J., & Edfeldt, A. (1986). Violence towards children in the United States and Sweden. *Child Abuse and Neglect, 10,* 501-510.

Hamberger, L. K., & Hastings, J. E. (1986). Personality correlates of men who abuse their partners: A cross-validation study. *Journal of Family Violence, 1,* 37-49.

Hamberger, L. K., & Hastings, J. E. (1988). Characteristics of abusive men suggestive of personality disorders. *Hospital and Community Psychiatry, 39,* 763-770.

Holtzworth-Monroe, A., & Hutchinson, G. (in press). Attributing negative intent to wife behavior: The attributions of maritally violent versus nonviolent men. *Journal of Abnormal Behavior.*

Hsu, L. K. G. (1990). *Eating disorders.* New York: Guilford.

Johann, S. L., & Osanka, F. (1989). *Representing . . . battered women who kill.* Springfield, IL: Charles C Thomas.

Johnson, B. (1989, February 13). Hedda's story. *People.*

Kalmuss, D. (1984). The intergenerational transmission of marital aggression. *Journal of Marriage and the Family, 46,* 11-19.

Lahey, B. B., Conger, R. D., Atkeson, B. M., & Treiber, F. A. (1984). Parenting behavior and emotional status of physically abusive mothers. *Journal of Consulting and Clinical Psychology, 52,* 1062-1071.

Leonard, K. E., & Senchak, M. (1990, August). *Alcohol and spousal aggression in marriage.* Paper presented at the 98th Annual Meeting of the American Psychological Association, Boston.

Levinson, D. (1988). Family violence in cross cultural perspective. In V. B. Van Hasselt, R. L. Morrison, A. S. Bellack, & M. Hersen (Eds.), *Handbook of family violence* (pp. 435-456). New York: Plenum.

Malamuth, N. M., Sockloskie, R. J., Koss, M. P., & Tanaka, J. S. (1991). Characteristics of aggressors against women: Testing a model using a national sample of college students. *Journal of Consulting and Clinical Psychology, 59,* 670-681.

Malone, J., O'Leary, K. D., & Tyree, A. (1989). Generalization and containment: Different effects of past aggression for husbands and wives. *Journal of Marriage and the Family, 51,* 687-697.

Margolin, G., Sibner, L. G., & Gleberman, L. (1988). Wife battering. In V. B. Van Hasselt, R. L. Morrison, A. S. Bellack, & M. Hersen (Eds.), *Handbook of family violence* (pp. 89-117). New York: Plenum.

Murphy, C. M., Meyer, S., & O'Leary, K. D. (1992). *Emotional vulnerability, psychopathology, and family of origin violence in men who assault female partners.* Unpublished manuscript, State University of New York, Stony Brook.

O'Farrell, T. J., & Choquette, K. A. (1990, August). *Marital violence in the year before and after spouse involved alcoholism treatment.* Paper presented at the 98th Annual Meeting of the American Psychological Association, Boston.

O'Leary, K. D. (1988). Physical aggression between spouses: A social learning theory perspective. In V. B. Van Hasselt, R. L. Morrison, A. S. Bellack, & M. Hersen (Eds.), *Handbook of family violence* (pp. 11-55). New York: Plenum.

O'Leary, K. D., Barling, J., Arias, I., Rosenbaum, A., Malone, J., & Tyree, A. (1989). Prevalence and stability of physical aggression between spouses: A longitudinal analysis. *Journal of Consulting and Clinical Psychology, 57,* 263-268.

O'Leary, K. D., & Jacobson, N. S. (1992). *Partner relational problems with physical abuse: DSM-IV literature summary.* Paper prepared for the American Psychiatric Association Task Force for DSM-IV.

O'Leary, K. D., Malone, J., & Tyree, A. (1992). *Physical aggression in early marriage: Relationship and pre-relationship effects.* Unpublished manuscript, State University of New York, Stony Brook.

O'Leary, K. D., & Vivian, D. (1990). Physical aggression in marriage. In F. Fincham & T. N. Bradbury (Eds.), *The psychology of marriage: Basic issues and applications* (pp. 323-348). New York: Guilford.

Pan, H. S., Neidig, P. H., & O'Leary, K. D. (1992a). *Gender differences in the factor structure of the Conflict Tactics Scale.* Unpublished manuscript, State University of New York, Stony Brook.

Pan, H. S., Neidig, P. H., & O'Leary, K. D. (1992b). *Predicting physical aggression of husbands against wives: A study of 8,320 military personnel.* Unpublished manuscript, State University of New York, Stony Brook.

Riggs, D. S., Murphy, C. M., & O'Leary, K. D. (1989). Intentional falsification in reports of interpartner aggression. *Journal of Interpersonal Violence, 4,* 220-232.

Riggs, D. S., & O'Leary, K. D. (1989). The development of a model of courtship aggression. In M. A. Pirog-Good & J. E. Stets (Eds.), *Violence in dating relationships: Emerging social issues* (pp. 53-71). New York: Praeger.

Riggs, D. S., & O'Leary, K. D. (1992). *Violence between dating partners: Background and situational correlates of courtship aggression.* Manuscript submitted for publication.

Rosenbaum, A., & Maiuro, R. (1990). Perpetrators of spouse abuse. In R. T. Ammerman & M. Hersen (Eds.), *Treatment of family violence* (pp. 280-309). New York: John Wiley.

Rosenbaum, A., & O'Leary, K. D. (1981). Marital violence: Characteristics of abusive couples. *Journal of Consulting and Clinical Psychology, 49,* 63-71.

Snell, J. E., Rosenwald, R. J., & Robey, A. (1964). The wife beater's wife: A study of family interaction. *Archives of General Psychiatry, 11,* 107-113.

Stark, E. (1992, May). *From dependency to empowerment: Framing and reframing the battered woman.* Paper presented at the Second Annual Conference: Domestic Violence: The

Family/Community Connection, State University of New York, Stony Brook, Division of Nursing.

Stark, E., & Flitcraft, A. (1988). Violence among intimates: An epidemiological review. In V. B. Van Hasselt, R. L. Morrison, A. S. Bellack, & M. Hersen (Eds.), *Handbook of family violence* (pp. 293-297). New York: Plenum.

Starr, R. H. (1988). Physical abuse of children. In V. B. Van Hasselt, R. L. Morrison, A. S. Bellack, & M. Hersen (Eds.), *Handbook of family violence* (pp. 119-155). New York: Plenum.

Stets, J. E. (1990). Verbal and physical aggression in marriage. *Journal of Marriage and the Family, 52,* 501-514.

Straus, M. A. (1979). Measuring intrafamily conflict and violence: The Conflict Tactics (CT) Scale. *Journal of Marriage and the Family, 41,* 75-88.

Straus, M. A. (1990). Social stress and marital violence in a national sample of American families. In M. A. Straus & R. J. Gelles (Eds.), *Physical violence in American families: Risk factors and adaptations to violence in 8,145 families* (pp. 181-201). New Brunswick, NJ: Transaction.

Straus, M. A., & Gelles, R. J. (1986). Societal change and change in family violence from 1975 to 1985 as revealed by two national surveys. *Journal of Marriage and the Family, 48,* 465-478.

Straus, M. A., Gelles, R. J., & Steinmetz, S. K. (1980). *Behind closed doors: Violence in the American family.* Garden City, NY: Anchor/Doubleday.

Walker, L. E. A. (1984). *The battered woman syndrome.* New York: Springer.

Widom, C. S. (1989). Does violence beget violence? A critical examination of the literature. *Psychological Bulletin, 106,* 3-28.

Williams, O. (1992, December). *Domestic violence and African-American women.* Paper presented at the NIMH Workshop on Violence Against Ethnic Women of Color: Research Issues, Bethesda, MD.

Wilson, G. T., O'Leary, K. D., & Nathan, P. N. (1992). *Abnormal psychology.* Englewood Cliffs, NJ: Prentice Hall.

Wolfe, D. A. (1985). Child abusive parents: An empirical review and analysis. *Psychological Bulletin, 97,* 462-482.

Wolfe, D. A. (1987). *Child abuse: Implications for child development and psychopathology.* Newbury Park, CA: Sage.

CHAPTER 2

Through a Sociological Lens
Social Structure and Family Violence

Richard J. Gelles

The core of the sociological perspective is the assumption that social structures affect people and their behavior. The major social structural influences on social behavior in general, and family violence in particular, are age, sex, position in the socioeconomic structure, and race and ethnicity. In addition, the structure of social institutions also influences social behavior. In the case of family violence, the structure of the modern family as a social institution has a strong overarching influence on the occurrence of family violence.

Social Facts and Social Influences

Age

Violence in intimate relationships follows the same general patterns with regard to age as does violence between nonintimates. The rates of violence (both victimization and offending) are highest for those between the ages of 18 and 30 years (Gelles & Straus, 1988; Straus, Gelles, & Steinmetz, 1980; U.S. Department of Justice, 1991; Wolfner & Gelles, 1993). Family violence, with the exception of the victimization of the elderly, is a phenomenon of youth, thus explanations for family violence need to consider issues such as life-span development, stage in the family life cycle, and human development if explanatory models are to reflect accurately the relationship between age and violence.

Sex

Interpersonal violence outside of intimate relationships takes place primarily between male offenders and male victims. The data on sex and family violence are somewhat different and often controversial. Much of the research on child maltreatment indicates that mothers are as, or more, likely to maltreat their children as are fathers (Burgdorf, 1980; National Center on Child Abuse and Neglect, 1988; Straus et al., 1980; Wolfner & Gelles, 1993). The sex difference, however, is not as clear as it might appear. First, the social construction of child maltreatment, especially the process of designating a perpetrator in official reports of child maltreatment, leaves females and mothers vulnerable to being identified as abusers and neglecters even if they are not directly responsible for the harm their children experience. Mothers are nearly always cited as offenders in cases of child neglect, not because they are the ones who directly caused harm to their children, but because cultural and societal views hold mothers responsible for the welfare of their children. Similarly, mothers are sometimes cited as maltreaters in official reports of child sexual abuse even when the perpetrator was the male partner or some other male, because child protective workers often assume that mothers have the responsibility for protecting their children from sexual abuse.

The data on physical abuse also indicate that females are nearly as, or more, likely than males to assault and abuse their children physically. However, as Margolin (1992) explains, these data fail to consider the different levels of responsibility males and females have for child care. When the level of responsibility for child care is controlled—for instance, comparing abuse committed by male and female baby-sitters (Margolin, 1991) or comparing abuse by single parents (Gelles, 1989)—males are actually more likely to be physical abusers than are females.

The data on physical violence and abuse between spouses are even more controversial than the data on child abuse (see Kurz, Chapter 5, this volume; Straus, Chapter 4, this volume). Some students of family violence, especially those who use a feminist perspective (see Kurz, Chapter 5, this volume; Ylló, Chapter 3, this volume), argue that females are vastly disproportional victims of adult intimate violence. Their point of view is supported by data on wife abuse derived from shelters and other helping agencies (see, for example, Dobash, Dobash, Wilson, & Daly, 1992). On the other hand, Murray Straus, among others, argues that there are far more women using violence toward men than the shelter data indicate. Although I cannot resolve this issue in this chapter, the data do suggest that males are the more likely offenders and females the more likely victims of family violence, consistent with a gender pattern of interpersonal violence found in other settings and groups.

Sex is also a factor in abuse of the elderly. Data indicate that women are the most likely victims of elder abuse. Data on offenders are somewhat more controversial. Steinmetz's (Chapter 14, this volume) conceptualization of elder abuse supports the claim that middle-aged females who are under stress from their caretaking obligations are the most likely abusers of the elderly. Pillemer's (Chapter 15, this volume) conceptualization that abuse is a result of the dependency of the offender is more neutral on which sex would be the most likely offender.

Position in the Social Structure

Wife abuse, child abuse, elder abuse, and other forms of family violence tend to occur in all social and economic groups. Violence and abuse can be found among truck drivers and physicians, laborers and lawyers, the employed and the unemployed, the rich and the poor. The fact that violence can be found in all types of homes leads some people to conclude that social factors, especially income and employment, are not relevant in explaining family violence. But although family violence does indeed cut across social and economic groups, it does not do so evenly. The risk of child abuse, wife abuse, and elder abuse is greater among those who are poor, who are unemployed, and who hold low-prestige jobs (Gelles & Straus, 1988; Pelton, 1978; Straus et al., 1980; Wolfner & Gelles, 1993). One of the mechanisms that explains why family violence is more likely to be found among those who are poor and unemployed or holding low-prestige jobs is social stress. The more stressful experiences individuals and families have to deal with, the greater the likelihood of the occurrence of some form of family violence (Milner & Chilamkurti, 1991; Starr, 1988; Straus, 1980a, 1990; Straus et al., 1980).

Race and Ethnicity

The data on family violence and race and ethnicity are somewhat contradictory. If one looks at official report data on child abuse, blacks and other minority racial groups are vastly overrepresented among those reported for child maltreatment (see, for example, American Association for Protecting Children, 1988; Gil, 1970). On the other hand, two national surveys of recognized and reported child maltreatment found that blacks were not overrepresented among those recognized for child maltreatment (Burgdorf, 1980; National Center on Child Abuse and Neglect, 1988). Other studies have found that blacks have lower rates of child maltreatment than do whites (Billingsley, 1969). Survey data indicate that blacks are more likely to use violence and abusive violence toward their children (Hampton & Gelles, 1991; Straus et al., 1980). This higher rate is the result of blacks having lower incomes and higher rates of unemployment than whites (Cazenave & Straus, 1979).

Official report data and survey data both agree that the rate of violence toward women is higher among blacks than among whites (Goetting, 1989; Hampton, Gelles, & Harrop, 1989).

The Second National Family Violence Survey, conducted in 1985, included an oversample of Hispanic families. The rates of husband-to-wife violence and parent-to-child violence among Hispanic respondents were significantly higher than those among non-Hispanic whites (Straus & Smith, 1990). As with blacks, the higher rate of violence in Hispanic homes is largely a function of the strong links among family violence, low income, urbanization, and youthfulness. Hispanic families are likely to have lower incomes than are white non-Hispanic families, are more likely to live in urban areas, and are younger than non-Hispanic whites.

I should point out that some official records, particularly official reports of child abuse and data from criminal justice agencies on wife abuse, reflect both the reality of the greater risk of abuse and violence in these groups *and* the fact that abuse and violence in these groups are overreported to official agencies. Newberger, Reed, Daniel, Hyde, and Kotelchuck (1977) and Hampton and Newberger (1985) found that poor and minority children are more likely to be correctly *and incorrectly* reported for child abuse, whereas white and middle- and upperclass families are much less likely to be correctly and incorrectly reported for abuse. Similarly, wife abuse and elder abuse in lowerincome and minority families is much more likely to come to the attention of the police and courts than is violence in more affluent homes.

Structure of the Family
as a Social Institution

The psychological perspective, because it looks for the causes of violence within the individual perpetrator, ignores the special and unique structure of the family as a social institution. The feminist perspective focuses only on the influence of gender and gender-structured relations on the institution of the family and the violence and abuse therein. The family, with the exception of the military in times of war and the police, is society's most violent social institution (Straus et al., 1980). The likelihood of being a victim of violence at the hands of a stranger or on the streets is measured in terms of risk per 100,000 people, but the risk of family violence is measured in terms of a rate per 100 individuals (Gelles & Straus, 1988). Thus a comprehensive perspective that explains family violence must consider the attributes of the family as a social institution that create such a high risk for violence.

In work published in 1979, Murray Straus and I identified the unique characteristics of the family as a social group that contribute to making the family a violence-prone institution (Gelles & Straus, 1979). Later, Straus, with his colleague Gerald Hotaling, noted the irony that these same characteristics we saw as making the family violence-prone also serve to make the family a warm, supportive, and intimate environment (Straus & Hotaling, 1980). Briefly, these factors are as follows:

1. *Time at risk:* The ratio of time spent interacting with family members far exceeds the ratio of time spent interacting with others, although the ratio varies depending on the stage in the family life cycle.

2. *Range of activities and interests:* Not only do family members spend a great deal of time with one another, the interaction ranges over a much wider spectrum of activities than does nonfamilial interaction.

3. *Intensity of involvement:* The quality of family interaction is also unique. The degree of commitment to family interaction is greater. A cutting remark made by a family member is likely to have a much larger impact than the same remark in another setting.

4. *Impinging activities:* Many interactions in the family are inherently conflict structured and have a "zero-sum" aspect. Whether a disagreement involves a decision about what television show to watch or what car to buy, there will be both winners and losers in family relations.

5. *Right to influence:* Belonging to a family carries with it the implicit right to influence the values, attitudes, and behaviors of other family members.

6. *Age and sex differences:* The family is unique in that it is made up of different ages and sexes. Thus there is the potential for battles between generations *and* between sexes.

7. *Ascribed roles:* In addition to the problem of age and sex differences is the fact that the family is perhaps the only social institution that assigns roles and responsibilities based on age and sex rather than interest or competence.

8. *Privacy:* The modern family is a private institution, insulated from the eyes, ears, and often rules of the wider society. Where privacy is high, the degree of social control will be low.

9. *Involuntary membership:* Families are exclusive organizations. Birth relationships are involuntary and cannot be terminated. There can be ex-wives and ex-husbands, but there are no ex-children or ex-parents. Being in a family involves personal, social, material, and legal commitment and entrapment. When conflict arises it is not easy to break off the conflict by fleeing the scene or resigning from the group.

10. *Stress:* Families are prone to stress. This is due in part to the theoretical notion that dyadic relationships are unstable (Simmel, 1950). Moreover, families are constantly undergoing changes and transitions. The birth of children, maturation of children, aging, retirement, and death are all changes recognized by family scholars. Moreover, stress felt by one family member (such as unemployment, illness, bad grades at school) is transmitted to other family members.

11. *Extensive knowledge of social biographies:* The intimacy and emotional involvement of family relations reveals a full range of identities to members of a family. Strengths and vulnerabilities, likes and dislikes, loves and fears are all known to family members. Although this knowledge can help support a relationship, the information can also be used to attack intimates and can lead to conflict.

Sociological Theories of Family Violence

Position in the social structure is clearly and strongly related to family violence. In order to illustrate how the sociological perspective applies and uses the empirical data on proximate correlates of family violence and the unique features of the family as a social institution, this section presents summaries of four primarily sociological theories of family violence: general systems theory, resource theory, exchange / social control theory, and subculture of violence theory.[1]

General Systems Theory

Murray Straus (1973) and Jean Giles-Sims (1983) developed and applied a social system approach to explain family violence. Here, violence is viewed as a system product rather than as the result of individual pathology. The family system operations can maintain, escalate, or reduce levels of violence in families. General systems theory describes the processes that characterize the use of violence in family interactions and explains how violence is managed and stabilized. Straus (1973) presents eight propositions to illustrate how general systems theory relates to family violence:

1. Violence between family members has many causes and roots. Normative structures, personality traits, frustrations, and conflicts are only some.
2. More family violence occurs than is reported.
3. Most family violence is either denied or ignored.
4. Stereotyped family violence imagery is learned in early childhood from parents, siblings, and other children.
5. The family violence stereotypes are continually reaffirmed for adults and children through ordinary social interactions and the mass media.
6. Violent acts by violent persons may generate positive feedback; that is, these acts may produce desired results.
7. Use of violence, when contrary to family norms, creates additional conflicts over ordinary violence.
8. Persons who are labeled violent may be encouraged to play out a violent role, either to live up to the expectations of others or to fulfill their own self-concepts of being violent or dangerous.

Giles-Sims (1983) elaborates Straus's basic model and identifies six temporal stages that lead to wife battering:

1. establishing the family system
2. the first incident of violence
3. stabilization of violence
4. the choice point
5. leaving the system
6. resolution or more of the same

Resource Theory

The resource theory of family violence assumes that all social systems (including the family) rest to some degree on force or the threat of force. The more resources—social, personal, and economic—a person can command, the more force he or she can muster. However, according to William Goode (1971), the more resources a person actually has, the less he or she will actually use force in an open manner. Thus a husband who wants to be the dominant person in the family but has little education, has a job low in prestige and income, and lacks interpersonal skills may choose to use violence to maintain the dominant position. In addition, family members (including children) may use violence to redress grievances when they have few alternative resources available.

Exchange/Social Control Theory

In earlier work I have elaborated on the basic propositions of an exchange theory of aggression and developed an exchange/social control model of family violence that proposes that wife abuse and child abuse are governed by the principle of costs and rewards (Gelles, 1983). Drawing from exchange theory I have noted that violence and abuse are used when the rewards are higher than the costs. Drawing from social control theories of delinquency, I have proposed that the private nature of the family, the reluctance of social institutions and agencies to intervene—in spite of mandatory child abuse reporting laws—and the low risk of other interventions reduce the costs of abuse and violence. The cultural approval of violence as both expressive and, in the case of disciplining children, instrumental behavior raises the potential rewards for violence.

Subculture of Violence Theory

The subculture of violence theory is perhaps the most fully developed and widely applied sociocultural explanation of violence (see Wolfgang & Ferracuti, 1967, 1982). This theory asserts that social values and norms provide meaning and direction to violent acts, and thus facilitate or bring about violence in situations specified by these norms and values. Subculture of violence theory explains why some sectors, or subcultures, of society or different societies are more violent than others, especially when they have cultural rules that legitimate or require violence.

The Attractiveness of
Psychological Explanations

The initial discussions of child abuse and wife abuse tended to overlook or downplay the relevance of social factors in explaining or helping to understand family violence. By and large, this was a consequence of the medical, or psychiatric, model that was applied by those who first discussed child abuse in the professional literature (see, for example, Kempe, Silverman, Steele, Droegemueller, & Silver, 1962;

Steele & Pollock, 1968). As Barbara Nelson (1984) points out, the first people to identify a problem often shape how others will perceive it (p. 13).

The early writings on family violence discounted social factors as playing any causal role in the etiology of abuse. As Steele and Pollock (1968) put it, "If all the people we studied were gathered together, they would not seem much different than a group of people picked by stopping the first several dozen people one would meet on a downtown street" (p. 92). They went on:

> Social, economic, and demographic factors . . . are somewhat irrelevant to the actual act of child abuse. Unquestionably, social and economic difficulties and disasters put added stress in people's lives and contribute to behavior which might otherwise remain dormant. But such factors must be considered incidental enhancers rather than necessary and sufficient causes. (p. 94)

For Steele and Pollock and other early students of child abuse, the explanation for abuse was that abusers suffered from significant psychopathology.

Leroy Schultz's (1960) examination of 4 cases of wife assault from a caseload of 14 spouse assaulters focused on mother-child dynamics as a means of explaining wife assault. Schultz noted that each assaulter was characterized by a domineering-rejecting mother relationship in which the child experienced primary rejection. The result was a passive-submissive individual who avoided conflict at all costs. Schultz noted that a uniformly poor mother-child relationship makes for a frustrated dependency in which the child's emotional needs are never met. He went on to explain that children who cannot permit aggressive impulses to break through during youth have difficulty as adults in entering into interpersonal relationships that do not duplicate their original dependency as children. These individuals seek to re-create dependent relationships with their spouses, but when their dependency needs are frustrated, the men tend to attack the objects of their frustration—their wives.

Current psychological explanations of child abuse, wife abuse, and family violence are considerably more sophisticated than the earlier notions of psychopathology or frustration-aggression arising out of disturbed patterns of mother-child relationships. Psychological theories of family violence also draw heavily on social learning as an explanation for child abuse, spouse abuse, elder abuse, and other forms of family violence (see O'Leary, 1988; also see Chapter 1, this volume). However, psychological explanations of violence continue to overlook and minimize the contributions of social and structural factors to the occurrence and persistence of violence and abuse in intimate relationships.

The notion that social factors are not relevant, or not as relevant as psychological factors, in explaining family violence is often manifested in assertions and statements such as "Family violence can be found in all social groups and in all income levels." Anecdotal examples of violence and abuse in wealthy families, or among physicians or lawyers, are also offered as proof that social factors play only a minimal causal role in family violence.

There continues to be a heavy psychological bias in most theoretical conceptualizations about the causes and explanations of child abuse, wife abuse, elder abuse, and other forms of family violence. The enduring stereotype of family violence is that the abuser is mentally disturbed or truly psychotic and that the victim is a defenseless innocent. The typical reaction to a description of a case of domestic violence or a photo of an abused woman or child is that "only a sick person" would do such a thing. The stereotype is so strong that unless the offender fits the profile of the mentally disturbed, psychotic alien and the victim is portrayed as innocent and defenseless, there is a tendency not to view the event as "abuse." The stereotype is so strong that some women who have been abused fail to define their experiences as abuse because the violence was not as severe as that depicted in such popular media accounts as the television movies *The Burning Bed* and *A Cry for Help: The Tracey Thurman Story*. Thus considerable public attention is focused on the most sensational cases of intimate violence. Horrible torture of women and children, sexual abuse in day-care centers, and the killing of babies and the elderly make news, not only because such cases are somewhat unusual (although less unusual than the public thinks), but because they fit the stereotype of what really is "family abuse."

We want to believe that the family is a safe, nurturant environment. We also do not want to see our own behavior and the behavior of our friends, neighbors, and relatives as improper. Thus most people want to envision "family violence" as terrible acts committed by horrible or bizarre people against innocents. This allows us to construct a problem that is perpetrated by "people other than us."

The theory that abusers are sick is often supported by a circular argument. Those who use the psychological level of analysis sometimes note that one of the character disorders that distinguishes child abusers is an "inability to control aggression." This seems a simple enough diagnosis. However, it is circular. How do we know that these people cannot control their aggression? Because they have abused their children. The abuse is thus the behavior to be explained *and* the means of explaining the behavior. When clinicians try to assess individuals without knowing whether or not they have abused their offspring or spouses, they find that they cannot accurately determine whether someone abused a family member based only on a psychological profile. In fact, only about 10% of abusive incidents are caused by mental illness. The remaining 90% are not amenable to purely psychological explanations (Steele, 1978; Straus, 1980b).

The Attractiveness of Feminist Theory

Feminist theory is becoming the dominant model for explaining violence toward women. There are significant strengths in the feminist explanation of wife abuse, as well as some important weaknesses. One major strength of the feminist approach is its "praxis" or "advocacy" approach. Feminist theory is about women's victimization as a social problem and the need to do something about the patterned, continuing, and harmful use of psychological and physical coercion to control and dominate women. To say that feminist theory is "politically correct" is to damn the theory and the theorists with faint praise. Feminist theory provides the explanation *and* the formulation to both explain and end violence toward women.

A second strength of feminist theory is the diverse, yet consistent, empirical support for the proposition that gender inequality explains violence toward women. A number of recent studies by different researchers who used different methodological approaches on different populations have all found that gender inequality explains variations in the incidence and rates of violence toward women. Rebecca Morley (in press) used both in-person interviews and mailed questionnaires to study wife abuse in Papua New Guinea. Her findings cast significant doubt on the traditional hypothesis that modernization and the resulting social disorganization of modernization produce increased risk of wife beating. Although modernization does produce new pressures, expectations, and changes in women's support systems, the underlying explanation for the abuse of women is the husband's perceived right to control his wife and a social structure that "allows" husbands to assert this right. Murray Straus (in press) analyzed data from the Second National Violence Survey as well as aggregate-level data to examine patterns of wife assault in the 50 U.S.

states. Straus's findings parallel Morley's New Guinea data. Social disorganization does not entirely explain variations in the rates of violence toward women in the United States. The greater the inequality between men and women and the greater the degree of social disorganization, the higher the rate of assault on wives.

Two additional researchers have employed data from newspapers to examine the abuse of women. Devi Prasad (in press) conducted a formal content analysis of newspaper articles on dowry-related violence in India, and Ko-Lin Chin (in press) used a less formal analysis of newspaper reports on violence toward "out-of-town brides" in the Chinese American community. The anecdotal data presented by Prasad and Chin add further weight to a gender inequality model of wife assault. The structurally inequitable positions of out-of-town Chinese brides and Indian women increase their risk of victimization.

The recent studies cited above support the earlier work of feminist scholars and sociologists who found that structured gender inequality is strongly associated with violence toward women. In addition, Straus and Morley both compare the explanatory power of competing theoretical models (social disorganization versus gender inequality) and find stronger support for the gender inequality model. Finally, the results come from a range of scholars who examined wife abuse using different methodologies and different theoretical approaches.

A final strength of the feminist perspective is that many feminist scholars, such as Yllö, Kurz, Dobash and Dobash, and Pagelow, are sociologists. They apply the sociological imagination, social facts, and sociological frames of reference to explaining violence toward women. Thus their approach is not entirely different from the theoretical approach used by sociologists, or those Yllö has labeled "family violence researchers."

The limitation of feminist theory is the other side of the coin of the theory's strength. Although the "gendered lens" provides a clear focus on violence toward women, the lens is a telephoto lens, not a wide-angle lens. The telephoto focus on violence toward women examines factors such as patriarchy, dominance, and control, and excludes from the vision other salient and important aspects of social structures and social institutions. The main problem with the feminist perspective is that it uses a single variable, patriarchy, to explain the existence of wife abuse. Moreover, the theory fails to account for the lack of variance of this single variable across time and cultures. Although the feminist perspective provides a politically attractive theory that is amenable to broad social action, it does not provide a useful theory to explain the complex nature of family violence. Feminist theory offers a single-variable analysis, albeit a powerful one, in a multivariable world. Moreover, feminist theory is an analysis of only one type of violence or victimization. The gendered lens does not, and apparently cannot, account for a wide range of objective phenomena that fall under the general label of "family violence." Neither Yllo (Chapter 3, this volume) nor other feminist scholars and theorists have been able to apply the feminist perspective to child abuse, sibling abuse, violence by women, or abuse of the elderly.

Summary

The sociological perspective provides the widest and most inclusive perspective from which to understand and explain family violence. A sociological perspective neither excludes nor diminishes the contributions of psychological or social psychological variables; rather, it places these variables within a wider explanatory framework that considers the impact of social institutions and social structures on social behavior. Similarly, sociological theory offers a more complex formulation for the varied phenomena of violence and abuse between intimates and is applicable to a wider range of victimization than is feminist theory.

Yet the sociological perspective has a major drawback. Because the sociological perspective *does not* focus on a single characteristic of social life (e.g., personality or gender inequality), sociological theories are by definition complex. The sociological theories reviewed in this chapter are complicated, and such theories do not lead to simple solutions, either in clinical or practice settings or in terms of social policy. One cannot easily use a sociological theory to inform clinical practice. Nor can one use it to develop a simple legislative package for a state or federal legislative body. Those who seek simple answers and simple solutions will find little of value in the sociological perspective.

Note

1. Two theoretical frameworks that have been applied to violence, symbolic interaction and conflict, are not reviewed here because they have not been widely applied to the study of family violence. Theories that are not primarily sociological, such as social learning theory (O'Leary, 1988), ecological theories (see Belsky, 1980; Garbarino, 1977), and sociobiological or evolutionary biology theory (see Burgess, 1979; Burgess & Draper, 1989; Daly & Wilson, 1988), are also not reviewed. In addition, this section does not review patriarchy or feminist theory, as this perspective is examined in Chapter 3 by Kersti Yllö.

References

American Association for Protecting Children. (1988). *Highlights of official child neglect and abuse reporting, 1986.* Denver: American Humane Association.

Belsky, J. (1980). Child maltreatment: An ecological integration. *American Psychologist, 35,* 320-335.

Billingsley, A. (1969). Family functioning in the low-income black community. *Casework, 50,* 563-572.

Burgdorf, K. (1980). *Recognition and reporting of child maltreatment.* Rockville, MD: Westat.

Burgess, R. L. (1979). *Family violence: Some implications from evolutionary biology.* Paper presented at the annual meetings of the American Society of Criminology, Philadelphia.

Burgess, R. L., & Draper, P. (1989). The explanation of family violence: The role of biological, behavioral, and cultural selection. In L. Ohlin & M. Tonry (Eds.), *Family violence* (pp. 59-116). Chicago: University of Chicago Press.

Cazenave, N., & Straus, M. A. (1979). Race, class, network embeddedness, and family violence: A search for potent support systems. *Journal of Comparative Family Studies, 10,* 280-299.

Chin, K.-L. (in press). Out-of-town brides: International marriage and wife abuse among Chinese immigrants. In R. J. Gelles (Ed.), Family violence [Special issue]. *Journal of Comparative Family Studies.*

Daly, M., & Wilson, M. (1988). *Homicide.* New York: Aldine DeGruyter.

Dobash, R. P., Dobash, R. E., Wilson, M., & Daly, M. (1992). The myth of sexual symmetry in marital violence. *Social Problems, 39,* 71-91.

Garbarino, J. (1977). The human ecology of child maltreatment. *Journal of Marriage and the Family, 39,* 721-735.

Gelles, R. J. (1983). An exchange/social control theory. In D. Finkelhor, R. J. Gelles, G. T. Hotaling, & M. A. Straus (Eds.), *The dark side of families: Current family violence research* (pp. 151-165). Beverly Hills, CA: Sage.

Gelles, R. J. (1989). Child abuse and violence in single parent families: Parent absence and economic deprivation. *American Journal of Orthopsychiatry, 59,* 492-501.

Gelles, R. J., & Straus, M. A. (1979). Determinants of violence in the family: Toward a theoretical integration. In W. R. Burr, R. Hill, F. I. Nye, & I. L. Reiss (Eds.), *Contemporary theories about the family* (Vol. 1, pp. 549-581). New York: Free Press.

Gelles, R. J., & Straus, M. A. (1988). *Intimate violence: The causes and consequences of abuse in the American family.* New York: Simon & Schuster.

Gil, D. (1970). *Violence against children: Physical child abuse in the United States.* Cambridge, MA: Harvard University Press.

Giles-Sims, J. (1983). *Wife-beating: A systems theory approach.* New York: Guilford.

Goetting, A. (1989). Patterns of marital homicide: A comparison of husbands and wives. *Journal of Comparative Family Studies, 20,* 341-354.

Goode, W. (1971). Force and violence in the family. *Journal of Marriage and the Family, 33,* 624-636.

Hampton, R. L., & Gelles, R. J. (1991). A profile of violence toward black children. In R. L. Hampton (Ed.), *Black family violence: Current research and theory* (pp. 21-34). Lexington, MA: Lexington.

Hampton, R. L., Gelles, R. J., & Harrop, J. (1989). Is violence in black families increasing? A comparison of 1975 and 1985 national survey rates. *Journal of Marriage and the Family, 51,* 969-980.

Hampton, R. L., & Newberger, E. H. (1985). Child abuse incidence and reporting by hospitals: The significance of severity, class, and race. *American Journal of Public Health, 75,* 56-60.

Kempe, C. H., Silverman, F. N., Steele, B. F., Droegemueller, W., & Silver, H. K. (1962). The battered-child syndrome. *Journal of the American Medical Association, 181,* 17-24.

Margolin, L. (1991). Abuse and neglect in nonparental child care: A risk assessment. *Journal of Marriage and the Family, 53,* 694-704.

Margolin, L. (1992). Beyond maternal blame: Physical child abuse as a phenomenon of gender. *Journal of Family Issues, 13,* 410-423.

Milner, J. S., & Chilamkurti, C. (1991). Physical child abuse perpetrator characteristics: A review of the literature. *Journal of Interpersonal Violence, 6,* 345-366.

Morley, R. (in press). Wife-beating and modernization: The case of Papua New Guinea. In R. J. Gelles (Ed.), Family violence [Special issue]. *Journal of Comparative Family Studies.*

National Center on Child Abuse and Neglect. (1988). *Study findings: Study of national incidence and prevalence of child abuse and neglect: 1988.* Washington, DC: U.S. Department of Health and Human Services.

Nelson, B. J. (1984). *Making an issue of child abuse: Political agenda setting for social problems.* Chicago: University of Chicago Press.

Newberger, E. H., Reed, R. B., Daniel, J. H., Hyde, J. N., Jr., & Kotelchuck, M. (1977). Pediatric social illness: Toward an etiologic classification. *Pediatrics, 60,* 178-185.

O'Leary, K. D. (1988). Physical aggression between spouses: A social learning perspective. In V. B. Van Hasselt, R. L. Morrison, A. S. Bellack, & M. Hersen (Eds.), *Handbook of family violence* (pp. 31-56). New York: Plenum.

Pelton, L. (1978). Child abuse and neglect: The myth of classlessness. *American Journal of Orthopsychiatry, 48,* 608-617.

Prasad, D. (in press). Dowry-related violence: A content analysis of news in selected newspapers. In R. J. Gelles (Ed.), Family violence [Special issue]. *Journal of Comparative Family Studies.*

Schultz, L. G. (1960). The wife assaulter. *Journal of Social Therapy, 6,* 103-111.

Simmel, G. (1950). *The sociology of Georg Simmel* (K. Wolf, Ed.). New York: Free Press.

Starr, R. H., Jr. (1988). Physical abuse of children. In V. B. Van Hasselt, R. L. Morrison, A. S. Bellack, & M. Hersen (Eds.), *Handbook of family violence* (pp. 119-156). New York: Plenum.

Steele, B. (1978). The child abuser. In I. Kutash, S. B. Kutash, L. B. Schlesinger, and Associates (Eds.), *Violence: Perspectives on murder and aggression* (pp. 285-300). San Francisco: Jossey-Bass.

Steele, B., & Pollock, C. (1968). A psychiatric study of parents who abuse infants and small children. In R. E. Helfer & C. H. Kempe (Eds.), *The battered child* (pp. 103-147). Chicago: University of Chicago Press.

Straus, M. A. (1973). A general systems theory approach to a theory of violence between family members. *Social Science Information, 12,* 105-125.

Straus, M. A. (1980a). Social stress and child abuse. In C. H. Kempe & R. E. Helfer (Eds.), *The battered child* (3rd ed., pp. 86-102). Chicago: University of Chicago Press.

Straus, M. A. (1980b). A sociological perspective on the causes of family violence. In M. R. Green (Ed.), *Violence and the family* (pp. 7-31). Boulder, CO: Westview.

Straus, M. A. (1990). Social stress and marital violence in a national sample of American families. In M. A. Straus & R. J. Gelles (Eds.), *Physical violence in American families:*

Risk factors and adaptations to violence in 8,145 families (pp. 181-201). New Brunswick, NJ: Transaction.

Straus, M. A. (in press). State-to-state differences in social inequality and social bonds in relation to assaults on wives in the United States. In R. J. Gelles (Ed.), Family violence [Special issue]. *Journal of Comparative Family Studies.*

Straus, M. A., Gelles, R. J., & Steinmetz, S. K. (1980). *Behind closed doors: Violence in the American family.* Garden City, NY: Anchor/Doubleday.

Straus, M. A., & Hotaling, G. T. (Eds.). (1980). *The social causes of husband-wife violence.* Minneapolis: University of Minnesota Press.

Straus, M. A., & Smith, C. (1990). Violence in Hispanic families in the United States: Incidence rates and structural interpretations. In M. A. Straus & R. J. Gelles (Eds.), *Physical violence in American families: Risk factors and adaptations to violence in 8,145 families* (pp. 341-367). New Brunswick, NJ: Transaction.

U.S. Department of Justice. (1991). *Criminal victimization in the United States.* Washington, DC: Government Printing Office.

Wolfgang, M., & Ferracuti, F. (1967). *The subculture of violence.* London: Tavistock.

Wolfgang, M., & Ferracuti, F. (1982). *The subculture of violence* (2nd ed.). London: Tavistock.

Wolfner, G., & Gelles, R. J. (1993). A profile of violence toward children. *Child Abuse and Neglect, 17,* 197-212.

CHAPTER 3

Through a Feminist Lens
Gender, Power, and Violence

Kersti A. Yllö

Violence within the family is as complex as it is disturbing. Compressed into one assault are our deepest human emotions, our sense of self, our power, and our hopes and fears about love and intimacy, as well as the social construction of marriage and its place within the larger society. Despite this complexity, the most fundamental feminist insight into all of this is quite simple Domestic violence cannot be adequately understood unless gender and power are taken into account.

Looking at domestic violence through a feminist lens is not a simple matter, however. Developing a theoretical, empirical, political, and personal understanding of violence requires us to analyze its complex gendered nature. This involves the psychologies of perpetrator and victim and their interactions, gendered expectations about family relationships and dynamics, and the patriarchal ideology and structure of society within which individuals and relationships are embedded. Although there is a range of feminist perspectives on each of these dimensions, there is broad consensus that each is profoundly shaped by gender and power.

Social action is the fundamental source of feminist insight into domestic violence. Feminist academic work, theoretical analyses, and methodological debates flow out of feminist practice. The feminist perspective, with its origins in a social movement, is strong on practical programs and critiques of prevailing perspectives. But it is not yet a fully developed, distinctive framework for the explanation of domestic violence, and in this limitation we are in good company, for no single

view is complete. I will argue, however, that although a feminist lens
may not be sufficient for seeing the full picture of domestic violence,
it is a necessary lens without which any other analytic perspective is
flawed. Gender and power are key elements of domestic violence,
whether one takes a sociological or a psychological perspective.

Focus on Domestic Violence

As social constructionists point out, the phenomena we study (including physical violence) are not simply "out there" to be discovered
through direct, objective observation (e.g., empirically). Rather, definitions of problems are socially created through ongoing controversy as
well as collaboration. Observation is always theory laden, and this is
especially true when the phenomenon under scrutiny is as politically
and emotionally fraught as violence (see Yllö, 1988).

The focus we choose for our work (including our theoretical formu-
lations, our empirical research, our policy recommendations, and our
social activism) is crucially important. As the title of this volume,
Current Controversies on Family Violence, suggests, the editors regard the
family as the overarching rubric for defining the problem. It then falls
to feminists, who tend to focus on *domestic violence* (a term that has
become synonymous with wife abuse), to explain why our analysis is
largely limited to woman abuse. In the recent *Handbook of Marriage and
the Family*, for example, Suzanne Steinmetz (1987) dismisses feminist
theory as "constricted" and of "limited utility as a theory of *family*
violence" (p. 749).

An important question that has been largely overlooked during the
20-year explosion of the family violence field is whether "family violence" is a unitary phenomenon that requires an overarching theory. I
would argue that feminist analysis has made an enormous contribution to our understanding of wife abuse, yet it has produced relatively
less insight into child abuse or elder abuse. However, I do not regard
this as evidence that feminist theory is constricted. It has made significant contributions to such areas as stranger rape, acquaintance rape,
sexual harassment in the workplace, and pornography. Further, this
analysis of violence against women (whether in the family or outside
it) rests within even broader feminist analysis of all aspects of women's
lives in patriarchal society.

In this sense, the feminist lens is truly a wide-angle lens rather than
a telephoto lens, as Gelles contends in Chapter 2 of this volume. His
view that feminism "uses a single variable, patriarchy, to explain the

existence of wife abuse" reflects a very limited conceptualization of patriarchy. Feminist theory does not regard patriarchy as a discrete, measurable variable (like age, sex, or socioeconomic status). Rather, patriarchy—the system of male power in society—is very complex and multidimensional. By focusing on patriarchy, feminism is no more a single-variable explanation than sociology, with its focus on social structure.

Feminist theory is not a narrow theory of one aspect of family violence. It is a very broad analysis of gender and power in society that has been fruitfully applied to domestic violence. I am not arguing that the study of violence against women should supplant the examination of family violence, but that we must recognize the distinctions as well as the linkages. The family as a social institution is undeniably a unique context that shapes the nature of the abuse within it. Whether we approach the problem with "gender" or "family" as our primary focus, I believe that we cannot understand one without the other.

Theoretical Lenses
(Or, What You See Is What You Get)

Over the past two decades, feminist theory and research have developed a picture of the family that reveals that social expectations regarding masculinity and femininity give relationships their shape. Whether it is our attitude toward love and sex, our ability and desire to communicate intimately, our need for connection versus autonomy, our involvement with our children, or our willingness to do the dishes—all of these are influenced (though not determined) by gender (Bernard, 1976; Chodorow, 1978; Tannen, 1990; Thorne & Yalom, 1982). However, in contrast to Sigmund Freud, Talcott Parsons, and the generations of psychologists and sociologists who followed them, feminists have argued that these distinctions are neither inherent nor functional. They are socially constructed and they create and maintain male power within the family and society.

Feminist analysis of domestic violence is firmly lodged in this broader theoretical and empirical framework. More than 15 years ago, Del Martin's ground-breaking treatise *Battered Wives* (1976) described violence as husbands' means of maintaining dominance within patriarchal marriage. In conjunction with the battered women's movement, which is built on this insight, feminist analysis grew and gained depth. Male violence was, for the first time, analyzed as a means of social control of women in general (Dobash & Dobash, 1979; Schechter, 1982).

During this same period, sociologists, led by Murray Straus, discovered family violence and initiated important research into the topic.
The field of sociology, and family sociology in particular, was just
emerging from functionalism at this point. The events of the day,
including the Vietnam War, the civil rights and student movements,
and the riots in our cities, called the functionalist model into question.
Instead of viewing society and its institutions as consensual systems
in equilibrium, sociologists began to focus on inequality, conflict,
violence, and change (Collins, 1975). Family sociologists, too, began to
look beyond the norms and roles of the static consensus model of
family relations. Sociological frameworks such as systems theory, resource and exchange theories, and the subculture of violence theory
(see Gelles, Chapter 2, this volume) all emerged during this period of
theoretical ferment.

"Family violence" became the dominant conceptual rubric in acade-
mia because the issue was pioneered by family sociologists (Gelles,
1974; Steinmetz & Straus, 1974). Up to this point, spouse abuse had
been viewed largely in terms of individual psychopathology. This
early sociological work was ground-breaking in its emphasis on social
forces. However, it was largely gender neutral. The patriarchal nature
of these social forces was not adequately incorporated into the theories
or empirical measures. The reality that the preponderance of the violence of the period (whether in the home, on the streets, or in the jungle)
was perpetrated by men was not central to the analyses.

The sociological theories reviewed by Gelles in Chapter 2 illustrate
some of the problems of looking at family violence without a feminist
lens. Several of the general systems model propositions obscure the
importance of gender. For example: "Stereotyped family violence imagery is learned in early childhood . . . [and is] continually reaffirmed
for adults and children through ordinary social interactions and the
mass media." Family violence imagery? The imagery of violence that
inundates our culture is of *masculine* violence. Male aggression is the
mainstay of our cultural images of violence, whether as fantasy (char-
acters such as the Terminator, Rambo, the Teenage Mutant Ninja Tur-
tles) or in reality (the Persian Gulf War, riots in Los Angeles, Yugosla-
via, Father Porter). The exceptions to this taken-for-granted backdrop
(e.g., *Thelma and Louise* and female soldiers in the Persian Gulf) get the
attention they do because they are exceptional.

Like systems theory, resource, exchange/control, and subculture of
violence theories ignore gender and are not as fruitful as they might
be if a feminist lens sharpened their focus. Resource and exchange

frameworks have contributed the important insights that power is based on resources and that violence is the ultimate resource for ensuring compliance. Unfortunately, the structural limits to women's access to key resources (such as income) as well as the cultural ideology of husband dominance are largely overlooked in the neutral/abstract formulation of these theories (Gillespie, 1971).

In the subculture of violence picture, men, as gendered human actors, are surprisingly invisible. The proposition that some sectors of society are more violent than others, especially when they have rules that legitimate or even require violence, would seem a useful start toward the analysis of male violence. However, this model is applied to subcultures such as the working class or particular race/ethnic groups. The reality that within these subcultures, as well as in the dominant culture, violence is overwhelmingly a male phenomenon is a nonissue. Is that fact so thoroughly taken for granted that it is not regarded as requiring explanation?

Although the theories outlined in Chapter 2 have been important in guiding sociological thinking about family violence, I would add conflict theory to the list because of its important influence on how violence is now conceptualized and measured. For the purposes of their research, Murray Straus and Richard Gelles initially conceptualized family violence as a form of conflict, which they regarded as a form of social conflict, more generally. Their theoretical underpinning came from conflict theorists such as Georg Simmel and Lewis Coser, and through this lens they saw the family as a social group in conflict (Sprey, 1969). Straus (1990) recently has restated this theoretical position, pointing out that conflict is inherent in families (as in other groups), with individuals "seeking to live out their lives in accordance with personal agendas that inevitably differ" (p. 30). He sees physical assault as a conflict tactic, defined as "the overt actions used by persons in response to a conflict of interests" (e.g., differing "personal agendas") (p. 30).

This conflict perspective offers important insight, but it, too, suffers from its lack of feminist lens. As Dobash, Dobash, Wilson, and Daly (1992) point out, "Such analysis obscures all that is distinctive about violence against wives which occurs in a particular context of perceived entitlement and institutionalized power asymmetry" (p. 83). The conflict perspective (sans feminism) obscures personal interests with gender interests. For example, when a husband forces his wife to have sex because it is her "wifely duty," is this just a conflict of personal interests? Surely we have a better understanding of the assault if we recognize that his "personal agenda" is socially constructed in a way that entitles him as a husband and legitimates his behavior. Conflict and personal interests are not gender neutral.

As Wini Breines and Linda Gordon (1983) emphasize in their review of family violence research, conflict is a "power struggle for the maintenance of a certain kind of social order" (p. 511). Family conflict occurs between members who hold very different positions in this social order. "Husband," "wife," "parent," and "child" are not neutral statuses whose occupants simply have differing personal agendas. They may all prefer different TV shows, but the conflict that ensues about the matter will likely be structured by expectations of gender and generational entitlement, not just personal preferences. When the issue is more serious (for example, a wife wanting to go back to school or to get a job), the gendered nature of the conflict will be even more salient.

There are many sociologists and psychologists who have contributed to the study of domestic violence. The theoretical assumptions of Straus and Gelles are emphasized here, however, because their impact on the empirical research in this field has been so profound. They developed the Conflict Tactics Scales (CTS), an instrument that dominates the family violence field to an extent rarely matched by other scales in other fields. Because the family violence field has been largely research (rather then theory) driven, the CTS has been adopted by a wave of researchers who have never explored, questioned, tested, or, often, even shared its underlying theoretical assumptions.

It is interesting to note that in Straus's (1990) recent theoretical discussion of the CTS, he explores several dimensions of the concept of conflict, but never mentions violence or explains why violence is best conceptualized as a conflict tactic (pp. 30-31). Straus and Gelles (1990) have consistently defined violence as "an act carried out with the intention or perceived intention of physically hurting another person" (p. 21). This definition is not clearly linked with their conflict of interest formulation, or with their actual measurement of violence.

The CTS would not require scrutiny in a theoretical chapter were it not for its consistent finding that wives are as violent as husbands in the home (Straus & Gelles, 1990, p. 104). This conclusion is fundamentally at odds with feminist analysis (as well as the real-world experiences of police, judges who issue restraining orders, emergency rooms, and shelters). Fuller discussions of the debate surrounding the CTS and "husband abuse" are available elsewhere (see DeKeseredy & Hinch, 1991; Dobash et al., 1992; Saunders, 1988; Straus, 1990; see also Kurz, Chapter 5, this volume; Straus, Chapter 4, this volume); however, I do want to raise a key question about the Conflict Tactics Scales.

Underlying the empirical debate is a theoretical issue that is rarely raised: Why begin with the assumption that violence is a conflict tactic? Instead of viewing violence as a conflict tactic, feminists suggest that it is better conceptualized as a tactic of coercive control to maintain the husband's power (Bograd, 1988, Hammer & Maynard, 1987; Jones & Schechter, 1992; Ptacek, 1988). Indeed, Gelles and Straus (1988) themselves recognize that "over and over again, case after case, interview after interview, we hear batterers and victims discuss how *power and control were at the core of events that led up to the use of violence*" (p. 92; emphasis added). Yet these core elements are missing in the "conflict of personal interests" approach to measuring violence.

The CTS is introduced to research subjects with the comment that all couples have disagreements that they try to settle in different ways. CTS questions about violent acts are at the end of a continuum of items such as "discussed an issue calmly," "cried," and "stomped out," about which husbands and wives are asked in parallel fashion. The CTS does not assess the meanings, contexts, or consequences of these individual acts. Further, and more significant in terms of the theoretical question I have raised, the CTS excludes, a priori, information on economic deprivation, sexual abuse, intimidation, isolation, stalking, and terrorizing—all common elements of wife battering and all rarely perpetrated by women.

The debate about the Conflict Tactics Scales and its controversial results has been heavily focused on empirical questions of reliability and validity, without adequate discussion of underlying theory. Dobash et al. (1992) present the challenge rather bluntly: "Those who claim that husbands and wives are equally violent have offered no conceptual framework for understanding why women and men should think or act alike" (p. 83). Through the conflict theory lens, gendered dimensions of violence are not seen, not measured, and (not surprisingly) not found.

The theories of violence discussed above are not inherently incompatible with feminist theory. In fact, they offer valuable insights (for example, regarding the relations among resources, power, and violence). Because these theories lack a feminist lens, however, they miss a crucial part of the domestic violence picture.

In the following section, I will discuss some of the important feminist work on domestic violence that is grounded in the empirically well-supported proposition that family relationships are profoundly shaped by gender and power—both interpersonal and institutional (for thorough reviews of feminist family scholarship, see Ferree, 1990; Sollie & Leslie, in press; Thompson & Walker, 1989).

A Close-Up of
Control, Intimacy, and Violence

To say, simply, that domestic violence is about gender and power may seem like nothing more than a sound bite. But it is far more than that—it is a concise expression of a complex body of feminist theory and research. A full discussion of this work would fill volumes; in this chapter I can only outline the coercive control view of domestic violence, consider some of its limitations, and suggest possible directions for fruitful development.

In her review essay on feminism and family research, Myra Marx Ferree (1990) states that "feminists agree that male dominance within families is part of a wider system of male power, is neither natural nor inevitable, and occurs at women's cost" (p. 866). Feminist work in family violence explores and articulates the ways in which violence against women in the home is a critical component of the system of male power. Violence grows out of inequality within marriage (and other intimate relations that are modeled on marriage) and reinforces male dominance and female subordination within the home and outside it (Schechter, 1988). In other words, violence against women (whether in the form of sexual harassment at work, rape by a date, or a beating at home) is a tactic of male control (Hanmer & Maynard, 1987). It is not gender neutral any more than the economic division of labor or the institution of marriage is gender neutral.

The conceptualization of violence as coercive control was not deduced from an abstract theoretical model and quantified. Rather, it grew inductively out of the day-to-day work of battered women/activists who struggled to make sense of the victimization they saw. As the shelter movement grew and survivors and activists joined together to discuss their experiences, a clearer vision of what domestic violence is and how to challenge it emerged (Schechter, 1982).

A control model of domestic violence, known as the "power and control wheel," developed by the Domestic Abuse Intervention Project in Duluth, Minnesota, is shown in Figure 3.1. This model has been used across the country in batterers' groups, support groups, and training groups (as well as in empirical studies). It provides a valuable, concise framework for seeing the interconnections between violence and other forms of coercive control, which I will refer to as *control tactics*. The wheel connects physical and sexual violence to the hub of power and control with a number of "spokes": minimization and denial, intimidation, isolation, emotional abuse, economic abuse, use of children, threats, and assertion of male privilege.

Figure 3.1. The Power and Control Wheel

SOURCE: Reprinted with permission from Minnesota Program Development, Inc., Domestic Abuse Intervention Project, 206 W. 4th Street, Duluth, MN 55806.

When one looks at these control tactics in a bit more detail, through research based on extensive interviews with battered women and batterers (Jones & Schechter, 1992; Ptacek, 1988; Yllö, Gary, Newberger, Pandolfino, & Schechter, 1992), the close-up picture of domestic violence that develops is one of domination rather than one of conflict of interest. The following is an interview excerpt from a study of women who were physically abused during their pregnancies (Yllö et al., 1992). It offers a view of events leading up to violence that differs markedly from the mutuality of the conflict tactics scenario. S., a

31-year-old white woman, describes the control and violence in her marriage that eventually resulted in a miscarriage:

> I didn't even realize he was gaining control and I was too dumb to know any better. . . . He was gaining control bit by bit until he was checking my pantyhose when I'd come home from the supermarket to see if they were inside out. . . . He'd time me. He'd check the mileage on the car. . . . I was living like a prisoner. . . . One day I was at Zayers with him . . . and I was looking at a sweater. He insisted I was looking at a guy. I didn't even know there was a guy in the area, because it got to the point that I, I had to walk like I had horse-blinders on. . . . You don't look anybody in the eye. You don't look up because you are afraid.

At one point, S. was insulted by a friend of her husband's and she was furious. She recalls:

> I told him, who the hell was he? And I threw a glass of root beer in his face. My husband gave me a back hand, so I just went upstairs to the bedroom and got into a nightgown. And he kept telling me to come downstairs and I said "No—just leave me alone." . . . He come up and went right through the door. Knocked the whole top panel off of the door and got into the room. Ripped the nightgown right off my back, just bounced me off every wall in that bedroom. Then he threw me down the stairs and . . . outside in the snow and just kept kicking me and saying it was too soon for me to be pregnant. . . . His friend was almost rooting him on.

What S. describes is far more than a conflict of personal agendas. The acts of physical abuse against S. are located in a context of male entitlement, control, intimidation, isolation, and emotional abuse. The violence enforces her subjection. As Schechter (1988) writes:

> Battering is a *pattern* of coercive control. . . . When a woman is battered, there is a pattern of unfair and unwarranted control being exercised over her life. Even as she resists her abuser's efforts, he continues to use coercion to dominate her. It is essential to understand this dynamic in order to understand why violence against women is so pervasive and powerful. (p. 243)

Schechter goes on to point out that when a batterer enforces his entitlement physically, he experiences a number of gains in the relationship. He gets his way, feels strong and manly, and has a partner catering to him in hopes of avoiding further violence (p. 244).

The coercive control model of domestic violence is an important theoretical alternative to the conflict tactics model. It identifies violence as a tactic of entitlement and power that is deeply gendered, rather than as a conflict tactic that is personal and gender neutral. It has deepened our understanding of family violence in substantial and significant ways. However, it is not the final analysis. Although it provides a potent description of violence and its context, it falls short of explaining it fully.

The coercive control model has rested on simple tenets of behavioral psychology and social exchange theory (a charge that has also been leveled at mainstream sociological approaches; see Breines & Gordon, 1983). As noted above, feminists have argued that men batter because they have much to gain through violence (Jones & Schechter, 1992; Schechter, 1988). This analysis parallels Gelles's (1983) exchange view, that "people hit and abuse other family members because they can. . . . People will use violence in the family if the costs of being violent do not outweigh the rewards" (p. 157). The similarity in psychological assumptions here is apparent, even though Gelles writes in gender-neutral terms.

My purpose is not to undermine the feminist paradigm, but rather to challenge us to develop it further. I agree that men do gain from violence, and in doing so they reinforce inequality within the home and beyond. What we are missing is an explanation of why a relatively small percentage of men batter, given the advantages to be gained. (And, by extension, we lack adequate intervention strategies to deal with those who do batter.) We have some answers in an empirical smorgasbord of variables (unemployment, stress, alcohol use, child abuse, and so on), yet we have little sense of the psychological dynamics leading to the decision to use violence. The rewards violence brings are, at least in part, subjectively determined. Why is a subordinate, cowering wife pleasing to some men, but not to others?

One intriguing effort to address these questions is the "feminist relational view of battering" developed by feminist therapists[1] at the Ackerman Institute (Goldner, Penn, Sheinberg, & Walker, 1990). These researchers are trying to explore the full subjective experience of batterers and the women they abuse without losing sight of male dominance in relationships and in society. Their work is not fully developed, but I want to highlight a few of their ideas that, I am sure, will be the subject of further debate. Goldner et al. (1990) argue that it is useful to

> understand male violence as simultaneously an instrumental and expressive act. Its instrumentality rests on the fact that it is a powerful method of social control, . . . a strategy that a man consciously "chooses." At another level violence can be understood as an impulsive, expressive act. . . . [Male violence] represents a conscious strategy of control, and a frightening disorienting loss of control. (p. 346)

In searching for the meaning of expressive violence, Goldner et al. don't rely on narrow, intrapsychic constructs. Instead, they follow recent gender theory, with its emphasis on the social construction of gender. This view holds that because "gender is relational and not essential, creating and recreating ourselves as gendered persons involves not a little struggle and ambivalence" (Hess; quoted in Ferree, 1990, p. 869). In sum, "the fundamental question is how the illusion of a gender dichotomy is constructed and maintained in the face of between-sex similarity and within-sex difference, and the answer is to be found in the constant and contentious process of en-gendering behavior as separate and unequal" (Ferree, 1990, p. 869).

Goldner at al. (1990) argue that this contentious process is a key to understanding intimate relationships, particularly violent ones. They have come to see battering as "a man's attempt to reassert gender difference and gender dominance, when his terror of not being different enough from 'his' woman threatens to overtake him" (p. 348). Although the gender struggle is central to masculine identity generally, Goldner et al. suggest that the fear takes extreme form in batterers and that it is grounded in families of origin in which gendered premises about masculinity and femininity are rigidly adhered to, especially by fathers (p. 351). Further, they suggest that these gender premises also shed light on the bond or alliance many battered women have with their abusers. We must not negate the importance of economic dependency and out-and-out terror that entrap so many battered women. However, we can do more, as feminists, to understand the bond that is separate from the bondage.

Caveats and Conclusions

There is, obviously, much more to be said about developing a full understanding of the dynamics of battering, and I believe that feminist work that incorporates coercive control and goes beyond it is very promising. As I challenge our thinking on this issue, I do want to state two important caveats First, it is crucial that psychological *explanations* of battering not serve as *excuses* for battering. Too often, factors such as a man's low self-esteem, poor impulse control, alcoholism, and traumatic childhood, or a couple's "mutual circular process," have served to relieve batterers of their responsibility for criminally assaulting their partners. Ironically, women's psychological problems have been seen as the cause of their victimization. Feminists charge that such analyses and the interventions based on them "*collude* with batterers by not making violence the primary issue or by implicitly legitimizing men's excuses for violence"(Adams, 1988, p. 177; see also Ptacek, 1988). As Goldner et al. (1990) write:

> Our attempt to discern and construct meaning in acts of violence does not overrule or substitute for our clear moral position regarding the acts themselves. Violence may be "explainable," but it is not excusable, and it may or may not be forgivable. That is up to the victim. (p. 345)

· The second caveat is that in developing a deeper insight into the subjective meaning of violence, we must not lose sight of the big picture that feminism has so clearly developed. Domestic violence is not just an individual problem, but a social and political one (Dobash & Dobash, 1992; Hanmer & Maynard, 1987). Violence is a means of social control of women that is at once personal and institutional, symbolic and material. The restrictions on women's psychic and physical freedom created by the fear and reality of male violence are inescapable. Efforts to understand more fully the psychology of violence are important and will, no doubt, contribute to our intervention efforts. However, they will do little to stanch the flow of violence in the absence of wider social action and fundamental social change on behalf of women. And in creating that social change, I believe, feminism makes its greatest contribution.

The final point I want to make is not about feminism or violence per se, but about the nature of the debate and controversy around these issues. I am disturbed by the deep cleavages that have resulted from attacks, counterattacks, and highbrow name-calling. Feminist scholars and activists with strong convictions are labeled ideologues and, most recently, "feminist fundamentalists" (Erickson, 1992). At the same time, feminists deepen the chasm by dismissing nonfeminist insights too quickly and hastily deciding who "gets it" and who doesn't. If our mutual goal is to understand the violence in order to stop it, then we must welcome the challenges other viewpoints pose and give them respectful consideration. My point that feminism is a necessary, but not sufficient, lens for understanding violence is a challenge to all of us to deepen our views.

Note

1. Although this theory is intriguing, I am concerned about its application in the context of conjoint treatment. Although Goldner et al. (1990) make reference to the criticisms leveled at couples therapy for domestic violence, they do not take the warnings seriously enough. Their commitment to a systemic approach overrides their safety concerns. See Bograd (1984, 1992), Dell (1989), and Willbach (1989) for fuller critiques of family systems treatment of battering.

References

Adams, D. (1988). Treatment models of men who batter: A profeminist analysis. In K. Yllö & M. Bograd (Eds.), *Feminist perspectives on wife abuse* (pp. 176-199). Newbury Park, CA: Sage.

Bernard, J. (1976). *The future of marriage*. New York: Bantam.

Bograd, M. (1984). Family systems approaches to wife battering: A feminist critique. *American Journal of Orthopsychiatry, 54*, 558-568.

Bograd, M. (1988). Feminist perspectives on wife abuse: An introduction. In K. Yllö & M. Bograd (Eds.), *Feminist perspectives on wife abuse* (pp. 11-26). Newbury Park, CA: Sage.

Bograd, M. (1992). Values in conflict: Challenges to family therapists' thinking. *Journal of Marital and Family Therapy, 18*, 245-256.

Breines, W., & Gordon, L. (1983). The new scholarship on family violence. *Signs, 8*, 490-531.

Chodorow, N. (1978). *The reproduction of mothering*. Berkeley: University of California Press.

Collins, R. (1975). *Conflict sociology*. New York: Academic Press.

DeKeseredy, W., & Hinch, R. (1991). *Woman abuse: Sociological perspectives*. Toronto: Thompson Educational Publishing.

Dell, P. (1989). Violence and the systemic view: The problem of power. *Family Process, 28*, 1-14.

Dobash, R. E., & Dobash, R. P. (1979). *Violence against wives: A case against the patriarchy*. New York: Free Press.

Dobash, R. P., & Dobash, R. E. (1992). *Women, violence, and social change*. New York: Routledge.

Dobash, R. P., Dobash, R. E., Wilson, M., & Daly, M. (1992). The myth of sexual symmetry in marital violence. *Social Problems, 39*, 71-91.

Erickson, B. (1992). Feminist fundamentalism: Reactions to Avis, Kaufman, and Bograd. *Journal of Marital and Family Therapy, 18*, 263-267.

Ferree, M. M. (1990). Beyond separate spheres: Feminism and family research. *Journal of Marriage and the Family, 52*, 866-884.

Gelles, R. J. (1974). *The violent home: A study of physical aggression between husbands and wives.* Beverly Hills, CA: Sage.

Gelles, R. J. (1983). An exchange/social control theory. In D. Finkelhor, R. J. Gelles, G. T. Hotaling, & M. A. Straus (Eds.), *The dark side of families: Current family violence research* (pp. 151-165). Beverly Hills, CA: Sage.

Gelles, R. J., & Straus, M. A. (1988). *Intimate violence: The causes and consequences of abuse in the American family.* New York: Simon & Schuster.

Gillespie, D. (1971). Who has the power? The marital struggle. *Journal of Marriage and the Family, 33*, 445-458.

Goldner, V., Penn, P., Sheinberg, M., & Walker, G. (1990). Love and violence: Gender paradoxes in volatile attachments. *Family Process, 29*, 343-364.

Hanmer, J., & Maynard, M. (1987). *Women, violence, and social control.* Atlantic Highlands, NJ: Humanities.

Jones, A., & Schechter, S. (1992). *When love goes wrong.* New York: HarperCollins.

Martin, D. (1976). *Battered wives.* New York: Pocket Books.

Ptacek, J. (1988). Why do men batter their wives? In K. Yllö & M. Bograd (Eds.), *Feminist perspectives on wife abuse* (pp. 133-157). Newbury Park, CA: Sage.

Saunders, D. G. (1988). Wife abuse, husband abuse, or mutual combat? A feminist perspective on empirical findings. In K. Yllö & M. Bograd (Eds.), *Feminist perspectives on wife abuse* (pp. 90-113). Newbury Park, CA: Sage.

Schechter, S. (1982). *Women and male violence: The visions and struggles of the battered women's movement.* Boston: South End.

Schechter, S., with Gary, L. (1988). A framework for understanding and empowering battered women. In M. Straus (Ed.), *Abuse and victimization across the life span* (pp. 240-253). Baltimore: Johns Hopkins University Press.

Sollie, D., & Leslie, L. (in press). *Feminism and family studies.* Newbury Park, CA: Sage.

Sprey, J. (1969). The family as a system in conflict. *Journal of Marriage and the Family, 31*, 699-706.

Steinmetz, S. K. (1987). Family violence: Past, present, and future. In M. B. Sussman & S. K. Steinmetz (Eds.), *Handbook of marriage and the family* (pp. 725-765). New York: Plenum.

Steinmetz, S. K., & Straus, M. A. (Eds.). (1974). *Violence in the family.* New York: Harper & Row.

Straus, M. A. (1990). The Conflict Tactics Scales and its critics: An evaluation and new data on validity and reliability. In M. A. Straus & R. J. Gelles (Eds.), *Physical violence in American families: Risk factors and adaptations to violence in 8,145 families* (pp. 49-73). New Brunswick, NJ: Transaction.

Straus, M. A., & Gelles, R. J. (Eds.). (1990). *Physical violence in American families: Risk factors and adaptations to violence in 8,145 families.* New Brunswick, NJ: Transaction.

Tannen, D. (1990). *You just don't understand: Women and men in conversation.* New York: William Morrow.

Thompson, L., & Walker, A. (1989). Gender in families: Women and men in marriage, work, and parenthood. *Journal of Marriage and the Family, 51*, 845-871.

Thorne, B., & Yalom, M. (1982). *Rethinking the family: Some feminist questions.* New York: Longman.

Willbach, D. (1989). Ethics and family therapy: The case management of family violence. *Journal of Marital and Family Therapy, 15*, 43-52.

Yllö, K. (1988). Political and methodological debates in wife abuse research. In K. Yllö
& M. Bograd (Eds.), *Feminist perspectives on wife abuse* (pp. 28-50). Newbury Park,
CA: Sage.
Yllö, K., Gary, L., Newberger, E. H., Pandolfino, J., & Schechter, S. (1992, October 18).
Pregnant woman abuse and adverse birth outcomes. Paper presented at the annual
meeting of the Society for Applied Sociology, Cleveland, OH.

Issues in
Definition and Measurement

At issue in Part I was the matter of how to conceptualize our topics of interest. In this section the issues are methodological: How do we operationalize and measure the topics we address?

All three controversies presented in Part II involve questions about violence between adult women and men. The first is about how we should understand and evaluate women's violence against men. Murray Straus argues that violence by women against men should be morally condemned and responded to as a social problem; Demie Kurz believes that Straus misdirects our attention and that only violence *against* women should be evaluated as a social problem requiring concern and social intervention. The second controversy moves the scene from family to college campuses. Mary Koss and Sarah Cook argue that date and acquaintance rape is a frequent occurrence on college campuses and that such rape is devastating in its consequences. Conversely, Neil Gilbert maintains that the incidence of such rape is overestimated and that the extent of its consequences is exaggerated. The third controversy is about how we should understand women's reactions to long-term victimization. Lenore Walker argues that abused women often develop a wide range of individual psychological troubles that she calls the battered woman's syndrome. Lee Bowker challenges this psychological focus and argues that the problems of abused women are social and political rather than individual.

Although Part II centers on controversies about definitions and measurements, differences in conceptual frameworks underlie specific disagreements. Not surprisingly, because all of the issues here concern the status of women as victims of male violence, controversies between feminist and other conceptual frameworks are a subtheme of all six chapters in this section. Straus, for example, uses a wide sociological conceptual lens that makes visible violence by women against their spouses. Although he maintains that his analysis is also feminist, Kurz labels Straus's framework as "irreconcilable with feminism." She believes the sociological lens distorts rather than clarifies, and that only the feminist lens correctly shows that we should be exclusively concerned with violence against women. Similarly, underlying the controversy about the prevalence and consequences of date rape is the difference between feminist and nonfeminist definitions of what constitutes violence against women. Koss and Cook, like Yllö (Chapter 3), would broaden the definition of what constitutes unacceptable violence toward women. They argue that rape occurs when a woman has unwanted sexual activity with a man "because he gave her drugs or alcohol to make her cooperate"; they maintain that a woman can be a victim of rape even if she, herself, does not label the experience as one of rape. Conversely, Gilbert believes that more traditional, and hence narrow, definitions of *consent* should be used; he argues that when women do not "feel victimized," or when they define themselves as victims of "miscommunication," rape has not occurred. In the final controversy presented in Part II, Walker argues that her psychological/ feminist perspective is "consistent with feminist theories about woman abuse," and she criticizes Bowker's sociological framework for containing "stereotyped behavioral expectations" for women.

In this section, readers can begin to see why conceptual frameworks matter. The particular disagreements throughout this volume are about specific issues, but differences in conceptual frameworks fuel the specific controversies. The chapters in Part II all revolve around specific methodological disputes: What is the behavior of interest? How do we define it? Where do we look for it? As these and many other chapters in this volume clearly show, operational definitions and research sample characteristics are important: What we look for and where we look determine "how much" of something we will find. For example, how common is date and acquaintance rape? The answer to that question depends in part on how we define *date and acquaintance rape*. Koss and Cook's definition leads them to find a great many such events; Gilbert's more narrow definition leads him to find far fewer instances. In the same way, the answer to another question depends on where we look for violence and on what kinds of violence we look for: Is women's violence against men a social problem? Straus looks at "all violence" in the general population, whereas Kurz focuses on the extreme violence known as wife abuse that comes to the attention of social service providers. Straus measures violence as a series of behaviorally defined variables; Kurz argues that violence cannot be understood as a series of variables because the meaning of violence depends on its context. Much like O'Leary (Chapter 1), Straus distinguishes between "mild" and "severe" violence; Kurz maintains that such distinctions are not warranted. Kurz and Straus reach diametrically opposed conclusions about the prevalence and meaning of women's violence against men, in no small part because they are looking at different phenomena.

The importance of definitions is also vividly illustrated in the third debate in this section, concerning the consequences of wife abuse. Although the explicit controversy is about the value of focusing on individual psychological troubles or on social and political conditions, the underlying disagreement is definitional. As defined by Walker, the "battered woman's syndrome" is not the same as "learned helplessness"; as defined by Bowker, the two are synonymous. As defined by Walker, "learned helplessness" is not equivalent to "passivity"; as defined by Bowker, it is. The perplexing question in all these debates is whether or not explicit controversies can be resolved when the "sides" rely on such different—and incompatible—definitions.

Although questions concerning how violence is defined and measured and how and where data are collected seem to be a long way from the world of family violence as an immediate practical and political problem, each of these spokespersons explicitly promotes a practical agenda. Straus, for example, uses most of his chapter to present a compilation of the evidence that women's violence exists. Yet this is not a mere methodological exercise, because the evidence allows him to advance his practical agenda: a complete cessation of violence *by* women that he believes would yield less violence done *to* women. Kurz also focuses much of her discussion on how to interpret research about women's violence toward men, but she does this to support her plea for readers to remain concerned with women as the victims of male violence. Likewise, Koss and Cook examine many studies supporting their argument that date and acquaintance rape is frequent and consequential. This, in turn, allows them to maintain that such rape "warrants further serious attention." In the opposing viewpoint, Gilbert's methodological comments support his practical agenda: to encourage public attention to those victims he believes are most in need of sympathy and services. Finally, Walker believes that public acceptance of the battered woman syndrome could yield very practical social service and legal benefits for abused women, whereas Bowker believes it is "social forces that we must target for change." In brief, although these controversies are explicitly about research methodology, all of these authors believe that there are very real and practical benefits associated with supporting their own sides of the controversies.

Furthermore, each of these authors is opposed—often vehemently—to the practical implications of supporting the "other side" of the controversy in which he or she is involved. Straus claims that failure to take women's violence seriously will lead to more violence against women; Kurz maintains that Straus's attention to violence by women has reduced public sympathy and resources for abused women. Koss and Cook argue that Gilbert's views have led the public to trivialize the very real consequences of date and acquaintance rape; Gilbert maintains that expanded definitions of rape trivialize extreme forms of rape and promote hostility between women and men. Walker criticizes Bowker's failure to accept the battered woman's syndrome because she believes this leads to blaming women for the violence they experience. Bowker counters that Walker's claim that the battered woman's syndrome is "typical" leads the public to assume that the problems of all abused women are individual and psychological, and therefore it misdirects our attention "toward the victim's personality."

How should readers evaluate the controversies presented in this section? Most of these authors use scientific evidence or currently accepted psychiatric categorizations to support their statements. At times, the content of these chapters might look like an ocean of numbers and technical terms that are resistant to evaluation by any but the most mathematically inclined and professionally trained. However, although it certainly is true that knowledge about scientific and professional standards for research are important bases for judging the quality of evidence, such knowledge is not sufficient. Simply stated, there is no way to prove that one or another underlying conceptualization or operationalization is correct. What is and what is not rape, a social problem, or the battered woman's syndrome is a matter of definition. True, decisions about the meaning of evidence rely on the application of the rules of research, but they also rely on logic and moral evaluation.

The task of judging the power of these arguments is essential; it is not possible to refuse evaluation and say simply that "all views" are correct. Either violence by women is a social problem or it is not; either date and acquaintance rape is an exaggerated social problem or it is not; either abused women typically do or typically do not suffer from battered woman's syndrome. It is no wonder that the debates in this section are among the most passionately argued in this volume: Depending on our evaluations of these controversies, practical and political choices logically follow.

CHAPTER 4

Physical Assaults by Wives
A Major Social Problem

Murray A. Straus

The first purpose of this chapter is to review research that shows that women initiate and carry out physical assaults on their partners as often as men do. A second purpose is to show that, despite the much lower probability of physical injury resulting from attacks by women, assaults by women are a serious social problem, just as it would be if men "only" slapped their wives or "only" slapped female fellow employees and produced no injury. One of the main reasons "minor" assaults by women are such an important problem is that they put women in danger of much more severe retaliation by men. They also help perpetuate the implicit cultural norms that make the marriage license a hitting license. It will be argued that, to end "wife beating," it is essential for women also to end the seemingly "harmless" pattern of slapping, kicking, or throwing things at male partners who persist in some outrageous behavior and "won't listen to reason."

The chapter focuses exclusively on physical assaults, even though they are not necessarily the most damaging type of abuse. One can hurt

AUTHOR'S NOTE: This chapter is based on a paper presented at the 1989 meeting of the American Society of Criminology. It is a pleasure to acknowledge the comments and criticisms of the members of the 1989-1990 Family Research Laboratory Seminar, and also those of Angela Browne, Glenda Kaufman Kantor, Coramae Mann, Daniel Saunders, Kirk R. Williams, and Kersti A. Yllö. However, this does not imply their agreement with the arguments presented in this chapter. Part of the data presented here are from the National Family Violence Resurvey, funded by National Institute of Mental Health grant R01MH40027 (Richard J. Gelles and Murray A. Straus, co-investigators) and by a grant for "family violence research training" from the National Institute of Mental Health (grant T32 MH15161).

a partner deeply—even drive the person to suicide—without ever lifting a finger. Verbal aggression may be even more damaging than physical attacks (Vissing, Straus, Gelles, & Harrop, 1991). This chapter is concerned only with physical assaults because, with rare exception, the controversy has been about "violence," that is, physical assaults, by wives.

Definition and Measurement of Assault

The National Crime Panel Report defines *assault* as "an unlawful physical attack by one person upon another" (U.S. Department of Justice, 1976). It is important to note that neither this definition nor the definition used for reporting assaults to the Federal Bureau of Investigation (1989) requires injury or bodily contact. Thus if a person is chased by someone attempting to hit the individual with a stick or to stab the person, and the victim escapes, the attack is still a felony-level crime—an "aggravated assault"—even though the victim was not touched. Nevertheless, in the real world, the occurrence of an injury makes a difference in what the police, prosecutors, and juries do. Consequently, injury will also be considered in this chapter.

Gender Differences in
Spouse Assault and Homicide Rates

National Family Violence Surveys

The National Family Violence Surveys obtained data from nationally representative samples of 2,143 married and cohabiting couples in 1975 and 6,002 couples in 1985 (information on the sample and methodology is given in Gelles & Straus, 1988; Straus & Gelles, 1986, 1990). Previously published findings have shown that, in both surveys, the rate of wife-to-husband assault was about the same (actually slightly higher) than the husband-to-wife assault rate (Straus & Gelles, 1986, 1990). However, the seeming equality may occur because of a tendency by husbands to underreport their own assaults (Dutton, 1988; Edleson & Brygger, 1986; Jouriles & O'Leary, 1985; Stets & Straus, 1990; Szinovacz, 1983). To avoid the problem of male underreporting, the assault rates were recomputed for this chapter on the basis of information provided by the 2,994 women in the 1985 National Family Violence Survey. The resulting overall rate for assaults by wives is 124 per 1,000 couples, compared with 122 per 1,000 for assaults by husbands *as reported by wives.* This difference is not great enough to be statistically significant. Separate rates were also computed for minor and severe assaults. The rate of minor assaults by wives was 78 per 1,000 couples, and the rate of minor assaults by husbands was 72 per 1,000. The severe assault rate was 46 per 1,000 couples for assaults by wives and 50 per 1,000 for assaults by husbands. Neither difference is statistically significant. As these rates are based exclusively on information provided by women respondents, the near equality in assault rates cannot be attributed to a gender bias in reporting.

As pointed out elsewhere, female assault rates based on the Conflict Tactics Scales (CTS) can be misleading because the CTS does not measure the purpose of the violence, such as whether it is in self-defense, nor does it measure injuries resulting from assaults (Straus, 1977, 1980; Straus, Gelles, & Steinmetz, 1980). That information must be obtained by additional questions, and the 1985 National Family Violence Survey included questions on who initiated violence and questions on injuries.

Injury adjusted rates. Stets and Straus (1990) and Brush (1990) provide data that can be used to adjust the rates to take into account whether the assault resulted in an injury. Stets and Straus found a rate of 3% for injury-producing assaults by men and 0.4% for injury-producing assaults by women. Somewhat lower injury rates were found by Brush for another large national sample—1.2% of injury-producing assaults by men and 0.2% for injury-producing assaults by women. An "injury adjusted" rate was computed using the higher of the two injury estimates. The resulting rate of injury-producing assaults by husbands is 3.7 per 1,000 (122 × .03 = 3.66), and the rate of injury-producing assaults by wives is much lower—0.6 per 1,000 (124 × .004 = 0.49). Thus the injury adjusted rate for assaults by men is six times greater than the rate of domestic assaults by women.

Although the injury adjusted rates correspond more closely to police and National Crime Victimization Survey statistics (see below), there are several disadvantages to rates based on injury (Straus, 1990b, pp. 79-83), two of which will be mentioned. One of the disadvantages is that the criterion of injury contradicts the new domestic assault legislation and new police policies. These statutes and policies premise restraining orders and encourage arrest on the basis of attacks. They do not require observable injury.

Another disadvantage of using injury as a criterion for domestic assault is that injury-based rates omit the 97% of assaults by husbands that do not result in injury but that are nonetheless a serious social problem. Without an adjustment for injury, the National Family Violence Survey produces an estimate of more than 6 million women assaulted by a male partner each year, of which 1.8 million are "severe" assaults (Straus & Gelles, 1990). If the injury adjusted rate is used, the estimate is reduced to 188,000 assaulted women per year. The figure of 1.8 million seriously assaulted women every year has been used in many legislative hearings and countless feminist publications to indicate the prevalence of the problem. If that estimate had to be replaced by 188,000, it would understate the extent of the problem and could handicap efforts to educate the public and secure funding for shelters and other services. Fortunately, that is not necessary. Both estimates can be used, because they highlight different aspects of the problem.

Other Surveys of Married and Dating Couples

Married and cohabiting couples. Although there may be exceptions that I missed, *every* study among the more than 30 describing some type of sample that is not self-selective (such as community random samples and samples of college student dating couples) has found a rate of assault by women on male partners that is about the same as the rate of assault by men on female partners. The space available for this chapter does not permit me to describe each of those studies, but they include research by respected scholars such as Scanzoni (1978) and Tyree and Malone (1991) and large-scale studies study such as the Los Angeles Epidemiology Catchment Area study (Sorenson & Telles, 1991), the National Survey of Households and Families (Brush, 1990), and the survey conducted for the Kentucky Commission on Women (Schulman, 1979).

The Kentucky study also brings out a troublesome question of scientific ethics, because it is one of several in which the data on assaults by women were intentionally suppressed. The existence of those data became known only because Hornung, McCullough, and Sugimoto (1981) obtained the computer tape and found that, among the violent couples, 38% were attacks by women on men who, as reported by the women themselves, had not attacked them. Some of the other studies that found approximately equal rates are cited in Straus and Gelles (1990, pp. 95-105).

Dating couples. Sugarman and Hotaling (1989) summarize the results of 21 studies that reported gender differences in assault. They found that the average assault rate was 329 per 1,000 for men and 393 per 1,000 for women. Sugarman and Hotaling comment that a "surprising finding . . . is the *higher* proportion of females than males who self-report having expressed violence in a dating relationship" (p. 8; emphasis added). Moreover, other studies published since their review further confirm the high rate of assault by women in dating relationships (see, e.g., Pirog-Good & Stets, 1989; Stets & Straus, 1990).

Samples of "battered women." Studies of residents in shelters for battered women are sometimes cited to show that it is only their male partners who are violent. However, these studies rarely obtain or report information on assaults by women, and when they do, they ask only about self-defense. Pagelow's (1981) questionnaire, for example, presents respondents with a list of "factors responsible for causing the battering," but the list does not include an attack *by* the woman, therefore precluding finding information on female-initiated assaults. One of the few exceptions is in the work of Walker (1984), who found that one out of four women in battering relationships had answered affirmatively that they had "used physical force to get something [they] wanted" (p. 174). Another is the study by Giles-Sims (1983) that found that in the year prior to coming to a shelter, 50% of the women reported assaulting their partners, and in the six months after leaving the shelter, 41.7% reported an assault against a spouse. These assaults could all have been in self-defense, but Giles-Sims's case study data suggest that this is not likely.

Government Crime Statistics

National Crime Victimization Survey. The National Crime Victimization Survey (NCVS) is an annual study of approximately 60,000 households, conducted for the Department of Justice by the Bureau of the Census. Analysis of the NCVS for the period 1973-1975 by Gaquin (1977-1978) found an extremely low rate of marital violence—2.2 per 1,000 couples. By comparison, the 1985 National Family Violence Survey found a rate of 161 per 1,000, which is 73 times higher. The NCVS rate for assaults by husbands is 3.9 per 1,000; the rate is 0.3 for assaults by wives. Thus, according to the NCVS, the rate of domestic assaults by husbands is 13 times greater than the rate of assaults by wives.

The extremely low rates of assaults by both husbands and wives found by the NCVS may be accounted for by the fact that NCVS interviews were conducted with both partners present, and victims may have been reluctant to respond out of fear of further violence. Perhaps even more important, the NCVS is presented to respondents as a study of crime. The difficulty with a "crime survey" as the context for estimating rates of domestic assault is that most people think of being kicked by their partners as wrong, but not a "crime" in the legal sense. It takes relatively rare circumstances, such as an injury or an attack by a former spouse who "has no right to do that," for the attack to be perceived as a "crime" (Langan & Innes, 1986). This is probably why the NCVS produces such totally implausible statistics as a 75% injury rate (compared with an injury rate of less than 3% in the two surveys cited earlier) and more assaults by former partners than by current partners. This is because, in the context of a crime survey, people tend to report attacks only when they have been experienced as "real crimes," because they resulted in injury or were perpetrated by former partners.

Police calls. Data on calls for domestic assaults to the police are biased in ways that are similar to the bias of the National Crime Victimization Survey. As in the NCVS, at least 93% of the cases are missed (Kaufman Kantor & Straus, 1990), probably because there was no injury or threat of serious injury great enough to warrant calling the police. Because the cases for which police are called tend to involve injury or chronic severe assault, and because that tends to be a male pattern, assaults by women are rarely recorded by police. Another reason assaults by women are rare in police statistics is that many men are reluctant to admit that they cannot "handle" their wives. These artifacts produce a rate of assaults by men that is hugely greater than the rate of assaults by women. Dobash and Dobash (1979), for example, found that only 1% of intrafamily assault cases in two Scottish cities were assaults by wives.

Spouse Homicide Rates

Homicide rates published by the FBI show that only 14% of homicide offenders are women (calculated from Federal Bureau of Investigation, 1989, unnumbered table at bottom of p. 9). However, the percentages of female offenders vary tremendously according to the relationships between offenders and victims. Female-perpetrated homicides of *strangers* occur at a rate that is less than a twentieth the male rate. The female share goes up somewhat for murders of *acquaintances*. As for murders of *family* members, women committed them at a rate that was almost half the rate of men in the period 1976-1979 and more than a third of the male rate during the period 1980-1984.

However, *family* includes all relatives, whereas the main focus of this chapter is couples. Two recent gender-specific estimates of the rates for partner homicide indicate that wives murder male partners at a rate that is 56% (Straus, 1986) and 62% (Browne & Williams, 1989) as great as the rate of partner homicides by husbands. This is far from equality, but it also indicates that, in partner relationships, even when the assaults are so extreme as to result in death, the rate for wives is extremely high, whereas, as noted above, for murders of strangers the female rate is only a twentieth of the male rate.

Self-Defense and Assaults by Wives

In previous work I have explained the high rate of attacks on spouses by wives as largely a *response* to or a defense against assault by the partner (Straus, 1977, 1980; Straus et al., 1980). However, new evidence raises questions about that interpretation.

Homicide

For lethal assaults by women, a number of studies suggest that a substantial proportion are self-defense, retaliation, or acts of desperation following years of brutal victimization (Browne, 1987; Browne & Williams, 1989; Jurik, 1989; Jurik & Gregware, 1989). However, Jurik (1989) and Jurik and Gregware's (1989) investigation of 24 cases in which women killed husbands or lovers found that the victim initiated use of physical force in 10 (40%) of the cases. Jurik and Gregware's Table 2 shows that only 5 out of the 24 homicides (21%) were in response to "prior abuse" or "threat of abuse/death." Mann's (1990) study of the circumstances surrounding partner homicides by wives shows that many women who murder their spouses are impulsive, violent, and have criminal records. Jurik (1989) and Jurik and Gregware (1989) also report that 60% of the women they studied had previous arrests. The widely cited study by Wolfgang (1958) refers to "victim-precipitated" homicides, but the case examples indicate that these homicides include cases of retaliation as well as self-defense.

National Family Violence Survey

Wife-only violence. Of the 495 couples in the 1985 National Family Violence Survey for whom one or more assaultive incidents were reported by a woman respondent, the husband was the only violent partner in 25.9% of the cases, the wife was the only one to be violent in 25.5% of the cases, and both were violent in 48.6% of the cases. Thus a minimum estimate of violence by wives that is *not* self-defense because the wife is the only one to have used violence in the past 12 months is 25%. Brush (1990) reports similar results for the couples in the National Survey of Families and Households.

Perhaps the real gender difference occurs in assaults that carry a greater risk of causing physical injury, such as punching, kicking, and attacks with weapons. This hypothesis was investigated using the 211 wives who reported one or more instances of a "severe" assault. The resulting proportions were similar: both, 35.2%; husband only, 35.2%; and wife only, 29.6%.

The findings just reported show that regardless of whether the analysis is based on all assaults or is focused on dangerous assaults, about as many women as men attacked spouses who had *not* hit them during the one-year referent period. This is inconsistent with the self-defense explanation for the high rate of domestic assault by women. However, it is possible that, among the couples where both assaulted, all the women were acting in self-defense. Even if that unlikely assumption were correct, it would still be true that 25-30% of violent marriages are violent solely because of attacks by the wife.

Initiation of attacks. The 1985 National Family Violence Survey asked respondents, "Let's talk about the last time you and your partner got into a physical fight and [the most severe act previously mentioned] happened. In that particular instance, who started the physical conflict, you or your partner?" According to the 446 wives involved in violent relationships, their partners struck the first blows in 42.3% of the cases, the women hit first in 53.1% of the cases, and the women could not remember or could not disentangle who hit first in the remaining 3.1% of the cases.

Similar results were obtained by five other studies. Bland and Orne's (1986) study of marital violence and psychiatric disorder in Canada found that wives initiated violence somewhat more often than did husbands. Gryl and Bird (1989) found that "respondents in violent dating relationships indicated that their partners initiated the violence 51% of the time; they initiated it 41% of the time; and both were equally responsible 8% of the time." Saunders (1989) analyzed data on the sequence of events in the 1975 National Family Violence Survey and found that women respondents indicated that they struck the first blow in 40% of the cases. Henton, Cate, Koval, Lloyd, and Christopher (1983) found that "in 48.7% . . . of the relationships, the respondent perceived that both partners were responsible for 'starting' the violence" (p. 472). A large-scale Canadian study found that women struck the first blow about as often as men. However, as in the case of the Kentucky survey mentioned earlier, the authors have not published the findings, perhaps because they are not "politically correct."

Is the High Rate of Assault by Wives Explainable as Self-Defense?

It is remarkable that every study that has investigated who initiates violence using methods that do not preclude the possibility of a wife beating, found that wives initiate violence in a large proportion of cases. However, caution is needed in interpreting these findings, for several reasons.

First, some respondents may have answered the question in terms of who began *the argument*, not who began *hitting*. Interviewers were instructed to rephrase the question in such cases. However, there may have been instances in which the misunderstanding of the question went unnoticed.

Second, if the wife hit first, that could still be in self-defense if her attack was in response to a situation that she defined as posing a threat of grave harm from which she could not otherwise escape (Browne, 1987; Jurik, 1989; Jurik & Gregware, 1989).

A third reason for caution is the limited data available in the National Family Violence Survey on the context of the assaults. Who initiates an assault and who is injured are important aspects of the contextual information needed for a full understanding of the gendered aspects of intrafamily assault, but they are not sufficient. For example, there may have been an escalation of assaults throughout the relationship, with the original attacks by the man. The fact that the most recent incident happened to be initiated by the female partner ignores the history and the context producing that act, which may be one of utter terror. This scenario is common in cases of women who kill abusive male partners. A battered woman may kill her partner when he is not attacking her, and thus may appear not to be acting in self-defense. As Browne (1987), Jurik (1989), and Jurik and Gregware (1989) show, the traditional criteria for self-defense use assumptions based on male characteristics that ignore physical size and strength differences between men and women and ignore the economic dependency that locks some women into relationships in which they have legitimate grounds for fearing for their lives.

The scenario described above is often recounted by clients of shelters for battered women. However, it is hazardous to extrapolate from the situation of women in those extreme situations to the pattern of assaults that characterizes couples in the general population as represented in the National Family Violence Survey. This issue is discussed more fully later in this chapter, in the section on the representative sample fallacy. For the moment, let us assume that many of the assaults initiated by wives are in response to fear derived from a long prior history of victimization. Even if that is the case, it is a response that tends to elicit further assaults by the male partner (Bowker, 1983; Feld & Straus, 1989; Gelles & Straus, 1988, chap. 7; Straus, 1974).

In the light of these qualifications and cautions, the self-defense explanation of the near equality between husbands and wives in domestic assaults cannot be rejected. However, one can conclude that the research on who hit first does not support the hypothesis that assaults by wives are primarily acts of self-defense or retaliation.

Gender and Chronicity of Assault

Although the prevalence rate of assaults by wives is about the same as that for husbands, husbands may engage in more *repeated* attacks. This hypothesis was investigated by computing the mean number of assaults among couples for which at least one assault was reported by a female respondent. According to these 495 women, their partners averaged 7.2 assaults during the year, and they themselves averaged six assaults. Although the frequency of assault by husbands is greater than the frequency of assault by wives, the difference is just short of being statistically significant. If the analysis is restricted to the 165 cases of severe assault, the husbands averaged 6.1 and the wives 4.28 assaults, which is a 42% greater frequency of assault by husbands and is also just short of being statistically significant. If one disregards the tests of statistical significance, these comparisons support the hypothesized greater chronicity of violence by husbands. At the same time, the fact that the average number of assaults by husbands is higher should not obscure the fact that the violent *wives* carried out an average of six minor and five severe assaults per year, indicating a repetitive pattern by wives as well as by husbands.

The Clinical Fallacy and
the Representative Sample Fallacy

The discrepancy between the findings from surveys of family problems and findings based on criminal justice system data or the experiences of women in shelters for battered women does not indicate that one set of statistics is correct and the other not. Both are correct. However, they apply to different groups of people and reflect different aspects of domestic assault. Most of the violence that is revealed by surveys of family problems is relatively minor and relatively infrequent, whereas most of the violence in official statistics is chronic and severe and involves injuries that need medical attention. These two types of violence probably have different etiologies and probably require different types of intervention. It is important not to use findings based on cases known to the police or shelters for battered women as the basis for deciding how to deal with the relatively minor and infrequent violence found in the population in general. That type of unwarranted generalization is often made; it is known as the *clinical fallacy*.

Representative community sample studies have the opposite problem, which can be called the *representative sample fallacy* (Straus, 1990b; see also Gelles, 1991). Community samples contain very few cases involving severe assaults every week or more often and injury. Men tend to be the predominant aggressors in this type of case, but representative sample studies cannot reveal that, because they include few if any such cases. Ironically, the types of cases that are not covered by community surveys are the most horrible cases and the ones that everyone wants to do something about. However, community surveys can tell us little about what to do about these extreme cases because the samples contain too few to analyze separately.

The controversy over assaults by women largely stems from survey researchers' assumptions that their findings on rates of spouse assault by men and women apply to cases known to the police and to shelters, and the similar unwarranted assumption by clinical researchers that the predominance of assaults by men applies to the population at large.

Both community sample data and clinical sample data are needed. Community sample data are essential for informing programs directed at the larger community, especially programs intended to prevent such cases in the first place or to prevent them from developing into "clinical cases." Conversely, it is essential to have research on clinical samples, such as those involved with the police or shelters for battered women, in order to have data that do apply to such cases and that therefore provide a realistic basis for programs designed to aid the victims and to end the most serious type of domestic violence.

Context and Meaning

The number of assaults by itself, however, ignores the contexts, meanings, and consequences of these assaults. The fact that assaults by women produce far less injury is a critical difference. There are probably other important differences between men and women in assaults on partners. For example, a man may typically hit or threaten to hit to force some specific behavior on pain of injury, whereas a woman may typically slap a partner or pound on his chest as an expression of outrage or in frustration because of his having turned a deaf ear to repeated attempts to discuss some critical issue (Greenblat, 1983). Despite this presumed difference, both are uses of physical violence for coercion.

A meta-analysis of research on gender differences in aggression by Eagly and Steffen (1986) brings out a related difference in context and meaning. These researchers found no *overall* difference in aggression by men and women, but less aggression by women if the act would produce harm to the target. These and other differences in context, meaning, and motivation are important for understanding violence by women against partners, but they do not indicate the absence of assault by women. Nor do differences between men and women in the histories, meanings, objectives, and consequences of assaults refute the hypothesis discussed below: that assaults by wives help legitimate male violence. Only empirical research can resolve that issue.

Violence by Wives
Increases the Probability of Wife Beating

There seems to be an implicit cultural norm permitting or encouraging minor assaults by wives in certain circumstances. Stark and McEvoy (1970) found about equal support for a wife hitting a husband as for a husband hitting a wife. Greenblat (1983) found that both men and women are *more* accepting of wives hitting husbands than of husbands hitting wives. Data from the National Family Violence Survey also show more public acceptance of a wife slapping a husband than of a husband slapping a wife. Greenblat suggests that this is because "female aggressors are far less likely to do physical harm"

(p. 247). These norms tolerating low-level violence by women are transmitted and learned in many ways. For example, even casual observation of the mass media suggests that just about every day, there are scenes depicting a man who makes an insulting or outrageous statement and an indignant woman who responds by "slapping the cad," thus presenting an implicit model of assault as a morally correct behavior to millions of women.

Let us assume that most of the assaults by wives fall into the "slap the cad" genre and are not intended to, and only rarely, cause physical injury. The danger to women is shown by studies that find that minor violence by wives increases the probability of severe assaults by husbands (Bowker, 1983; Feld & Straus, 1989; Gelles & Straus, 1988, pp. 146-156). Sometimes this is immediate and severe retaliation. Regardless of whether that occurs, however, a more indirect and probably more important effect may be that such morally correct slapping acts out and reinforces the traditional tolerance of assault in marriage. The moral justification of assault implicit when a woman slaps or throws something at a partner for doing something outrageous reinforces his moral justification for slapping her when *she* is doing something outrageous, or when she is obstinate, nasty, or "not listening to reason" as he sees it. To the extent that this is correct, one of the many steps needed in primary prevention of assaults on wives is for women to forsake even "harmless" physical attacks on male partners and children. Women must insist on nonviolence from their sisters, just as they rightfully insist on it from men.

It is painful to have to recognize the high rate of domestic assaults by women. Moreover, the statistics are likely to be used by misogynists and apologists for male violence. The problem is similar to that noted by Barbara Hart (1986) in the introduction to a book on lesbian battering: "[It] is painful. It challenges our dream of a lesbian utopia. It contradicts our belief in the inherent nonviolence of women. And the disclosure of violence by lesbians . . . may enhance the arsenal of homophobes. . . . Yet, if we are to free ourselves, we must free our sisters" (p. 10). My view of recognizing violence by wives is parallel to Hart's view on lesbian battering. It is painful, but to do otherwise obstructs a potentially important means of reducing assaults by husbands—raising the consciousness of women about the implicit norms that are reinforced by a ritualized slap for outrageous behavior on the part of their partners.

It follows from the above that efforts to prevent assaults by husbands must include attention to assaults by wives. Although this may seem like "victim blaming," there is an important difference. Recognizing that assaults by wives are one of the many causes of wife beating does not justify such assaults. It is the responsibility of husbands as well as wives to refrain from physical attacks (including retaliation), at home as elsewhere, no matter what the provocation.

Conclusions

Ending assaults *by* wives needs to be added to efforts to prevent assaults *on* wives for a number of reasons. Perhaps the most fundamental reason is the intrinsic moral wrong of assaulting a spouse, as expressed in the fact that such assaults are criminal acts, even when no injury occurs. A second reason is the unintended validation of the traditional cultural norms tolerating a certain level of violence between spouses. A third reason is the danger of escalation when wives engage in "harmless" minor violence. Feld and Straus (1989) found that if the female partner also engaged in an assault, it increased the probability that assaults would persist or escalate in severity over the one-year period of their study, whereas if only one partner engaged in physical attacks, the probability of cessation increased. Finally, assault of a spouse "models" violence for children. This effect is as strong for assaults by wives as it is for assaults by husbands (Jaffe, Wolfe, & Wilson, 1990; Straus, 1983, 1992a; Straus et al., 1980).

It should be emphasized that the preventive effect of reducing minor assaults by wives has not been proven by the evidence in this chapter. It is a plausible inference and a hypotheses for further research. Especially needed are studies to test the hypothesis that "harmless" assaults by wives strengthen the implicit moral justification for assaults by husbands. If the research confirms that hypothesis, it would indicate the need to add reduction of assaults by wives to efforts to end wife beating, including public service announcements, police arrest policy, and treatment programs for batterers. Such changes must be made with extreme care for a number of reasons, not the least of which is to avoid implying that violence by women justifies or excuses violence by their partners. Moreover, although women may assault their partners at approximately the same rate as men assault theirs, because of the greater physical, financial, and emotional injury suffered, women are the predominant victims (Stets & Straus, 1990; Straus et al., 1980). Consequently, first priority in services for victims and in prevention and control must continue to be directed toward assaults by husbands.

Response to Demie Kurz's Chapter

Chapter 5 of this volume, by Demie Kurz, is representative of a number of allegedly feminist criticisms of the research showing roughly equal rates of assault by wives and husbands. These critics argue that the family violence approach and the feminist approach are irreconcilable. On the contrary, what is irreconcilable are these critics' erroneous depiction of family violence research as ignoring gender and power and their narrow and erroneous depiction of feminism as a single causal factor theory. This response therefore applies to that literature as well as to the immediate example of Kurz's chapter. This literature misrepresents both family violence and feminist approaches. It also contains many factual errors.

How can so many errors occur and be repeated so often? Elsewhere, I discuss several possibilities, including the possibility that the errors are deliberate distortions intended to discredit the scientific findings by discrediting the researchers whose studies revealed the equal rates of assault (Straus, 1992b). In this response, I will show that the literature represented by Kurz's chapter also seems to be operating on the principle that an erroneous assertion becomes true if it is repeated often enough. Following are some examples.

Kurz is one of many who state or imply that family violence researchers ignore the fact that male violence results in more injury than does female violence. This is truly incredible, because that very point has been emphasized in every one of my books and papers on this issue since the 1970s.

Kurz implies that family violence researchers want to give priority to violence by women, whereas my publications over many years (some of which she cites) have consistently stated the opposite. To take the most recent example, my closing words in this chapter are that "first priority in services for victims and in prevention and control must continue to be directed toward assaults by husbands."

A truly amazing statement by Kurz is that I "misrepresent the nature of marriage as a partnership of equals." In fact, a central focus of my research since the early 1970s has been studies showing male dominance and its pernicious effects, including violence against women (Coleman & Straus, 1986; Kolb & Straus, 1974; Straus, 1973, 1976, 1994; Straus et al., 1980; Yllö & Straus, 1990).

Many of the issues for which Kurz and others contrast the "family violence" approach with the "feminist approach" are issues we agree are important contributions of the feminist approach. What is wrong is presenting them as contradicting the approach of family violence researchers. Quite the opposite. A paper I presented in 1973 was the sociological work that first introduced most of the feminist approaches to assaults on women that Kurz presents (see Straus, 1976). Almost every time Kurz uses the phrase "feminists argue," it can be replaced by citations to publications in which "Straus argues." These feminist issues include institutionalized male power, cultural norms legitimating male violence against women, and economic inequality between men and women that locks women into violent marriages. These contributions were widely cited until I published "politically incorrect" data on violence by women and was therefore excommunicated from feminist ranks. However, I remain one of the faithful, and have never accepted the excommunication.

The only evidence in Kurz's chapter that seems to refute the 30 or more studies showing that women assault partners at about the same rate as men is from police records and the National Crime Victimization Survey. However, for the reasons I have described in this chapter, police and NCVS statistics are not valid as measures of the extent to which women assault their partners. The inappropriateness of using NCVS and police statistics for this purpose has been acknowledged by the Department of Justice (Langan & Innes, 1986), which is currently trying to redesign the NCVS to correct the problem.

As for the Conflict Tactics Scales, ostensibly feminist critiques of this instrument contain so many factual errors that the authors could not have examined the CTS firsthand. To take just three examples from errors in many of these "critiques": First, the CTS is said to measure only violence used to settle a conflict. On the contrary, the introductory instructions ask respondents to describe what happens "when they disagree, get annoyed with the other person, or just have spats or fights because they're in a bad mood or tired or for some other reason." Second, the results are questionable because men may underreport their own violence, but the statistics in this chapter are based on interviews with wives. Third, Kurz says the CTS ignores verbal abuse, but Verbal Aggression is one of the three scales in the CTS.

In addition to factual errors, there are conceptual errors. For example, it is claimed that the CTS is invalid "because the continuum of violence in the scales is so broad that it fails to discriminate among the different kinds of violence." Rather, it is the broad continuum that enables one to identify cases on the basis of the severity of the violence. Perhaps the most important conceptual error is the belief that the CTS is deficient because it does not measure the consequences of physical assault (such as physical and emotional injury) or the causes (such as a desire to dominate). This is akin to thinking that a spelling test is inadequate because it does not measure why a child spells badly, or does not measure possible consequences of poor spelling, such as low self-esteem or low evaluations by employers. The concentration of the CTS on acts of physical assault is deliberate and is one of its strengths. Only by having separate measures of assaults, injuries, and context can one, for example, show that acts of violence by men result in more injury than when the same acts are committed by women (Stets & Straus, 1990; Straus, 1990a, 1990b).

The attacks on the CTS are examples of blaming the messenger for the bad news. Moreover, no matter what one thinks of the CTS, at least four studies that did *not* use the CTS also found roughly equal rates of violence by women.

Like all tests and scales, the CTS is not perfect. Nevertheless, numerous reviews by scholars who are not interested in blaming the messenger agree that the CTS is the best available instrument (see, e.g., reviews by Grotevant & Carlson, 1989; Hertzberger, 1991). Its use in many studies since 1973 has established its validity and reliability. No other scale meets this standard. New evidence on validity and reliability is published almost monthly by research scholars who are using the CTS in many countries. My own use of the CTS has produced strong support for several aspects of feminist theory. It is time for other feminist scholars to take advantage of this instrument to do likewise.

It is almost beyond belief that Kurz and certain other allegedly feminist critics can ignore or dismiss the many studies that have data on samples that are representative of the general public (compared with clinical samples) and that, without exception, find nearly equal rates of violence by women.

Perhaps even more serious is the implied excusing of assaults by women because they result from frustration and anger at being dominated. This is parallel to the excuses men give to justify hitting their wives, such as a woman's being unfaithful. Kurz also excuses the "slap the cad" type of violence by women as defensive behavior, even though the example in my chapter to which she refers does not imply a physical attack, or threat of such an attack, by a male partner.

In my opinion, major parts of Kurz's chapter and other similar critiques are not feminist critiques, but justifications of violence by women in the guise of feminism. This is a betrayal of the feminist ideal of a nonviolent world. In addition, excusing violence by women and denying overwhelming research evidence may have serious side effects. It may undermine the credibility of feminist scholarship and

contribute to a backlash that can also undermine progress toward the
goal of equality between men and women.

References

Bland, R., & Orne, H. (1986). Family violence and psychiatric disorder. *Canadian Journal
    of Psychiatry, 31,* 129-137.
Bowker, L. H. (1983). *Beating wife-beating.* Lexington, MA: Lexington.
Browne, A. (1987). *When battered women kill.* New York: Free Press.
Browne, A., & Williams, K. R. (1989). Exploring the effect of resource availability and
    the likelihood of female-perpetrated homicides. *Law and Society Review, 23(1),*
    75-94.
Brush, L. D. (1990). Violent acts and injurious outcomes in married couples: Methodo-
    logical issues in the National Survey of Families and Households. *Gender & Society,*
    4, 56-67.
Coleman, D. H., & Straus, M. A. (1986). Marital power, conflict and violence. *Violence
    and Victims, 1,* 141-157.
Dobash, R. E., & Dobash, R. P. (1979). *Violence against wives: A case against the patriarchy.*
    New York: Free Press.
Dutton, D. G. (1988). *The domestic assault of women: Psychological and criminal justice
    perspectives.* Boston: Allyn & Bacon.
Eagly, A. H., & Steffen, V. J. (1986). Gender and aggressive behavior: A meta-analytic
    review of the social psychological literature. *Psychological Bulletin, 100,* 309-330.
Edleson, J. L., & Brygger, M. P. (1986). Gender differences in reporting of battering
    incidents. *Family Relations, 35,* 377-382.
Federal Bureau of Investigation. (1989). *Crime in the United States.* Washington, DC: U.S.
    Department of Justice.
Feld, S. L., & Straus, M. A. (1989). Escalation and desistance of wife assault in marriage.
    Criminology, 27, 141-161.
Gaquin, D. A. (1977-1978). Spouse abuse: Data from the National Crime Survey. *Vic-
    timology, 2,* 632-642.
Gelles, R. J. (1991). Physical violence, child abuse, and child homicide: A continuum of
    violence or distinct behaviors? *Human Nature, 2,* 59-72.
Gelles, R. J., & Straus, M. A. (1988). *Intimate violence: The causes and consequences of abuse
    in the American family.* New York: Simon & Schuster.
Giles-Sims, J. (1983). *Wife battering: A systems theory approach.* New York: Guilford.
Greenblat, C. S. (1983). A hit is a hit is a hit . . . or is it? Approval and tolerance of the
    use of physical force by spouses. In D. Finkelhor, R. J. Gelles, G. T. Hotaling, &
    M. A. Straus (Eds.), *The dark side of families: Current family violence research* (pp. 235-
    260). Beverly Hills, CA: Sage.
Grotevant, H. D., & Carlson, C. I. (1989). *Family assessment: A guide to methods and
    measures.* New York: Guilford.
Gryl, F. E., & Bird, G. W. (1989). *Close dating relationships among college students: Differences
    by gender and by use of violence.* Paper presented at the annual meeting of the
    National Council on Family Relations, New Orleans.
Hart, B. (1986). Preface. In K. Lobel (Ed.), *Naming the violence: Speaking out about lesbian
    battering* (pp. 9-16). Seattle, WA: Seal.

Henton, J., Cate, R., Koval, J., Lloyd, S., & Christopher, S. (1983). Romance and violence in dating relationships. *Journal of Family Issues, 4*, 467-482.

Hertzberger, S. D. (1991). The Conflict Tactics Scales. In D. J. Keyser & R. C. Sweetland (Eds.), *Test critiques, 8*. Kansas City: Test Corporation of America.

Hornung, C. A., McCullough, B. C., & Sugimoto, T. (1981). Status relationships in marriage: Risk factors in spouse abuse. *Journal of Marriage and the Family, 43*, 675-692.

Jaffe, P. G., Wolfe, D. A., & Wilson, S. K. (1990). *Children of battered women: Issues in child development and intervention planning*. Newbury Park, CA: Sage.

Jouriles, E. N., & O'Leary, K. D. (1985). Interspousal reliability of reports of marital violence. *Journal of Consulting and Clinical Psychology, 53*, 419-421.

Jurik, N. C. (1989, November). *Women who kill and the reasonable man: The legal issues surrounding female-perpetrated homicide*. Paper presented at the 41st Annual Meeting of the American Society of Criminology, Reno, NV.

Jurik, N. C., & Gregware, P. (1989). *A method for murder: An interactionist analysis of homicides by women*. Tempe: Arizona State University, School of Justice Studies.

Kaufman Kantor, G., & Straus, M. A. (1990). Response of victims and the police to assaults on wives. In M. A. Straus & R. J. Gelles (Eds.), *Physical violence in American families: Risk factors and adaptations to violence in 8,145 families* (pp. 473-486). New Brunswick, NJ: Transaction.

Kolb, T. M., & Straus, M. A. (1974). Marital power and marital happiness in relation to problem solving ability. *Journal of Marriage and the Family, 36*, 756-766.

Langan, P., & Innes, C. A. (1986). *Preventing domestic violence against women* (Bureau of Justice Statistics Special Report). Washington, DC: U.S. Department of Justice.

Mann, C. R. (1990). Black female homicide in the United States. *Journal of Interpersonal Violence, 5*, 176-201.

Pagelow, M. D. (1981). *Woman-battering: Victims and their experiences*. Beverly Hills, CA: Sage.

Pirog-Good, M. A., & Stets, J. E. (Eds.). (1989). *Violence in dating relationships: Emerging social issues*. New York: Praeger.

Saunders, D. G. (1989, November). *Who hits first and who hurts most? Evidence for the greater victimization of women in intimate relationships*. Paper presented at the 41st Annual Meeting of the American Society of Criminology, Reno, NV.

Scanzoni, J. (1978). *Sex roles, women's work, and marital conflict*. Lexington, MA: Lexington.

Schulman, M. (1979, July). *A survey of spousal violence against women in Kentucky* (Study No. 792701, conducted for Kentucky Commission on Women, sponsored by the U.S. Department of Justice, Law Enforcement Assistance Administration). Washington, DC: Government Printing Office.

Sorenson, S. B., & Telles, C. A. (1991). Self-reports of spousal violence in a Mexican-American and non-Hispanic white population. *Violence and Victims, 6*, 3-15.

Stark, R., & McEvoy, J., III. (1970, November). Middle class violence. *Psychology Today, 4*, 52-65.

Stets, J. E., & Straus, M. A. (1990). Gender differences in reporting marital violence and its medical and psychological consequences. In M. A. Straus & R. J. Gelles (Eds.), *Physical violence in American families: Risk factors and adaptations to violence in 8,145 families* (pp. 151-166). New Brunswick, NJ: Transaction.

Straus, M. A. (1973). A general systems theory approach to a theory of violence between family members. *Social Science Information, 12*, 105-125.

Straus, M. A. (1974). Leveling, civility, and violence in the family. *Journal of Marriage and the Family, 36*, 13-29.

Straus, M. A. (1976). Sexual inequality, cultural norms, and wife-beating. *Victimology, 1,* 54-76.

Straus, M. A. (1977, March). Normative and behavioral aspects of violence between spouses: Preliminary data on a nationally representative USA sample. In *Violence in Canadian Society.* Symposium sponsored by Simon Fraser University, Department of Criminology, at the University of New Hampshire Family Research Laboratory, Durham.

Straus, M. A. (1980). Victims and aggressors in marital violence. *American Behavioral Scientist, 23,* 681-704.

Straus, M. A. (1983). Ordinary violence, child abuse, and wife-beating: What do they have in common? In D. Finkelhor, R. J. Gelles, G. T. Hotaling, & M. A. Straus (Eds.), *The dark side of families: Current family violence research* (pp. 213-234). Beverly Hills, CA: Sage.

Straus, M. A. (1986). Domestic violence and homicide antecedents. *Domestic Violence, 62,* 446-465.

Straus, M. A. (1990a). The Conflict Tactics Scales and its critics: An evaluation and new data on validity and reliability. In M. A. Straus & R. J. Gelles (Eds.), *Physical violence in American families: Risk factors and adaptations to violence in 8,145 families* (pp. 49-73). New Brunswick, NJ: Transaction.

Straus, M. A. (1990b). Injury and frequency of assault and the "representative sample fallacy" in measuring wife beating and child abuse. In M. A. Straus & R. J. Gelles (Eds.), *Physical violence in American families: Risk factors and adaptations to violence in 8,145 families* (pp. 75-91). New Brunswick, NJ: Transaction.

Straus, M. A. (1992a). Children as witnesses to marital violence: A risk factor for lifelong problems among a nationally representative sample of American men and women. In D. F. Schwarz (Ed.), *Children and violence: Report of the Twenty-Third Ross Roundtable on Critical Approaches to Common Pediatric Problems in collaboration with the Ambulatory Pediatric Association.* Columbus, OH: Ross Laboratories.

Straus, M. A. (1992b). Sociological research and social policy: The case of family violence. *Sociological Forum, 7,* 211-237.

Straus, M. A. (1994). State-to-state differences in social inequality and social bonds in relation to assaults on wives in the United States. *Journal of Comparative Family Studies, 25.*

Straus, M. A., & Gelles, R. J. (1986). Societal change and change in family violence from 1975 to 1985 as revealed by two national surveys. *Journal of Marriage and the Family, 48,* 465-479.

Straus, M. A., & Gelles, R. J. (Eds.). (1990). *Physical violence in American families: Risk factors and adaptations to violence in 8,145 families.* New Brunswick, NJ: Transaction.

Straus, M. A., Gelles, R. J., & Steinmetz, S. K. (1980). *Behind closed doors: Violence in the American family.* Garden City, NY: Anchor/Doubleday.

Sugarman, D. B., & Hotaling, G. T. (1989). Dating violence: Prevalence, context, and risk markers. In M. A. Pirog-Good & J. E. Stets (Eds.), *Violence in dating relationships: Emerging social issues.* New York: Praeger.

Szinovacz, M. E. (1983). Using couple data as a methodological tool: The case of marital violence. *Journal of Marriage and the Family, 45,* 633-644.

Tyree, A., & Malone, J. (1991). *How can it be that wives hit husbands as much as husbands hit wives and none of us knew it?* Paper presented at the annual meeting of the American Sociological Association.

U.S. Department of Justice. (1976). *Dictionary of criminal justice data terminology.* Washington, DC: National Criminal Justice Information Service.

Vissing, Y. M., Straus, M. A., Gelles, R. J., & Harrop, J. W. (1991). Verbal aggression by parents and psychosocial problems of children. *Child Abuse and Neglect, 15,* 223-238.

Walker, L. E. A. (1984). *The battered woman syndrome.* New York: Springer.

Wolfgang, M. E. (1958). *Patterns of criminal homicide.* Philadelphia: University of Pennsylvania Press.

Yllö, K. A., & Straus, M. A. (1990). Patriarchy and violence against wives: The impact of structural and normative factors. In M. A. Straus & R. J. Gelles (Eds.), *Physical violence in American families: Risk factors and adaptations to violence in 8,145 families.* New Brunswick, NJ: Transaction.

CHAPTER 5

Physical Assaults by Husbands
A Major Social Problem

Demie Kurz

Are women violent toward men? This question has been asked repeatedly, particularly in recent years as the issue of domestic violence has gained national recognition. The women's movement, which brought the issue of battered women to public attention in the late 1970s, claims that it is men who are violent (Dobash & Dobash, 1992; Schechter, 1982; Tierney, 1982). Currently, advocates for battered women in many professions and organizations accept this analysis, and use it to promote change in the legal, medical, and social service responses to battered women (American College of Physicians, 1986; Attorney General's Task Force on Family Violence, 1984; Johnson, 1985; Koop, 1985).

However, among social scientists there has been a lot of controversy about the nature of violence in intimate relationships, particularly the question of whether women are violent toward men. A number of social scientists identify with the feminist tradition and argue that women are the victims of violence in relationships with men (Bowker, 1986; Breines & Gordon, 1983; Dobash & Dobash, 1979; Kurz, 1989; Loseke, 1992; Pagelow, 1981; Stanko, 1985; Wardell, Gillespie, & Leffler, 1983; Yllö & Bograd, 1988; see also Yllö, Chapter 3, this volume). These researchers claim that, historically, the law has promoted women's subordination and condoned husbands' use of force in marriage. Other social scientists, the "family violence" researchers, argue that the real problems are "spouse abuse" and "family violence" (see, e.g., Gelles, 1974; Gelles & Cornell, 1985; Gelles & Straus, 1988; McNeely & Robinson-Simpson, 1987; Schwartz, 1987; Shupe, Stacey, & Hazelwood, 1987; Steinmetz, 1977-1978; Stets, 1990; Stets & Straus, 1990; Straus, 1980a;

88

Straus & Gelles, 1990; Straus, Gelles, & Steinmetz, 1980; see also St___s, Chapter 4, this volume). These researchers believe that women as well as men are violent, and some claim that women "initiate and carry out physical assaults on their partners as often as men do" (Straus, Chapter 4, this volume).

This debate over men's and women's use of violence has significant consequences for popular and academic conceptions of battered women, and for social policy. How a problem is framed determines the amount of concern that is generated for that problem as well as the solutions that are proposed. Research findings influence whether the media and the public take battered women seriously, or whether they view them as equally blameworthy partners in "family violence." Feminists fear that a focus framing the problem as "spouse abuse" will lead to decreased funding for shelters, a diversion of resources to "battered men," and/or increased arrests of women in "domestic disputes" under mandatory arrest policies. More generally, feminists fear that a focus on "spouse abuse" diverts attention from the causes of violence against women—inequality and male dominance.

In this chapter I argue that the feminist point of view best explains the nature and the extent of violence between men and women in intimate relationships. Feminists argue that violence between intimates takes place within a context of inequality between men and women in marriage, whereas family violence researchers promote a gender-neutral view of power in intimate relationships. I will compare the evidence and theories presented by the proponents of each perspective, and I will argue that the family violence view is based on false assumptions about the nature of marriage and of equality between men and women.

A Feminist Perspective on Violence in Intimate Relationships

Feminist researchers argue that women are the victims of male violence. They support their point of view with official crime statistics, data from the criminal justice system and hospitals, interviews with victims of battering and batterers, and historical evidence. Looking at such data, which, as Straus notes in Chapter 4 of this volume, are biased toward finding extreme victimization, it is clear that women are overwhelmingly the victims of violence. The National Crime Victimization Survey of 1982 reported that 91% of all violent crimes between spouses were directed at women by husbands or ex-husbands, whereas only 5% were directed at husbands by wives or ex-wives (cited in Browne, 1987, p. 7). Analysis of these data over time provides similar results (Gaquin, 1977-1978; Schwartz, 1987). In their study of police records in Scotland, Dobash and Dobash (1979) found that when gender was known, women were targets in 94% and offenders in 3% of cases. Other studies based on data from the criminal justice system show similar results (Kincaid, 1982; McLeod, 1984; Quarm & Schwartz, 1985; Watkins, 1982).

Data on injury patterns confirm that it is women, not men, who sustain injuries in conflicts between males and females in intimate relationships. Brush (1990), in an analysis of data from the National Survey of Families and Households, found that women were significantly more likely to be injured than were men in disputes involving violent tactics. Berk, Berk, Loseke, and Rauma (1983), based on their examination of police records, conclude that in 95% of cases it is the woman who is injured and that, even when both partners are injured, the woman's injuries are nearly three times as severe as the man's. Data from hospitals show women to be overwhelmingly the injured parties (Kurz, 1987, 1990; McLeer & Anwar, 1989; Stark, Flitcraft, & Frazier, 1979). These data lead feminist researchers to reject the concept of "spouse abuse," the idea that women are equally as violent as men.

Feminists claim that the use of violence by men to control female intimates has long been condoned by major social institutions. The first law in the United States to recognize a husband's right to control his wife with physical force was an 1824 ruling by the Supreme Court of Mississippi permitting the husband "to exercise the right of moderate chastisement in cases of great emergency" (quoted in Browne, 1987, p. 166). This and similar rulings in Maryland and Massachusetts were based on English common law, which gave a husband the right of "correction" of his wife, although he was supposed to use it in moderation.

> In 1871 wife beating was made illegal in Alabama. The court stated: The privilege, ancient though it be, to beat her with a stick, to pull her hair, choke her, spit in her face or kick her about the floor, or to inflict upon her like indignities, is not now acknowledged by our law. . . . the wife is entitled to the same protection of the law that the husband can invoke for himself. (quoted in Browne, 1987, p. 167)

A North Carolina court made a similar decision in 1874, but limited the kinds of cases in which the court should intervene:

If no permanent injury has been inflicted, nor malice, cruelty nor dangerous violence shown by the husband, it is better to draw the curtain, shut
out the public gaze, and leave the parties to forget and forgive. (quoted
in Browne, 1987, p. 167)

Until recent legal reforms were enacted, the "curtain rule" was widely
used by the legal system to justify its nonintervention in cases of wife
abuse.

The law and the nature of marriage have changed dramatically since
the early twentieth century; however, feminists claim that these institutions continue to condone violence against women. Although new
laws have criminalized battering, we do not know whether these laws
will be enforced (Buzawa & Buzawa, 1990; Kurz, 1992). A recent study
suggests that even police who receive training in how to make a
criminal response to battering cases may continue to view battered
women as unfortunate victims of personal and social problems such
as poverty and, in the absence of strong police department support,
view arrests as low priority and not part of their "real" work (Ferraro,
1989). To the extent that these laws are not viewed seriously, the legal
system will continue to treat battering as an individual problem, rather
than as criminal behavior.

As for marriage, feminists argue that it still institutionalizes the
control of wives by husbands through the structure of husband-wife
roles. As long as women are responsible for domestic work, child care,
and emotional and psychological support, and men's primary identity
is that of provider and revolves around employment, the husband has
the more important status and also controls the majority of decisions
in the family. It is through such a system, coupled with the acceptance
of physical force as a means of control, that, in the words of Dobash
and Dobash (1979), the wife becomes an "appropriate victim" of physical and psychological abuse. Feminists argue further that the use of
violence for control in marriage is perpetuated not only through norms
about a man's rights in marriage, but through women's continued
economic dependence on their husbands, which makes it difficult for
wives to leave violent relationships. This dependence is increased by
the lack of adequate child care and job training, which would enable
women to get jobs with which they could support themselves.

Citing interview data from men and women that demonstrate that
battering incidents occur when husbands try to make their wives
comply with their wishes, feminist researchers believe that men still
use violence as a way to control female partners. Based on data from
interviews with 109 battered women, Dobash and Dobash (1979)

demonstrate how, over the course of their marriages, batterers increasingly control wives through intimidation and isolation, findings confirmed by other interview studies (Pagelow, 1981; Walker, 1984). Violence, therefore, is just one of a variety of controls that men try to exercise over female partners; others are anger and psychological abuse (Adams, 1988; Dobash & Dobash, 1979; Mederos, 1987). Interviews with batterers show that men believe they are justified in their use of violence, particularly when their wives do not conform to the ideal of the "good wife" (see Adams, 1988; Dobash & Dobash, 1979; Ptacek, 1988).

Some researchers have also found that male dominance is a factor in other types of violence in the family. For example, Bowker, Arbitell, and McFerron (1988) found that 70% of wife beaters also physically abused their children; these researchers argue that the most important cause and context of child abuse is current abuse of a woman by a male intimate. They also found that the severity of wife beating predicted the severity of child abuse, and that the greater the degree of husband dominance, the greater the likelihood of child abuse. Similarly, Stark and Flitcraft (1985), in their review of medical records, found that children whose mothers were battered were more than twice as likely to be physically abused as were children whose mothers were not battered. They also believe that purposive violence by male intimates against women is the most important context for child abuse. Thus to understand and prevent child abuse it is important to consider that, among other factors, male dominance has a significant impact on fathers' treatment of children (Margolin, 1992).

Finally, feminists have shown how, in addition to the law and the family, a variety of institutions condone male dominance and reinforce battering on an ongoing, everyday basis. Some have demonstrated how this occurs through the labeling and processing of abused women by frontline workers who have the most contact with these women. Stark et al. (1979) argue that because of patriarchal medical ideologies and practices, health care practitioners fail to recognize battering and instead label battered women as having psychological problems. These researchers claim that the actions of health care workers serve to perpetuate battering relationships and argue that the medical system duplicates and reinforces the patriarchal structure of the family. In my own work, I have documented how individual staff in emergency rooms come to define battered women as not "true medical cases," but "social" ones, and feel they make extra work and trouble for medical practitioners (Kurz, 1987, 1990). Battered women who do not look like "typical victims" are frequently not recognized as battered and are sent back home, without any recognition of or attention to their battering.

Other studies address the issue of how violence against women is taught and reinforced in institutions such as the military (Russell, 1989) and sports (Messner, 1989). Sanday (1991) and others (e.g., Martin & Hanmer, 1989) have studied the ways in which fraternity practices and rituals, in promoting loyalty to a brotherhood of men, legitimate gang rape and other types of violence against women. Kanin (1984) suggests that the college date rapists he studied came from a more highly sexualized subculture than did non-date rapists.

Family Violence Research and the Feminist Critique

In stark contrast to feminist researchers, family violence researchers focus on "spouse abuse," on women's as well as men's use of violence. They claim that women as well as men are perpetrators of physical violence (McNeely & Mann, 1990; McNeely & Robinson-Simpson, 1987; Steinmetz, 1977-1978; Steinmetz & Lucca, 1988), and some claim that women are as violent within the family as men (Stets & Straus, 1990; Straus, Chapter 4, this volume; Straus & Gelles, 1986). In this section I argue that when researchers claim that women are as violent as men, they do so on the basis of faulty data and flawed assumptions about gender and the family.

Family violence researchers typically base their claims about women's use of violence on data collected using the Conflict Tactics Scales (CTS) (Straus, 1979), an instrument that requires respondents to identify conflict tactics they have used in the previous year. These range from nonviolent tactics (calm discussion) to the most violent tactics (use of a knife or gun). Using the CTS, family violence researchers find similar percentages of husbands and wives using violent tactics (e.g., Straus, Chapter 4, this volume; Straus & Gelles, 1986; Straus et al., 1980). On the basis of these data, one family violence researcher concluded that there is a "battered husband syndrome" (Steinmetz, 1977-1978, 1987). Findings based on the CTS have been replicated by a number of researchers both in the United States and abroad (Brinkerhoff & Lupri, 1988; Nisonoff & Bitman, 1979; Stets, 1990), including for dating relationships (Arias, Samios, & O'Leary, 1987; DeMaris, 1987; Lane & Gwartney-Gibbs, 1985).

Straus (Chapter 4, this volume) cites findings from the 1985 National Family Violence Survey, based on women's responses to the Conflict

Tactics Scales, that show that both wife and husband were violent in 48.6% of cases, the husband only was violent in 25.9% of cases, and the wife only was violent in 25.5% of cases. Straus concludes from these data that "regardless of whether the analysis is based on all assaults or is focused on dangerous assaults, about as many women as men attacked spouses who had *not* hit them during the one-year referent period." Citing other studies that show the same results, he concludes that these figures are "inconsistent with the self-defense explanation for the high rate of domestic assault by women."

Feminist researchers argue that the data showing that women are as violent as men, particularly data based on the Conflict Tactics Scales, are misleading and flawed (Berk et al., 1983; Breines & Gordon, 1983; Dobash & Dobash, 1979; Dobash, Dobash, Wilson, & Daly, 1992; Pleck, Pleck, Grossman, & Bart, 1977-1978; Saunders, 1989). Feminists believe that the validity of the CTS is undermined because the continuum of violence in the scales is so broad that it fails to discriminate among different kinds of violence (Dobash & Dobash, 1979; Dobash et al., 1992; Stark & Flitcraft, 1985). For example, the CTS contains the item "bit, kicked, or hit with a fist." Thus a woman who bites is equated with a man who kicks or hits with a fist. Another item, "hit or tried to hit with an object," which is counted as severe violence, is similarly ambiguous. Critics also argue that the scale does not take into account self-defense.

In support of their position, feminists also point to the findings of studies in which women were asked about their use of violence. For example, Saunders (1988) found that in the vast majority of cases, women attributed their use of violent tactics to self-defense and fighting back. Emery, Lloyd, and Castleton (1989), in an interview study based on a small sample of women who were victims of dating violence, found that most of the women spoke of self-defense. Some women also spoke of using violence in frustration and anger at being dominated by their partners and in retaliation for their partners' violent behavior.

Further, feminists point out that the CTS focuses narrowly on counting acts of violence. Such a focus draws attention away from related patterns of control and abuse in relationships, including psychological abuse and sexual abuse, and does not address other means of nonviolent intimidation and domination, including verbal abuse, the use of suicide threats, and the use of violence against property, pets, children, or other relatives. Similarly, the conception of violence as a "conflict tactic" fails to convey the connection between the use of violence and the exercise of power. In Chapter 3 of this volume, Yllö argues that violence is better conceptualized as a "tactic of coercive control to maintain the husband's power."

In addition to their view that women commit as many violent acts as men, family violence researchers also claim that women initiate violence as frequently as men do. They draw this conclusion on the basis of responses to a question in the National Family Violence Survey about who initiated conflicts in the relationship. The National Family Violence Survey, based on the CTS, found that in 53% of cases wives reported that they hit first; their partners initiated the violence in 42% of cases (Straus, Chapter 4, this volume). These findings have led family violence researchers to a new focus on women's use of violence (Straus, Chapter 4, this volume). Even though husbands use more serious types of violence, these researchers now claim that violence by women against their husbands must be considered a serious problem.

Let us briefly examine the logic of the family violence position that women initiate violence as often as do men. In Chapter 4 of this volume, Straus turns our attention to occasions when a woman slaps a man. He refers to a "typical case" in which a woman uses acts of violence and assumes that a man who is acting like a "cad" has done something offensive to a woman: "Let us assume that most of the assaults by women fall into the 'slap the cad' genre and are not intended to, and only rarely, cause physical injury." He then focuses on the woman's "assaults" and goes on to argue that a woman who "slaps the cad" is in effect provoking her partner by providing him with a justification for hitting:

> Such morally correct slapping acts out and reinforces the traditional tolerance of assault in marriage. The moral justification of assault implicit when a woman slaps or throws something at a partner for something outrageous reinforces his moral justification for slapping her when *she* is doing something outrageous, or when she is obstinate, nasty, or "not listening to reason" as he sees it.

After claiming that assaults by wives are one of the "causes" of assaults by husbands, he concludes with a stern warning that all women must forsake violence:

> One of the many steps needed in primary prevention of assaults on wives is for women to forsake even "harmless" physical attacks on male partners and children. Women must insist on nonviolence from their sisters, just as they rightfully insist on it from men.

In a few sentences, Straus proceeds from women's defensive behavior to a focus on women as provoking the violence. What is wrong with this logic? Although eliminating violence should be a high-priority goal for all men, women, and children, this reframing of the issue puts the blame and responsibility for the violence on the woman. Targeting women's behavior removes the focus from what men might be doing to women. What does it mean that he is acting like a "cad"? Does this refer to unwanted sexual advances, belittling of the woman, verbal intimidation, drunken frenzy? Who is responsible here? Focusing on the woman's behavior provides support for typical excuses and justifications by batterers, such as "She provoked me to do this" (Ptacek, 1988).

Another problem with asking a single question about who initiated the violence is that it does not focus on the meaning and context of female violence against male partners. For example, there were no questions asked about women's motives for striking first. We know that male physical and sexual violence against women is often preceded by name-calling and other types of psychological abuse (Browne, 1987), and that women may view these behaviors as early warning signs of violence and hit first in hopes of preventing their partners from using violence (Saunders, 1989). Hanmer and Saunders (1984) have noted that many women hit first because of a "well-founded fear" of being beaten or raped by their husbands or male intimates. Thus, even when women do initiate violence, it may very well be an act of self-defense.

In my view there are many reasons it would be better if we all could be nonviolent—it may well be true that violence provokes more violence. However, we must understand the power dynamics behind the use of violence in particular types of relationships—we must examine who feels entitled to use violence and why. The feminist perspective addresses these critical questions about the context of violence.

A brief examination of the theoretical perspective of family violence researchers shows the faulty assumptions that guide their interpretation of the data. As one would expect from their findings, as well as their use of the terms *family violence* and *spouse abuse*, family violence researchers take a family systems approach to analyzing husbands' and wives' use of violence. They believe that the origins of the problem of violence lie in the nature of the family, not in the relationship between husband and wife (Gelles, 1983; Gelles & Straus, 1988), and that violence affects all family relationships. According to Straus et al. (1980):

A fundamental solution to the problem of wife-beating has to go beyond a concern with how to control assaulting husbands. It seems as if violence is built into the very structure of the society and family system itself. . . . It [wife beating] is only one aspect of the general pattern of family violence, which includes parent-child violence, child-to-child violence, and wife-to-husband violence. (p. 44)

Family violence researchers believe that violence in the contemporary American family is caused by a variety of social structural factors, including stresses from difficult working conditions, unemployment, financial insecurity, and health problems (see, e.g., Gelles & Cornell, 1985; Gelles & Straus, 1988; Straus et al., 1980). They also believe that husbands and wives are affected by wider social norms condoning violence as a means of solving conflict, and they see evidence of the cultural acceptance of violence in television programming, folklore, and fairy tales (Straus, 1980b), as well as in surveys showing widespread public acceptance of violence. Straus and his colleagues also cite sexism as a factor in family violence; although they believe men and women are equally violent, they believe women are more victimized by family violence because of "the greater physical, financial, and emotional injury" women suffer (Straus, Chapter 4, this volume).

Proponents of the family violence perspective make some important points about the prevalence of violence in American society; however, from a feminist perspective, the family violence view is seriously flawed. Although cultural norms of violence and stressful living conditions may influence individuals' use of violence, these wider cultural norms and social conditions are mediated by the norms of particular institutions. In the case of the institution of marriage, norms promoting male dominance in heterosexual relationships and males' right to use force have a direct influence on behavior in marriage.

Family violence researchers do acknowledge male dominance when they argue that sexism is an important factor in domestic violence and that women are the ones who are most seriously hurt in battering relationships. However, from a feminist perspective, sexism is not just *a* factor in domestic violence. For feminists, gender is one of the fundamental organizing principles of society. It is a social relation that enters into and partially constitutes all other social relations and activities, and pervades the entire social context in which a person lives. Thus feminists criticize family violence researchers for equating "spouse abuse," elder abuse, and child abuse, because from that perspective women constitute just one group among a number of kinds of victims. Feminists believe that wife abuse should be compared with related types of violence against women, such as rape, marital rape, sexual harassment, and incest (Wardell et al., 1983), all of which are also products of male dominance.

Feminists argue that family violence researchers disregard the influence of gender on marriage and heterosexual relationships and see power in the family as a gender-neutral phenomenon. Family violence researchers claim that "violence is used by the most powerful family member as a means of legitimizing his or her dominant position" (Straus et al., 1980, p. 193). They believe that power can as equally be held by a wife as by a husband. They also argue that "even less powerful members of the family tend to rely on violence as a reaction to their own lack of participation in the family decision-making process" (Straus et al., 1980, p. 193).

This view of the exercise of power as gender-neutral misrepresents the nature of marriage as a partnership of equals. As discussed above, marriage has been and still is structured so that husbands have more power than wives. Men are the primary wage earners and women, as those responsible for child rearing and household work, do not typically have the same bargaining power as their husbands. Thus power is not gender-neutral; it is structured into the institution of marriage in such a way that women are disadvantaged.

To conclude, the basic assumptions of the family violence and feminist approaches to domestic violence are irreconcilable. Further, each group has voiced strong disagreements with the other. Family violence researchers argue that the legitimate sociological approach to the issue of violence in the family should be a "multicausal" one; they believe that the feminist approach is biased by a single-minded focus on gender (Straus, 1991). Further, family violence researchers criticize feminist work as "political" (Gelles, 1983; Straus, 1991) and charge that they have been harassed for studying violent women (Gelles & Straus, 1988, p. 106; Straus, 1991). They believe that findings about women's violence have been "suppressed" because they are not "politically correct" (Straus, Chapter 4, this volume). Such statements posit a conspiracy of feminists to keep the "truth" from being known, rather than an understanding that different theories and methods lead to different conclusions.

Feminists fear that the family violence approach will reinforce existing popular conceptions that women cause their own victimization by provoking their male partners. They fear that such views will lead to policy outcomes that are harmful to women. Family violence researchers acknowledge that their research has been used to provide testimony against battered women in court cases and to minimize the need for shelters (Gelles & Straus, 1988, p. 90; Straus & Gelles, 1986, p. 471), however, they argue that this is less "costly" than the "denial and suppression" of violence by women (Straus & Gelles, 1986, p. 471). The question is, Costly for whom?

Feminists are concerned that if funders come to believe that family violence is a "mutual" occurrence between "spouses," or that there is a "battered husband syndrome," there will be decreased support for shelters for battered women. Feminists also fear a diversion of resources to shelters for "battered men." A recent *New York Times* article on a proposed shelter for battered men cited Straus' work as providing evidence that women assault men (Lewin, 1992). Men's rights groups cite the "battered husband syndrome" when lobbying for custody and child support issues from a men's rights perspective (Ansberry, 1988; Fathers for Equal Rights Organization, 1988; McNeely & Robinson-Simpson, 1987).

Feminists also fear that the family violence perspective will reinforce the individualist bias in the field of counseling—that counselors will focus on clients' individual and personal problems without identifying the inequality between men and women that is the context for battering (Adams, 1988). They disagree with those family violence proponents who argue that violence is caused primarily by frustration, poor social skills, or inability to control anger (Hotaling, Straus, & Lincoln, 1990; Shupe et al., 1987; Steinmetz, 1987). Finally, feminists worry that a belief in "spouse abuse" or a "battered husband syndrome" will encourage police who operate under mandatory arrest statutes to arrest women in "domestic disputes."

Conclusion

In this chapter I have argued that women are typically victims, not perpetrators, of violence in intimate relationships. I have shown how norms and practices of male dominance promote the use of violence by men toward female intimates. The proponents of the family violence perspective, in arguing that women are violent toward men, disregard gender and its determining role in structuring marital and other heterosexual relationships.

Data on the use of conflict tactics and acts of violence must be interpreted in the context of power differences in male-female relationships. Abstracted from their context, data on who initiates and uses violence promote faulty conclusions. To interpret violence in the family, we must understand how gender shapes the exercise of power in heterosexual relationships.

References

Adams, D. (1988). Treatment models of men who batter: A profeminist analysis. In K. Yllö & M. Bograd (Eds.), *Feminist perspectives on wife abuse* (pp. 176-199). Newbury Park, CA: Sage.

American College of Physicians. (1986). Position statements of the American College of Physicians. *Philadelphia Medicine, 82*, 496.

Ansberry, C. (1988, May 5). Calling sexes equal in domestic violence, article stirs clash among rights groups. *Wall Street Journal.*

Arias, I., Samios, M., & O'Leary, K. D. (1987). Prevalence and correlates of physical aggression during courtship. *Journal of Interpersonal Violence, 2*, 82-90.

Attorney General's Task Force on Family Violence. (1984). *Final report.* Washington, DC: Department of Justice.

Berk, R. A., Berk, S. F., Loseke, D. R., & Rauma, D. (1983). Mutual combat and other family violence myths. In D. Finkelhor, R. J. Gelles, G. T. Hotaling, & M. A. Straus (Eds.), *The dark side of families: Current family violence research* (pp. 197-212). Beverly Hills, CA: Sage.

Bowker, L. H. (1986). *Ending the violence.* Holmes Beach, FL: Learning Publications.

Bowker, L. H., Arbitell, M., & McFerron, J. R. (1988). On the relationship between wife beating and child abuse. In K. Yllö & M. Bograd (Eds.), *Feminist perspectives on wife abuse* (pp. 158-174). Newbury Park, CA: Sage.

Breines, W., & Gordon, L. (1983). The new scholarship on family violence. *Signs, 8*, 490-531.

Brinkerhoff, M., & Lupri, E. (1988). Interspousal violence. *Canadian Journal of Sociology, 13*, 407-434.

Browne, A. (1987). *When battered women kill.* New York: Free Press.

Brush, L. D. (1990). Violent acts and injurious outcomes in married couples: Methodological issues in the National Survey of Families and Households. *Gender & Society, 4*, 56-67.

Buzawa, E. S., & Buzawa, C. G. (1990). *Domestic violence: The criminal justice response.* Newbury Park, CA: Sage.

DeMaris, A. (1987). The efficacy of a spouse abuse model in accounting for courtship violence. *Journal of Family Issues, 8*, 291-305.

Dobash, R. E., & Dobash, R. P. (1979). *Violence against wives: A case against the patriarchy.* New York: Free Press.

Dobash, R. P., & Dobash, R. E. (1992). *Women, violence, and social change.* New York: Routledge.

Dobash, R. P., Dobash, R. E., Wilson, M., & Daly, M. (1992). The myth of sexual symmetry in marital violence. *Social Problems, 39*, 71-91.

Emery, B., Lloyd, S., & Castleton, A. (1989). *Why women hit: A feminist perspective.* Paper presented at the annual meeting of the National Council on Family Relations, New Orleans.

Fathers for Equal Rights Organization, Inc. (1988, February). *Father's Review, 1.*

Ferraro, K. (1989). Policing woman battering. *Social Problems, 36*, 61-74.

Gaquin, D. A. (1977-1978). Spouse abuse: Data from the National Crime Survey. *Victimology, 2*, 632-642.

Gelles, R. J. (1974). *The violent home: A study of physical aggression between husbands and wives.* Beverly Hills, CA: Sage.

Gelles, R. J. (1983). An exchange/social control theory. In D. Finkelhor, R. J. Gelles, G. T. Hotaling, & M. A. Straus (Eds.), *The dark side of families: Current family violence research* (pp. 151-165). Beverly Hills, CA: Sage.

Gelles, R. J., & Cornell, C. (1985). *Intimate violence in families.* Beverly Hills, CA: Sage.

Gelles, R. J., & Straus, M. A. (1988). *Intimate violence: The causes and consequences of abuse in the American family.* New York: Simon & Schuster.

Hanmer, J., & Saunders, S. (1984). *Well-founded fear: A community study of violence to women.* London: Hutchinson.

Hotaling, G. T., Straus, M. A., & Lincoln, A. (1990). Intrafamily violence and crime outside the family. In M. A. Straus & R. J. Gelles (Eds.), *Physical violence in American families: Risk factors and adaptations to violence in 8,145 families* (pp. 431-470). New Brunswick, NJ: Transaction.

Johnson, N. (1985). Police, social work, and medical responses to battered women. In N. Johnson (Ed.), *Marital violence* (pp. 109-123). London: Routledge & Kegan Paul.

Kanin, E. (1984). Date rape: Unofficial criminals and victims. *Victimology, 9*, 95-108.

Kincaid, P. J. (1982). *The omitted reality: Husband-wife violence in Ontario and policy implications for education.* Maple, Ontario: Learners Press.

Koop, C. E. (1985). Introduction. Centers for Disease Control (Ed.), *Surgeon general's workshop on violence and public health: Sourcebook.* Atlanta, GA: U.S. Public Health Service.

Kurz, D. (1987). Responses to battered women: Resistance to medicalization. *Social Problems, 34*, 501-513.

Kurz, D. (1989). Social science perspectives on wife abuse: Current debates and future directions. *Gender & Society, 3*, 501-513.

Kurz, D. (1990). Interventions with battered women in health care settings. *Victims and Violence, 5*, 243-256.

Kurz, D. (1992). Battering and the criminal justice system: A feminist view. In E. S. Buzawa & C. G. Buzawa (Eds.), *Domestic violence: The criminal justice response* (pp. 21-38). Westport, CT: Auburn House.

Lane, K. E., & Gwartney-Gibbs, P. A. (1985). Violence in the context of dating and sex. *Journal of Family Issues, 6*, 45-59.

Lewin, T. (1992, April 20). Battered men sounding equal-rights battle cry. *New York Times,* p. 12.

Loseke, D. R. (1992). *The battered woman and shelters: The social construction of wife abuse.* Albany: State University of New York Press.

Margolin, L. (1992). Beyond maternal blame: Physical child abuse as a phenomenon of gender. *Journal of Family Issues, 13*, 410-423.

Martin, P. Y., & Hanmer, R. (1989). Fraternities and rape on campus. *Gender & Society, 3*, 457-473.

McLeer, S., & Anwar, R. (1989). A study of battered women presenting in an emergency department. *American Journal of Public Health, 79*, 65-66.

McLeod, M. (1984). Women against men: An examination of domestic violence based on an analysis of official data and national victimization data. *Justice Quarterly, 1*, 171-193.

McNeely, R. L., & Mann, C. (1990). Domestic violence is a human issue. *Journal of Interpersonal Violence, 5,* 129-132.
McNeely, R. L., & Robinson-Simpson, G. (1987). The truth about domestic violence: A falsely framed issue. *Social Work, 32,* 485-490.
Mederos, F. (1987). *Theorizing continuities and discontinuities between "normal" men and abusive men: Work in progress.* Paper presented at the Third National Family Violence Research Conference, University of New Hampshire, Durham.
Messner, M. (1989). When bodies are weapons: Masculinity and violence in sport. *International Review of Sociology of Sport, 25,* 203-220.
Nisonoff, L., & Bitman, I. (1979). Spouse abuse: Incidence and relationship to selected demographic variables. *Victimology, 4,* 131-140.
Pagelow, M. D. (1981). *Woman-battering: Victims and their experiences.* Beverly Hills, CA: Sage.
Pleck, E., Pleck, J. H., Grossman, M., & Bart, P. (1977-1978). The battered data syndrome: A comment on Steinmetz's article. *Victimology, 2,* 680-684.
Ptacek, J. (1988). Why do men batter their wives? In K. Yllö & M. Bograd (Eds.), *Feminist perspectives on wife abuse* (pp. 133-157). Newbury Park, CA: Sage.
Quarm, D., & Schwartz, M. (1985). Domestic violence in criminal court. In C. Schweber & C. Feinman (Eds.), *Criminal justice politics and women: The aftermath of legally mandated change* (pp. 29-46). New York: Haworth.
Russell, D. (1989). Sexism, violence, and the nuclear mentality. In D. Russell (Ed.), *Exposing nuclear phallacies* (pp. 63-74). New York: Plenum.
Sanday, P. R. (1991). *Fraternity gang rape: Sex, brotherhood, and privilege on campus.* New York: New York University Press.
Saunders, D. G. (1988). Wife abuse, husband abuse, or mutual combat? In K. Yllö & M. Bograd (Eds.), *Feminist perspectives on wife abuse* (pp. 90-113). Newbury Park, CA: Sage.
Saunders, D. G. (1989, November). *Who hits first and who hurts most? Evidence for the greater victimization of women in intimate relationships.* Paper presented at the 41st Annual Meeting of the American Society of Criminology, Reno, NV.
Schechter, S. (1982). *Women and male violence: The visions and struggles of the battered women's movement.* Boston: South End.
Schwartz, M. D. (1987). Gender and injury in spousal assault. *Sociological Focus, 20,* 61-75.
Shupe, A., Stacey, W., & Hazelwood, R. (1987). *Violent men, violent couples: The dynamics of domestic violence.* Lexington, MA: Lexington.
Stanko, E. (1985). *Intimate intrusions.* London: Routledge & Kegan Paul.
Stark, E., & Flitcraft, A. (1985). Women-battering, child abuse and social heredity: What is the relationship? In N. Johnson (Ed.), *Marital violence* (pp. 147-171). London: Routledge and Kegan Paul.
Stark, E., Flitcraft, A., & Frazier, W. (1979). Medicine and patriarchal violence: The social construction of a "private" event. *International Journal of Health Services, 9,* 461-493.
Steinmetz, S. K. (1977-1978). The battered husband syndrome. *Victimology, 2,* 499-509.
Steinmetz, S. K. (1987). Family violence: Past, present, and future. In M. B. Sussman & S. K. Steinmetz (Eds.), *Handbook of marriage and the family* (pp. 725-765). New York: Plenum.
Steinmetz, S. K., & Lucca, J. (1988). Husband battering. In V. B. Van Hasselt, R. L. Morrison, A. S. Bellack, & M. Hersen (Eds.), *Handbook of family violence* (pp. 233-246). New York: Plenum.

Stets, J. E. (1990). Verbal and physical aggression in marriage. *Journal of Marriage and the Family, 52,* 501-514.

Stets, J. E., & Straus, M. A. (1990). Gender differences in reporting marital violence and its medical and psychological consequences. In M. A. Straus & R. J. Gelles (Eds.), *Physical violence in American families: Risk factors and adaptations to violence in 8,145 families* (pp. 151-166). New Brunswick, NJ: Transaction.

Straus, M. A. (1979). Measuring intrafamily conflict and violence: The Conflict Tactics (CT) Scale. *Journal of Marriage and the Family, 41,* 75-88.

Straus, M. A. (1980a). A sociological perspective on the prevention of wife beating. In M. A. Straus & G. T. Hotaling (Eds.), *The social causes of husband-wife violence* (pp. 211-234). Minneapolis: University of Minnesota Press.

Straus, M. A. (1980b). Victims and aggressors in marital violence. *American Behavioral Scientist, 23,* 681-704.

Straus, M. A. (1991). New theory and old canards about family violence research. *Social Problems, 38,* 180-197.

Straus, M. A., & Gelles, R. J. (1986). Societal change and change in family violence from 1975 to 1985 as revealed by two national surveys. *Journal of Marriage and the Family, 48,* 465-479.

Straus, M. A., & Gelles, R. J. (1990). How violent are American families? Estimates from the National Family Violence Resurvey and other studies. In M. A. Straus & R. J. Gelles (Eds.), *Physical violence in American families: Risk factors and adaptations to violence in 8,145 families* (pp. 95-132). New Brunswick, NJ: Transaction.

Straus, M. A., Gelles, R. J., & Steinmetz, S. K. (1980). *Behind closed doors: Violence in the American family.* Garden City, NY: Anchor/Doubleday.

Tierney, K. (1982). The battered women movement and the creation of the wife beating problem. *Social Problems, 29,* 207-220.

Walker, L. E. A. (1984). *The battered woman syndrome.* New York: Springer.

Wardell, L., Gillespie, D. L., & Leffler, A. (1983). Science and violence against wives. In D. Finkelhor, R. J. Gelles, G. T. Hotaling, & M. A. Straus (Eds.), *The dark side of families: Current family violence research* (pp. 69-84). Beverly Hills, CA: Sage.

Watkins, C. R. (1982). *Victims, aggressors, and the family secret: An exploration into family violence.* St. Paul: Minnesota Department of Public Welfare.

Yllö, K., & Bograd, M. (Eds.). (1988). *Feminist perspectives on wife abuse.* Newbury Park, CA: Sage.

CHAPTER 6

Facing the Facts

Date and Acquaintance Rape Are Significant Problems for Women

Mary P. Koss
Sarah L. Cook

In 1987, when Koss, Gidycz, and Wisniewski published their epidemiological study of sexual assault on college campuses, funded by the National Institute of Mental Health, their findings startled the scientific community and the nation at large. Results indicated that, since their fourteenth birthdays, 27% of college women recalled an incident that met the legal definition of rape, including attempts. In a 12-month period, 76 per 1,000 college women experienced one or more attempted or completed rapes. Of these rapes, 8 of 10 involved someone the victim knew, and more than half (57%) of all the rapes involved a date. Many people have trouble believing that this level of assault could exist without coming to the attention of police, parents, or institutional authorities. One of them is University of California social welfare professor Neil Gilbert, who wonders why rape, if it is as common as Koss and colleagues suggest, has not been routinely reported to justice authorities. But before we can discuss the problems related to reporting rape, and thus the problems that the study faced and surmounted, we must consider how rape is defined.

Definitions of Rape

The FBI defines rape as attempted or completed vaginal intercourse with a female, forcibly and against her will (Federal Bureau of Investigation, 1991). This definition is used *only* for the collection of federal crime statistics. State laws govern the adjudication of rape cases, unless the crime occurs on federal government property, when federal rape law would apply. Both federal and state rape laws have been reformed since the 1970s and are more contemporary than the FBI definition in that they (a) are gender neutral, meaning either men or women can be victims of rape; (b) cover anal and oral penetration as well as vaginal intercourse and include insertion of objects other than the penis; and (c) extend to nonforcible assaults if intercourse is obtained with someone unable to consent because of mental illness, mental retardation, or intoxication (Estrich, 1987; Michigan Statutes Annotated, 1980; Searles & Berger, 1987). Social scientists distinguish several types of rape, including stranger rape, acquaintance rape, date rape, and marital rape. *Acquaintance rape* refers to assaults committed by anyone who is not a complete stranger. *Date rape* is a specific type of acquaintance rape that involves a victim and a perpetrator who have some level of romantic relationship between them. However, the essential meaning of the word *rape* is unaffected by the relationship of the parties, except in the handful of states that still maintain a spousal exclusion limiting a woman's rights to charge her husband with rape. Other than this exception, legally, date and acquaintance rapes are rape.

Gilbert has proclaimed that "radical feminists have distorted the definition of rape and created a bogus epidemic" (quoted in Hendrix, 1991). His thoughts echo criticisms first raised by journalist Stephanie Gutmann (1991) in *Playboy* magazine and, most recently, by free-lance writer Cathy Young (1992). Criticism centers on the national college student survey, although this study has stood unchallenged in the professional literature since its 1987 publication in a leading peer-reviewed psychology journal and has since been joined by additional empirical papers based on the same data set that were also deemed worthy of publication (Gidycz & Koss, 1990, 1992; Koss & Dinero, 1988, 1989; Koss, Dinero, Seibel, & Cox, 1988; Malamuth, Koss, Sockloskie, & Tanaka, 1991; Risin & Koss, 1987; White & Koss, 1992). Critics focus mainly on the definitions of rape used in the research and assert that the scope of victimization found is so large only because it is based on a radical and elastic new definition of rape. Gutmann (1990) writes, "If, (as some researchers propose), we broadly define rape to include sex a woman subsequently regrets or even subjection to sexual innuendo, almost every woman has been raped" (p. 50). Although educational materials may exist that promote broad interpretations of the term *rape*, critics err in the assumption that these definitions undergird the empirical data base. The definition of rape used in the national survey was consistent with the statutes of most North American jurisdictions; the rape rate included only instances of unwanted sexual penetration, perpetrated by force, threat of harm, or when the victim was intoxicated.

In Chapter 7 of this volume, Gilbert questions the item used to ascertain information about unwanted penetration that occurred when a woman was intoxicated. Although rape when incapacitated is a legitimate component of the legal definition, for the sake of discussion it is helpful to examine what happens to the prevalence figures when these instances are removed. Removing this item from the calculations of rape prevalence among the 3,187 women students in the national sample studied by Koss and colleagues (1987), lowers the attempted rape figure from 12% to 8% and the completed rape figure from 16% to 11%. Even with the focus limited only to instances where unwanted penetration was attempted or obtained forcibly, a total of 20% of college women, or one in five, qualify as rape victims since their 14th birthday. This level of victimization is still very substantial and invalidates Gilbert's implication that date and acquaintance rapes are mainly misunderstandings promoted by alcohol use.

The Critics Redefine Rape

To rectify the alleged problems with definitions of sexual assault, critics make several suggestions. Even though it would be outrageous to ask a car thief, Well, you did take the car, but did you *mean* to steal it? Gutmann (1991) suggests that adding a dimension of intent to the definition of sexual assault would clarify the definition. In order for a man to be guilty, Gutmann argues, he must have intended to rape the women. But as Muehlenhard, Powch, Phelps, and Giusti (1992) point out, "If, for a man to be guilty of rape, he must interpret 'no' to mean 'no,' but if he always interprets 'no' as foreplay, then he can never be guilty of rape!" (p. 32). Gilbert (1991b) criticizes a "radical feminist effort to impose new norms governing intimacy between the sexes" (p. 61) and complains that "the awesome complexity of human interaction is reduced to 'No means no.' " Apparently, Gilbert believes that young men should reject a face-value interpretation of the word *no*. He characterizes as "inconvenient" Muehlenhard and Hollabaugh's (1988) findings that 39% of college women surveyed admitted on occasion to having said no when they meant yes, but he fails to recognize the converse: The majority of women (61%) have never engaged in token resistance. Men must ask themselves, given the terrible consequences, is the risk warranted of interpreting no to mean yes when the majority of women who say no mean no?

Gilbert and others also believe that women should identify their experiences with the label "rape" in order to be included in prevalence estimates (Gilbert, 1991a, 1991b; Young, 1992). Yet, failure to embrace the correct legal term for a victimization certainly does not mean that the incident itself never happened. In making this assertion, critics reveal their unfamiliarity with victimization survey methodology. It has long been known to survey experts that the general public is unaware of correct definitions of legal terms such as *rape, larceny, burglary,* and *robbery.* Often people's ideas of what constitutes rape are based on rape myths conveyed by pornography, "dirty" jokes, movies, and rock videos—images that are hardly designed to give the public an accurate understanding of the range of sexual assault (Muehlenhard et al., 1992).

Some women who have endured sex against their will may fail to realize that legal standards for rape have been met, but this does not mean that they view the incidents' impacts positively or even neutrally. In fact, half of the rape victims identified in the national survey considered their experiences to be rape or some crime similar to rape. Only 10% of women contended that they did not feel victimized by the experience. The same phenomenon has been encountered in studies of community samples of women (Russell, 1990; Wyatt, 1992). Many who did not initially label their experiences as rape contacted researchers at a later date to report incidents they now understood to be rape, after the legal definition had been fully explained to them.

Keeping Rape a Secret

Although it would be wonderful if the last decade had produced supportive environments across the country on every college campus so that rape victims could make reports without fear, Gilbert's suggestion that this state exists is quite utopian. Furthermore, there are no data to support his suggestion. To the contrary, a telephone survey released in April 1992 of a representative sample of 4,009 adult women found that recent rape victims have greater fear than women raped in earlier years about the possibility of their names being made public (National Victims Center, 1992). Half of all rape victims in this study stated that they would be much more likely to report if there were laws prohibiting name and address disclosure by the media. Rape victims fear having their identities made public because of the long historical tradition in Western culture of denigrating them as unmarriageable, damaged goods.

Another reason victims hesitate to report to police is concern that their allegations of rape will be discredited, or that they will be blamed for setting themselves up for victimization (Feldman-Summers & Norris, 1984; Ruback, Greenberg, & Westcott, 1984; Williams, 1984). The skepticism of critics like Gilbert perfectly demonstrates the disclosure climate that victims wish to avoid. Thus it is not surprising that less than 5% of college student rape victims reported their assaults to the police and almost half told no one at all (Koss et al., 1987). Extreme reluctance to disclose victimization also has been replicated by other investigators using a random sample at a large midwestern university (Pirog-Good & Stets, 1989). Unfortunately, the latest nationally representative data continue to show that the reporting rate for rape remains low, at 16% (National Victims Center, 1992).

Rape or Rapette?

It has been said that the term *date rape* is an oxymoron, because the word *date* connotes mutuality and pleasure whereas the word *rape* implies powerlessness and humiliation. The juxtaposition of the two words modifies the traditional sense of outrage associated with the word *rape,* and the term *date rape* comes to signify "rapette" in many minds. It is viewed as something like rape, but certainly not as traumatizing as "real rape" perpetrated by a violent stranger (Estrich, 1987). This viewpoint is inconsistent with both empirical data and the law.

The thought that one will be killed or seriously injured is equally as common among women who are raped by dates as it is among those raped by total strangers (National Victims Center, 1992). And even though the women in the national survey were sufficiently free of emotional impairment to function as college students, the evidence still suggests that their rapes were traumatic for them. Afterward, 27% of victims thought about suicide to the point that they considered the methods they would use to kill themselves (Koss et al., 1988). Furthermore, the scores on standard measures of psychological symptoms for all rape victims averaged one standard deviation higher than those for nonvictimized women, and were similar to the scores of students who were seeking counseling services on campus (Koss et al., 1988). The psychological distress generated by the rape was equal, regardless of whether the rapist was a complete stranger, casual acquaintance, or steady date. Yet even these data may underestimate the impact of rape on victims, because those most affected may have dropped out of school, thereby becoming unavailable to participate in the survey.

Another finding that suggests rapette to critics is that approximately 40% of the victims reported having sex again with the men who raped them. Unfortunately, the data did not allow us to differentiate between future sexual contacts with spouse or boyfriend that were not forced from additional rapes by the same perpetrator. Shotland (1989, 1992) theorizes that women's responses to date rape may depend upon the context of the relationship. Among college-aged rape victims, 22% were raped by casual dates and 31% by steady dates (the remainder were raped by strangers, nonromantic acquaintances, and husbands or other relatives; Koss et al., 1988). Shotland (1992) suggests that a woman is more likely to continue a relationship after an assault if she has had a lengthy relationship with the perpetrator than if she has dated him only casually and has little emotional investment in the relationship. A woman who is raped on a first date is more likely to assume that her date is totally responsible for the assault than is a woman who is raped by a steady date who has never aggressed toward her before, in which case she may assume more responsibility for the assault (Shotland, 1992). But whether it was after the first incident or possibly after others occurred, 87% of the victims eventually ended their relationships with the men who raped them (Koss et al., 1988).

The Bigger Picture: Rape Among Community Women

The 15% completed rape prevalence rate from the national study of college students does not stand alone in the literature; rather, it is part of a bigger picture filled in by other investigators (for a review, see Koss, 1993). First, the results are replicated by other studies of college students. Estimates of completed rape frequency in the 12% range have been reported in two representative samples of individual institutions, including a southern state university (Yegidis, 1986) and a midwestern state university (Koss & Oros, 1982). Estimates as high or higher than 12% for unwanted intercourse have been reported in more than 10 additional studies lacking representative sampling methods, and there are *no* studies that have reported substantially lower or higher rates of *rape* among college students (see Craig, 1990, for a review; Gilbert correctly notes in Chapter 7 of this volume that this review contains a range of figures, but that is because the article is not limited to studies that focused on rape). Second, the results of the national study that critics view as inflated in fact show lower rates than do data from community surveys of women that include a broader sociodemographic range of participants than is found in college samples. The rape prevalence estimates in seven recent representative studies of adult women residing in communities across the United States were 24% in Minnesota (Burt, 1979), 24% in San Francisco (Russell, 1982), 28% among college-educated women aged 18-39 in Los Angeles (Sorenson, Stein, Siegel, Golding, & Burnam, 1987); 25% for African American and 20% for white women in Los Angeles County (Wyatt, 1992), and 23% in Charleston, South Carolina (Kilpatrick, Saunders, Veronen, Best, & Von, 1987). In a recently released telephone survey of more than 4,000 women in a nationally representative sample, the rate of rape was reported to be 14%, even though this rate excluded rapes of women unable to consent (National Victims Center, 1992).

Among the lowest estimates in the literature is a 6% figure from rural North Carolina (George, Winfield, & Blazer, 1992). Because this estimate was obtained using a methodology identical to that used by Sorenson et al. (1987), the difference cannot be attributed to measurement, but must substantially reflect true differences in prevalence rates according to sociodemographic, social, and religious characteristics. The political and religious conservatism of the South is well known, as are the generally higher rates of crime and drug abuse in California. Also, Sorenson et al.'s higher estimate was obtained from college-educated respondents, and, paradoxically, advanced education is related to somewhat higher reporting of all kinds of victimization, including rape, perhaps because such respondents are less intimidated by the "testlike" nature of a survey (Koss, 1992). Hence it is reasonable to suggest that both extremes in the magnitude of prevalence estimates represent the effects of social context on the risk of victimization (George et al., 1992; White & Sorenson, 1992b).

In spite of this wealth of data, Gilbert (1991b) concludes that the national study estimates have provoked a "phantom epidemic." To reach this conclusion, Gilbert has to ignore not only the literature reviewed above, but also the entire body of research by Kanin and colleagues that documents a 20%-25% prevalence rate for sexual assault among college students going back over a 20-year period (Shotland, 1989). In addition, the evidence that Gilbert (1991b) uses to support his charges is flawed. Specifically, he erroneously compares Koss's and Russell's *lifetime* prevalence rates with *12-month* incidence rates derived from the National Crime Victimization Survey (NCVS) published by the U.S. Bureau of Justice Statistics (BJS; see, e.g., BJS, 1992). Even if figures for comparable periods had been compared, Gilbert would have found NCVS estimates lower than those obtained independent of the federal government. The most important and consistent finding of sexual assault research spanning more than a decade is that *all* representative studies reporting incidence estimates of rape *uniformly exceed* NCVS estimates (Koss, 1992; Muehlenhard et al., 1992). Experts and even the compilers of the NCVS themselves now agree that their methodology undermines self-disclosure of sexual assault and results in underdetection of rape (Harlow, 1991; Koss, 1992; National Victims Center, 1992; Russell, 1984).

Incidents of sexual assault are undetected in the NCVS for at least five reasons (detailed treatment of these issues can be found in Koss, 1992). First, compilers of the NCVS concede that "violence or attempted violence involving family members or close friends is under-reported in the NCS [*sic*] . . . because some victims . . . are reluctant to implicate family members or relatives, *who in some instances may be present during the interview*" (BJS, 1984, p. 10; emphasis added). Second, NCVS interviewers are not trained to handle sensitive issues and are not consistently matched in ethnicity or gender with respondents, thereby undermining rapport and trust. Third, the NCVS is presented as a survey of crimes. As discussed previously, if a woman does not understand that her experience fits the legal definition of rape, she may fail to report it. Fourth, the screening question for rape has been vaguely worded, as opposed to the screening questions for all other crimes. To detect rape, interviewers, until 1991, asked: "Did anyone TRY to attack you in *some other way?*" (BJS, 1992, p. 108; italic emphasis added). The rationale behind this item was that "each victim defines for herself. . . . no one in the survey is ever asked directly if she has been raped" (BJS, 1985, p. 2). This vague wording stands in marked contrast to the mode of inquiry used for other crimes, such as the following typical item: "Were you knifed, shot at, or attacked with some other weapon by anyone at all?" (BJS, 1992, p. 108). Fifth, the NCVS adopts the outdated FBI definition of rape, which excludes incidents that are legitimately rape under state statutes, such as crimes where the offender is the legal or common-law spouse of the victim; where oral, anal, digital, or object penetration occurred; and where the victim was incapacitated and unable to consent. Recent NCVS revisions involve question content (BJS, 1991) but fail to address other survey shortcomings (Koss, 1992).

Recognizing Psychosocial and Economic Costs

There are many ways for women to be victimized, including crimes such as purse snatching, mugging, stalking, sexual touching, shooting, and rape by strangers or acquaintances. Although less likely than men to be victims of all violent crimes except rape, women's estimates of their vulnerability to crime appear to be heavily influenced by their perceived risk of rape (Riger, LeBailly, & Gordon, 1981). Among women younger than 35, rape is feared even more than murder, assault, or robbery (Warr, 1985). In a study conducted by Gordon and Riger (1989), one-third of women interviewed in several urban centers across the United States cited the fear of physical harm, especially rape, as their most common concern; the remainder worried about rape at least occasionally. In response to their fear, more than half of the women reacted with self-isolation; they stayed inside and avoided visiting friends or going out for evening entertainment. When they did go out, more than half of women surveyed (51%) stated that they always went with a friend or two as protection, compared with 4% of men (Gordon & Riger, 1991). Most of the men surveyed (90%) denied taking any steps to reduce their vulnerability to crime, even though they lived in the same neighborhoods as the female respondents (Gordon & Riger, 1989). These findings suggest that contemporary women in the United States live their lives under the threat of sexual violation, and this fear constitutes a special burden not shared by men.

Overwhelmingly, the actions taken by the women interviewed in Gordon and Riger's study were intended to protect them from assaults by strangers. Today, after an explosion of sexual assault research in the past decade, it is widely accepted that women have more reason to fear violence from acquaintances and those they know more intimately than from strangers on the street. The implications for women's and men's lives are frightening and, at the very least, disconcerting. The traditional "social order" between men and women is upset, leaving the rules of dating and other social interactions in limbo. Women may feel that they must restrict their lives to a greater extent—socially, intellectually, recreationally, and spiritually—to protect themselves from date and acquaintance rape. Men and women are forced to examine and redefine sexual roles and scripts that contribute to sexual assault. These implications threaten the status quo and may provoke anxiety, fear, confusion, and doubt. Nonetheless, they cannot be ignored.

Because the true scope of rape has been hidden until recently, it is difficult to estimate the psychosocial and economic costs of sexual assault. Gordon and Riger's (1991) study illustrates that these costs spread beyond the directly victimized and affect nonvictimized women as well. We do not yet know the full effects of bypassing opportunities because of fear of rape on women's achievement of their potentials, health, and economic well-being. What is known is that the costs are even higher for the women who are direct victims. Psychologically, rape devastates many victims. Economically, it exacts a toll in terms of dollars spent for health and mental health care plus time lost from work or school. Victims of sexual assault often experience fear, anxiety, and depression in addition to difficulty in sexual relationships and other psychological and physical symptoms (Gidycz & Koss, 1991, 1992). Almost one-third develop rape-related post-traumatic stress disorder (PTSD) at some point in their lives (National Victims Center, 1992). For some victims the symptoms of PTSD do not recede for many years, and they continue to be plagued by persistent reexperiencing of the assaults in the form of dreams or flashbacks, the necessity of avoiding reminders of the assaults, and difficulty in sleep and concentration. Community studies of adult women have revealed that PTSD is more likely to develop following rape than for any other trauma studied, including other violent crimes, and major civilian disasters such as hurricanes (Kilpatrick et al., 1987; Norris, 1992). Further, rape-related PTSD dramatically increases women's risk for alcohol and drug abuse problems (National Victims Center, 1992).

Violence also affects women's perceptions of their health and their utilization of medical services. Koss, Koss, and Woodruff (1991) found that women with histories of severe victimization (sexual and/or physical assaults) saw themselves as less healthy, perceived more physical complaints and symptoms of emotional distress, experienced less physical and mental well-being, and engaged in more injurious health behaviors than did women without such histories. They utilized medical services at rates 33-100% higher then nonvictims in the year of victimization, at a cost 2.5 times higher than that for nonvictims. Among the chronic disorders more prevalent among victimized women are pelvic pain, gastrointestinal disorders, headaches and other forms of chronic pain, urinary tract symptoms, and premenstrual syndrome (Koss & Heslet, 1992).

The Role of Science in Prevention

Much of the criticism leveled against sexual assault research also targets prevention efforts, which Gilbert (Chapter 7, this volume) labels "dysfunctional consequences of advocacy research." According to Gilbert, neither mutual respect nor reasonable discussion can now occur between the sexes because of the negative climate created by what he considers to be inflated rape prevalence estimates. However, the evidence fails to support either that the figures are inflated or that a communication impasse exists. Turk and Muehlenhard found that 61% of a college sample were now willing to define as rape sexual intercourse that proceeded after objections were stated (cited in Muehlenhard et al., 1992). This movement toward consensus on a definition of sexual assault is most likely the result of a dramatic increase in awareness and dialogue regarding sexual assault.

Gilbert's views here are not surprising, given his recent opposition to child sexual abuse prevention education (Berrick & Gilbert, 1991), but they are misdirected. The inadequacy in prevention efforts is not in program content, but in program evaluation. Colleges and universities are responding on a continuum from revising sexual assault policies to hiring education and prevention coordinators. Many programs have been developed, but hardly any have been empirically evaluated. Furthermore, what little research does exist has been accepted too uncritically in the sexual assault prevention literature (Rozee, Bateman, & Gilmore, 1991). Without solid empirical evaluation of these programs, it cannot be known whether they truly affect second-order change, which in this case would be reflected by a reduction in the incidence of sexual assault (Rappaport, Seidman, & Davidson, 1979).

The next step for sexual assault prevention programs is critical assessment of program impact, which is an area ripe for basic and applied research. Several questions need to be answered about a prevention approach before a plan for evaluation can be developed. They include the following: (a) At what level of prevention does the program aim? Is the intent to stop the occurrence of the incidents (primary prevention), to minimize their impacts (secondary prevention), or to promote healing among those already affected (tertiary prevention)? (b) Who (group or individual) is the target of the intervention? (c) What is the intended effect of the intervention and at what level is the effect expected—individual, group, setting/mediating structure, or meso-system (Seidman, 1987)? Beyond answering questions of program efficacy, prevention research aids in illuminating existing models or in developing new models of sexual aggression. Seidman (1987) has noted, "Prevention intervention research provides fertile ground for discovery, hypothesis-generation, and theory-comparison. . . . in the course of observing our interventions unfold, we can begin to discover the patterns of causality and linkages between variables and their contextual embeddedness" (p. 3). There is an urgent need for sexual assault prevention research. Collaborations between university researchers and community and university sexual assault educators could fill this need.

Rules of Advocacy Research

Psychological research can and should play an integral role in the development of public policy (Reppucci, 1985). At the same time, scientists must be cognizant of their responsibilities when disseminating policy-applicable research results (Weithorn, 1987). Justice David L. Bazelon (1982) implores psychologists to avoid the sin of nondisclosure in this task by focusing on more than conclusory statements, disclosing underlying values, and admitting uncertainties and divisions of opinion that may exist about research findings. Although it is up to the reader to judge whether sexual assault research avoids these pitfalls, it is our view that the majority of sexual assault research, when held to these standards, fares well. When discrepant estimates of sexual assault surface, differences are taken to be real, not discounted as bucking conventional wisdom, as Gilbert charges in his chapter in this volume. Likewise, values are explored (see White & Sorenson, 1992a, for thoughtful discussions of these issues). The purpose of research into sexual aggression is scientific understanding to facilitate primary prevention, early intervention, and treatment of sexual assault.

Research that is widely disseminated for the public's use runs a risk of being misused and misrepresented. No scientist can guarantee that his or her research will always be appropriately used, but the misuse of it does not invalidate the original findings. Gilbert is wrong to fault empirical research that used a legally based definition of rape because some prevention programs and educational efforts have arisen that incorporate broad definitions. This is like holding the car manufacturer responsible for a purchaser's reckless driving. Just as scientists have responsibilities when disseminating research, so do those who critique research. Overgeneralized and emotional statements, such as Gilbert's comment that research findings "indict all men as rapists," appear to be made by someone who objects to research findings, rather than by someone involved in the research process. It is important to realize that the "question of advocacy can be raised both about those claiming that virtually everyone has been victimized and about those arguing that 'real' violence is relatively uncommon" (Berliner, 1992, p. 121).

Conclusion

This chapter has placed the findings of a national study of rape among college students in the context of relevant research to illustrate that the study findings are not isolated or spurious, nor do they constitute "highly sophisticated advocacy research." Rather, they are alarming findings that warrant further serious attention. The scientific community can respond to controversies in intimate violence in several productive ways. These include further exploring the implications of widespread violence, examining discrepant research findings, developing and testing alternative hypotheses, and advancing scientific knowledge by refining theories regarding sexual assault. Criticizing existing research by misrepresenting the findings and by confusing empirical research with advocacy and educational efforts reveals little regard for scholarship and hinders understanding.

References

Bazelon, D. L. (1982). Veils, values, and social responsibility. *American Psychologist, 37,* 115-121.

Berliner, L. (1992). Facts or advocacy statistics: The case of acquaintance rape. *Journal of Interpersonal Violence, 7,* 121-126.

Berrick, J. D., & Gilbert, N. A. (1991). *With best intentions: The child sexual abuse prevention movement.* New York: Guilford.

Burt, M. R. (1979). *Attitudes supportive of rape in American culture* (Final report to National Institute of Mental Health, National Center for the Prevention and Control of Rape). University of Minnesota, Minneapolis.

Craig, M. E. (1990). Coercive sexuality in dating relationships: A situational model. *Clinical Psychology Review, 10,* 395-423.

Estrich, S. (1987). *Real rape: How the legal system victimizes women who say no.* Cambridge, MA: Harvard University Press.

Federal Bureau of Investigation. (1991). *Uniform crime reports.* Washington, DC: U.S. Department of Justice.

Feldman-Summers, S., & Norris, H. (1984). Differences between rape victims who report and those who do not report to a public agency. *Journal of Applied Social Psychology, 14,* 562-573.

George, L. K., Winfield, I., & Blazer, D. G. (1992). Sociocultural factors in sexual assault: Comparison of two representative samples of women. In J. W. White & S. B. Sorenson (Eds.), Adult sexual assault [Special issue]. *Journal of Social Issues, 48,* 105-125.

Gidycz, C. A., & Koss, M. P. (1990). A comparison of group and individual sexual assault victims. *Psychology of Women Quarterly, 14,* 325-342.

Gidycz, C. A., & Koss, M. P. (1991). The effects of acquaintance rape on the female victim. In A. Parrot & L. Bechhofer (Eds.), *Acquaintance rape: The hidden crime* (pp. 270-284). New York: John Wiley.

Gidycz, C. A., & Koss, M. P. (1992). Predictors of long-term sexual assault trauma among a national sample of victimized college women. *Violence and Victims, 6,* 177-190.

Gilbert, N. (1991a, June 27). The campus rape scare. *Wall Street Journal,* p. 10.

Gilbert, N. (1991b). The phantom epidemic of sexual assault. *Public Interest, 103,* 54-65.

Gordon, M. T., & Riger, S. (1989). *The female fear.* New York: Free Press.

Gordon, M. T., & Riger, S. (1991). *The female fear: The social cost of rape.* Urbana: University of Illinois Press.

Gutmann, S. (1990, October). Date rape: Does anyone really know what it is? *Playboy,* pp. 48-56.

Gutmann, S. (1991). "It sounds like I raped you!" How date-rape re-education fosters confusion, undermines personal responsibility, and trivializes sexual violence. In O. Pocs (Ed.), *Human sexuality* (pp. 217-221). Guilford, CT: Dushkin.

Harlow, C. W. (1991). *Female victims of violent crime* (Report No. NCJ-126826). Washington, DC: U.S. Department of Justice, Bureau of Justice Statistics.

Hendrix, K. (1991, July 9). Defining controversy: Professor raises furor by claiming date rape statistics are inflated. *Los Angeles Times,* pp. E1-E2.

Kilpatrick, D. G., Saunders, B. E., Veronen, L. J., Best, C. L., & Von, J. M. (1987). Criminal victimization: Lifetime prevalence, reporting to the police, and psychological impact. *Crime & Delinquency, 33,* 479-489.

Koss, M. P. (1992). The underdetection of rape: Methodological choices that influence incidence estimates. In J. W. White & S. B. Sorenson (Eds.), Adult sexual assault [Special issue]. *Journal of Social Issues, 48,* 61-75.

Koss, M. P. (1993). Detecting the scope of rape: A review of prevalence research methods. *Journal of Interpersonal Violence, 8,* 198-222.

Koss, M. P., & Dinero, T. E. (1988). Predictors of sexual aggression among a national sample of male college students. In R. A. Prentky & V. L. Quinsey (Eds.), Human sexual aggression: Current perspectives [Special issue]. *Annals of the New York Academy of Sciences, 528,* 133-147.

Koss, M. P., & Dinero, T. E. (1989). A discriminant analysis of risk factors among a national sample of college women. *Journal of Consulting and Clinical Psychology, 57,* 242-250.

Koss, M. P., Dinero, T. E., Seibel, C. A., & Cox, S. L. (1988). Stranger and acquaintance rape: Are there differences in the victim's experience? *Psychology of Women Quarterly, 12,* 1-24.

Koss, M. P., Gidycz, C. A., & Wisniewski, N. (1987). The scope of rape: Incidence and prevalence of sexual aggression and victimization in a national sample of higher education students. *Journal of Consulting and Clinical Psychology, 55,* 162-170.

Koss, M. P., & Heslet, L. (1992). The somatic consequences of violence against women. *Archives of Family Medicine, 1,* 53-59.

Koss, M. P., Koss, P., & Woodruff, W. J. (1991). Deleterious effects of criminal victimization on women's health and medical utilization. *Archives of Internal Medicine, 151,* 342-347

Koss, M. P., & Oros, C. (1982). The sexual experiences survey: A research instrument investigating sexual aggression and victimization. *Journal of Consulting and Clinical Psychology, 50,* 455-457.

Malamuth, N. M., Koss, M. P., Sockloskie, R., & Tanaka, J. (1991). The characteristics of aggressors against women: Testing a model using a national sample of college students. *Journal of Consulting and Clinical Psychology, 59,* 670-681.

Michigan Statutes Annotated. (1980). 28.788 (1) (h) (Callaghan) (Cum. Supp.).

Muehlenhard, C. L., & Hollabaugh, L. C. (1988). Do women sometimes say no when they mean yes? The prevalence and correlates of women's token resistance to sex. *Journal of Personality and Social Psychology, 54*, 872-879.

Muehlenhard, C. L., Powch, I. G., Phelps, J. L., & Giusti, L. M. (1992). Definitions of rape: Scientific and political implications. In J. W. White & S. B. Sorenson (Eds.), Adult sexual assault [Special issue]. *Journal of Social Issues, 48*, 23-44.

National Victims Center. (1992). *Rape in America: A report to the nation.* Arlington, VA: Author.

Norris, F. H. (1992). Epidemiology of trauma: Frequency and impact of different potentially traumatic events on different demographic groups. *Journal of Consulting and Clinical Psychology, 60*, 409-418.

Pirog-Good, M. A., & Stets, J. E. (1989). The help-seeking behavior of physically and sexually abused college students. In M. A. Pirog-Good & J. E. Stets (Eds.), *Violence in dating relationships: Emerging social issues* (pp. 108-125). New York: Praeger.

Rappaport, J., Seidman, E., & Davidson, W. (1979). Demonstration research and manifest vs. true adoption: The natural history of a research project to divert adolescents from the legal system. In R. F. Munoz, L. R. Snowden, & J. G. Kelly (Eds.), *Social and psychological research in community settings* (pp. 101-144). San Francisco: Jossey-Bass.

Reppucci, N. D. (1985). Psychology in the public interest. In A. M. Rogers & C. J. Scheirer (Eds.), *The G. Stanley Hall Lecture Series* (Vol. 5, pp. 125-156). Washington, DC: American Psychological Association.

Riger, S., LeBailly, R. K., & Gordon, M. T. (1981). Community ties and urbanites' fear of crime: An ecological investigation. *American Journal of Community Psychology, 9*, 653-665.

Risin, L. I., & Koss, M. P. (1987). The sexual abuse of boys: Frequency and descriptive characteristics of victimizations reported by a national sample of male students. *Journal of Interpersonal Violence, 2*, 309-323.

Rozee, P. D., Bateman, P., & Gilmore, T. (1991). The personal perspective of acquaintance rape prevention: A three-tier approach. In A. Parrot & L. Bechhofer (Eds.), *Acquaintance rape: The hidden crime* (pp. 337-354). New York: John Wiley.

Ruback, R. B., Greenberg, M. S., & Westcott, D. R. (1984). Social influence and crime victim decision making. *Journal of Social Issues, 40*, 51-76.

Russell, D. E. H. (1982). The prevalence and incidence of forcible rape and attempted rape of females. *Victimology, 7*, 81-93.

Russell, D. E. H. (1984). *Sexual exploitation: Rape, child sexual abuse, and workplace harassment.* Beverly Hills, CA: Sage.

Russell, D. E. H. (1990). *Rape in marriage.* Bloomington: Indiana University Press.

Searles, P. R., & Berger, R. J. (1987). The current status of rape reform legislation: An examination of state statues. *Women's Rights Law Reporter, 10*, 25-43.

Seidman, E. (1987). Toward a framework for primary prevention research. In J. Steinberg & M. Silverman (Eds.), *Preventing mental disorders: A research perspective* (Report No. ADM 87-1192, pp. 2-19). Rockville, MD: U.S. Department of Health and Human Services.

Shotland, R. L. (1989). A model of the causes of date rape in developing and close relationships. In C. Hendrick (Ed.), *Close relationships* (pp. 247-270). Newbury Park, CA: Sage.

Shotland, R. L. (1992). A theory of the causes of courtship rape: Part 2. In J. W. White & S. B. Sorenson (Eds.), Adult sexual assault [Special issue]. *Journal of Social Issues, 48*, 127-143.

Sorenson, S. B., Stein, J. A., Siegel, J. M., Golding, J. M., & Burnam, M. A. (1987). Prevalence of adult sexual assault: The Los Angeles Epidemiologic Catchment Area Study. *Journal of Epidemiology, 126*, 1154-1164.

U.S. Bureau of Justice Statistics. (1984). *Criminal victimization in the United States, 1982.* Washington, DC: U.S. Department of Justice.

U.S. Bureau of Justice Statistics. (1985). *The crime of rape* (Report No. NCJ-96777). Washington, DC: U.S. Department of Justice.

U.S. Bureau of Justice Statistics. (1991). *National Crime Survey: Redesign phase III basic screen questionnaire (NCS-1X).* Washington, DC: U.S. Department of Justice.

U.S. Bureau of Justice Statistics. (1992). *Criminal victimization in the United States, 1990.* Washington, DC: U.S. Department of Justice.

Warr, M. (1985). Fear of rape among urban women. *Social Problems, 32*, 239-250.

Weithorn, L. A. (1987). Professional responsibility in the dissemination of psychological research in legal contexts. In G. Melton (Ed.), *Reforming the law: Impact of child development research* (pp. 253-279). New York: Guilford.

White, J. G., & Koss, M. P. (1992). Courtship violence: Incidence in a national sample of higher education students. *Violence and Victims, 6*, 247-256.

White, J. W., & Sorenson, S. B. (Eds.). (1992a). Adult sexual assault [Special issue]. *Journal of Social Issues, 48*(1) 1-195.

White, J. W., & Sorenson, S. B. (1992b). A sociocultural view of sexual assault: From discrepancy to diversity. In J. W. White & S. B. Sorenson (Eds.), Adult sexual assault [Special issue]. *Journal of Social Issues, 48*, 187-195.

Williams, L. S. (1984). The classic rape: When do victims report? *Social Problems, 31*, 459-467.

Wyatt, G. E. (1992). The sociocultural context of African American and white American women's rape. In J. W. White & S. B. Sorenson (Eds.), Adult sexual assault [Special issue]. *Journal of Social Issues, 48*, 77-91.

Yegidis, B. L. (1986). Date rape and other forced sexual encounters among college students. *Journal of Sex Education and Therapy, 12*, 51-54.

Young, C. (1992, May 31). Women, sex and rape: Have some feminists exaggerated the problem? *Washington Post*, p. C-1.

CHAPTER 7

Examining the Facts
Advocacy Research Overstates the Incidence of Date and Acquaintance Rape

Neil Gilbert

The *Ms.* magazine Campus Project on Sexual Assault directed by Dr. Mary Koss is one of the largest, most widely disseminated, and most frequently cited studies of rape on college campuses in the United States. Funded by the National Institute of Mental Health, this research effort was endorsed with the imprimatur of a respected federal agency. Often quoted in newspapers and journals, on television, and during the 1991 Senate hearings on sexual assault, the *Ms.* findings have gained a degree of authority by process of repetition. Most of the time, however, those who cite the research findings take them at face value, understanding neither where the numbers come from nor what they actually represent. This is, in part, because this study benefits from the powerful aura of scientific research. Prefaced by sophisticated discussions of the intricate research methods employed, the findings are presented in a virtual blizzard of data supported by a few convincing case examples and numerous references to lesser-known studies. But footnotes do not a scholarly endeavor make, and the value of quantitative findings depends upon how accurately the research variables are measured, how well the sample is drawn, and the analysis to which the data are subject. Despite the respected funding source, frequent media acknowledgment, and aura of scientific respectability, a close

AUTHOR'S NOTE: An earlier version of this chapter appeared as "Realities and Mythologies of Rape" in *Society* (May/June 1992).

examination of this study reveals serious flaws that cast grave doubt on the credibility of its findings.

The *Ms.* study involved a survey of 6,159 students at 32 colleges. As Koss operationally defines the problem, 27% of the female college students in their study had been victims of rape (15%) or attempted rape (12%) an average of two times between the ages of 14 and 21. Using the same survey questions, which she claims represent a strict legal description of the crime, Koss calculates that during a 12-month period, 16.6% of college women were victims of rape or attempted rape and that more than one-half of these victims were assaulted twice (Koss, 1988; Koss, Gidycz, & Wisniewski, 1987; Warshaw, 1988). It is interesting to note that in reporting the findings in Chapter 6 of this volume, Koss and Cook indicate that the annual rate of rape and attempted rape for college women is 7.6%. What they do not tell the reader is that this one-year incidence rate is based on a different definition of rape from the one used to calculate the 27% rate reported between the ages of 14 and 21. They also fail to indicate that the 16.6% annual rate is based on the definition emphasized in the original research (Koss, 1988; Koss et al., 1987). If victimization continued at this annual rate over four years, one would expect well over half of college women to suffer an incident of rape or attempted rape during that period, and more than one-quarter of them to be victimized twice. There are several reasons for serious researchers to question the magnitude of sexual assault conveyed by the *Ms.* findings.

To begin with, there is a notable discrepancy between Koss's definition of rape and the way most of the women she labels as victims interpreted their experiences. When they were asked directly, 73% of the students whom Koss categorizes as victims of rape did not think that they had been raped. This discrepancy is underscored by the subsequent behavior of a high proportion of those identified as victims, 42% of whom had sex again with the men who supposedly raped them. Of those categorized as victims of attempted rape, 35% later had sex with their purported offenders (Koss, 1988; Koss et al., 1987).

Rape and attempted rape were operationally defined in the *Ms.* study (Koss, 1988) by five questions, three of which referred to the threat or use of "some degree of physical force." The other two questions, however, asked: "Have you had a man attempt sexual intercourse (get on top of you, attempt to insert his penis) when you didn't want to by giving you alcohol or drugs, but intercourse did not occur?" and "Have you had sexual intercourse when you didn't want to because a man gave you alcohol or drugs?" Some 44% of all the women identified as victims of rape and attempted rape in the previous year were so labeled because they responded positively to these awkward and vaguely worded questions.

What does having sex "because" a man gives you drugs or alcohol signify? A positive response does not indicate whether duress, intoxication, force, or the threat of force was present; whether the woman's judgment or control was substantially impaired; or whether the man purposefully got the woman drunk in order to prevent her resistance to sexual advances. It could mean that a woman was trading sex for drugs or that a few drinks lowered the respondent's inhibitions and she consented to an act she later regretted. Koss assumes that a positive answer signifies that the respondent engaged in sexual intercourse against her will because she was intoxicated to the point of being unable to deny consent (and that the man had administered the alcohol for this purpose). The item could have been clearly worded to denote "intentional incapacitation of the victim," but as the question stands it would require a mind reader to detect whether any affirmative response corresponds to this legal definition of rape.

Unable to answer this problem, Koss and Cook (Chapter 6, this volume) take the question as originally reported, "Have you had sexual intercourse with a man when you didn't want to because he gave you drugs or alcohol?" (Koss, 1988; Koss et al., 1987) and add the words "to make you cooperate." Rather than helping the case, however, this revised version suggests that instead of being too drunk to deny consent, the respondent actually cooperated in the act of intercourse after taking drugs or alcohol.

Finally, there is a vast disparity between the Ms. study findings and the rates of rape and attempted rape that come to the attention of various authorities on college campuses. The number of rapes formally reported to the police on major college campuses is remarkably low— on the order of two to five incidents a year in schools with thousands of women (or fewer than 1 per 1,000 female students in moderate-sized colleges). It is generally agreed that many rape victims do not report their ordeals because of the embarrassment and callous treatment frequently experienced at the hands of the police. Over the last decade, however, rape crisis counseling and supportive services have been established on virtually every major campus in the country. Highly sensitive to the social and psychological violations of rape, these services offer a sympathetic environment in which victims may come forward for assistance, without having to make official reports to the police. Although these services usually minister to more victims than are reported to the local police, the numbers remain conspicuously low compared with the incidence rate of rape and attempted rape on college campuses as Koss defines the problem.

Applying Koss's finding of an annual incidence rate of 166 in 1,000 women (each victimized an average of 1.5 times) to the population of 14,000 female students at the University of California, Berkeley, in 1990, for example, one would expect about 2,000 women to have experienced 3,000 incidents of rape or attempted rape that year. On the Berkeley campus, 2 rapes were reported to the police in 1990, and between 40 and 80 students sought assistance from the campus rape counseling service. Although this represents a serious problem, its dimensions (3-6 cases in 1,000) are a fraction of the number (166 cases in 1,000) claimed by the *Ms.* study.

What accounts for these problems and discrepancies? Koss offers several explanations, some of which appear to derive from new data or additional analysis. Therefore, it is important to distinguish between the data originally reported in 1987-1988 and later versions of the findings. The findings from the *Ms.* study were originally described in three articles, one by Koss and two coauthors in a 1987 issue of the *Journal of Consulting and Clinical Psychology*, the second (an expanded version of that article) authored by Koss as a chapter in the 1988 book *Rape and Sexual Assault*, and the third, by Koss, Dinero, Seibel, and Cox, in a 1988 issue of the *Psychology of Women Quarterly*; also published in 1988 was Robin Warshaw's book *I Never Called It Rape: The* Ms. *Report on Recognizing, Fighting, and Surviving Date and Acquaintance Rape*, with an afterword by Koss describing the research methods used in the *Ms.* project on which the book was based.

Two of the articles reported that only 27% of the students whom Koss (1988; Koss et al., 1987) classified as rape victims believed they had been raped; the third article provided additional data on how all these supposed victims labeled their experiences (Koss et al., 1988). The findings reported here indicate that (a) 11% of the students said they "don't feel victimized"; (b) 49% labeled the experience "miscommunication"; (c) 14% labeled it "crime, but not rape"; and (d) 27% said it was "rape." Although there was no indication that other data might have been available on this question, three years later a surprisingly different distribution of responses was put forth. In answer to questions raised (Gilbert, 1991a, 1991b) about the fact that most of the victims did not think they had been raped, Koss (1991a) reported that the students labeled as victims viewed the incident as follows: "One quarter thought it was rape, one quarter thought it was some kind of crime but did not believe it qualified as rape, one quarter thought it was sexual abuse but did not think it qualified as a crime, and one quarter did not feel victimized." In a later paper, the gist of these new findings was revised, with Koss (1991c) recounting: "One quarter thought it was some kind of crime, but did not *realize* it qualified as rape; one quarter thought it was *serious* sexual abuse, but did not know it qualified as a crime" (p. 9; emphasis added).

Finally, with the lack of both accuracy and candor typical of advocacy research, Koss and Cook (Chapter 6, this volume) report, "In fact, half the rape victims identified in the national survey considered their experience to be rape or some crime similar to rape." The lack of accuracy is reflected in the fact that, as noted above, the data originally reported show not "half," but only 41%, of respondents labeling their experience as "rape" or as "a crime, but not rape" (Koss et al., 1988). The lack of candor is reflected in the fact that Koss and Cook fail to tell the reader that 49% of the women labeled their experience as "miscommunication."

These inconsistencies in the reported findings aside, the additional data are difficult to interpret. If one-quarter thought their incidents involved a crime, but not rape, what kind of crime did they have in mind? Were they referring to illegal activity at the time, such as underage drinking or drug use? Despite Koss's elaboration on the data originally reported, at least one version of the findings reveals that 60% of the students either did not feel victimized or thought the incident was a case of miscommunication. Although in the second version many more of the students assessed the sexual encounters in negative terms, the fact remains that 73% did not think they were raped.

Concerning the 42% of purported victims who had sex afterward with their supposed assailants, again new data appear to have surfaced. Describing this finding in her chapter in *Rape and Sexual Assault*, Koss (1988) originally noted, "Surprisingly, 42% of the women indicated that they had sex again with the offender on a later occasion, *but it is not known if this was forced or voluntary*; most relationships (87%) did *eventually* break up subsequent to the victimization" (p. 16; emphasis added). Three years later, in a letter to the *Wall Street Journal*, Koss (1991b) is no longer surprised by this finding and evidently has new information revealing that when the students had sex again with the offenders on later occasions they were raped a second time and that the relationships broke up not "eventually" (as do most college relationships), but immediately after the second rape. Referring to this group's behavior, Koss explains: "Many victims reacted to the first rape with self-blame and thought that if they tried harder to be clear they could influence the man's behavior. Only after the second rape did they realize the problem was the man, not themselves. Afterwards, 87% of the women ended the relationship with the man who raped them." As a further explanation of the students' behavior, Koss (1991b) suggests that because many of the students were sexually inexperienced, they "lacked familiarity with what consensual intercourse should be like."

These explanations are not entirely convincing. It is hard to imagine that many 21-year-old college women, even if sexually inexperienced, are unable to judge if their sexual encounters are consensual. As for the victims blaming themselves and believing they might influence the men's behavior if they tried harder the second time, Koss offers no data from her survey to substantiate this process of reasoning. Although research indicates there is a tendency for victims of rape to blame themselves (Craig, 1990), there is no evidence that this induces them to have sex again with their assailants. One might note that there are cases of battered wives who stay with their husbands under insufferable circumstances, but it is not apparent that the battered woman syndrome applies to a large proportion of female college students (for discussion of this syndrome see Walker, Chapter 8, this volume).

With regard to the operational definition of rape used in the *Ms.* study and described in the earlier reports, Koss (1990, 1991a, 1991b) continues to claim that the study measures the act of "rape legally defined as penetration against consent through the use of force, or when the victim was purposely incapacitated with alcohol or other drugs." No explanation is offered for how the researcher detects the "intentional incapacitation of the victim" from affirmative answers to questions such as, Did you have unwanted sex because a man gave you alcohol? Although those responses account for about 40% of the incidents classified as rape and attempted rape, when describing the study to the Senate Judiciary Committee (Koss, 1990) and in other writings (Koss, 1991c), the examples of typical items used to define rape do not include these questions.

In reviewing the research methodology for the *Ms.* study, Koss (1988; Koss et al., 1987) explains that previous reliability and validity studies conducted on the 10-item Sexual Experience Survey instrument showed that few of the female respondents misinterpreted the questions on rape. Examining these earlier studies, however, one finds that the Sexual Experience Survey (SES) instrument originally referred to (Koss & Oros, 1982) differed from the revised version used in the *Ms.* study in at least one important respect: The original SES instrument contained neither of the questions dealing with rape or attempted rape "because a man gave you alcohol or drugs." In a brief report on the assessment of validity, Koss and Gidycz (1985) note: "To explore the veracity of the self-reported sexual experiences, the Sexual Experiences Survey [original wording] was administered to approximately 4000 students" (p. 422), which suggests that the findings on validity would not include the vague items on "intentional incapacitation" absent from the original version of the SES instrument.

Finally, the vast discrepancy between Ms. study figures and the number of students generally seen by rape counseling services or reported to authorities on college campuses is accounted for by the assertion that most college women who are sexually violated by an acquaintance do not recognize themselves as victims of rape. According to Koss (1991b), "Many people do not realize that legal definitions of rape make no distinctions about the relationship between victim and offender." Contrary to this claim, findings from the U.S. Bureau of Justice Statistics (1989, 1991) suggest that the crime of being raped by an acquaintance may not be all that difficult to comprehend; in recent years 33-45% of the women who said they were raped identified their assailants as acquaintances.

In support of the findings from the Ms. project, additional studies are invoked as sources of independent verification. Some of these studies used different definitions of forced sexual behavior (including verbal persuasion and psychological coercion) and involved small or nonrepresentative samples that are inadmissible for making serious estimates about the size of the problem (e.g., Ageton, 1983). Others are referred to without explanation or critical examination. Thus, for example, Koss and Cook (Chapter 6, this volume) cite two studies using representative samples that show the prevalence rate of rape for college students in the 12% range, a figure not too far from the 15% reported in the Ms. findings. One of these studies, conducted by Koss and Oros (1982), used the original version of the SES instrument to measure rape, which excluded items dealing with "intentional incapacitation of the victim." The second study defined rape as forced oral sex or intercourse, where the use of "force" included verbal persuasion (Yegidis, 1986). "This study showed," according to the researcher, "that most of the sexual encounters were forced through verbal persuasion-protestations by the male to 'go further' because of sexual need, arousal, or love" (Yegidis, 1986, p. 53). According to this definition, the conventional script of nagging and pleading—"Everyone does it," "If you really loved me, you'd do it," "I need it," "You'll like it,"—is transformed into a version of rape. After verbal persuasion, the form of "force" experienced most frequently by students was "use of alcohol or drugs," though the study neither elaborates on this category nor claims that it reflects intentional incapacitation of the victim (Yegidis, 1986).

Claiming that the *Ms.* survey's estimates of rape prevalence "are well-replicated in other studies," Koss (1991c, p. 8) refers us to Craig's (1990) discerning review of the literature to confirm the consistency of prevalence data on college students. This is a curious citation, given that Craig is in fact of a different opinion. Analyzing the problems of definition, Craig notes that they "vary from use of force to threat of force, to use of manipulative tactics such as falsely professing love, threatening to leave the woman stranded, or attempting to intoxicate the woman" (p. 403). Even when studies use the same general definitions, their authors often develop idiosyncratic measures to operationalize the terms, all of which leads Craig to conclude "that this lack of consistency limits the comparability of studies and makes replication of results difficult" (p. 403).

Advocacy Numbers: What Do They Mean?

The *Ms.* study is a highly sophisticated example of advocacy research. Under the veil of social science, elaborate research methods are employed to persuade the public and policymakers that a problem is vastly larger than commonly recognized. This is done in several ways: (a) by measuring a problem so broadly that it forms a vessel into which almost any human difficulty can be poured; (b) by measuring a group highly affected by the problem and then projecting the findings to society at large; (c) by asserting that a variety of smaller studies and reports with different problem definitions, methodologies of diverse quality, and varying results form a cumulative block of evidence in support of current findings; and (d) when research is criticized, by changing definitions and revising data in the hope that no one will examine the facts as originally reported.

Advocacy research is not a phenomenon unique to studies of rape on campus. It is practiced in a wide variety of substantive problem areas and supported by groups that, as Peter Rossi (1987) suggests, share an "ideological imperative" that maintains that findings politically acceptable to the advocacy community are more important than the quality of research from which they are derived, playing fast and loose with the facts is justifiable in the service of a noble cause, and data and sentiments that challenge conventional wisdom are to be condemned or ignored. Denounced for expressing objectionable sentiments, for example, folk singer Holly Dunn's hit, "Maybe I Mean Yes

(When I Say No)" was clearly out of tune with the feminist rhetoric, "No means no." The controversy over these lyrics ignored Muehlen-hard and Hollabaugh's (1988) inconvenient findings that 39% of the 610 college women they surveyed admitted to having said no to sexual advances when they really meant yes and fully intended to have their way.

Although advocacy studies do little to elevate the standards of social science research, they sometimes serve a useful purpose in bringing grave problems to public attention. No matter how it is measured, rape is a serious problem that creates an immense amount of human suffer-ing. One might say that even if the rape research magnifies this prob-lem in order to raise public consciousness, it is being done for a good cause, and in any case the difference is only a matter of degree. So why make an issue of the numbers?

However, the issue is not that advocacy studies simply overstate the incidence of legally defined rape, but the extent to which this occurs and what it means. After all, the difference between boiling and freez-ing is "only a matter of degree." The tremendous gap between esti-mates of rape and attempted rape that emerge from data collected annually by the U.S. Bureau of Justice Statistics (BJS; 1991) and the figures reported in advocacy studies have a critical bearing on our understanding of the issue at stake.

The BJS surveys, actually conducted by the Census Bureau, inter-view a random sample of about 62,000 households every six months. The confidentiality of responses is protected by federal law, and re-sponse rates amount to 96% of eligible units. The interview schedule asks a series of screening questions such as the following: Did anyone threaten to beat you up or threaten you with a knife, gun or some other weapon? Did anyone try to attack you in some other way? Did you call the police to report something that happened to you that you thought was a crime? Did anything happen to you which you thought was a crime, but you did not report to the police? A positive response to any of these screening items is followed up by further questions: What actually happened? How were you threatened? How did the offender attack you? What injuries did you suffer? When, where did it happen, what did you do, and so forth.

BJS findings reveal that 1.2 women in 1,000 over 12 years of age were victims of rape or attempted rape. This amounts to approximately 135,000 female victims in 1989. No trivial number, that annual figure translates into a lifetime prevalence rate of roughly 5-7%, which sug-gests that as many as 1 out of 14 women is likely to experience an incident of rape or attempted rape sometime over the course of her life.

As in other victimization surveys, there are problems of subject recall, definition, and measurement in the BJS studies that, as Koss (1991a) and others (e.g., Jencks, 1991; Russell, 1984) have pointed out, lead to underestimation of the amount of sexual assault.[1] Assuming that the BJS survey underestimated the problem by 50%, that is, it missed one out of every two cases of rape or attempted rape in the sample, the lifetime prevalence rate would rise to approximately 10-14%. Although an enormous level of sexual assault, at that rate the BJS estimates would still be dwarfed by the findings of Koss and Russell's studies, which suggest that one in two women will be victimized an average of twice in her lifetime. This brings us to the crux of the issue, which is that the huge differences between federal estimates and advocacy research findings have implications that go beyond matters of degree in measuring the size of the problem.

If 27% of female college students actually suffer an average of two incidents of rape or attempted rape by the time they are 21, the lifetime prevalence rate of these offenses is so high that one is ineluctably driven to conclude that rape occurs so frequently as to be almost a norm in sexual relations and that most men are rapists. This is a view advanced by a small but vocal group of advocates. "The truth that must be faced," according to Russell (1984), "is that this culture's notion of masculinity—particularly as it is applied to male sexuality— predisposes men to violence, to rape, to sexually harass, and to sexually abuse children" (p. 220). In a similar vein, Koss (1988) notes that her findings support the view that sexual violence against women "rests squarely in the middle of what our culture defines as 'normal' interaction between men and women" (p. 23). Catherine MacKinnon (1991), one of the leading feminists in the rape crisis movement, offers a vivid rendition of the theme that rape is a social disease afflicting most men. Writing in the *New York Times*, she advises that when men charged with the crime of rape come to trial, the court should ask, "Did this member of a group sexually trained to woman-hating aggression commit this particular act of woman-hating sexual aggression?"

Some Dysfunctional Consequences

Advocacy research not only promulgates the idea that most men are rapists, it provides a form of "scientific" legitimacy for the promotion of social programs and individual behaviors that act on this idea. When asked if college women should view every man they see as a potential rapist, a spokeswoman for the student health services at the University of California, Berkeley, told the *Oakland Tribune*, "I'm not sure that would be a negative thing" (quoted in Brydoff, 1991). This echoes the instruction supplied in one of the most popular college guidebooks on how to prevent acquaintance rape. "Since you can't tell who has the potential for rape by simply looking," the manual warns, "be on your guard with every man" (Parrot, 1988, p. 3). Experts on date rape advise college women to take their own cars on dates or to have a backup network of friends ready to pick them up, to stay sober, to inform the man in advance what the sexual limits will be that evening, and to prepare for the worst by taking a course in self-defense beforehand (Warshaw, 1988). These instructions imply that dating men is a dangerous affair.

Beyond taking courses in self-defense, the implications drawn from advocacy research sometimes recommend more extreme measures. During a public lecture titled *The Epidemic of Sexual Violence Against Women*, Diana Russell (1991) was asked by a member of the audience whether, in light of the ever-present danger, women should start carrying guns to protect themselves against men. Russell stated that personal armament was a good idea for women, but that they should probably take lessons to learn how to hit their targets; her response was greeted by loud applause.

But not all feminists, or members of the rape crisis movement, agree with the view that all men are predisposed to be rapists. Gillian Greensite (1991), founder of the Rape Prevention Education program at the University of California, Santa Cruz, writes that the seriousness of this crime "is being undermined by the growing tendency of some feminists to label all heterosexual miscommunication and insensitivity as acquaintance rape" (p. 15). (One is reminded that 50% of the students Koss defined as victims of rape labeled their experiences "miscommunication.") This tendency, Greensite observes, "is already creating a climate of fear on campuses, straining relations between males and females" (p. 68).

Heightened confusion and strained relations between men and women are not the only dysfunctional consequences of advocacy research that inflates the incidence of rape to a level that indicts most men. According to Koss's data, rape is an act that most educated women do not recognize as such when it has happened to them, and after which almost half of the victims continue their relationships with the alleged rapists. Characterizing this type of sexual encounter as rape trivializes the trauma and pain suffered by the many women who are truly victims of this crime, and may ultimately make it more difficult to convict their assailants. In exaggerating the statistics on rape, advocacy research conveys an interpretation of the problem that advances neither mutual respect between the sexes nor reasonable dialogue about assaultive sexual behavior.

It is difficult to criticize advocacy research without giving an impression of caring less about the problem than those engaged in magnifying its size. However, one may be deeply concerned about the problem of rape and still wish to see a fair and objective analysis of its dimensions. Advocacy studies have, in their fashion, rung the alarm. Before the rush to arms, a more precise reading of the data is required if we are to draw an accurate bead on this problem and attack it successfully.

Note

1. As Jencks (1991) points out, because the BJS surveys are conducted almost the same way every year, the biases that lead to underestimation are likely to be constant, so these figures provide quite a reliable guide to trends in sexual assault over time. In this regard it is interesting to note that the BJS data show the rates of rape declining by about 30% between 1978 and 1988 (Gilbert, 1991b; Jencks, 1991; U.S. Bureau of the Census, 1989; U.S. Bureau of Justice Statistics, 1991).

References

Ageton, S. (1983). *Sexual assault among adolescents.* Lexington, MA: Lexington.

Brydoff, C. (1991, May 30). Professor: Rape figures are inflated. *Oakland Tribune,* p. 1.

Craig, M. E. (1990). Coercive sexuality in dating relationships: A situational model. *Clinical Psychology Review, 10,* 395-423.

Gilbert, N. (1991a, June 27). The campus rape scare. *Wall Street Journal,* p. 10.

Gilbert, N. (1991b). The phantom epidemic of sexual assault. *Public Interest, 103,* 54-65.

Greensite, G. (1991, Fall). Acquaintance rape clarified. In *Student Guide, University of California at Santa Cruz.* Santa Cruz: University of California.

Jencks, C. (1991, Winter). Is violent crime increasing? *American Prospect, 4,* 98-109.

Koss, M. P. (1988). Hidden rape: Sexual aggression and victimization in a national sample of students in higher education. In A. W. Burgess (Ed.), *Rape and sexual assault II* (pp. 1-25). New York: Garland.

Koss, M. P. (1990). Testimony in Senate hearings on women and violence. In *Women and violence: Hearings before the Committee on the Judiciary, United States Senate, 101st Congress, Second Session, Part 2* (pp. 27-43). Washington, DC: Government Printing Office.

Koss, M. P. (1991a, July 17). Statistics show sexual assaults are more prevalent than many realize. *Los Angeles Daily Journal,* p. 6.

Koss, M. P. (1991b, July 25). [Letter to the editor]. *Wall Street Journal,* p. 21.

Koss, M. P. (1991c). *Rape on campus: Facing the facts.* Unpublished manuscript.

Koss, M. P., Dinero, T. E., Seibel, C. A., & Cox, S. L. (1988). Stranger and acquaintance rape: Are there differences in the victim's experience? *Psychology of Women Quarterly, 12*, 1-24.

Koss, M. P., & Gidycz, C. (1985). Sexual experiences survey: Reliability and validity. *Journal of Consulting and Clinical Psychology, 53*, 422-423.

Koss, M. P., Gidycz, C. A., & Wisniewski, N. (1987). The scope of rape: Incidence and prevalence of sexual aggression and victimization in a national sample of higher education students. *Journal of Consulting and Clinical Psychology, 55*, 162-170.

Koss, M. P., & Oros, C. (1982). The sexual experiences survey: A research instrument investigating sexual aggression and victimization. *Journal of Consulting and Clinical Psychology, 50*, 455-457.

MacKinnon, C. (1991, December 15). The Palm Beach hanging. *New York Times*, p. 15.

Muehlenhard, C. L., & Hollabaugh, L. C. (1988). Do women sometimes say no when they mean yes? The prevalence and correlates of women's token resistance to sex. *Journal of Personality and Social Psychology, 54*, 872-879.

Parrot, A. (1988). *Acquaintance rape and sexual assault prevention training manual*. Ithaca, NY: Cornell University.

Rossi, P. (1987). No good applied social research goes unpunished. *Society, 25*(1), 73-79.

Russell, D. E. H. (1982). *Rape in marriage*. New York: Macmillan.

Russell, D. E. H. (1984). *Sexual exploitation: Rape, child sexual abuse, and workplace harassment*. Beverly Hills, CA: Sage.

Russell, D. E. H. (1991, November 25). *The epidemic of sexual violence against women: A national crisis*. Seabury Lecture, University of California, Berkeley.

U.S. Bureau of the Census. (1989). *Statistical abstract of the United States, 1987*. Washington, DC: Government Printing Office.

U.S. Bureau of Justice Statistics. (1991). *Criminal victimization in the United States, 1989*. Washington, DC: U.S. Department of Justice.

Warshaw, R. (1988). *I never called it rape: The Ms. report on recognizing, fighting, and surviving date and acquaintance rape*. New York: Harper & Row.

Yegidis, B. L. (1986). Date rape and other forced sexual encounters among college students. *Journal of Sex Education and Therapy, 12*, 51-54.

CHAPTER **8**

The Battered Woman Syndrome Is a Psychological Consequence of Abuse

Lenore E. A. Walker

The study of battered women and battering relationships has developed over the past 20 years, beginning with a sociological and epidemiological understanding of those involved in battering relationships (Straus, Gelles, & Steinmetz, 1980) and then moving to psychological understanding of battered women (Walker, 1979, 1984), men who batter women (Sonkin, Martin, & Walker, 1985) and the dynamics of battering relationships (Blackman, 1989; Browne, 1987; Walker, 1984, 1989a, 1989b). By the early 1980s we had learned, from the women themselves, how they overcame the often major obstacles in their paths, and researchers and clinicians could more accurately describe the dynamics of abusive relationships (Walker, 1979, 1984). Since the dynamics of battering relationships have become known, it has been easier to identify the specific psychological effects that can come from living in an abusive relationship (Bograd, 1988; Carmen, Reiker, & Mills, 1984; Dutton, 1992; Herman, 1992; Saunders, 1986; Schechter, 1982; Walker, 1979, 1984, 1989a, 1989b, 1991, 1992). It is the constellation of these psychological effects that make up what is called the *battered woman syndrome* (BWS).

This chapter argues that battered woman syndrome exists and presents evidence that (a) the syndrome is part of a recognized pattern of psychological symptoms called *post-traumatic stress disorder* (PTSD) reported in the psychological literature to be produced by repeated exposure to trauma such as the physical, sexual, and/or serious psychological assault experienced by battered women; (b) the syndrome is consistent with feminist theoretical explanations of abuse of women; (c) the syndrome is useful in developing appropriate intervention programs that assist battered women to recover from their victimization; and (d) the syndrome is accepted by others who can offer battered women assistance, such as those in the medical, psychological, and legal communities.

The alternative argument, posited by Bowker in Chapter 9 of this volume, seems to deny that a woman may be psychologically affected in a particular and recognizable way by the abuse she experiences, that she may adopt certain psychological symptoms that assist her in coping with the "crazy-making" situation she experiences, and that she may be unable to cease using these coping strategies even when they are no longer useful. The point of view presented in this chapter recognizes these coping strategies as part of the clinical symptoms observed in BWS, which is a legitimate psychological construct that can affect different women in different ways, depending upon a particular woman's previous exposure to other oppressors, mental health status, available support systems, frequency and severity of the abuse, and a quality best described as "hardiness" of the individual woman.

As with many other clinical syndromes, all symptoms are not observable in all situations, and many are evident only under certain kinds of stress. Some symptoms are more likely to be potentiated when battering interacts with other forms of oppression, such as racism, poverty, homophobia, physical debility, or other mental illnesses. It is easy to confuse a clinical syndrome with theoretical explanations for the dynamics of abuse, such as the cycle theory of violence and the psychosocial construct of learned helplessness, both of which can precipitate coping strategies that are then labeled as clinical responses by psychologists. Although some find this labeling process stigmatizing and unhelpful, I would argue that placing the psychological impact from abuse into the context of other stress responses actually avoids the typical victim blaming that frequently blocks women from receiving appropriate community assistance.

Learned Helplessness

Although theoretical understanding of the dynamics of battering are dealt with at different points in this chapter, it is important to clarify the concept of learned helplessness to avoid further confusion with the forthcoming discussions of BWS. *Learned helplessness* describes the process by which organisms learn that they cannot predict whether what they do will result in a particular outcome (Seligman, 1975). It does *not* mean they learn to behave in a helpless way. The name Seligman gave to his theory is unfortunately confusing, although a careful reading of his and others' work, including my applications to battered women, can clarify this point. Seligman's (1975) experiments in the laboratory and my own applications in studies of more than 400 battered women (Walker, 1984) support the clinical observation that there are measurable changes in the perceptions of people who are exposed to repeated, inescapable, aversive stimulation (see Barnett & LaViolette, 1993, for a review of research studies identifying learned helplessness in battered women). One consequence for those who develop learned helplessness is the loss of their belief that they can reliably predict that a particular response will bring about their safety. This is called a lack of response-outcome contingencies, in behavioral psychology language, and describes the loss of ability to predict normally expected contingent outcomes when a particular response is made. In the case of battered women with learned helplessness, they do not respond with total helplessness or passivity; rather, they narrow their choice of responses, opting for those that have the highest predictability of creating successful outcomes. Even if learned helplessness were another way of labeling the BWS, which it is not, the process does not suggest the alleged helplessness or inherent weakness of battered women.

What Is Battered Woman Syndrome?

BWS is a group of usually transient psychological symptoms that are frequently observed in a particular recognizable pattern in women who report having been physically, sexually, and/or seriously psychologically abused by their male (and, sometimes, female) domestic partners. Analysis of the women's reports of the abuse indicates that the violence has been used as a means of exerting power and control over the women's behavior, often without regard for the women's rights in the situation. The pattern of symptoms in BWS is similar enough to the category of post-traumatic stress disorder found in the *Diagnostic and Statistical Manual of Mental Disorders*, third edition, revised (DSM-III-R; American Psychiatric Association, 1987) that it is considered a subcategory of PTSD (Herman, 1992; Root, 1992; Walker, 1991, in press), as are rape trauma syndrome (Koss & Harvey, 1991), combat veteran's syndrome (Figley, 1985), child sexual abuse accommodation syndrome (Summit, 1983; Walker, 1990), battered child syndrome (Helfer & Kempe, 1974; Mones, 1991; Terr, 1990), and similar psychological syndrome reactions in other crime victims and sequelae from other traumatic incidents, including natural causes such as earthquakes, fires, and airplane crashes (Figley, 1985; Ochberg, 1988).

The notion that human beings systematically prepare in a particular way for "fight or flight" when feeling scared in a dangerous situation was first proposed in the early days of psychology by classic theorists such as William James. Many of the earliest psychologists attempted to measure such responses to danger and looked at the cost such preparation might have for victims' other functions. In this context, *fight* refers to the body's and mind's preparedness to take on a challenging and dangerous situation, often included in the study of the high arousal of the autonomic nervous system. Recent studies of stress and its impact on mental and physical health include the study of the effects of such high arousal on anxiety, panic disorders, phobias, hypertension, and other physiological components of stress and anxiety. Spielberger (1991), for example, presents data on the rate of heart attacks and cancer that develop upon repeated exposure to certain types of stressors. Although battered women do cope with their abuse, often protecting themselves and their families, sometimes the cost is an almost constant state of high arousal that keeps their bodies and minds running at full speed.

Flight refers to running away; physically, if possible, or mentally, when physical escape is impossible. The typical psychological flight coping responses of high avoidance of further harm and pain include depression and other often very sophisticated ways to keep the batterer as calm as possible for as long as possible. The psychological defenses or avoidance techniques of denial, minimization, repression, and dissociation described later in this chapter are also avoidance coping strategies. In my research study of 400 battered women, the average battering relationship lasted six years, approximately the same length of time all subsequently terminated relationships lasted in 1980. Avoidance techniques reported by Bowker's (1986) sample of 1,000 battered women would probably be classified in this response category (see Bowker, Chapter 9, this volume).

Unlike other functional or organic mental health problems studied, normal responses to fear usually abate on their own without much intervention once the feared object is gone or the situation is resolved. However, for some victims the continuous fear or perception of danger, leading to descriptions such as learning "how to walk on eggshells," may create a residual effect where the woman continues to believe the danger is present because it is still in her mind. Thus, for some battered women, the BWS symptoms continue even when they are no longer adaptive to the situation, because the fear stimulus is still mentally present. Flashbacks, dissociative experiences, reliving the abusive incidents mentally, and intrusive thoughts of the violence are all psychological symptoms of BWS and have been found in the battered women studied (Herman, 1992; Walker, 1984, 1989b). These are similar to responses made by rape victims, incest survivors, and others exposed to traumatic events that take away their power and control. Unless the symptoms are addressed, such cognitive and memory changes may perpetuate the effects from abuse and prevent women from becoming survivors. Often women do not need any further intervention beyond safety from future abuse and good support from family, friends, or battered women shelter staff and advocates to move into survivor status, even with severe PTSD and BWS symptoms. Others may need specific interventions, such as Survivor Therapy (Walker, in press).

Contemporaneous to the study of battered women, there began a whole new area of studies that documented the psychological impact of trauma on an individual who has been exposed to single-incident or repeated traumatic events, including combat in war, rape, and earthquakes (Figley, 1985; Ochberg, 1988). Specialists in the study of the psychological effects of trauma identified and named the various syndromes or collections of psychological symptoms that are frequently found in those trauma victims studied. Any person, with a normal or pathological history, could be expected to develop such symptoms from exposure to the trauma. Thus a normal person who experiences an abnormal stressor can be expected to develop a PTSD syndrome such as BWS. Many of the reactions described by the respondents to Bowker's (1986) study would fit within this definition.

Diagnosing PTSD
and Battered Woman Syndrome

BWS, like other subcategories of PTSD, does not appear by name as a separate category in the psychiatric diagnostic system found in the DSM-III-R, although BWS does appear in the ninth edition of the World Health Organization's *International Classification of Diseases*. For a variety of reasons, including the rapidly growing data base that identified numerous other PTSD syndromes, the American Psychiatric Association's task force decided not to specify any subcategories by name, but rather created a generic diagnostic category with psychosocial stressors listed under Axis IV to construct the primary PTSD traumatic event(s). Thus to diagnose BWS formally, the generic criteria for PTSD as listed in the DSM-III-R must be met.

Although some object to the use of a clinical diagnosis for battered women, for fear of pathologizing the effects directly attributable to the abuse the women have experienced, for many battered women it is a relief to find out that the changes in the way they have been thinking, feeling, and acting have a name, are common to other trauma victims, are usually transient or respond to brief treatment such as survivor therapy (Walker, in press), and prove that they are not really "crazy" as is often suggested by their abusive partners.

Post-Traumatic Stress Disorder
Diagnostic Criteria

PTSD first appeared as a diagnostic category in the DSM-III in 1980 and was slightly revised for the DSM-III-R in 1987. For a clinician to make a BWS diagnosis, he or she must also find that the subject meets the PTSD criteria that are minimal in nature; a woman with BWS often has more than the minimum symptoms required for PTSD. A recent study of more than 4,000 trauma victims, including a large sample of battered women, found that only 4% could not be diagnosed using the present PTSD criteria (D. Kilpatrick, personal communication, 1992). Many of these women had been misdiagnosed with more serious personality disorders as well as separate diagnoses of depression and anxiety disorders that really were associated with the PTSD (see Herman, 1992). My research indicated that 59% of the women who responded told a mental health clinician about the abuse and, despite meeting the criteria for PTSD and BWS, they still got other diagnostic labels rather than the one specific to the reactions to the abuse (Walker, 1984).

There are five criteria for the diagnosis of PTSD using the DSM system:

1. presence of a stressor that could cause a traumatic response (battering)
2. symptoms lasting for more than one month
3. measurable cognitive and memory changes
4. at least three measurable avoidance symptoms
5. at least two measurable arousal symptoms

The first two of these are threshold criteria; the last three are specific patterns of symptoms that correspond to the expected fight or flight trauma reaction.

Threshold criteria. First, the traumatic event must be of sufficient magnitude that it would be expected to cause similar symptoms in almost any normal person who experienced it. Second, the symptoms must last for more than one month. The first is important as it differentiates the PTSD from other diagnoses of mental illness by insisting that a normal person can develop it as a result of adaptation to survive abnormal experiences. The second category assures that someone who is having a difficult emotional reaction to a traumatic event but recovers spontaneously within four weeks will not be mislabeled as having PTSD.

Symptoms corresponding to fight or flight trauma. Cognitive and memory distortions make up the first group of symptoms listed in the PTSD criteria. *Cognitive distortions* take many forms, including difficulty in concentration and confused thinking. The insistence of the batterer that he monopolizes the woman's perceptions may result in her believing his twisting of the truth. The pessimistic thinking style of those who develop learned helplessness, where the woman becomes unable to predict whether her responses will result in a particular outcome, particularly one that will better protect her, is another example of a cognitive disorder that can result in poor judgment (Abramson, Garber, & Seligman, 1978).

The isolation of the severely battered woman and her inability to know whom to trust also contributes to a narrowing of her perceived options. However, it is not magic that changes these negative thoughts to more positive ones; it is a more optimistic outlook that comes from feelings of empowerment (Seligman, 1990). Sometimes this happens with greater success on the job, sometimes it comes about because conditions change with the children, sometimes the legal system empowers her through an order of protection, and sometimes it takes place because the woman becomes less isolated—perhaps through television, a new friend, or some other social support, such as a battered woman advocate. Numerous research studies have documented the cognitive distortions that occur in battered women (see Barnett & LaViolette, 1993; Campbell, 1989; Claerhout, Elder, & Janes, 1982; Edleson, Eisikovits, Guttman, & Sela-Amit, 1991; Frieze, 1979; Lanius & Jensen, 1987; Walker, 1984, 1991).

Memory distortions in PTSD can take two major forms: *intrusive* memories of the trauma that frighten the woman and magnify her terror and *partial psychogenic amnesia* that causes her to forget much of the painful experiences. Both of these coping strategies can be worked on in self-help groups or those that are facilitated by therapists in shelters or mental health offices. Earlier beliefs that battered women shouldn't talk about the abuse only encouraged the repression of the pain; such repression takes continued effort that is better spent in planning a new life. Often those battered women who have also been victims of child sexual abuse learn to dissociate from the experience to reduce their ability to feel the pain. Those who dissociate, or split their minds from their bodies, may also develop psychogenic amnesia for parts of the abuse. Although there is much discussion today in the literature concerning the role of memory acquisition, integration, and retrieval in PTSD, most clinicians (Courtois, 1988) and researchers (Briere, 1989) document memory changes in abuse victims.

Intrusive memories can occur spontaneously, without any conscious thoughts about the abusive incidents. They often occur when the woman is quietly at rest and may cause her to engage in frenetic, hysterical types of activities or obsessive thinking to avoid the frightening spontaneous thoughts. Kilpatrick (1990) found that the single factor that best predicted female alcohol and drug abusers is whether or not they were abuse victims. He suggests that the chemical substances are used by such women to continue to keep away the intrusive memories that prolong the experience of terror, abuse, and its subsequent pain. The memories can also intrude during the woman's dreams, whether they specifically reenact parts of past battering incidents or re-create her feelings of vulnerability and terror.

Some intrusive memories are so vivid that the woman believes that the abuse is reoccurring, usually reexperienced through *flashbacks* or *dissociative* experiences in BWS. It is common for a battered woman to have flashbacks to fragments of some previous abusive incidents when she senses that the batterer is about to begin another acute battering incident. This magnifies the fear and causes the woman to perceive each successive battering incident as more dangerous than if it were the first one to occur. Dissociation, or the ability to separate one's mind from the experiences of one's body, is a psychological defense mechanism that protects abuse victims from cognitively knowing the full experience of the trauma. Some liken it to a trance experience; in any case, it is a different level of consciousness that permits mental emphasis to be placed on something other than the abuse that is occurring. When the intrusive memories of the abuse become too overwhelming, the battered woman, particularly if she has also been sexually abused, is often able to dissociate from the reexperience, too. Intrusive memories may also be recognized when there is actual physiological discomfort at the memories elicited by a conditioned-like response to something that serves as a reminder to the battered woman of the abuse. This connection to the highly emotional feelings experienced at the time of the abusive event is experienced frequently by abuse victims, perpetuating the effects of the trauma.

High avoidance, depression, and other flight symptoms make up the second set of BWS symptoms that measure avoidance responses and numbing of feelings. They include a variety of ways of avoiding the situation, including physically leaving whenever possible and, when this is not possible, using psychological defense mechanisms, usually unconsciously, to leave the situation mentally. Most battered women are aware that leaving the man does not stop the violence. Rather, he may well keep his threats to make sure that no other man ever has her, if he cannot have her. To get the women to return to them, batterers use stalking, finding, harassing, and persuading. Many battered women try to avoid thinking about the violence by conscious attempts not to deal with it other than by keeping the man as calm as possible as well as unconscious attempts through coping strategies such as minimization, denial, repression, and dissociation, described earlier. Some battered women become so mentally confused that they cannot concentrate on the extent of their fears; others become obsessed about trying to reduce the probability that they will be seriously hurt. Often this means giving in to the batterer's demands to become more isolated from other meaningful people in their lives, feeling estranged from others, and avoiding places or activities that might get him more upset or remind themselves of the abuse.

The woman with BWS demonstrates less interest in significant activities that she used to like, has begun to feel different from, and estranged from, other people, and believes that she will not live as long as others. She no longer experiences the same range of feelings as she did prior to the abuse. In some cases, a more serious depression occurs that may receive a separate clinical diagnosis (McGrath, Keita, Strickland, & Russo, 1990). As described earlier, some women use alcohol and other drugs to numb their feelings, another form of avoidance that blocks pain. In most cases these symptoms can clear up spontaneously, sometimes prior to or at the point of separation; other times, they are reduced after the woman becomes safe from the abuser. Bowker's (Chapter 9, this volume) suggestion that a U-shaped curve or "psychogenesis" is responsible for the result of lessening the depression ignores the similarity with the natural cycle of clinical depression that is frequently present in situation-based depressions as measured by clinicians. Seligman's (1975) original experiments were designed to learn more about exogenous depressions by producing them situationally in the laboratory. I suggest that Seligman produced PTSD, which has depression as one of its three essential components.

High arousal, anxiety-based symptoms, and other fight symptoms make up the third set of symptoms that often develops in women trying to protect themselves from further abuse. *Sleep problems,* such as too little or too much sleep and difficulties in falling asleep and in staying asleep, are common. Battered women report difficulties in falling asleep and in staying asleep, particularly awakening easily after several hours of sleep. Sometimes this pattern has been established by the batterer, who won't let her go to sleep as he forces her to pay attention to him or else he wakes the sleeping woman when he isn't sleeping and verbally harasses her for several hours. *Eating problems* are also present, whether the battered woman can't eat because of the high stress or because the man actually controls what kind of food and how much of it she eats. This is particularly common when children are present, especially teenagers over whom he wants to gain more control.

Hypervigilance to cues of danger and *exaggerated startle response* are two other high-arousal PTSD criteria that are commonly found in battered women. Much like the instinctive survival response of animals who have survived a forest fire to recognize the slightest smell of fire, battered women often recognize the early warning signs that another acute battering incident is about to occur. Sometimes they are able to use this early warning system as a signal to better protect themselves. Other times they are likely not to pay attention to it (using avoidance symptoms described earlier), hoping that they are just being silly or rationalizing that they are overreacting. This lack of validation or faith in their own ability to recognize danger is facilitated by society's institutions that invalidate and ignore battered women's pleas for help or provide ineffective assistance. Despite the low response rate of most institutions and those from whom battered women sought help in my study (Walker, 1984), more than 50% of the battered women interviewed still said they would continue to seek help. Both the startle response and hypervigilance to danger cues are the most resistant to change; long after the woman has found safety, she may still react with hypervigilance and startle when she is scared. Sometimes these responses win her the label of "hysterical"; other times she is simply ignored and invalidated. Most women who have ended up killing their abusers in self-defense tried to no avail to get someone to listen to their fears (Blackman, 1989; Browne, 1987; Walker, 1989b, 1992).

Irritability and even *angry responses* by a battered woman are also included in this list of high-arousal symptoms. Some have suggested that someone with BWS must behave consistent with the stereotype of the passive and ineffective battered woman, which is not part of the criteria. In fact, consistent with Bowker's (1986) research, most of the empirical and clinical research suggests that battered women have a well-developed ability to keep the man as calm as possible for as long as possible, often by not paying attention to their own needs and not feeling or expressing their anger at the injustice of their treatment. Indeed, many battered women do block these legitimate angry feelings so they often come out slowly, in indirect ways, or through irritability at times when it is less dangerous to express such angry feelings. Bowker does not acknowledge the terrible psychological and physical costs of feeling terror as experienced by these women.

As I have written elsewhere, sometimes women, believing that their abuse is inevitable, try to avoid being killed or more seriously harmed by attempting to control where and when they will be beaten (Walker, 1979, 1984, 1989b, 1991, in press). In fact, the belief that escape from abuse is difficult or impossible for some women is borne out by crime statistics that indicate more than 70% of reported incidents of battering occurred after the woman left the relationship (U.S. Crime Survey, 1990). Nonetheless, most battered women, even those with BWS, do attempt to defend themselves in a variety of successful and unsuccessful ways.

Physiological reactivity, especially when situations remind the woman of prior violent episodes, is commonly seen in most battered women with BWS (Cotton, 1990). Often women who are not in need of emergency room services do not seek medical attention right after an acute battering incident but do seek help during the calm period when they are able to experience the various aches and pains in their bodies that often are associated with high stress. Koss (1992) found that post-assault victims made twice as many visits to physicians as did non-victims, and the most severely victimized women's costs were 2.5 times higher than those of nonvictimized women. Chronic pelvic pain, headache, back pain, facial pain and TMJ, gastrointestinal complaints, and chronic illnesses are all reported after abuse. These high-anxiety symptoms may also appear as panic reactions in which the woman's psychological terror is expressed in body symptoms that mimic suffo-cation, heart palpitations and other indications of a heart attack, and general debilitation of an emergency nature. Women who have been sexually as well as physically abused are more likely to have such serious physiological and panic reactions.

Consistency With Feminist Theories About Woman Abuse

Feminist analysis of woman abuse holds that men beat women in order to gain power and control over them. It is understood that any woman can be battered, no matter what her demographic class, racial or ethnic group, or prior mental health status. Feminists place the responsibility for violence against a woman on the individual man who commits the abuse, although there is an understanding that situational factors in society, particularly unchecked misogyny, support woman abuse. Although many battered women have been forced into taking sole responsibility for stopping men's violence because of the system's lack of support, the feminist position is that it is the man's, not the woman's, responsibility to stop the violence. Bowker's essay in this volume comes dangerously close to insisting that because *some* battered women are strong enough to stop the violence, *all* women should be expected to become strong enough from the experience to escape from it and therefore be personally responsible for getting on with their lives. Feminist philosophy states that the personal is political, and the transformation of society is seen as the primary way to stop violence against women.

Feminists also insist that traditional psychotherapy does not help most battered women to heal and get on with their lives, because of both the inability of therapists to recognize and deal effectively with clients' experiences of violence and the need for societal change to eliminate those factors that perpetuate the violence. A recent study of psychologists' experiences with their own personal abuse demonstrates that therapists personally experience the same frequencies and gender ratios as the general public for sexual harassment, physical abuse, and sexual abuse within and outside of families (Pope & Feldman-Sommers, 1992). The researchers report that 12% of the female therapists studied were battered by an adult partner in a relationship, 30% were incest survivors, and more than 40% experienced sexual harassment in school or on the job.

Interestingly, battered women's perceptions of the inadequacies of therapists to understand their experience of violence are supported by a recent study by Hansen, Harway, and Cervantes (1991), who found that both female and male family therapists were equally unable to perceive the seriousness of domestic violence; 40% of those they surveyed were even unable to confront the conflict using analogue studies with cases that actually eventually escalated to homicide. These researchers' results may be unique to those who practice family therapy, or perhaps they may account for some therapists' continued denial, repression, minimization, and lack of empathy with victims as a way to keep from dealing with their own personal histories of abuse. It is interesting that Bowker's (Chapter 9, this volume) analysis of his case study of Sara indicates that his attitude is similar to those described by well-intentioned but inadequate therapists who demonstrate a lack of awareness of the psychological cost of the struggle that women go through to survive the abuse. Bowker seems to infer from Sara's recovery that the violence was not so dangerous or debilitating to her. Many women who demonstrate BWS make recoveries similar to Sara's. The point is that with proper assistance women's recovery may be easier, and they may not have to do it themselves.

Feminist Non-Woman-Blaming Theories

It is important to remember that the early literature suggested that battered woman certainly must be masochistic (Shainess, 1984) or at least wanted or deserved the abuse because of some internal personality defect or willful provocative behavior (Snell, Rosenwald, & Robey, 1964) even though there were only a few clinical cases to support these diagnostic conclusions. PTSD-BWS is a more accurate diagnosis than masochism or the more current personality disorder diagnostic categories. Rejection of BWS because some clinicians may misdiagnose the symptoms as a personality disorder, denying its existence in the face of clinical data or even trying to prove that there are no detrimental psychological effects from battering that women cannot overcome with a strong will, is another form of victim blaming. Even today, most mental health professionals do not take the battered woman seriously (Hansen et al., 1991). The politicization of the study of battered women as part of the feminist and battered women's movement helped focus the issues on women's oppression in general, rather than on specific women's individual behavior (Chesler, 1972; Schechter, 1982). Thus the PTSD-BWS diagnostic category is consistent with the feminist viewpoint that women do not seek out abusive partners, that any normal woman can fall prey to a batterer, that even normal women remain in abusive situations for a period of time, and that the abuse is not the woman's fault, no matter how obnoxious or mean her behavior toward the man. It is the only diagnostic category in the DSM-III-R diagnostic system that accepts the normality of the person's reactions prior to exposure to the trauma.

It is important to note that there is no discussion of self-esteem in the PTSD-BWS criteria. This is because the construct of self-esteem is not a unitary one, as Bowker (Chapter 9, this volume) contends. Data from my 1984 study show that battered women feel good about many of their qualities, including their ability to best protect themselves in very dangerous situations. Rosewater (1985a, 1985b) and Dutton (1992) found that battered women's MMPI scores indicate low ego strength, often thought to be one component of self-esteem. Bowker's hypothesis of a curvilinear relationship to self-esteem, that waxes and wanes according to nonmeasurable environmental stimuli, is probably more accurately clinically described as situation based, caused by the cycle of violence. The woman is more likely to perceive herself in control during the early phase, the *tension-building period*, when she can do things to help keep the batterer calm, and the third phase, the *loving contrition* or *absence of tension period*, which brings with it the rewards of the relationship, and sees the batterer as being in control during the second phase, the *acute battering incident*. My research has identified these three phases of the violence cycle in two-thirds of the 1,600 acute battering incidents evaluated for more than 400 battered women (see Walker, 1984, for further discussion and data). If indeed battered women respond to the immediate situation with coping strategies designed to best protect themselves and their children, then it is important to pay attention to what activities they can engage in at the different phases of the cycle.

Using the PTSD-BWS category can meet the challenge from feminists to avoid pathologizing the individual woman by taking into account the situational context that affects her behavior, yet also can acknowledge the honesty of the serious psychological effects that violence has upon her ability to function. It is not victim blaming, in that the woman is expected to be just like other women and not somehow provoking or seeking out her own abuse. It also helps lead to the design of effective treatment programs that emphasize changes in the environment, so that she is safe and the violence stops, rather than changes in her behavior.

Implications of
Battered Woman Syndrome for Intervention

The feminist analysis insists that safety and protection from an abusive man, a feminist support system, and advocacy will be sufficient for most women to recover from their battering experiences. It does not deny that there are negative effects from being exposed to horrendous violence.

The issue of the residual negative psychological effects that do occur in many women from being exposed to violence over a repeated period of time remains important. If the battered woman's coping strategies that were successful during the abusive relationship no longer work in a nonabusive situation, then appropriate therapeutic intervention is important to have as an available option. Hansen et al. (1991) demonstrate that therapists need better diagnostic techniques to help guide them in choosing interventions. Most therapists are not yet aware of the seriousness of these battering dynamics, nor do they understand the difference between providing special interventions for trauma victims and providing interventions for those with other psychological problems that may cause similar symptoms (Dutton, 1992; Herman, 1992; Koss & Harvey, 1991; McGrath et al., 1990; Walker, in press). Advocates must also learn how to identify those battered women who may have a more difficult time recovering once they are free from their abusers. Sometimes these women are identifiable as they have a difficult time just terminating the relationship and staying away from the man even though they have all available support systems. BWS is a way to acknowledge the origin of these women's difficulties as well as to guide the intervention process.

A woman who has developed a personality disorder needs different types of treatment methods than does someone who needs some supportive counseling after becoming safe from the batterer. Having a diagnosis such as PTSD-BWS available tells the therapist to set up a treatment program moving toward the goal of empowerment and self-efficacy, such as feminist therapy (Dutton, 1992; Walker, 1991) or a combination of trauma and feminist therapy, survivor therapy (Walker, in press) rather than other possible goals and options. The woman's strengths are identified and she is encouraged to utilize them. Deficits are neither emphasized nor clinically addressed until much later in treatment. The woman must feel like an egalitarian partner in her therapy; authoritarian methods are not useful. Many feminist therapy techniques are appropriate for this type of treatment (see Brown, 1992; Brown & Root, 1990; Dutton, 1992; Root, 1992; Rosewater & Walker, 1985; Walker, 1991).

It is the combination of the feminist political gender analysis and the new field of trauma studies that has resulted in the understanding of the psychological effects of domestic violence as BWS and helped psychologists and other mental health professionals to design effective intervention programs.

Implications of
Battered Woman Syndrome for Legal Issues

If woman abuse is considered a violation of the woman's civil rights, then emphasis on legal remedies is more clearly indicated than is therapy (Gondolf, 1990; McConnell, 1991). In fact, there have been numerous changes in the legal system to protect women from abuse more effectively (see Walker, 1989b, 1992). These changes include pro-arrest policies and vigorous prosecution of violent men at the earliest moment of detection. (For more on arrest policies, see Berk, Chapter 20, this volume; Buzawa & Buzawa, Chapter 21, this volume.) Often, the woman is too afraid or does not have the emotional ability to be a witness at such a trial, and then a psychologist, mental health specialist, or battered woman advocate who has examined the woman and found evidence of BWS can testify as to the psychological probability of the woman's having been abused by the defendant. In many jurisdictions, it is not possible to present evidence of more than one battering incident during such a prosecution. However, an expert witness who can testify as to the presence of BWS through evaluation of the client would be able to tell the court about other instances of abuse that would be consistent with the development of the syndrome that caused her to become so fearful of testifying herself. Thus a successful prosecution is more likely, with the possible outcome of a referral to a special program for abusive men or prison for the perpetrator.

Psychological testimony on BWS is also useful in cases where the woman is on trial for the commission of a crime, whether she has carried out a criminal act because of coercion and duress from the man or she has killed him in what she claims is self-defense. Again, testimony about presence of BWS may (a) help the judge or jury to understand her state of mind, including a reasonable perception of imminent danger, and (b) add to her credibility about the abuse, especially important when there are no witnesses, prior police reports, or medical records of treatment from injuries (Price, 1985).

In civil cases where the woman is suing for damages because of injuries suffered when she was battered and divorce cases where prenuptial agreements and equitable distribution of marital assets are at issue, the woman who can put on evidence of BWS will have an advantage toward proving her case. Introduction of BWS testimony has been accepted in most courts and, in fact, appears as language in new state statutes that provide a battered woman with the right to introduce the testimony on her own behalf, particularly in homicide cases where she admits to the killing but claims she was justified in protecting herself or her children. There has been an attempt to get the legislative language to be broad enough also to include battered women who may not demonstrate the diagnosable symptoms.

BWS has also been used improperly in the courts by mental health practitioners who are not trained in understanding abuse issues, especially in child custody disputes (Cahn, 1991). Some do not link the use of the syndrome to the PTSD diagnosis and trauma field knowledge base (Deed, 1991; Liss & Stahly, 1993). Others use it as a substitute for a description of the dynamics of abuse, much as the earlier definitions of child abuse syndromes have been used (Gondolf, 1990). Still others use the syndrome as an excuse for their own stereotyped misunderstandings of battered woman. In a recent trial in Oklahoma, a psychologist mistakenly testified to the definition of BWS as including the notion that the woman had to be a slave to the man before he would apply such a label to her. Obviously, such ignorance must be dealt with through education and training, whether or not the concept of BWS is accepted.

Conclusions

I have argued in this chapter that BWS is a collection of psychological symptoms that occur in a pattern consistent with PTSD, listed in the common nosology systems used by mental health professionals. In suggesting that most battered women are like Joan of Arc, Bowker (Chapter 9, this volume) forgets the history of women victims who had to meet men's tests of fortitude and strength. Women accused of being witches in New England were placed in similar no-win situations when they were tested by being dunked under water—if they survived, it demonstrated they were possessed and they were put to death; if they drowned, it proved they were not witches, but they were dead anyway. Bowker's pull-yourself-up-by-your-own-bootstraps theory is great for those who can make it, but battered women deserve whatever assistance they need to heal and get on with their lives. Stories like those Bowker relates about Sara are told over and over each day by women who do their best with minimal resources. However, there are numerous points of female stereotyped behavioral expectations in Bowker's rendition of Sara's story for which feminists would take him to task. Bowker's naive belief that women should take the responsibility to save themselves and still stay sweet, nonangry, and loving toward men is invalidating and insulting to the many women who have escaped and survived in any way they could. Injustice has been committed against battered women, and they have the right to be as angry as they need to be about it for as long as it helps them to recover. BWS is consistent with feminist theories about woman abuse in that it does not blame the victim for her abuse but, rather, accepts trauma theory explanations for the development of the psychological symptoms. Understanding the mental health implications of helping the woman eliminate coping strategies that are no longer necessary once she is out of the abusive situation, the therapist who understands BWS can develop appropriate intervention plans, such as those used in feminist therapy or survivor therapy systems. Finally, BWS is recognized by the legal field as an important tool for assisting women to become better protected from violence, for developing justification and duress defenses should they commit criminal offenses while their state of mind is affected by the abuse, and for helping them recover financial compensation for damages in civil and divorce actions. Like PTSD, BWS exists and has potential to be used as protection for battered women and to help them heal when used properly.

In conclusion, Bowker's chapter in this volume is not a rebuttal to my remarks here. I do not state anywhere that battered women have personality disorders, nor do I state that the BWS is part of their personalities. Rather, I have stated that there are psychological effects to being battered, that such effects are predictable and have a name, BWS, and that they may be temporary and may abate with safety, or may be more long-lasting and need special intervention. Furthermore, Bowker's argument is ill informed, because he does not examine any of the recent literature on the BWS. Indeed, although I began BWS in my 1984 book, Bowker cites only my 1979 work. Therefore, he cannot be challenging the battered woman syndrome.

References

Abramson, L. Y., Garber, J., & Seligman, M. E. P. (1978). Learned helplessness in humans: Critique and reformulation. *Journal of Abnormal Psychology, 87,* 49-74.

American Psychiatric Association. (1987). *Diagnostic and statistical manual of mental disorders* (3rd ed., rev.). Washington, DC: Author.

Barnett, O. W., & LaViolette, A. D. (1993). *It could happen to anyone: Why battered women stay.* Newbury Park, CA: Sage.

Blackman, J. (1989). *Intimate violence: A study of injustice.* New York: Columbia University Press.

Bograd, M. (1988). Power, gender and the family: Feminist perspectives on family systems theory. In M. A. Dutton-Douglas & L. E. A. Walker (Eds.), *Feminist psycho-*

therapies: Integration of therapeutic and feminist systems (pp. 118-133). Norwood, NJ: Ablex.

Bowker, L. H. (1986). *Ending the violence.* Holmes Beach, FL: Learning Publications.

Briere, J. (1989). *Therapy for adults molested as children: Beyond survival.* New York: Springer.

Brown, L. S. (1992). Personality disorders. In L. S. Brown & M. S. Ballou (Eds.), *Personality and psychopathology: Feminist reappraisals.* New York: Guilford.

Brown, L. S., & Root, M. P. P. (Eds.). (1990). *Diversity and complexity in feminist therapy.* New York: Haworth.

Browne, A. (1987). *When battered women kill.* New York: Free Press.

Cahn, N. R. (1991). Civil images of battered women: The impact of domestic violence on child custody decisions. *Vanderbilt Law Review, 44,* 1041-1097.

Campbell, J. C. (1989). A test of two explanatory models of women's responses to battering. *Nursing Research, 38,* 18-24.

Carmen, E. H., Reiker, P. P., & Mills, T. (1984). Victims of violence and psychiatric illness. *American Journal of Psychiatry, 141,* 378-383.

Chesler, P. (1972). *Women and madness.* New York: Avon.

Claerhout, S., Elder, J., & Janes, C. (1982). Problem-solving skills of rural battered women. *American Journal of Community Psychology, 10,* 605-612.

Cotton, D. H. G. (1990). *Stress management: An integrated approach to therapy.* New York: Brunner/Mazel.

Courtois, C. (1988). *Healing the incest wound.* New York: W. W. Norton.

Deed, M. (1991). Court-ordered child custody evaluations: Helping or victimizing vulnerable families? *Psychotherapy, 11,* 76-84.

Dutton, M. A. (1992). *Healing the trauma of woman battering: Assessment and intervention.* New York: Springer.

Edleson, J. L., Eisikovits, Z. C., Guttman, E., & Sela-Amit, M. (1991). Cognitive and interpersonal factors in woman abuse. *Journal of Family Violence, 6,* 167-182.

Figley, C. (1985). *Trauma and its wake.* New York: Brunner/Mazel.

Frieze, I. H. (1979). Perceptions of battered wives. In I. H. Frieze, D. Bar-Tal, & J. S. Carroll (Eds.), *New approaches to social problems: Applications of attribution theory* (pp. 79-108). San Francisco: Jossey-Bass.

Gondolf, E. W. (1990). The human rights of women survivors. *Response to Victimization of Women and Children, 13*(2), 6-8.

Hansen, M., Harway, M., & Cervantes, N. (1991). Therapists' perceptions of severity in cases of family violence. *Violence and Victims, 6,* 225-235.

Helfer, R. E., & Kempe, C. H. (Eds.). (1974). *The battered child* (2nd ed.). Chicago: University of Chicago Press.

Herman, J. L. (1992). *Trauma and recovery.* New York: Basic Books.

Kalmuss, D. S. (1984). The intergenerational transmission of marital aggression. *Journal of Marriage and the Family, 46,* 11-19.

Kilpatrick, D. (1990, August). *Violence as a precursor of women's substance abuse: The rest of the drugs-violence story.* Paper presented at a symposium during the annual meeting of the American Psychological Association, Boston.

Koss, M. P. (1992). Medical consequences of rape. *Violence Update, 3*(1), 1-11.

Koss, M. P., & Harvey, M. R. (1991). *The rape victim: Clinical and community interventions* (2nd ed.). Newbury Park, CA: Sage.

Lanius, M. H., & Jensen, B. L. (1987). Interpersonal problem-solving skills in battered, counseling, and control women. *Journal of Family Violence, 2,* 151-162.

Liss, M. B., & Stahly, G. B. (1993). Domestic violence and child custody. In M. Hansen & M. Harway (Eds.), *Battering and family therapy: A feminist perspective* (pp. 200-216). Newbury Park, CA: Sage.

McConnell, J. E. (1991, May). *Beyond metaphor: Battered women, involuntary servitude and the Thirteenth Amendment.* Paper presented at the International Victimology Conference, Institute for Sociology and the Law, Onati, Spain.

McGrath, E., Keita, G. P., Strickland, B., & Russo, N. F. (Eds.). (1990). *Women and depression: Risk factors and treatment issues* (Final report of the APA National Task Force on Women and Depression). Washington, DC: American Psychological Association.

Mones, P. (1991). *When a child kills: Abused children who kill their parents.* New York: Simon & Schuster.

Ochberg, F. M. (Ed.). (1988). *Post-traumatic therapy.* New York: Brunner/Mazel.

Pope, K. S., & Feldman-Summers, S. (1992). National survey of psychologists' sexual and physical abuse history and their evaluation of training and competence in these areas. *Professional Psychology: Research and Practice, 23,* 353-361.

Price, R. L. (1985). Battered woman syndrome: A defense beginning to emerge. *New York Law Journal, 194,* 104.

Root, M. P. P. (1992). Reconstructing the impact of trauma on personality. In L. S. Brown & M. S. Ballou (Eds.), *Personality and psychopathology: Feminist reappraisals.* New York: Guilford.

Rosewater, L. B. (1985a). Feminist interpretations of traditional testing. In L. B. Rosewater & L. E. A. Walker (Eds.), *Handbook of feminist therapy: Women's issues in psychotherapy* (pp. 266-273). New York: Springer.

Rosewater, L. B. (1985b). Schizophrenic, borderline or battered? In L. B. Rosewater & L. E. A. Walker (Eds.), *Handbook of feminist therapy: Women's issues in psychotherapy* (pp. 215-225). New York: Springer.

Rosewater, L. B., & Walker, L. E. A. (Eds.). (1985). *Handbook of feminist therapy: Women's issues in psychotherapy.* New York: Springer.

Saunders, D. G. (1986). When battered women use violence: Husband abuse or self-defense? *Violence and Victims, 1,* 47-60.

Schechter, S. (1982). *Women and male violence: The visions and struggles of the battered women's movement.* Boston: South End.

Seligman, M. E. P. (1975). *Helplessness: On depression, development and death.* San Francisco: Freeman.

Seligman, M. E. P. (1990). *Learned optimism: The skill to conquer life's obstacles, large and small.* New York: John Wiley.

Shainess, N. (1984). *Sweet suffering: Woman as victim.* Indianapolis: Bobbs-Merrill.

Snell, J., Rosenwald, R., & Robey, A. (1964). The wife-beater's wife: A study of family interaction. *Archives of General Psychiatry, 11,* 107-112.

Sonkin, D. J., Martin, D., & Walker, L. E. A. (1985). *The male batterer: A treatment approach.* New York: Springer.

Spielberger, C. (1991). *Psychosocial and personality risk factors in heart disease and cancer.* Paper presented at the annual meeting of the New York State Psychological Association, Montauk, NY.

Straus, M. A., Gelles, R. J., & Steinmetz, S. K. (1980). *Behind closed doors: Violence in the American family.* Garden City, NY: Anchor/Doubleday.

Summit, R. (1983). The child sexual abuse accommodation syndrome. *Child Abuse and Neglect, 7,* 177-193.

Terr, L. (1990). *Too scared to cry: Psychic trauma in childhood.* New York: Harper & Row.

U.S. Crime Survey. (1990). *Report.* Washington, DC: U.S. Department of Justice.

Walker, L. E. A. (1979). *The battered woman.* New York: Harper & Row.

Walker, L. E. A. (1984). *The battered woman syndrome.* New York: Springer.

Walker, L. E. A. (1989a). Psychology and violence against women. *American Psychologist, 44,* 695-702.

Walker, L. E. A. (1989b). *Terrifying love: Why battered women kill and how society responds.* New York: HarperCollins.

Walker, L. E. A. (1990). Psychological assessment of sexually abused children for legal evaluation and expert witness testimony. *Professional Psychology: Research and Practice, 21,* 344-353.

Walker, L. E. A. (1991). Post-traumatic stress disorder in women: Diagnosis and treatment of battered woman syndrome. *Psychotherapy, 28,* 21-29.

Walker, L. E. A. (1992). Battered woman syndrome and self-defense. *Notre Dame Journal of Law, Ethics, and Public Policy, 6,* 321-334.

Walker, L. E. A. (in press). *Abused women and Survivor Therapy: A practical guide for the psychotherapist.* Washington, DC: American Psychological Association.

CHAPTER 9

A Battered Woman's Problems
Are Social, Not Psychological

Lee H. Bowker

Lenore Walker publicized the battered woman syndrome in her 1979 book, *The Battered Woman*. The key elements of her theory are that marital violence follows a three-stage cycle (tension building, acute battering, and the batterer's loving contrition) and that the victim's experience of repeated cycles of violence produce in her a condition of learned helplessness. The woman's motivation to respond decreases, giving way to passivity. She believes that nothing she can do will alter her situation. She experiences diminished self-confidence, and is likely to suffer anxiety and depression.

The battered woman syndrome is taken by many to be a psychological construct, a property of the personalities of battered women. In this essay, I argue that the syndrome is really a shorthand term for a variety of conditions that hold battered women captive in violent marriages, conditions that exist in the social system more than in the personalities of battered women. Walker (1979) characterizes her theory as psychosocial, not exclusively psychological, implying that it is the product of interaction between the social and personality systems. By positing the battered wife's helplessness as *learned*, she signals that it is derived from the social system, with its structural and cultural components (norms, values, and beliefs). In the chapter she has written for this volume, Dr. Walker shifts ground, limiting the battered woman syndrome to the personality system. This is unfortunate, as it removes her conception of the syndrome even further from an accurate, multisystem model of the experiences of battered wives than was the case in her ground-breaking 1979 formulation.

Are Battered Women Helpless?

I shall begin my examination of the battered woman syndrome with a consideration of the alleged helplessness of the battered woman. Just how helpless is the battered woman? My research involved in-depth interviews with 146 formerly battered women from southeastern Wisconsin, each of whom had ended the violence from her husband and continued to live with him for at least one year after the final incident of violence occurred (see Bowker, 1983). This was later expanded to a national sample of 1,000 battered and formerly battered women using a questionnaire and voluntarily submitted case histories (see Bowker, 1986). I hypothesized that battered women were not nearly as passive as they had been portrayed in the literature. Instead, they were active agents in trying to make their environments safer. I saw the length of time it took them to free themselves from abuse as a reflection of the intransigence of their husbands' penchant for domination and the lack of support from traditional social institutions rather than as evidence of the women's passivity or helplessness.

Given that scientists usually find what they are looking for in a study, I was not surprised to find that the battered women I studied actively resisted their victimization. What did surprise me was the vast array of personalized strategies and help sources used by the battered women to end the violence in their lives. Perhaps other researchers have focused on such women's apparent helplessness because they did not probe in interviews for detailed information about how the women tried to free themselves from the abuse. Let us look briefly at what the battered women in my national sample did to try to end their victimization.

The 1,000 battered women in my study resorted to seven major personal strategies to end the battering. Each of these personal strategies was used at least once by a majority of the women in the sample. Of the 1,000 women, 716 tried to talk the men out of battering them, 752 attempted to extract promises that the men would never batter them again, 868 avoided the men physically or avoided certain topics of conversation, 651 hid or ran away when attacked, 855 covered their faces and vital organs with their hands or used other passive defenses, 758 threatened to call the police or to file for divorce unless the battering ceased, and 665 fought back physically (counterviolence). Some personal strategies were tried only once because they proved ineffective. Avoidance was the category of personal strategy that was most likely to be used repeatedly. A total of 591 women reported using avoidance more than 10 times, 480 of them in excess of 20 times. Counterviolence was the least likely to be used extensively, with only 199 women fighting back physically on more than 10 occasions.

Many women tried fighting back physically only once or twice, because they found that it led to an escalation of the man's violence against them. In rating the effectiveness of these personal strategies, a mere 52 of the 665 women who tried fighting back found it to be very effective, compared with 397 who found it increased their spouses' violence against them. Counterviolence was the most dangerous of all the personal strategies, but every one of the strategies led to increased violence against some of the women in the sample. For example, threatening to call the police or to file for divorce led to increased violence for 229 women, and passive defense stimulated abusers to increase their violence against 156 of the women. The most successful personal strategies were avoidance and hiding or running away, which were rated as very effective by 115 and 99 of the women, respectively.

Faced with the limited effectiveness of personal strategies, most of the battered women turned to informal sources of help for personal support, advice, sheltering, and increased social pressure on the batterer. Members of the women's families (626) and friends (622) were commonly sought out. Less often used were in-laws (377) and neighbors (287). All of these help sources were effective for some women, but ineffective for the majority who tried them. Thus the women generally progressed to involvement with the formal institutions of society.

The women in the study were asked about their experiences with eight formal help sources, how often they used them, and their estimate of the help sources' effectiveness in decreasing or ending the violence. The eight formal help sources were the police, physicians and nurses, the clergy, lawyers, district attorneys, social service or counseling agencies, women's groups, and battered women's shelters. The police were called at least once in 533 of the relationships, and social service or counseling agencies were involved in 504 of the relationships, generally offering supportive counseling to the abused women, as their husbands usually refused to cooperate. Lawyers also received heavy use (431 women), not counting the district attorneys who became involved in another 118 cases. Physicians and nurses were seen by 334 of the battered women, members of the clergy by 332, and the newly created help sources of women's groups and battered women's shelters were utilized by 207 and 219 of the women, respectively. The formal help sources that were most likely to be rated as very or somewhat effective by the women who used them were women's groups (60%), battered women's shelters (56%), lawyers (50%), and social service or counseling agencies (47%) (for details on these help sources, see Bowker & Maurer, 1985, 1986, 1987). The women who ended the violence in their lives almost always combined effective formal help sources with informal social support and the personal strategies that worked best for them.

This doesn't sound very much like helpless women, does it? These were victimized women, to be sure; most of the women in the sample were horribly victimized over many years. The student or professional reading about learned helplessness might conclude that all battered women are helpless. Nothing could be further from the truth. The data presented above show that many battered women work very hard to free themselves from violence, even though a number of them are committed to remaining with their abusive partners for life or at least for a very long time. It is not possible to say exactly what proportion of battered women do so, for the studies I have conducted have used samples of volunteers, not random samples that are representative of an identifiable national or regional population. However, we can say with certainty that battering does not always produce a degree of learned helpfulness that immobilizes the victim for endless periods of time. Otherwise, how could we explain the fact that so many previously battered women are now living free of violence?

Part of the solution to this mystery is that the decline of self-esteem suffered by battered women is not linear, but curvilinear. That is to say, the women's self-esteem is initially depressed by battering, and it falls lower and lower as the battering continues. Then, when all seems hopeless, a spark of innate health ignites growth in the personalities of the victims. I call this reemergence of health *psychogenesis*, because it is often hard to find any external stimulus for this change. The U-shaped curve of self-esteem bottoms out and the battered women begin to become stronger, at first tentatively and then accelerating their personal growth until they succeed in ending the violence in their lives.

Why did the women's groups and battered women's shelters receive the highest effectiveness ratings from the abused women? There are a number of specific reasons, such as the superiority of the role-modeling techniques that are used by formerly battered women who have become paraprofessionals leading women's groups and serving as counselors and administrators in battered women's shelters. When you total up these specificities, it becomes clear that feminist help sources are successful because they are able to nurture the personality growth of the women who seek them out; they fan the flames ignited through psychogenesis (Bowker & Maurer, 1985).

Effective as they are, women's groups and battered women's shelters do not usually reach women who are at the bottom of the U-shaped curve of self-esteem. Except for women who come to them as a result of emergency intervention through a third party, such as the police, their clients have already moved themselves up to a modest degree on the far side of the self-esteem curve. They have previously taken a number of actions to rid themselves of abuse, actions that belie any characterization of them as passive and helpless. They have developed a readiness for the further growth that will ensure their triumph over the aggressors who have abused them. Women's groups and shelters offer them the support and insight necessary to accelerate their recovery from the abuse.

In the interview study, the formerly battered women were revealed as strong and healthy, for they continued to grow and develop after the violence was vanquished. Truly they can now be seen as victims who have become victors. Their original self-esteem has been regained and they have gone beyond that to a higher level of personality integration and to what is often referred to as strength of character.

If Battered Women Aren't Helpless, Why Do They Continue to Be Battered?

There are worse things than battering! At least that is what battered women who continue to live with abusive spouses are telling us. What could possibly be worse than battering, you say? Here are some answers from battered women.

Worse battering. Trying to get away, if unsuccessful, is likely to lead to escalated violence, perhaps homicide. The torture and killing of pets are other commonly seen methods of "teaching her a lesson."

Harm to the children. Most battered women and a few of their aggressors try to protect their children from the worst of the violence. Few battered women would be willing to leave their children unprotected in the care of a batterer, and many do not have sufficient resources to take their children with them if they leave. In addition, many batterers threaten that they will gain full legal custody of the children if their wives leave. This would deprive the battered women of their children forever, in addition to endangering the mental and physical health of the children by placing them in the care of the batterers.

Retaliation against parents or other close relatives. Some batterers make a point of threatening to kill their in-laws if their wives ever leave them.

Starvation and homelessness. Many batterers are careful to keep their wives in economic chains. No property is in the women's names, nor are checking and savings accounts. With no money available to them, how can the women leave without starving? Where will they stay if their husbands have socially isolated them from friends and relatives? Those who do have friends with whom they could stay often fear endangering their friends by hiding out at their homes. My own experiences with having a car windshield smashed by beer bottles and a menacing visit from a man who had a long history of successful play as a lineman on the football team at the Washington State Penitentiary exemplify the danger of helping a battered wife.

Shame, failure, and public sin. It is common for battered women to take responsibility for the continuation of even a violent marriage. The shame of admitting failure can be very great for these women. In the case of women who are members of certain traditional religions, staying in violent marriages and protecting the children as best they can are the only way to avoid being defined as sinfully irresponsible.

Loss of social identity and one's entire way of life. Violence, like alcoholism and dependence on controlled substances, has a way of creeping into an otherwise comfortable life, increasingly polluting it but never changing it too much all at once. Thus victims maintain their social identities through most if not all of the violence. For a woman, ending the violence often means losing all that is familiar in her life. If her husband has some standing in the community, leaving him entails a loss of that social standing until she can build a new life in which she has her own place in society.

Escaping from the violence may mean that a woman must leave all but a few of her belongings behind, knowing that she probably will never see most of them again. Her husband may destroy her favorite things in a rage when he realizes that she is free. In extreme cases, battered women have to take the same precautions as people in the federal witness protection program. A few of the women in my national study reported saving secretly for years, then leaving in the middle of the night for another state, followed by a complete change of identity, right down to a new social security number. For women who have had to go this far to escape victimization, one of the penalties is never seeing friends and relatives again. If you met a woman who had almost saved up enough money to escape, you might label her a helpless person. You would be wrong, as you would learn one day when she disappeared without a trace.

Most of us have never been in a situation like this, so it is difficult for us to have empathy for severely battered women—sympathy, yes, but not empathy. To empathize means that one really knows what it feels like to be a battered woman—the terror, disorientation, confusion, and feelings of worthlessness and failure. Readers may wonder how it can be true that battered women would have to fear escalated violence, harm to their children, retaliation against their parents, starvation, homelessness, shame, and loss of social identity. This is possible only because we live in a society whose institutions are slow to move to the aid of abused women.

Not All Battered Women
Develop the Battered Woman Syndrome

To believe that all battered women suffer from the battered woman syndrome is to deny their fundamental humanity. Their humanity entails freedom of choice, admittedly within somewhat inflexible boundaries set by their oppressors, other intimidators, and various social institutions. Their vast diversity as unique individuals implies that they will experience a very wide range of reactions to abuse. All battered women will react to the abuse they suffer, but not all will develop symptoms that fit the pattern of the battered woman syndrome. Furthermore, some of the women who do develop BWS symptoms experience the symptoms for only a short time. It is important to realize that most battered women begin to recover from these symptoms as soon as they (and their children, if there are any) are safe. BWS symptoms are therefore fundamentally different from the long-lasting symptoms that characterize so many of the psychiatric disorders listed in the American Psychiatric Association's *Diagnostic and Statistical Manual of Mental Disorders* (1987).

All of us who are teachers know that teaching does not invariably lead to learning by our students. Sometimes we use poor teaching strategies, and other times we are insensitive to the varieties of learning styles among the women and men in our classes. Students are all too aware of these limitations in teaching effectiveness, which they reflect in the teaching evaluation forms that they complete at the close of every semester. Many students exercise their freedom of choice to ignore even those teachers whose strategies are flawless and who are perfectly attuned to the diversity of learning styles among their students.

This analogy helps us to understand the effects of the batterer's psychological, economic, social, sexual and physical abuse on his wife or other intimate partner. In the first place, batterers vary in their technical competence at intimidation. Some are extremely skilled at predation, having polished their strategies by abusing many individuals, male and female, throughout their lives. Others know little about how to dominate others beyond what they learn from televised football games, movies, and stories they hear from their male friends at work. Batterers who have a firm grasp of the strategies that are effective in dominating and intimidating their victims still may not be sensitive to the particular learning style of their current partner or to the fact that strategies of abuse must be attuned to the specifics of each situation. What cows the victim today may be the stimulus for her to file for divorce tomorrow, or to kill the abuser while he is sleeping.

Continuing with our analogy, battered wives may choose not to learn to be helpless no matter how effective their husbands are at teaching helplessness. It is possible that everyone has a breaking point, although we know of many heroines and heroes in history who have chosen death rather than domination, helplessness, betrayal, or recantation. Joan of Arc is one of the most famous women to have made this choice. Her reward for showing outstanding strength of character was to be burned at the stake by men whose domination of the entire social system was challenged by her actions.

Is it not possible that one of the reasons so many previously battered women who are still living with their former abusers report no batterings in the past year (Straus, Gelles, & Steinmetz, 1980) is that they have refused to learn to be helpless and instead have taught their husbands to be more respectful of their basic human rights? Thus might the students become teachers and the victims become victors in their struggle for a reasonable balance of power in their marriages.

I shall illustrate this thesis with a brief case history from one of the battered women I have known. Her name and identifying characteristics have been modified to protect her privacy. Sara was born into an unstable, abusive family. Her father dominated both Sara and her mother, but did not provide Sara with adequate parental nurturance and support. This pattern continued, eventually culminating in the extensive misuse of psychoactive substances by both parents, which no doubt explains why Sara began to misuse alcohol and other drugs shortly after she entered her teenage years. The instability of her home life gave her a strong need for a protector, which she conceptualized at that time as a fatherlike person.

When Sara was sexually molested by three of the older men she knew, she did not report it to her parents or the police. Forced to act as the only responsible parent at home to her father, mother, and siblings, she dreamed of escape. Her dream became a reality when she dropped out of school and ran off with a man nearly twice her age. Her parents made no attempt to force her to return home or to block her marriage. The dream soon turned into a nightmare of drug abuse, alcoholism, rape, battering, and additional psychological, economic, and social abuse. At least three other lovers followed, each appearing at first to be a protector and later revealing himself to be an abuser. Sara was battered while she was pregnant; one night she spontaneously aborted because of the severity of the blows to her stomach. Then, at 23 years of age, she physically disabled her current abuser, moved to another state, and enrolled in college—all with no financial help or emotional support from her parents or other family members. It was at this point that I made her acquaintance and, with her permission, gathered enough independent evidence to convince me that her memory of the past 10 years of her life was accurate.

That Sara was a severely battered woman there can be no doubt; nor is there doubt that she suffered marital rape on numerous occasions. Like all battered women, her psychological suffering was immense and intense, yet she never became helpless. She never gave up. Compelled to give in for the moment by violence, she nevertheless continued her resistance the next day and eventually freed herself from each of the abusive relationships in which she was victimized, beginning with her first molestation at the age of 10. Her lovers used every trick at their disposal to prevent her from leaving the relationship. They succeeded only in delaying her exit. She chose poor partners because of the lack of support from family, friends, and social institutions, not because she was self-destructive or victimization-prone, those psychologizing terms so often used by people to blame the victim for her own victimization. For example, the police refused to arrest the batterer when she called them, and her minister told her to submit to her husband's demands because it was God's will.

Sara's emergence from these serial victimizations and her refusal to learn to be helpless rekindle our faith in the power and innate health of human beings. The flame of Joan of Arc's spirit could not be obscured by the incineration of her body. Only death at the hands of one of her abusers would have kept Sara from her ultimate triumph over all of them. How many American women who have freed themselves from abuse and now live lives without fear are like Sara? We do not know. The methodological complexities and the cost of answering this question make it unlikely that we will ever find out.

The most amazing thing about Sara is that she remains a compassionate, loving human being. She continues to be open to initiating relationships and to trusting people of both sexes until they prove themselves unworthy of that trust, a remarkable achievement that few of us could hope to match were we subjected to the horrible suffering that was part of Sara's life. Although perhaps still having a weak spot for men who are somewhat older than herself, she shows a normal ability to form meaningful relationships with men as well as women. Sara is always willing to help someone else, yet she is a formidable opponent in a fight. Meeting her for the first time, you would think that she was raised in a supportive, middle-class home and was never abused by anybody. Her goal is to complete a college degree, supporting herself by working three-quarters time so that she won't be saddled by high loan payments after she graduates. She intends to become a counselor or administrator in a battered women's shelter, where her interpersonal skills, her knowledge of the internal workings of battering relationships, and her power as a role model for battered women who are just beginning to gain the strength necessary to become free of violence will assure her of success.

Examples of heroic women such as Sara can't tell us how many battered women never learn to become helpless. They do prove, however, that even very severe battering and molestation during the formative years of adolescence as well as later adulthood do not invariably result in the development of learned helplessness and the battered woman syndrome. Each claim that an individual's perceptions and behavior have been significantly altered by the battered woman syndrome must be evaluated on its own merits. In survivors like Sara, we have the potential for developing a much better understanding of how some women overcome the effects of abuse and refuse to be taught to be helpless. At the same time, we must realize that survivors like Sara are as unusual as women who truly learn to be helpless as a result of battering. Both are at the extremes of the distribution of reactions to abuse. In between are the millions of women who have freed themselves from abuse with more scars than Sara *appears* to have but less helplessness than we would expect if we believed in the learned helplessness version of the battered woman syndrome. They somehow became free of the violence, but, except for the 1,000 women who shared their experiences with me, we don't know how they did it. Their important stories have yet to be told.

I recommend that major funding agencies such as the National Institute of Mental Health place a high priority on research to discover how formerly battered women have ended their victimization and reconstructed their lives. The widespread dissemination of these results in the media, the public schools, and institutions of higher education would enable millions of women to avoid future victimization and help a similar number of currently battered women to escape from victimizing relationships or to force their abusers to reduce their demands for dominance.

Summary

In this chapter, I have argued that the battered woman syndrome is not primarily a property of the personalities of battered women, as portrayed by Lenore Walker in this volume and elsewhere. Instead, it is a summary term for the many social, psychological, economic, and physical variables that tend to hold women in abusive relationships for extended periods of time. Learned helplessness arises in oppressive relationships from which the victims cannot easily escape. If some battered women appear to have been taught by their batterers to be helpless, it probably is a signal that they have not yet been taught how to resist this negative indoctrination and how to force abusers to become more egalitarian without necessarily having to leave them or to kill them.

I have presented data that show that battered wives continue to resist their husbands actively throughout their marriages, exploring different combinations of personal strategies and help sources until they are successful in freeing themselves from the violence. These data show that a great many battered women cannot be characterized as helpless for any appreciable period of time. I have listed six of the many reasons most battered women do not immediately leave abusive mates. The apparent battered woman syndrome that we observe in many victimized wives is a misleading construct for most of these women to the extent that it directs our attention toward the victim's personality and away from the array of forces that may be thought of as conspiring to immobilize battered women and to force them to remain in abusive situations. It is these forces that we must target for change so that battered women will no longer be constrained in their efforts to become free of violence.

I concluded this essay with the case history of Sara, a remarkable woman who exemplifies the positive extreme of the continuum of responses to battering, as far as one can get from learned helplessness. Like the survivors of the Nazi and Stalinist death camps, prisoners of war, and those who have lived through major natural disasters, Sara inspires each of us to confront our own misfortunes actively. The more we can learn about how many women in our world cope with tragedy and go on to live successful and productive lives, making important contributions to our society, the better we will be able to teach other victims and potential victims to secure a violence-free future for themselves, and the more money we will be able to divert from relatively ineffective services to the help sources that battered women have found to be most effective in aiding them in their fight to become free of violence and male domination.

References

American Psychiatric Association. (1987). *Diagnostic and statistical manual of mental disorders* (3rd ed., rev.). Washington, DC: Author.

Bowker, L. H. (1983). *Beating wife-beating.* Lexington, MA: Lexington.

Bowker, L. H. (1986). *Ending the violence.* Holmes Beach, FL: Learning Publications.

Bowker, L. H., & Maurer, L. (1985). The importance of sheltering in the lives of battered wives. *Response to the Victimization of Women and Children, 7,* 2-11.

Bowker, L. H., & Maurer, L. (1986). The effectiveness of counseling services utilized by battered women. *Women and Therapy, 5,* 65-82.

Bowker, L. H., & Maurer, L. (1987). The medical treatment of battered wives. *Women and Health, 12,* 25-45.

Straus, M. A., Gelles, R. J., & Steinmetz, S. K. (1980). *Behind closed doors: Violence in the American family.* Garden City, NY: Anchor/Doubleday.

Walker, L. E. A. (1979). *The battered woman.* New York: Harper & Row.

PART III

Issues in Causes

Examining causation is the nexus of all research, theory, and social intervention for family violence or any other social problem. Of course, the types of causal connections that are of interest are determined by conceptual frameworks. Feminist frameworks emphasize the conditions and characteristics associated with gender inequality, sociological perspectives stress the importance of social conditions and social experiences, and psychological frameworks focus on individual characteristics. Most of the chapters in Part III tilt toward a social psychological framework in that they emphasize how social experiences create individual-level characteristics that cause violence.

We include three specific debates here. The first applies to all forms of violence: Does alcohol or drug use cause violence? Jerry Flanzer argues that alcohol is *the* critical cause of violence; Richard Gelles maintains that alcohol and other drugs might be associated with violence but that these are not the cause of violence. The second debate concerns child abuse: Do abused children grow up to become abusive parents? Byron Egeland argues that exposure to violence is a "significant" risk factor leading to violence, whereas Joan Kaufman and Edward Zigler maintain that this intergenerational hypothesis is "overstated and oversimplified." Finally, for the first and only time in this volume, we turn to a question about elder abuse: What is the relationship between "dependency" and such abuse? Suzanne Steinmetz believes that the "stress, frustration, and feelings of burden" experienced by the dependent elderly's caregivers result in abusive treatment. Hence she argues that the dependence of *elders* causes their abuse. Karl Pillemer, conversely, believes that the more typical situation involves caregivers who, because of mental illness, alcoholism, or some other individual trouble, are dependent on the elder persons they abuse. Hence he believes that the dependence of *caregivers* is the causal connection to abuse.

Although the chapters in Part III concern disagreements about the causes of violence, they illustrate how specific controversies can be fueled by definitional disagreements. First, readers will notice that these spokespersons do not always explicitly define their key concepts. Gelles, for example, observes that Flanzer never defines such terms as *alcoholism, substance abuse,* and *alcohol intake.* Second, definitional disagreements can occur between common definitions and authors' definitions because authors sometimes define their topics in ways that are *not* similar to popular definitions. For example, although the common interest in alcohol is on the immediate effects of alcohol on the *abuser,* when Flanzer claims that "alcohol causes violence" he is including the *intergenerational* effects of alcohol use and the consequences of alcohol use by *all* family members. In the same way, although the common image of child abuse is of physical assault or physical neglect, Egeland enlarges the definition to include parents who are labeled by researchers as "hostile/rejecting" or "psychologically unavailable." As Kaufman and Zigler note, any such definitional expansions automatically increase the level of associations that will be found. In brief, although this section focuses on controversies surrounding the *causes* of violence, different conceptualizations and definitions are important. Whether or not we believe that alcoholism, childhood victimization, elder dependency, or caregiver dependency causes abusive behavior depends in part on how we conceptualize and measure these things.

As with the controversies discussed in Part II, answers to questions about what causes violence also depend on research methodology. And here, most authors *emphasize* the methodological problems in the existing research. Gelles, for example, questions the validity of research findings associating violence with the use of alcohol and other drugs. According to him, these prior studies typically have failed to define key variables and often have inappropriately generalized information from nonrepresentative samples to the general population. In the controversy surrounding elder abuse, Steinmetz notes that research has used varying social service, legal, and research definitions of *elder abuse;* both Steinmetz and Pillemer emphasize the confusing consequences of sampling differences. Finally, in the controversy surrounding the transmission of child abuse, authors on both sides emphasize the problems that arise from relying on "retrospective" studies; they also note the problems inherent in using only information from people who come to the attention of social service providers. It therefore seems that we can extend Pillemer's comment about research on elder abuse. That research—and all research surrounding family violence—is only in its "toddler stage." Most spokespersons, therefore, are hesitant to make sweeping claims because the present state of knowledge is woefully flawed and inadequate.

The controversies addressed in this section are not as deep as those surrounding debates about definition and measurement. As with controversies in conceptualization, these authors often share basic agreements. So, although Flanzer argues that his comments serve to "negate" Gelles's sociological perspective on alcohol or other drug use, he nonetheless acknowledges the importance of cultural ideas about alcohol "within the violent pervasive American culture." For his part, Gelles does not deny that alcohol use is often "associated" with violence; rather, he questions the basis for that association. It is clear that there is much that Egeland shares with Kaufman and Zigler. These authors agree that the simplistic and popularized form of the notion of intergenerational transmission of violence must be discarded—it is just plain wrong to believe that abused children *will most assuredly* grow up to be abusers. Their disagreements are about the extent to which the experience of abuse serves as a risk factor predicting abusive behavior and about what types of "mediating" factors influence the transmission of abuse. Finally, Steinmetz and Pillemer agree that some elderly persons are dependent on their abusers and that others are abused by their dependent offspring. Their disagreements concern how many of which kinds of abused elderly there are.

Although these arguments are complex and often subtle, judgments about them must be made, because even subtle differences can have not-so-subtle practical implications. Although we might well agree with Steinmetz that "in a society as rich as ours, the issue should not be *which* population is in greatest need of limited resources," our real world is one of trade-offs. Attention to, and thus money for, some types of research and social services diverts attention, and funds, from other types. Not surprisingly, each of the controversies discussed in Part III could be—and often is— reframed into questions about where we should concentrate our research attention and practical action. For example, if Flanzer is judged as correct in his assertion that "alcoholism is very high on the list" of causes of family violence, it follows that we need more research on alcoholism and that efforts to stop alcoholism also would prevent violence. On the other hand, if Gelles is judged as correct in his assertion that "if substances are linked to violence at all, it is through a complicated set of individual, situational, and social factors," then we should not be so focused on the single factor of alcohol.

In the same way, how we evaluate the controversy about the "intergenerational transmission of violence" would lead us to choose a particular path for research and practical action. The more we agree with Egeland that experiencing violence is an "important" risk factor, the more we should specifically work to break this cycle. The more we agree with Kaufman and Zigler that for abused children the "pathway to abusive parenting is far from inevitable," the more we should think about, examine, and attend to possibly more important causes of violence. In addition, the more we agree with Egeland, the more we should look for the "social" mediators in the transmission of violence, whereas Kaufman and Zigler would lead us to examine how "genetic" factors mediate abuse. Finally, if we believe Steinmetz's prediction that in the future we will see an increase in the number of abused dependent elderly, we should support research on and programs to relieve the caregiver stress that causes violence. But the more we agree with Pillemer that programs to relieve caregiver stress would help a very small portion of abused elderly persons, the more we would support his agenda for more research, social services, and legal interventions to eliminate the dependency of abusers. In an ideal world, of course, we would give attention and resources to all forms of violence. In our real world, we do not. Decisions about research agendas and practical action follow from our evaluations of controversies such as those addressed here.

The chapters in Part III are perhaps the most difficult in this volume to evaluate, because each controversy involves a "popular," "commonsense" view about the causes of violence. As the spokespersons themselves note, the "demon rum" explanation for violence, the intergenerational cycle of violence theory, and the image of abused elderly as childlike and dependent are widely believed. Because "common knowledge" is sometimes more "common" than "knowledge," we leave it to the reader to decide whether or not the popular is the most compelling. The question here is how the belief, the folklore, the commonsense understanding of the social world holds up to logical, political, and moral scrutiny.

CHAPTER 10

Alcohol and Other Drugs Are Key Causal Agents of Violence

Jerry P. Flanzer

Alcoholism causes family violence. Just as high alcohol intake leads to cirrhosis of the liver, brain damage, and heart failure, so does high alcohol intake lead to violence in the family. At first glance at this assertion, the reader may be in shock, even outraged. Certainly one knows of alcoholics who are not prone to be abusive in the family, and certainly one knows of violent families where alcohol does not appear to be in the picture. Nevertheless, I remind the reader that there are other causes for cirrhosis of the liver, brain damage, and heart failure—but alcohol is certainly high on the list. Similarly, I agree that family violence has other causes. However, alcoholism, in its varying forms, is very high on the list.

Gelles, in Chapter 11 of this volume, argues that cultural/social context will dictate responsive behavior to alcohol use, and thereby he attempts to minimize the "alcohol-cause" argument. The following should serve to negate or, at the very least, to question his premise.

Substance abuse, alcohol abuse in particular, frequently emerges as the prominent risk factor contributing to myriad family problems. Despite media attention, alcoholism (alcohol dependence and abuse) continues to account for the overwhelming majority of the substance abuse problems in the United States and, not surprisingly, remains the most frequently mentioned form of substance abuse contributing to family problems in general and family violence specifically (for documentation, see Ackerman, 1988, who reports a higher incidence of all types of abuse occurring in alcoholic families). Although the folklore across centuries and cultures refers to the link between alcoholism and family violence in all its forms (child abuse and severe neglect, sibling abuse, spouse abuse, and elder abuse), social scientists have begun to investigate the link between alcoholism and family violence seriously only in the past few decades. The link is becoming clear, whether one refers to the actual occurrence of violence in the home or to the intergenerational and developmental consequences of living in a home with a family culture of alcoholism and violence. In this chapter I take the broad view of the intergenerational effect of alcoholism on family violence, going beyond the specific concern of the immediate effects of alcohol to the more general concern of long-term effects. Similarly, I take into account the alcohol intake of all family members, not just that of the perpetrator of the abuse.

My task in this chapter is to focus on the intermeshed behaviors of family violence and alcoholism. First, let's look at the common inter-active behaviors among and between the alcoholic/abusive perpetra-tor, the victim, and resultant dynamic function within the family. And then let's look at the how these and other factors lead to support for my argument of a causal connection.

Similar clinical portraits are being noted by numerous authors. Table 10.1 represents an attempt to portray the commonalities of behavioral responses and purposes that alcoholism and family violence both share for the perpetrator, the victim, and the family as a whole. The responses may be broadly defined as defense mechanisms, issues of parenting, tolerance levels, projection, loyalty, communication pat-terns, control/mastery over others, affection needs, responses to stress, depression, and thought patterns.

Repeated clinical observations of the behaviors of abusers and their victims have led to a consensus among experts about the behavioral sets of the participants. Universally, all abusers, whether hitters or drinkers, project blame onto others: "It's not my fault"; "She deserves that." Universally, all perpetrators (alcoholics/abusers) tend to be jealous and possessive of targeted victims. The slightest suspicion of a spouse's relationship with another, for example, brings tirades and recriminations. Often, abusers expect children to behave as their par-ents, or expect spouses to take care of everything. These role expecta-tions are impossible to meet. If one questions an abuser about a critical incident, one finds that he or she does not always remember the details and may even "black out" the incident altogether. Regardless, the abuser is not abusive all the time. In fact, he or she might otherwise be a model citizen.

Victims tend to be socially isolated, ashamed to show their physical and emotional scars, and unwilling to expose their plight to others. Part of this social isolation is caused by the victim's internalization of

TABLE 10.1 Commonalities of Behavioral Response Among Family
Members Experiencing Alcoholism and Family Violence

Response	Perpetrator	Victim	Family Function
Defense mechanisms	denial of the problem; minimizing, rationalizing, isolating	denial of the problem; minimizing, rationalizing, isolating	denial of the problem; rationalizing, isolating
Parenting	autocratic	enmeshed, infantilized	parentification
Tolerance	low frustration, increasingly aggressive, controlling	high frustration, increasingly hurt	increasing tolerance
Projection	blaming others	accepting blame, feeling shame	family inferiority
Loyalty	secretive	secretive, loyal	keeping the family intact
Communication	decreasing empathic communication	distancing to avoid abuse	minimizing pain through rigidifying communication patterns
Control	solidifying power	decreasing power	unequal power relationships
Affection	less intimate	less intimate	rigidifying affectionate relationships to avoid pain
Stress	increasingly provocative, restrictive	increasingly alarmed, timid	stress reduction
Depression	defending against depression, low self-esteem	building depression, lowering self-esteem	depression, eventual destabilization
Thought patterns	increasing impulsivity	increasing magical thinking	external rescue fantasies

blame. The victim mistakenly agrees with the abuser—"I deserve it."
Invariably, the victim believes strongly in family loyalty. Family secrets
are guarded to an extreme; maintenance of family integrity is desired
at all costs. The perpetrator's violent and alcoholic behavior blocks the
development of intimacy and masks the abuser's frightening feelings

of low self-esteem. These deleterious behaviors also block feelings of dependency and the extreme fear of being "swallowed up" that is linked to concerns of losing one's identity. The perpetrator maintains the illusion of superiority and control over his or her own life and that of the victim and, in so doing, actually creates the opposite effect.

All parties become more disoriented. At first, they must structure time to maintain functional family relationships. But they generally find themselves losing identity, through, first, the total enmeshment and then the total lack of involvement, or disengagement, with one another. Some families, having lived only with drinking and violence, have accepted this as the norm for family life, and even when they want to change, they do not know the truly "normal" ways to act. They pretend, and act as they have observed others to be. Thus, as is observed with crisis-prone individuals, they appear rigid and adhere strictly to authority.

Children growing up in violent homes evidence many of the same symptoms as children growing up in alcoholic homes. Clinicians have reported similar portraits among and between these two groups of children: emotional triangulations, secrets and isolation, stressed relationships, failing finances, and hopelessness. Children in alcoholic homes appear to have the same litany of maladaptive behaviors as child abuse victims, including juvenile delinquency, low self-esteem, suicide attempts, overrepresentation among clients of psychotherapists, sexual dysfunction, and marital difficulties (Berry & Boland, 1977; Edwards, 1982; Flanzer, 1981, 1982; Flanzer & Sturkie, 1987; Polch, Armor, & Braiker, 1981).

Given the string of clinical similarities, one may wonder if we are dealing with the same population. Are these essentially the same families, looked at from a different angle, if you will? Could it be that one abuse is contributing to or causing the other? Or are these two abuses mutually exclusive, but only by chance frequently occur among the same families? Or are these two forms of abuse symptomatic of yet a third factor? I believe it is plausible that alcoholism and other addictive drugs may be a primary cause of violence in families.

I am aware, as is the reader, that there are many families in which alcoholism or some form of family violence appears to occur without the appearance of the other. Not all alcoholic families appear to include physical, sexual, or emotional abuse, and not all violence in families appears to be triggered by drinking or the taking of drugs. But with further exploration of the history of the family, I suggest that this mutually exclusive occurrence is rare and not the norm. So the question may be, How can it happen that family violence occurs without drinking or drug use? I maintain that the pattern of effects of alcohol-ism/drug abuse on increasing family violence emerges with clarity when one broadens the definition of *alcoholism and drug abuse*. If re-searchers would examine the periods and cycles of abuse, abstinence and withdrawal, cognitive and neurological damage to individual family members, the frequency of alcohol or other drug (AOD) use, and AOD effects on family interaction and development, they would see that they have missed the presence of AOD in the preponderance of their studies. In other words, alcoholism, or other substance depend-ence or abuse, may be more than a contributory factor to family violence, it may actually be one of the primary causes of violence in the family.

In trying to prove a causal relationship, three properties must be demonstrated (Denzin, 1980, p. 213):

1. *Association:* Proof of significant associations or correlations of the key variable must be shown. The researcher must show that the causal vari-ables in the "symptom" produced variations in the dependent variable.

2. *Time:* A clear temporal relationship, wherein one factor precedes the other, must be shown. The researcher must show that the causal variable occurs before the dependent variable.

3. *Intervening variables:* An explanation of the relationship of intervening factors as catalysts or products must show that this causal system is not spurious—not the product of other variables.

Association

Byles (1978) was among the first to report alcoholism to be highly associated with spouse battering among 139 persons appearing in family court. Similar alcohol-spouse abuse associations were found by Cleek and Pearson (1985) in their divorce study, Wilson and Orford (1978) in their review, and Stewart and DeBlois (1981) in their study of abused mothers of children in psychiatric settings. Alcoholism and child abuse and neglect have been shown to appear together in a host of studies and clinical reviews. Studies of child-abusing families simi-larly have shown varying rates of alcoholism among family members.

These studies have used a variety of clinical and research method-ologies. They also have been inconsistent as to their definitions of key variables, such as the actual definitions of the levels or degrees of child abuse and neglect, spouse abuse, and alcohol abuse and dependency. These differences make comparisons across studies and subsequent clinical reviews difficult. Still, the trends are evident. The correlations between alcohol and child abuse increase when we include the drinking patterns of all family members and not just those of the perpetrators. Samples of incestuous fathers have been shown to have a range of associations between alcoholism and incest of from 20-25% (Gebhard, Gagnon, Pomeroy, & Christenson, 1965; Meiselman, 1978) to 50% (Virkunnen, 1974). Samples of perpetrators of physical abuse show a range of association between alcoholism and physical abuse of 23% (Black & Mayer, 1980) to 42-65% (Behling, 1971). Positive correlations—the greater amount of alcohol abuse correlated with greater severity of child abuse and neglect—have been found in a DWI sample (Spieker & Mousakitis, 1977) and in an adolescent abuse sample (Flanzer, 1980). Such associations might even be underestimates: Both of these studies also note that many of the most severe drinkers no longer have the opportunity to be perpetrators or victims, as they have lost their families. Evidence of a curvilinear relationship between levels of abuse exists. Downs and Miller (1986) found that having an alcoholic father might be related to being a victim of sexual abuse by a significant other. This finding seems to "delink" alcoholism as a direct cause, allowing speculation about a "secondary" relationship, but it strengthens the argument that when alcoholism is present in a system it supports an abusive relationship.

Time

Two timing issues need to be addressed: First, was there any drinking *before, during,* or *instead of* the violence incident? Second, is there any pattern connecting drinking and abuse viewed over long periods of time?

Several researchers report timing variables that link drinking to the abusive event. For example, Nau (1967) found 57% of the male abusers in his sample and 42% of the female abusers to have been intoxicated during the abusive incidents. Glazier (1971) and Gil (1973) found 13% of their abusing sample to be intoxicated during the abusive events. In a study of adolescent abusing parents, I found nearly half to be drinking instead of hitting their children, and most of the others to be drinking after abusive events (Flanzer, 1982). The examination of the relationship between the two abuses over a long period of time helps us to realize that either a continuous or a delayed effect may be occurring over years within families, and timing may be different during different phases of the life cycle or between generations.

Many researchers have reported intergenerational findings, in which abused children grew up to be alcoholic adults, with varying samples. Behling (1971) found that 88% of an alcoholic sample had been abused; Black and Mayer (1980) found 47% of their sample had been abused as children; Covington (1986) and Lundy (1986) report similar findings. Miller, Downs, and Gondoli (1987) have reported that the alcoholic women in a population of women sexually abused in childhood tended to have been sexually abused as children over longer periods of time than did the nonalcoholic women in that population. Researchers also have found that being raised in alcoholic homes is related to becoming a perpetrator of child abuse (Behling, 1971; Famularo, Stone, Barnum, & Wharton, 1986). So, in these studies, one abuse appears to precede the other intergenerationally, thus supporting the broader definition of a relationship between alcohol and violence.

Intervening Variables

There are a number of intervening variables to be considered, including the following:

- alcohol as an instigator of violence
- alcohol as a disinhibitor of social control
- alcohol's destruction of the normal growth and development of the individual and the family system
- alcohol as a rationalization for violence
- alcohol's alteration of brain functioning

Alcohol can instigate violence. Violent behavior results from a combination of the situation, the drug, and the individual's personality (Niven, 1986; cited in Miller & Potter-Efron, 1990). Miller and Potter-Efron (1990) suggest that psychological disorders or reactions to environmental stressors may cause the aggressive behavior more than the actual physiological effects of the abused drugs. For the aggression-instigating condition, an imbibing individual may be physiologically unable to attend to the ambiguous cues and complexity of behaviors that normally mediate social behavior. This individual, who in effect has tunnel vision, sees only immediate and limited cues that in themselves might instigate aggressive behavior (Taylor & Leonard, 1983; cited in Miller & Potter-Efron, 1990). In some cases, the individual's ability to distinguish between aggressive/instigating and aggressive/

inhibiting cues becomes impaired, and the vulnerability to engage in aggressive behavior increases.

Alcohol causes disinhibition that can lead to violence. Much of the literature suggests that alcohol reduces inhibitions, which results in a higher likelihood of aggressive behavior. An individual harboring intense underlying anger that has been contained by psychological defense mechanisms can become physically aggressive and intimidating as a result of the disinhibiting effects of alcohol. Miller and Potter-Efron (1990) also support a major contention, as do I, that the abused drugs act as disinhibitors of pent-up underlying anger. This disinhibition can cause the drinking or drug-abusing person to do things that he or she would not ordinarily do were he or she not abusing drugs or alcohol.

Alcohol destroys normal growth and development of the individual and the family system. Steinglass, Bennett, Wolin, and Reiss (1987) pay particular attention to the regulatory and central organizing functions of alcoholism and alcohol-related behaviors on the structure of family life. The alcohol-involved family life is skewed toward short-term stability at the expense of long-term growth. The family accommodates to the demands of alcoholism, and distortions occur that shape family growth and development. This restructuring of family life establishes a milieu that tolerates and accommodates to violence.

Alcohol may serve as a rationalization for violence, allowing the perpetrator to avoid taking responsibility for his or her actions. Intense drinking by the perpetrator or the victim (spouse) often leads to increased marital conflict, the drinking party's lack of responsibility, and other environmental (often employment or financial) stressors.

Alcohol alters brain functioning. The ingestion of alcohol over time results in the laceration of brain matter. The changes in the brain/ neurotransmitter system as a result of drinking may be a causative agent in the relationship between alcohol and violent behavior, especially during periods of withdrawal. "Withdrawal syndrome" is the brain's reaction to the absence of alcohol. Withdrawal symptoms include increased irritability, quick temper, and anger. Being in a hyper-irritable state, the drinker does not need much stimulus to react with anger.

Conclusion

In the matter of alcohol and family violence, the case for causality rests on evidence of association, timing, and the presence of intervening variables. The high frequency of association is strengthened by the expansion of the definition to include clinical relationship over time. As researchers take more careful clinical histories, they find evidence of AOD involvement in families prior to their presentation as "violent families." At the present state of knowledge, the strongest case for the causative relationship between AOD and violence are the five intervening variables presented above.

Well-functioning persons have greater capacity for autonomy than do malfunctioning persons. Individuals living under the intense anxiety of double abuse are likely to be less autonomous, less differentiated, less able to process perceptions on an objective level, more enmeshed, and governed by their abusive relationships and perceptions. Thereby, they are also more at risk for the occurrence of any dysfunctional, invasive behaviors of others. Stated in other terms, they are vulnerable to accepting external others' (the predominant culture's) belief systems and norms, being less able to govern their behavior by their own internal, moral, and self-worth/integral beliefs. This may account for abusive behaviors surrounding drinking within the violent pervasive American culture, and for less provocative behavior surrounding drinking in more "depressed" and/or less violence-tolerating cultures. The violent perpetrator, stressed by AOD, is less likely to be able to manage anxiety in the external world and, supported by the external world's acceptance of violence, more likely to exacerbate his or her dysfunctional behavior. He or she will drink more *and* hit more. The "context"—the "culture"—is the catalyst, the condition in which the cause, alcoholism, operates. I contend that AOD intake, abuse, and dependency are key causative agents for violence in the family. Although this position is in opposition to current mainstream thinking, the clinical experience of many therapists, as well as the evidence presented here, certainly warrants further testing of this position.

References

Ackerman, R. J. (1988). Complexities of alcohol and abusive families. *Focus on Chemically Dependent Families, 11*(3), 15.

Behling, D. W. (1971, June). *History of alcohol abuse in child abuse cases reported at Naval Regional Medical Center.* Paper presented at the National Child Abuse Forum, Long Beach, CA.

Berry, R. E., & Boland, J. P. (1977). *The economic cost of alcohol abuse.* New York: Free Press.

180   ISSUES IN CAUSES

Black, R., & Mayer, J. (1980). Parents with special problems: Alcoholism and opiate addiction. In C. H. Kempe & R. E. Helfer (Eds.), *The battered child* (3rd ed.). Chicago: University of Chicago Press.

Byles, J. A. (1978). Violence, alcohol problems and other problems in the disintegrating family. *Journal of Studies on Alcohol, 39*, 551-553.

Cleek, M. G., & Pearson, T. A. (1985). Perceived causes of divorce: An analysis of interrelationships. *Journal of Marriage and the Family, 47*, 179-183.

Covington, S. S. (1986). Facing the clinical challenges of women alcoholics: Physical, emotional and sexual abuse. *Focus on Family, 9*(3), 10-11, 37, 42-44.

Denzin, N. K. (1980). *Sociological methods: A sourcebook.* Chicago: Aldine.

Downs, W., & Miller, B. (1986). *Childhood abuse and alcohol histories.* Paper presented at the annual meeting of the American Society on Criminology, Atlanta, GA.

Edwards, G. (1982). *The treatment of drinking problems.* New York: McGraw-Hill.

Famularo, R., Stone, K., Barnum, R., & Wharton, R. (1986). Alcoholism and severe child maltreatment. *American Journal of Orthopsychiatry, 56*(3), 481-485.

Flanzer, J. P. (1980). Alcohol-abusing parents and their battered adolescents. In M. Galanter (Ed.), *Currents in alcoholism* (Vol. 3, pp. 529-538). New York: Grune & Stratton.

Flanzer, J. P. (1981). The vicious circle of alcoholism and family violence. *Alcoholism, 1*(3), 30-32.

Flanzer, J. P. (1982). *The many faces of family violence.* Springfield, IL: Charles C Thomas.

Flanzer, J. P., & Sturkie, D. K. (1987). *Alcohol and adolescent abuse.* Holmes Beach, FL: Learning Publications.

Gebhard, P. H., Gagnon, J., Pomeroy, W., & Christenson, C. (1965). *Sex offenders.* New York: Harper & Row.

Gil, D. (1973). *Violence against children: Physical child abuse in the United States.* Cambridge, MA: Harvard University Press.

Glazier, A. E. (1971). *Child abuse: A community challenge.* Buffalo, NY: Henry Stewart.

Lundy, C. (1986). Social role enactment and the onset, maintenance and cessation of alcohol dependence in women. *Dissertation Abstracts International, 46*(10), 3158-A.

Meiselman, K. C. (1978). *A psychological study of causes and effects of child sexual abuse with treatment recommendations.* San Francisco: Jossey-Bass.

Miller, B. A., Downs, W. R., & Gondoli, D. M. (1987). Childhood sexual abuse incidents for alcoholic women versus a random household sample. *Violence and Victims, 2*, 157-172.

Miller, M. M., & Potter-Efron, R. T. (1990). Aggression and violence associated with substance abuse. In R. T. Potter-Efron & P. S. Potter-Efron (Eds.), *Aggression, family violence, and chemical dependency* (pp. 1-36). New York: Haworth.

Nau, E. (1967). Kindesmishandlung [Child abuse]. *Mschr. Kinderheilk, 115*, 192-194.

Niven, R. (1986). Adolescent drug abuse. *Hospital and Community Psychiatry, 37*, 6596-6607.

Polch, J. M., Armor, D. J., & Braiker, H. B. (1981). *The course of alcoholism.* New York: John Wiley.

Spieker, G., & Mousakitis, C. (1977). *Alcohol abuse and child abuse and neglect.* Paper presented at the 27th Annual Meeting of the Alcohol and Drug Problems Association of North America, New Orleans.

Steinglass, P., Bennett, L., Wolin, S., & Reiss, D. (1987). *The alcoholic family.* New York: Basic Books.

Stewart, M. A., & DeBlois, S. C. (1981). Wife abuse among families attending a child psychiatric clinic. *Journal of the American Academy of Child Psychiatry, 20,* 845-862.

Taylor, S., & Leonard, K. E. (1983). Alcohol and human physical aggression. In R. Green & E. Donnerstein (Eds.), *Aggression: Theoretical and empirical reviews* (Vol. 2, pp. 77-111). New York: Academic Press.

Virkunnen, M. (1974). Incest offenders and alcoholism. *Medicine Science and Law, 14,* 124-128.

Wilson, C., & Orford, J. (1978). Children of alcoholics: Report of a preliminary study and comments on the literature. *Journal of Studies on Alcohol, 39,* 121-142.

CHAPTER 11

Alcohol and Other Drugs Are Associated With Violence— They Are Not Its Cause

Richard J. Gelles

The "demon rum" explanation for violence and abuse in the home is one of the most pervasive and widely believed explanations for family violence in the professional and popular literature. Addictive and illicit drugs, such as cocaine, crack, heroin, marijuana, and LSD, are also considered causal agents in child abuse, wife abuse, and other forms of family violence.

That alcohol and substance abuse may be related to, or may directly cause, family violence is not a new idea. William Hogarth's etching *Gin Lane*, done in the early 1700s, presents a graphic visual portrayal of the abuses and neglect that befall children whose parents abuse alcohol (for a copy of this etching, see Radbill, 1974). Not surprisingly, Hogarth's etching also implies that only certain types of alcohol, in this case gin, which was used primarily by the lower classes, are related to abuse and neglect. Social workers in the United States in the 1800s believed alcohol was the cause of child maltreatment, and the prohibition movement in the United States in the 1920s was partially based on the assumption that drinking led to the mistreatment of children (Gordon, 1988).

Both conventional wisdom and scholarly presentations, such as the preceding chapter by Jerry Flanzer, argue not only that there is a substantial association between alcohol and drug use and violence in the home, but that the substances themselves are direct causal agents. The key to the argument that alcohol causes violent behavior is the proposition that alcohol acts as a *disinhibitor* to release violent tendencies. The proposition is based on a causal link between alcohol and the human brain. Alcohol is viewed by many as a "superego solvent" that reduces inhibitions and allows violent behavior to emerge. Crack, cocaine, heroin, LSD, and marijuana have also been postulated as direct causal agents that reduce inhibitions, unleash violent tendencies, and/or directly elicit violent behavior.

There is substantial support for the notion that alcohol and drug use is related to violence in general, and to family violence in particular. Research on homicide, assault, child abuse, and wife abuse all find substantial associations between alcohol use and abuse and violence (Byles, 1978; Coleman & Straus, 1983; Gelles, 1974; Gillen, 1946; Guttmacher, 1960; Leonard, Bromet, Parkinson, Day, & Ryan, 1985; Kaufman Kantor & Straus, 1989; Miller, 1990; Snell, Rosenwald, & Robey, 1964; Wolfgang, 1958). In his chapter, Flanzer reviews a number of studies that demonstrate an association between alcohol use and misuse and family violence. Research on drug use and abuse is much more suggestive and anecdotal than is the research on alcohol and violence. In our own survey of violence in American families, we found that parents who reported "getting high on marijuana or some other drug" at least once a year also reported higher rates of violence and abusive violence toward their children (Wolfner & Gelles, 1993).

Alcohol and Violence:
Arguments and Evidence Against
the Theory of Disinhibition

It is my contention that, with the exception of the data I discuss in the following section on amphetamines and violence, there is little evidence to support the claim that alcohol and drugs act as disinhibitors and are of primary importance in explaining family violence. Stated another way, there is little scientific evidence to support the theory that alcohol and drugs such as cocaine and crack have chemical and pharmacological properties that directly produce violent and abusive behavior. Evidence from cross-cultural research, laboratory studies, blood tests of men arrested for wife beating, and survey research all indicates that although alcohol use may be associated with intimate violence, alcohol is not a primary cause of the violence.

Evidence From Cross-Cultural Research

The best evidence against the disinhibitor theory of alcohol comes from cross-cultural studies of drinking behavior. Craig MacAndrew and Robert Edgerton (1969) reviewed the cross-cultural evidence on how people react to drinking. If the pharmacological properties of alcohol are the direct causes of behavior after drinking, then there should be very little variation in drinking behavior across cultures. If alcohol acts chemically on the human brain, then it should have the same general behavioral consequences across societies. Contrary to what one would expect using a pharmacological explanation, Mac-Andrew and Edgerton found that drinking behavior varies greatly from culture to culture. In some cultures, individuals drink and become passive; in others, individuals drink and become aggressive. What explains the cross-cultural variation? The differences in drinking behavior appear to be related to what people in each society *believe* about alcohol. If the cultural belief is that alcohol is a disinhibitor, then people who drink tend to become disinhibited. If the cultural belief is that alcohol is a depressant, drinkers become passive and depressed.

Because in our society the belief is widespread that alcohol and drugs release violent tendencies when people drink or believe they are drunk, people are given, according to MacAndrew and Edgerton (1969), a "time-out" from the normal rules of social behavior. Because family violence is widely considered deviant and inappropriate behavior, there is a desire to "hush up" or rationalize abusive behavior in families. The desire of both offenders and victims to cover up family violence and the belief that alcohol is a disinhibitor combine to provide a socially acceptable explanation for violence. "I didn't know what I was doing, I was drunk," is a frequent explanation for wife beating and sometimes child beating. Victims of family violence often explain the perpetrator's actions by noting, "My husband is a Dr. Jekyll and Mr. Hyde—when he drinks he is violent, but when he is sober, he is no problem." In the end, the social expectations about drinking and drinking behavior in our society teach people that if they want to avoid being held responsible for their violence, they can either drink before they are violent or at least say they were drunk.

Laboratory Experiments

The social psychologist Alan Lang and his colleagues put Mac-Andrew and Edgerton's cross-cultural findings about alcohol, disinhibition, and violence to a test. Lang and his colleagues reasoned that if drinking behavior was learned, a researcher could manipulate a situation to produce "drunken behavior" even if the people involved were not actually drinking alcohol. Lang selected vodka as the alcoholic beverage he would use in his laboratory experiments because the taste of vodka could not be differentiated from "decarbonated" tonic water.

Lang and his colleagues performed an experiment in which college student subjects were assigned randomly to one of four groups (Lang, 1981; Lang, Goeckner, Adesso, & Marlatt, 1975). Two groups received tonic water, and the other two groups received tonic water and vodka. Subjects in one set of groups (one group receiving tonic water only and one receiving vodka and tonic) were accurately told what they were drinking. The other two groups were misled, so that the tonic water only drinkers believed they were drinking vodka and tonic and the vodka and tonic drinkers believed they were drinking only tonic water that had been decarbonated.

Lang and his associates measured aggression by assessing the intensity and duration of shocks subjects believed they were administering to Lang's associates.[1] Lang and his colleagues also measured fine motor skills by having subjects try to place shaped objects into shaped holes.

The researchers found that although drinking (whether the subjects correctly knew they were drinking or not) was related to fine motor skills, drinking was related to aggression only as a function of expectancy. In other words, the most aggressive subjects—the ones who gave the most and strongest shocks—were those who *thought* they were drinking, regardless of whether their glasses actually contained alcohol. Lang (1981) has also reviewed the results of numerous other laboratory experiments; he concludes that it is *expectancy* that determines how people behave when they are, or believe they are, drinking.

Blood Tests of Men Arrested for Wife Beating

A third piece of evidence regarding the association between alcohol and violence comes from the work of Morton Bard. Bard and his colleague Joseph Zacker (1974) trained police officers to observe, record, and intervene in cases of domestic assault. In 1,388 cases of domestic assault, one or both partners were drinking in 56% of the incidents. Drinking was as common in cases of verbal disputes as in physical assaults. Bard (personal communication, 1974), however, found that although nearly half of the assaultive men said they were drinking at the time of the assaults, when blood alcohol tests were administered it was found that less than 20% of the men were legally intoxicated. Thus, although alcohol was *associated* with the violence, there is less than compelling evidence that the men were actually physically affected by the amount of alcohol they consumed. One drink can affect motivation and coordination, but it usually takes two drinks in an hour to bring about a blood level of .10—the general legal limit of intoxication.

Survey Research

Additional evidence on the link between drinking and violent behavior comes from survey research. Murray Straus and his colleagues examined data from two national surveys of family violence. The first survey found that there was a strong relationship between alcohol use and family violence (Coleman & Straus, 1983). However, extreme levels of alcohol use were *not* related to high levels of violence. Physical violence in families actually *declined* for those who reported the highest incidence of being drunk.

Glenda Kaufman Kantor and Murray Straus (1987) examined data from the second National Family Violence Survey and found that, contrary to the earlier study, excessive drinking was associated with higher levels of wife abuse. The rate of husband-to-wife violence was highest among binge drinkers, next highest among those who reported that they drank alcohol from three times a week up to daily and who had three or more drinks each time they drank, and was lowest among those who reported that they abstained from drinking alcohol. These data seem to provide support for at least the theory that drinking is associated with violence. However, Kaufman Kantor and Straus also examined drinking behavior *at the time of the violent incident.* Their analysis of the data clearly demonstrate that alcohol *was not* used immediately prior to the violent conflict in the majority (76%) of the cases. One or both partners were drinking at the time of the violent episode in 24% of the cases. The violent male was drinking at the time of the incident in 14% of the cases, the victimized female in 2% of the cases, and both were drinking in 8% of the cases.

Thus, although the survey research demonstrates a substantial association between drinking and violence, alcohol use per se is not a necessary or sufficient cause of family violence.

Drugs and Violence

Drugs other than alcohol have been implicated as direct causes of human violent behavior. The issue of a possible link between drug use and abuse and violence is emotion laden, and fact is often mixed with myth. One problem is that, with regard to family violence, research on child or wife abuse rarely includes information on the use of drugs, other than alcohol (Kaufman Kantor & Straus, 1989). A second problem is that there are many different drugs that have been implicated in acts of violence, and each drug implicated has a different physiological effect. The drugs implicated include marijuana, phencyclidine (PCP), cocaine, opiates, hallucinogens such as LSD, stimulants, and sedative-hypnotics (Miller & Potter-Efron, 1990). The available research on the different types of drugs and their possible effects on violent behavior has found some consistent evidence.

Cannabis or marijuana use is frequent among juvenile offenders and violent juvenile offenders, and some investigators attribute fearfulness, panic, and intense aggressive impulses to marijuana use (Nicholi, 1983). On the other hand, marijuana is generally classified as a drug that produces a euphoric effect, and it may actually reduce rather than increase the potential for violent behavior. Some researchers have found that the higher the dose of marijuana, the lower the likelihood of violent behavior (Taylor & Leonard, 1983).

Although popular accounts of LSD usage suggest that LSD "trips" can lead to violent behavior, research tends to suggest that the physiological effects of this drug are antithetical to violent behavior (Johnson, 1972).

Opiates, such as heroin, have also been linked to criminal and violent acts. Crime rates for opiate users are unusually high, and violence may often be part of the criminal act. However, any link between opiates and violent behavior appears to be more of a result of the fact that opiate addicts commit crimes to obtain money for drug purchases rather than a function of the drug itself. Opiates are commonly used for sedation and anesthetics.

Cocaine is an extremely volatile drug with a short and intense effect. Although the intensity of the cocaine or crack rush is great and the effects varying, there appears to be little evidence that cocaine or crack is actually causally related to aggressive behavior (Johnson, 1972; Miller & Potter-Efron, 1990).

One drug does stand out as a possible cause of human violent behavior—amphetamines. Amphetamines raise excitability and muscle tension, and this may lead to impulsive behavior. The behavior that follows from amphetamine use is related to both the dosage and the preuse personality of the user. High-dosage users who already have aggressive personalities are likely to become more aggressive when using this drug (Johnson, 1972). Interestingly, studies of nonhuman primates, in this case stump-tailed macaques, have found that monkeys do become more aggressive when they receive dosages of d-amphetamine (Smith & Byrd, 1987). Based on his program of research with monkeys and amphetamine use, Neil Smith estimates that as many as 5% of instances of physical child abuse may be related to amphetamine use and abuse (Smith & Byrd, 1987).

Methodological Issues

Despite the evidence against the theory of alcohol and most drugs as the primary cause of intimate violence, other researchers and clinicians, such as Flanzer (Chapter 10, this volume), continue to assert that alcohol and drugs cause violence. Although the literature linking alcohol and drug use and abuse to various forms of family violence appears abundant and consistent, there are a number of important methodological limitations in the current research that both undermine the claim for a strong and consistent association between alcohol and drug use and violence and, more important, limit the ability to make causal inferences about the link between alcohol and other drug use and violent behavior.

Definitions

The first problem is one of defining of the key terms. The main variables in studies that link alcohol and drug use and abuse to family violence are often inadequately defined. The majority of investigators who study the relationship between substance use and abuse and family violence fail to appreciate the problems that arise in defining *family violence, child abuse, child maltreatment, wife abuse, spouse abuse,* and *elder abuse.*

Abuse and violence. The terms *violence, abuse, domestic violence, intimate violence,* and *family violence* are often used interchangeably in reports on alcohol, drugs, and violence. In many cases, the terms are used without definitions at all. In addition, investigators examining the association between drinking and/or drug use and child abuse often examine more than one form of maltreatment—physical abuse, sexual abuse, and/or neglect. Because each specific form of maltreatment has a relatively low base rate, and because the forms of abuse overlap—that is, some children are both physically and sexually abused—many researchers use *child abuse* or *child maltreatment* as a global construct and include various forms of maltreatment under the general term. When physical abuse and neglect are combined under the same term, it is impossible to know whether an association between alcohol and/or drug use and maltreatment is the result of alcohol and drugs producing disinhibition and thus violent behavior, whether the alcohol and drug abuse is itself considered a sign of neglect, or whether the alcohol and drug use led to neglect because of the debilitating effects of chronic or excessive alcohol and/or drug use.

Most studies of alcohol use and child maltreatment cannot be compared with one another because of the wide variation of nominal definitions of *maltreatment* employed by investigators. Some researchers study violence toward children, others focus on sexual abuse, and still others examine the full range of acts of commission and omission under the concept of *child maltreatment*. The varying definitions of abuse and neglect result in wide variations in the associations reported between drinking and drug use and child abuse and neglect.

To a lesser extent, the same definitional problems affect the study of spouse abuse, woman abuse, or what some call "domestic violence." Definitions of *wife abuse* typically focus on acts of damaging physical violence directed toward women by their spouses or partners. Some investigators broaden the definition to include sexual abuse, marital rape, and even pornography.

"Violence," the core concept in studies that attempt to test the hypothesis of a causal relation between alcohol and violence, has also proven to be difficult to define. The word *violence* is frequently used interchangeably with *aggression,* although *violence* refers to a physical act, whereas *aggression* refers to any malevolent act that is intended to hurt another person. The hurt may not be only physical, but may be emotional injury or material deprivation. Second, because of the negative connotation of the term *violence,* some investigators try to differentiate between hurtful violence and more legitimate acts. Thus William Goode (1971) tries to distinguish between legitimate acts of force and illegitimate acts of violence. Spanking a child who runs into the street might be considered "force," whereas beating the same child would be "violence." Attempts to clarify the concept of violence have demonstrated the difficulty of distinguishing between legitimate and illegitimate acts. Offenders, victims, bystanders, and agents of social control often accept and tolerate many acts between family members that would be considered illegitimate if committed by strangers.

Measuring abuse and violence. Although there is considerable variation in the nominal definitions of *abuse* and *violence*, there is quite a bit of similarity in the way researchers operationally define these terms. Abuse and violence are typically seen as taking place in those instances in which the victim becomes known and labeled by a professional or official agency. Thus studies that examine the relationship between alcohol and child abuse typically obtain a sample of abused children or abusive parents from clinical caseloads or official reports of child maltreatment. Studies that focus on wife assault obtain samples from clinical caseloads, programs for battered men, or shelters for battered women.

The major problem with operationally defining *violence* and *abuse* through the use of clinical cases or official report data is that the operational definitions overlook the systematic biases in the process by which cases of abuse are either officially labeled or come to clinical attention. For example, Newberger, Reed, Daniel, Hyde, and Kotelchuck (1977) argue that poor, lower-class, and minority children with injuries seen in public hospitals are more likely to be labeled "abused" than are middle- or upper-class children seen in physicians' private practices.

A significant limitation of using clinical cases or official reports of abuse as the means of operationalizing the variables *maltreatment, abuse,* or *violence* is that the strength of the association between alcohol and other drug use and violence may be artificially increased by a selective labeling process. Physicians, social workers, police officers, and other social service and criminal justice personnel who believe that alcohol and drug abuse *cause* family violence may be preferentially susceptible to labeling an incident "child abuse" or "wife abuse" if alcohol or another substance is involved. If alcohol or substance use is absent, the same incident or injury may well be labeled an "accident." Sarah Fenstermaker Berk and Donileen Loseke (1980) found that police were more likely to make arrests in cases of domestic violence when the offender was drinking than when he was not drinking. Thus studies that use police records, court cases, social service records, and official registry data of child abuse and wife abuse probably overrepresent incidents in which alcohol and drugs were involved. These are the types of samples used in the majority of research studies cited by Flanzer in Chapter 10. As noted earlier, if the study is examining child neglect and cases are drawn from official registries, the alcohol and drug use may have been the defining factor that led the caretaker to be reported for neglecting his or her child.

Alcohol and drug use. There are similar problems with the nominal and operational definitions of *alcohol and drug use* and *abuse.* The terms *alcohol use, alcohol abuse, alcoholism, drug use, drug dependency,* and *excessive use* are often used interchangeably in studies, and the terms are often either not precisely defined or not defined at all. Flanzer himself uses these terms interchangeably in his chapter in this volume and never actually defines what he means by *alcoholism, substance abuse,* or *alcohol intake.* Paul Roman (1991) points out that an overarching problem with all research on alcohol use and abuse is that the jargon of *alcoholism, alcohol abuse, responsible drinking, problem drinking,* and all other such concepts are not effectively and consensually defined and measured. Just as some studies use the general term *child maltreatment,* some studies use the general term *substance abuse* to encompass use and abuse of a range of substances—alcohol, cocaine, marijuana, heroin, and so on. The use of a general construct for substance use and abuse ignores the differing pharmacological properties of the substances.

Furthermore, when studies actually do attempt to define and measure alcohol or drug use and abuse, they tend to use a single-item measure. Some studies use a single self-report measure of drinking, drug use, drinking problems, or drug problems—for instance, an item that asks whether the respondent has an alcohol problem. In other studies, it is not at all clear how the diagnoses of alcoholism or alcohol problems were made. Kenneth Leonard and Theodore Jacob (1988) note that it appears that someone—the offender, his or her spouse, or some social agency—simply categorizes the offender with respect to drinking habits.

Few studies attempt to distinguish between the amount of alcohol or a drug that is consumed and the frequency of consumption. Very few studies actually collect direct data on alcohol or drug use, such as using blood or saliva tests to assess the presence of alcohol or drugs in the body. Thus, because self-reports or classifications of alcohol or drug use are not validated against an objective measure, the validity of these classifications in many studies is questionable.

An additional measurement dilemma is that some studies assess history of alcohol and drug use and correlate this with violence; other studies measure alcohol or drug use for a specific period of time, for instance, the past six months or year; still other studies measure alcohol or substance use at the time of a (or the most recent) violent incident.

When data are obtained on drinking or drug use at the time of the violent incident, researchers rarely obtain a measure of whether the perpetrator has a pattern of drinking or substance use. Conversely, some studies focus on the alcohol or drug problem, but do not measure whether the offender actually was using the substance at the time of the violent incident. This latter shortcoming is especially important, because such studies can shed no light on the disinhibition hypothesis about alcohol, drugs, and violence.

Research Designs

Flanzer (Chapter 10, this volume) explains that there are three criteria that must be satisfied in order to demonstrate a causal relationship. He also argues that the research linking alcohol, drugs, and violence satisfies the criteria of causality. I believe that research not only fails to satisfy the three criteria, it fails to satisfy the fourth criteria of "theoretical rationale" as well.

Association. Research design problems in many of the studies that examine drinking, drugs, and family violence limit the ability to determine whether significant associations exist. The main limitation of many studies is that the investigators fail to use a control or comparison group, or, if a comparison group is employed, it is not an appropriate group. Numerous studies simply collect data on the alcohol or drug use of a clinical population of abusers or abused. These studies identify the proportion of offenders who have alcohol problems or drug problems. Even if the proportions are quite high—greater than 50%—it is impossible to know whether these proportions are higher than would be found among other individuals in the clinical population who do not use violence against family members. When comparison groups are employed, investigators often fail to establish baseline measures of family violence. Thus a study that compares alcohol use in a sample of individuals seen in therapy for marital violence to a sample of individuals seen in therapy for marital distress cannot establish a valid association unless there is a baseline measure of marital violence obtained from the presumed nonviolent distressed couples. Even when baseline data on violence are collected from a comparison group, the group itself may be inappropriate for comparison because of variations in significant social, demographic, or psychological variables.

Even when the studies employ control or comparison groups, the actual associations between alcohol and family violence are quite variable. Flanzer points out in his chapter that estimates of the association between alcohol use and child molestation range from 19% to 49%. The relationship between alcohol use and wife abuse is similarly variable, depending on the study and study methodology. Thus, although the available evidence does demonstrate an association, it does not demonstrate a uniformly strong association between substance use and family violence.

Time order. Because the vast majority of studies of drinking, drugs, and family violence are cross-sectional, where data are collected at only one point in time, investigators have difficulty in meeting the time order condition of causality. In brief, this means that the investigators cannot demonstrate that the alcohol or drug use preceded the violent or abusive behavior. It is at least plausible that the drinking or drug use that is correlated with violence commenced *after* the onset of the violent and abusive behavior. Unless investigators examine the pattern of drinking and drug use over time, they cannot determine whether or not the drinking or drug use preceded the violent or abusive behavior.

Intervening variables or spuriousness. Few studies attempt to rule out spuriousness in the relationship between drinking and other drug use and family violence. As noted above, one plausible spurious variable is that drinking may be the determining factor in whether a case is identified as child maltreatment or whether an arrest is made in the case of wife abuse. Another plausible source of spuriousness is that a social factor, such as poverty or marital conflict, may be simultaneously related to the likelihood of substance abuse and violent and abusive behavior. Finally, the relationship between drinking and drug use and family violence may be spurious; it may be simply a function of expectancy effects. Because individuals in our culture assume that alcohol and drugs reduce inhibitions and increase the likelihood of violent or untoward sexual behavior, the cultural expectancy, and not the chemical properties of the substances, may explain the association between drinking and drug use and family violence.

Theoretical rationale. The final threat to the validity of the claim for a causal relationship between alcohol and other drug use and family violence is the inadequacy of the theoretical rationale. The key theoretical link that is used to explain the purported relationship is that alcohol and some drugs chemically affect the brain and break down or reduce inhibitions, and thus cause violent behavior. The preceding sections reviewed the body of research that undermines the claim that the use of alcohol and certain drugs leads to violence by reducing inhibitions.

Conclusion

It is clear that there is no simple link between substance use and family violence. The relationship cannot be explained simply by stating that alcohol or certain drugs "release inhibitions" and cause violent behavior. Even in the case of amphetamines, which have the most direct psychopharmacological relationship to violence (meaning the direct effects of the substance on behavior; Goldstein, 1985), the effect depends on dosage and preuse personality. The influence of substances on the likelihood of violence is mediated by social factors, such as income, education, and occupation; cultural factors, such as attitudes about violence, drugs, alcohol, and the effects of alcohol; and personality factors.

Except for the evidence that appears to link amphetamine use to family violence, the portrait of the alcohol- and drug-crazed partner or parent who impulsively and violently abuses a family member is a distortion. If substances are linked to violence at all, it is through a complicated set of individual, situational, and social factors.

Note

1. The students were told that they were going to engage in a learning experiment and that they were "teachers" who were responsible for teaching "students" words and sounds. The "students" sat in another room and were "wired" to a shock panel controlled by the experimental subjects. The "students" acted as if they were shocked, but no actual shock was administered.

References

Bard, M., & Zacker, J. (1974). Assaultiveness and alcohol use in family disputes. *Criminology*, 12, 281-292.
Berk, S., & Loseke, D. (1980). "Handling" family violence: The situated determinants of police arrest in domestic disturbances. *Law and Society Review*, 15, 317-346.

Byles, J. A. (1978). Violence, alcohol problems and other problems in the disintegrating family. *Journal of Studies on Alcohol, 39,* 551-553.

Coleman, D. H., & Straus, M. A. (1983). Alcohol abuse and family violence. In E. Gottheil, K. Druley, T. Skoloda, & H. Waxman (Eds.), *Alcohol, drug abuse and aggression* (pp. 104-124). Springfield, IL: Charles C Thomas.

Gelles, R. J. (1974). *The violent home: A study of physical aggression between husbands and wives.* Beverly Hills, CA: Sage.

Gillen, J. (1946). *The Wisconsin prisoner: Studies in crimogenesis.* Madison: University of Wisconsin Press.

Goldstein, P. J. (1985). The drugs/violence nexus: A tripartite conceptual framework. *Journal of Drug Issues, 15,* 492-506.

Goode, W. J. (1971). Force and violence in the family. *Journal of Marriage and the Family, 33,* 624-636.

Gordon, L. (1988). *Heroes of their own lives: The politics and history of family violence.* New York: Viking.

Guttmacher, M. (1960). *The mind of the murderer.* New York: Farrar, Straus, & Cudahy.

Johnson, R. (1972). *Aggression in man and animals.* Philadelphia: W. B. Saunders.

Kaufman Kantor, G., & Straus, M. A. (1987). The drunken bum theory of wife beating. *Social Problems, 34,* 213-230.

Kaufman Kantor, G., & Straus, M. A. (1989). Substance abuse as a precipitant of wife abuse victimizations. *American Journal of Alcohol Abuse, 15,* 173-189.

Lang, A. R. (1981, February). *Drinking and disinhibition: Contributions from psychological research.* Paper presented to the Social Research Group of the University of California at Berkeley School of Public Health and the National Institute on Alcohol Abuse and Alcoholism-sponsored conference, "Alcohol Disinhibition: The Nature and Meaning of the Link," Berkeley.

Lang, A. R., Goeckner, D. J., Adesso, V. J., & Marlatt, G. A. (1975). Effects of alcohol on aggression in male social drinkers. *Journal of Abnormal Psychology, 84,* 508-518.

Leonard, K. E., Bromet, E. J., Parkinson, D. K., Day, N. L., & Ryan, C. M. (1985). Patterns of alcohol use and physically aggressive behavior. *Journal of Studies on Alcohol, 46,* 279-282.

Leonard, K. E., & Jacob, T. (1988). Alcohol, alcoholism, and family violence. In V. B. Van Hasselt, R. L. Morrison, A. S. Bellack, & M. Hersen (Eds.), *Handbook of family violence* (pp. 383-406). New York: Plenum.

MacAndrew, C., & Edgerton, R. B. (1969). *Drunken comportment: A social explanation.* Chicago: Aldine.

Miller, B. A. (1990). The interrelationship between alcohol and drugs and family violence. In M. De La Rosa, E. Y. Lambert, & B. Gropper (Eds.), *Drugs and violence: Causes, correlates, and consequences* (pp. 177-207). Washington, DC: Government Printing Office.

Miller, M. M., & Potter-Efron, R. T. (1990). Aggression and violence associated with substance abuse. In R. T. Potter-Efron & P. S. Potter-Efron (Eds.), *Aggression, family violence, and chemical dependency* (pp. 1-36). New York: Haworth.

Newberger, E. H., Reed, R. B., Daniel, J. H., Hyde, J. N., Jr., & Kotelchuck, M. (1977). Pediatric social illness: Toward an etiologic classification. *Pediatrics, 60,* 178-185.

Nicholi, A. (1983). The non-therapeutic use of psychoactive drugs. *New England Journal of Medicine, 308,* 925-933.

Radbill, S. (1974). A history of child abuse and infanticide. In R. E. Helfer & C. H. Kempe (Eds.), *The battered child* (2nd ed., pp. 3-21). Chicago: University of Chicago Press.

Roman, P. M. (1991). Preface. In P. M. Roman (Ed.), *Alcohol: The development of sociological perspectives on use and abuse* (pp. 1-18). New Brunswick, NJ: Rutgers Center on Alcohol Studies.

Smith, E. O., & Byrd, L. (1987). External and internal influences on aggression in captive group-living monkeys. In R. J. Gelles & J. Lancaster (Eds.), *Child abuse and neglect: Biosocial dimensions* (pp. 175-199). Hawthorne, NY: Aldine de Gruyter.

Snell, J., Rosenwald, R., & Robey, A. (1964). The wife-beater's wife: A study of family interaction. *Archives of General Psychiatry, 11,* 107-113.

Taylor, S., & Leonard, K. E. (1983). Alcohol and human physical aggression. In R. Green & E. Donnerstein (Eds.), *Aggression: Theoretical and empirical reviews* (Vol. 2, pp. 77-111). New York: Academic Press.

Wolfgang, M. (1958). *Patterns in criminal homicide.* New York: John Wiley.

Wolfner, G., & Gelles, R. J. (1993). A profile of violence toward children: A national study. *Child Abuse and Neglect, 17,* 197-212.

CHAPTER 12

A History of Abuse Is a Major Risk Factor for Abusing the Next Generation

Byron Egeland

Over the more than 30 years since Kempe, Silverman, Steele, Droege-mueller, and Silver's (1962) description of the "battered child syndrome," a tremendous amount has been written about the causes of child maltreatment. Much of the early writing reported that abusing parents were themselves abused, which led to the belief in the transmission of abuse or a cycle of abuse across generations. This notion of the intergenerational transmission of abuse was one of the earliest and most widely accepted theories of abuse. Spinetta and Rigler (1972) note that "one of the basic factors in the etiology of child abuse draws unanimity: abusing parents were themselves abused or neglected physically or emotionally as children" (p. 298). It continues to be accepted as a significant factor in the etiology of abuse. Widom (1989) notes that it currently is the "premier" hypothesis in the field of abuse and neglect. The popularity and longevity of the intergenerational hypothesis is the result of many factors, including the fact that it makes intuitive sense and thus has popular appeal.

Support for the notion that child maltreatment is transmitted across generations has also come from the general belief in the cycle of violence—violence begets violence. There is considerable evidence from research on delinquent behavior (e.g., McCord, 1983); homicides (Ressler & Burgess, 1985); aggressive, violent behavior in young children (Egeland, Sroufe, & Erickson, 1983; George & Main, 1979); and family violence to support the notion of a cycle of violence. In the area of family violence, Roy (1977) found that 80% of abusive husbands had been abused as children or had witnessed their fathers abusing their mothers. Straus, Gelles, and Steinmetz (1980) found that men and women who grew up in violent homes were far more likely to abuse their spouses than were men and women who grew up in nonviolent homes. Straus et al. conclude that each generation learns to be violent by participating in a violent family. In general, there is considerable evidence to support the notion that violence breeds violence (Widom, 1989).

Despite the popular belief in the cycle of violence, an increasing number of professionals are raising questions about the intergenerational hypothesis. In the area of child abuse, Kaufman and Zigler (1987) argue that the rate of transmission across generations is overstated, at least in the popular press (see Kaufman & Zigler, Chapter 13, this volume). In addition, they warn that popularizing the intergenerational hypothesis will have negative consequences and unnecessarily raise fears in prospective parents who have histories of having been abused. In the remainder of this chapter I will review the literature on the findings regarding the intergenerational hypothesis and argue that it is an important risk factor in the etiology of child maltreatment. In addition, I will briefly review the factors that have been found to be associated with breaking the cycle of abuse.

Empirical Support for
the Intergenerational Hypothesis:
Retrospective Studies

The bulk of the empirical evidence in support of the intergenerational hypothesis in the area of child maltreatment has come from retrospective studies. This approach involves looking backward in time as abusing parents are studied after they have been identified as having abused their own children. Investigators using the retrospective approach, with or without comparison groups of nonabusive parents, usually find that a large majority of abusing parents were abused as children (Herrenkohl, Herrenkohl, & Toedter, 1983; Oliver & Taylor, 1971; Steele & Pollock, 1974). For example, Steele and Pollock (1974) found that all 60 abusing parents in their study were abused as children. They conclude that a basic factor in the "genesis" of child abuse is the treatment the parents received during their childhood.

One reason Kaufman and Zigler (1987) claim that the case for the intergenerational hypothesis is overstated is that the findings from retrospective research overestimate the rate of transmission of abuse across generations. The problem with the retrospective approach is that it cannot determine what proportion of adults who were maltreated as children are providing adequate care for their own children. The retrospective approach provides information about the percentage of abusers who were abused as children, but it does not provide information about the caregiving behavior of all individuals who were abused. It appears that the majority of abusing parents were themselves abused, but it may also be the case that the majority of parents who were abused as children are providing adequate care. Looking backward, the rate of abuse across generations is high; looking forward, using a prospective approach, the rate is likely to be lower. Unfortunately, there has never been a true prospective study, where a group of abused children were followed into adulthood and the quality of their parenting assessed. Following a group of abused children into adulthood would no doubt uncover a rate of abuse across generations that would be lower than the 100% rate found by Steele and others who have used retrospective data. It is important that investigators be cautious in interpreting the findings of retrospective studies.

As noted above, Kaufman and Zigler (1987) argue that the retrospective approach leads to an overestimate of the rate of transmission. Perhaps this is true, but there may also be reasons the retrospective approach may result in an *underestimate* of the rate of transmission. It is possible that interviewing parents about their own childhoods may result in an underestimate of the actual number who were abused. Zeanah and Zeanah (1989) point out that some parents who were abused as children believe that physical punishment and neglect are normal, or at least acceptable. If asked if they were abused as children, some abused adults would say no because they believe that the harsh treatment they received from their parents is acceptable. An indeterminable number of parents whose treatment as children could be considered abuse do not perceive themselves as having been abused.

A second reason for underreports of maltreatment during childhood is that some parents describe their own parents and childhood experiences in idealized fashion. Main and Goldwyn (1984) and others have found that some abused parents describe their parents in global and positive terms and, when encouraged to give examples of the care they received as children, are unable to describe specific situations. These parents have idealized their childhood experiences. Main and Goldwyn describe the process of idealization as part of a defensive strategy that individuals develop to cope with the trauma of abuse. Idealization is one form of dissociation, which is a mechanism sometimes used by individuals to cope with traumatic experiences. Other dissociative symptoms include an inability to recall traumatic experiences, the extreme forms of which are psychogenic amnesia, fugue states, and multiple personality disorder. Thus idealization and other factors that cause underreporting of a history of having been abused as a child may lead to underestimates of the rate of transmission.

Prospective Investigations of Maltreatment Across Generations

It is difficult to judge the accuracy of Kaufman and Zigler's (1987; Chapter 13, this volume) estimated rate of transmission of abuse of 30%, because it is based on only three quasi-prospective investigations. In reviewing these investigations, one could find reasons to support an argument for a higher rate.

Two of the three prospective studies found an 18% rate of transmission of abuse across generations (Hunter, Kilstrom, Kraybill, & Loda, 1978; Straus, 1979). My colleagues and I found a rate of 40% using a broader definition of *maltreatment* that included parents who were psychologically unavailable (Egeland, Jacobvitz, & Sroufe, 1988). There are a number of reasons the 18% rate found by Straus (1979) and Hunter et al. (1978) is an underestimate. Straus's early study, which is basically a retrospective study, consisted of a large national sample of two-parent families with children between the ages of 3 and 17. His rate of 18% is likely an underestimate because the sample was limited to two-parent families with children over age 3. In fact, much child abuse takes place in single-parent families, and much abuse occurs prior to age 3. In addition, parents were identified as having histories of abuse if they indicated that they were physically punished during adolescence. Adolescence is a period when physical punishment is *least* likely to occur. The majority of parents who were abused as children were probably omitted from the "history of punishment" category.

There were also reasons Hunter et al. (1978) found a low rate (18%) of intergenerational transmission. They studied mothers of premature or ill newborns and found that 10 out of the sample of 255 mothers were reported for substantiated instances of abuse or neglect during their babies' first year of life. Of these 10 mothers, 9 reported family histories of abuse or neglect. Looking backward in this way, support of the intergenerational hypothesis seems strong (90% rate of transmission). Hunter and Kilstrom (1979) further report that of 49 families in which a parent reported having been abused as a child, 9 abused their infants, resulting in an 18% rate of transmission.

The findings from Hunter and Kilstrom's investigation illustrate how the retrospective versus the prospective approach can affect the apparent rate of transmission—90% versus 18%. Moreover, the low figure of 18% was affected by a number of factors; for instance, the families were followed for only one year. Had the sample been followed beyond the infancy period, it is likely that more cases of abuse would have been reported. The peak period of abuse is the toddler and preschool period. The criterion for current abuse status was a confirmed report of abuse registered in the state welfare agency, whereas information on parents' histories of abuse was based on their self-reports in interviews. How many parents who reported having been abused as children were confirmed child protection cases? The criteria for history of abuse were much less stringent than the criterion used to determine current abuse status, which would result in a lower rate.

Based on findings from the Mother-Child Project, a longitudinal study of high-risk parents and their children, I found a rate of maltreatment across generations of 40% (Egeland, 1988), which is slightly higher than the 30% estimated by Kaufman and Zigler (1987). My data are based on a sample of 267 first-time pregnant women who were enrolled in their last trimester of pregnancy and who have been followed over the past 16 years. The mothers were considered at risk for caregiving problems because of their low SES, youthfulness, unmarried status, and lack of support.

Within this high-risk sample, 44 cases of maltreatment were identified, which included physical abuse ($N = 24$), neglect ($N = 24$), hostile/rejecting ($N = 19$), and psychologically unavailable ($N = 19$) patterns of caretaking. Overlap among these four categories of maltreatment was considerable; for example, 15 of the 19 children who experienced hostile/rejecting mothers were also physically abused. In addition, there was an "other" problem group that consisted of mothers who were not the primary caretakers of their children. One mother in this group traveled with a circus and saw very little of her child, and others had basically abandoned their children for other reasons.

Mothers in all maltreatment groups were identified on the basis of information obtained from mother interviews, home visits, and observations of mother and child in home and laboratory situations. These data were obtained at regular intervals, starting at birth and continuing through preschool. The maltreatment groups were formed based on data collected through the preschool period. A total of 18 assessments occurred between the neonatal period and 48 months of age.

Independent of the identification of mothers who were maltreating their children, we determined the quality of care the mothers received when they were children. At the time of the 48- and 54-month assessments, each mother was asked a series of questions about her childhood and family of origin, including whether or not she was reared by a relative or placed in a foster home. She was asked about how she was disciplined and whether or not she was beaten or physically abused, sexually molested, or neglected. On the basis of the responses, 47 mothers were identified as having been maltreated as children. Women who were not abused were further divided into those who were emotionally supported as children (35 women) and the remainder of the sample. Emotionally supportive families were described as loving, concerned, and encouraging.

Of the 47 mothers who were abused as children, 16 (34%) were currently maltreating their children and 3 (6%) were in the other problems group, resulting in a 40% rate of maltreatment across generations. Within this group of 47 mothers who were abused as children, 13 mothers reported having been sexually abused as children by a family member. Of these, 6 (46%) maltreated their children, and 2 were having other problems (15%). Altogether, 61% of the mothers who reported having been sexually abused as children were maltreating their children.

From the total sample of 47 mothers who were abused as children, a sizable proportion (40%) were maltreating their children; however, it is important to note that the majority of the abused parents provided adequate care. A history of abuse is a major risk factor for abusing, but it is not a guarantee that abuse will occur in the next generation. There are many additional risk factors that need to be considered in order to understand the causes and varied "courses" of child maltreatment.

There is also evidence to support the transmission of good-quality caregiving across generations. Of the 35 mothers judged to have emotionally supportive parents, only 1 was currently maltreating her child. All of the mothers in the sample, including those who were emotionally supported as children, were currently poor and had other characteristics and life circumstances that placed them at risk for maltreating their children. Despite their risk status, only one (3%) of the mothers who was loved, nurtured, and emotionally supported as a child was currently maltreating her child. These findings suggest that good-quality care and nurturance reduce the likelihood of abuse in the next generation, even for parents who are at risk for abuse because of adverse environmental and life circumstances. Being raised in a warm and accepting environment serves as a protective factor against maltreatment in the next generation.

Of the mothers who grew up in homes where there was no evidence of maltreatment or emotional support (those in the middle range of caregiving), 9% were currently maltreating their children and 9% were in the other problems group. These findings support the argument that abuse may be the result of factors other than a history of abuse. As we have seen, there are many exceptions to the continuity of caregiving across generations. Many parents who were abused provide adequate care, and some parents who were not abused as children become abusers. These exceptions, especially those who broke the cycle of abuse, are an important group to study. By comparing parents who broke the cycle of abuse with those who were abused and continue to abuse their children, we can better understand the process involved in the transmission of abuse across generations, which may lead to effective prevention and intervention programs.

In summary, my colleagues and I have found the rate of transmission of abuse to be 40%, which I believe to be a conservative estimate. Regardless of whether the rate of transmission is 30%, as estimated by Kaufman and Zigler (1987), or higher, as we and others have found, the association is substantial and should not be ignored by researchers or practitioners in the field. A transmission rate of 40% is at least 13 times greater than the highest national estimate of the rate of child abuse.

Breaking the Cycle of Abuse

Much of our research having to do with the transmission of abuse across generations has focused on the question, Why do some abused individuals break the cycle of abuse? To answer this question, my colleagues and I compared mothers who were abused in childhood and who abused their children (continuity group) to mothers who were abused but provided adequate care for their own children (exception group). I will summarize these findings, which have been reported in detail elsewhere (Egeland, 1988; Egeland et al., 1988).

One set of variables that distinguished mothers who broke the cycle of abuse from those in the continuity group had to do with the availability of emotionally supportive individuals. Mothers who broke the cycle were, as children, more likely to have had foster parents or relatives who provided them with emotional support. Even though a woman was abused as a child, there was someone there for nurturance and support. Another relationship variable distinguishing the two groups was the mother's relationship with a husband/boyfriend. Most of the mothers who broke the cycle were in intact, stable, and satisfying relationships. One mother who gave birth at age 18 and who continues to live with the father of the child described the father as supportive and accepting. She described how she has come to trust him and how, within this trusting relationship, she has changed her expectations regarding close relationships. At times, she reported, she becomes frustrated and upset in disciplining her child, but she is able to seek help and support from her mate.

Another relationship variable that distinguished the continuity and exception groups was involvement in psychotherapy as an adolescent or young adult. A number of mothers who broke the cycle of abuse were in long-term, intensive psychotherapy. One of our mothers who was most severely abused as a child was removed from her mother at age 11 and placed in a succession of foster homes. In the third foster home, she took pills to get high, which was interpreted as a suicide attempt. Because there were limited treatment options in the rural area where she lived, she was sent to a hospital that treated chemically dependent adults. During her two-year stay in the hospital she received a great deal of emotional support from other patients, along with intensive psychotherapy. Through therapy and support, the mother became aware of her child-rearing history and how it might affect the child care she provided her children.

This mother described her abusive experiences in an integrated and coherent fashion. The experiences were reported with much emotion, and she provided specific examples to support her view of her parents. This integration of the abusive experience into her view of herself was typical of mothers who broke the cycle of abuse. Mothers who broke the cycle of abuse seemed to be aware of how their early experiences affected their expectations regarding relationships. They were aware of the effects of their childhood histories of abuse on their current feelings about themselves and significant others, particularly their children. In general, they were more insightful in their understanding of themselves and seemed to have better understanding of their relationships with their children than did mothers who did not break the cycle.

Mothers who did not break the cycle of abuse seemed to dissociate or "split off" the abusive experience rather than integrating it into a view of themselves. Many of these mothers idealized their pasts, unrealistically describing their parents and childhood experiences as all good. Such descriptions were basically fantasy; they were incongruent with actual experiences. One of the mothers went on at length about the great time she had as a child with her father. She described him as a wonderful man, but she could not give any specific examples of childhood activities with her father. We later learned that he had a serious drinking problem and that he abandoned the family when she was 2 years old. Other mothers seemed "detached" from their parents and childhoods. They had difficulty recalling childhood experiences and avoided talking about their parents. It was common for these mothers to make comments such as "I am having trouble remembering" or "My mind just goes blank when I try to remember my childhood." They talked about their histories of abuse in a vague, disconnected fashion, as if the abuse never really happened to them. Typically, they displayed little emotion when describing their abusive experiences.

Even though these findings are very tentative, it appears that some mothers who were abused as children coped with the traumatic experience by "splitting off" or dissociating. They repeated the abusive pattern in their relationships with their children because they did not see the connection between their current behaviors and their pasts. Because they dissociated from their own experiences, they did not associate the pain they felt as children with the pain they inflicted on their own children. The abusive experiences were not memories on which they could reflect; instead, the early experiences were repeatedly acted out (Egeland & Erickson, 1991).

Briere (1987) found that women who have been sexually abused often dissociate or "split off" this traumatic experience. Putnam, Guroff, Silberman, Barban, and Post (1986), in a study of multiple personality disorder, an extreme form of dissociation, found a high incidence of severe physical and sexual abuse in their sample. Despite very little empirical knowledge about dissociation as a coping strategy for dealing with traumatic experience, and even less about the role it may play in explaining the intergenerational transmission of abuse, there are a number of interesting hypotheses that need to be investigated.

There are other mechanisms that may help us understand the processes by which maltreatment is transmitted across generations. We have hypothesized that attachment theory may "explain the cycle of abuse" (Egeland et al., 1988). Bowlby (1980) notes that the early caregiver-infant attachment relationship is a prototype of later relationships. During the course of the first year of life, infants form strong emotional relationships with their primary caregivers. This attachment is necessary for the survival of the infant. As part of this relationship, the infant develops representational models or, to use Bowlby's term, inner working models of self and significant others. At an early age, the child constructs a cognitive model that best fits the reality experienced. As the child grows older, new relationships are assimilated into existing models as long as the new experiences don't deviate too greatly from the existing models. These models are maintained largely outside of awareness, and they provide the child with a set of expectations about self and relationships that in turn influence the child's behavior in relationships. Zeanah and Anders (1987) have noted that inner working models compel an individual to re-create experiences congruent with his or her relationship history. Sroufe (1983) observed children in preschool who were classified as secure or anxiously attached in infancy and found support for this notion that the children re-created relationships with their teachers that were consistent with their earlier relationships with their primary caregivers.

A child who has a history of abuse expects others to be rejecting, hostile, and unavailable. A child who has been neglected (physically, emotionally, or both) expects others to be unresponsive, unavailable, and not willing to meet his or her needs. Maltreated children bring these expectations to relationships, and they respond to others in a fashion consistent with their expectations.

Zeanah and Zeanah (1989) make the argument that early patterns of relating and the development of inner working models have more far-reaching consequences than do specific traumatic events. The child's subjective view of the abusive experience forms the basis of the inner working model. It is the "meaning context" of the maltreating behavior that forms the theme of what is internalized and becomes a "working model." The violence per se is not passed on from one generation to the next; rather, the ongoing theme of the caregiving relationship is transmitted. Based on recent studies using the Adult Attachment Interview, Zeanah and Zeanah (1989) have identified rejection, role reversal, and fear as major themes underlying different types of inner working models of individuals who were maltreated. Based on my own work, I would add emotionally unresponsive parenting as a major theme. My colleagues and I have identified a type of emotionally unresponsive parent that we call "psychologically unavailable"; we have found this form of maltreatment to have devastating effects on the development of young children (Egeland & Sroufe, 1981; Egeland et al., 1983).

Conclusion

One danger in attempting to view the intergenerational hypothesis from a pro or con perspective is the implication that there are only two points of view on this issue. It is not an "either/or" question. There are multiple etiologies of child maltreatment that have different impacts for each parent who maltreats his or her child. A history of maltreatment is one piece in this complex puzzle.

From the above review of the literature in the area of intergenerational transmission of child maltreatment, it seems safe to conclude that a history of having been maltreated is a major risk factor for maltreatment in the next generation. Many abusers were abused; however, many who were abused are providing good-quality care for their children. Rather than debating the validity of the intergenerational hypothesis of child abuse, we should be focusing on understanding the mechanism involved in the transmission of violence and how the cycle is broken. Perhaps we need further research to determine the exact rate of transmission, but clearly the research emphasis should be on determining the factors associated with breaking the cycle of abuse. Such a focus could lead eventually to effective prevention and intervention programs.

References

Bowlby, J. (1980). *Attachment and loss: Vol. 3. Loss, sadness, and depression.* New York: Basic.

Briere, J. (1987, January). *The longterm clinical correlates of childhood sexual victimization.* Paper presented at the annual meeting of the New York Academy of Sciences, New York.

Egeland, B. (1988). Intergenerational continuity of parental maltreatment of children. In K. D. Browne, C. Davies, & P. Stratton (Eds.), *Early prediction and prevention of child abuse* (pp. 87-102). New York: John Wiley.

Egeland, B., & Erickson, M. F. (1991). Rising above the past: Strategies for helping new mothers break the cycle of abuse and neglect. *Zero to Three, 11*(2), 29-35.

Egeland, B., Jacobvitz, D., & Sroufe, L. A. (1988). Breaking the cycle of abuse. *Child Development, 59*(4), 1080-1088.

Egeland, B., & Sroufe, L. A. (1981). Developmental sequelae of maltreatment in infancy. In R. Rizley & D. Cicchetti (Eds.), *New directions for child development: Developmental perspectives in child maltreatment* (pp. 77-92). San Francisco: Jossey-Bass.

Egeland, B., Sroufe, L. A., & Erickson, M. F. (1983). The developmental consequences of different patterns of maltreatment. *Child Abuse and Neglect, 7,* 459-469.

George, C., & Main, M. (1979). Social interactions of young abused children: Approach, avoidance, and aggression. *Child Development, 50*(2), 306-318.

Herrenkohl, E. C., Herrenkohl, R. C., & Toedter, L. J. (1983). Perspectives on the inter-generational transmission of abuse. In D. Finkelhor, R. J. Gelles, G. T. Hotaling, & M. A. Straus (Eds.), *The dark side of families: Current family violence research* (pp. 305-316). Beverly Hills, CA: Sage.

Hunter, R. S., & Kilstrom, N. (1979). Breaking the cycle in abusive families. *American Journal of Psychiatry, 136,* 1320-1322.

Hunter, R. S., Kilstrom, N., Kraybill, E. N., & Loda, F. (1978). Antecedents of child abuse and neglect in premature infants: A prospective study in a newborn intensive care unit. *Pediatrics, 61,* 629-635.

Kaufman, J., & Zigler, E. (1987). Do abused children become abusive parents? *American Journal of Orthopsychiatry, 57,* 186-192.

Kempe, C. H., Silverman, F. N., Steele, B. F., Droegemueller, W., & Silver, H. K. (1962). The battered-child syndrome. *Journal of the American Medical Association, 181,* 17-24.

Main, M., & Goldwyn, R. (1984). Predicting rejection of her infant from mother's representation of her own experience: Implications for the abused-abusing inter-generational cycle. *Child Abuse and Neglect, 8,* 203-207.

McCord, J. (1983). A forty year perspective on effects of child abuse and neglect. *Child Abuse and Neglect, 7,* 265-270.

Oliver, J. E., & Taylor, A. (1971). Five generations of ill-treated children in one family pedigree. *British Journal of Psychiatry, 119,* 473-480.

Putnam, F. W., Guroff, J. J., Silberman, E. K., Barban, L., & Post, R. M. (1986). The clinical phenomenology of multiple personality disorder: Review of 100 recent cases. *Journal of Clinical Psychiatry, 47*(6), 285-293.

Ressler, R. K., & Burgess, A. W. (1985). The men who murdered. *FBI Law Enforcement Bulletin, 54,* 2-6.

Roy, M. (Ed.). (1977). *Battered women: A psychosocial study of domestic violence.* New York: Van Nostrand Reinhold.

Spinetta, J. J., & Rigler, D. (1972). The child abusing parent: A psychological review. *Psychological Bulletin, 77,* 296-304.

Sroufe, L. A. (1983). Infant-caregiver attachment and adaptation in the preschool: The roots of competence and maladaptation. In M. Perlmutter (Ed.), *Development of cognition, affect, and social relations* (pp. 41-81). Hillsdale, NJ: Lawrence Erlbaum.

Steele, B. J., & Pollock, C. B. (1974). A psychiatric study of parents who abuse infants and small children. In R. E. Helfer & C. H. Kempe (Eds.), *The battered child* (2nd ed., pp. 80-133). Chicago: University of Chicago Press.

Straus, M. A. (1979). Family patterns and child abuse in a nationally representative sample. *International Journal of Child Abuse and Neglect, 3,* 213-225.

Straus, M. A., Gelles, R. J., & Steinmetz, S. K. (1980). *Behind closed doors: Violence in the American family.* Garden City, NY: Anchor/Doubleday.

Widom, C. S. (1989). Does violence beget violence? A critical examination of the litera-ture. *Psychological Bulletin, 106,* 3-28.

Zeanah, C. H., & Anders, T. F. (1987). Subjectivity in parent-infant relationships: A discussion in internal working models. *Infant Mental Health Journal, 8,* 237-250.

Zeanah, C. H., & Zeanah, P. D. (1989, May). Intergenerational transmission of maltreat-ment: Insights from attachment theory and research. *Psychiatry, 52,* 177-196.

CHAPTER 13

The Intergenerational Transmission of Abuse Is Overstated

Joan Kaufman
Edward Zigler

The intergenerational hypothesis states that maltreated children are likely to become abusive parents. It is common in the popular press to see assertions that 99% of all abused children become abusive parents (Kaufman, 1987), with this belief held by many legal and mental health professionals as well (Widom, 1989). Although being maltreated as a child puts one at risk for becoming abusive, the path between the two points is far from direct or inevitable (Kaufman & Zigler, 1987, 1988, 1989; Widom, 1989). The aim of this chapter is to demonstrate that the intergenerational hypothesis in its popularized form is overstated and oversimplified. A sample of empirical studies will be reviewed, and an estimate of the true rate of transmission presented. Mediating factors that affect the likelihood of abuse being transmitted across generations will also be outlined, together with a discussion of the manner in which genetic and environmental factors may interact to increase the likelihood of a given abused child becoming an abusive parent (for a comprehensive review of the literature, see Kaufman & Zigler, 1987; Widom, 1989).

Studies Cited in Support of the Intergenerational Hypothesis

There are many papers cited in support of the intergenerational hypothesis that do no more than make assertions of its validity, without providing any substantive evidence (Bleiberg, 1965; Blue, 1965;

Corbett, 1964; Harper, 1963; Kempe, 1973; Wasserman, 1967). Many other papers cited in the literature base their conclusions on information obtained regarding the childhoods of identified abusers, without comparable data on any comparison subjects (Fontana, 1968; Galdston, 1965; Green, Gaines, & Sandgrund, 1974; Kempe, Silverman, Steele, Droegemueller, & Silver, 1962; McHenrey, Girdany, & Elmer, 1963; Oliver & Taylor, 1971; Paulson & Blake, 1969; Silver, Dublin, & Lourie, 1969; Steele & Pollack, 1968). Although these studies were valuable in generating hypotheses about the possible relationship between a history of abuse and abusive parenting, they cannot be considered conclusive, because no comparison subjects were utilized. Individuals with histories of abuse who did not maltreat their children were not studied, making it impossible to determine what proportion of individuals with histories of abuse repeat the cycle and what proportion do not.

The studies conducted to examine the intergenerational hypothesis that have used comparison subjects report transmission estimates that range from 18% to 70% (Altemeier, O'Connor, Vietze, Sandler, & Sherrod, 1982; Conger, Burgess, & Barrett, 1979; Egeland & Jacobvitz, 1984; Egeland, Jacobvitz, & Sroufe, 1988; Gaines, Sandgrund, Green, & Powers, 1978; Herrenkohl, Herrenkohl, & Toedter, 1983; Hunter & Kilstrom, 1979; Quinton, Rutter, & Liddle, 1984; Smith & Hanson, 1975; Spinetta, 1978; Straus, 1979). The controlled study that produced the lowest transmission estimate (Hunter & Kilstrom, 1979) and the one that produced the highest (Egeland & Jacobvitz, 1984) are detailed below. In reviewing these two studies, we place our emphasis on demonstrating how variation in aspects of research design affect the rates of transmission derived. Research elements to be examined include (a) the subjects studied (identified abusers versus high-risk populations), (b) the research designs employed (retrospective versus prospective), (c) the types of data sources utilized to substantiate claims of past and current abuse, (d) the duration of follow-up, and (e) the definitions of *history of abuse* and *current abuse* utilized. At the conclusion of this section, we present an estimate of the true rate of transmission.

Hunter and Kilstrom (1979) conducted one of the controlled studies that produced the lowest transmission rate estimate (18%). This same rate is reported by Straus (1979) as well. Hunter and Kilstrom conducted a prospective, longitudinal study of 282 parents of newborns admitted to a regional intensive care nursery for premature infants; this population was selected because premature infants have been found to be at increased risk for child abuse (Elmer & Gregg, 1967).

Information about the parents' childhoods, mothers' pregnancies, children's health, and families' social networks was obtained through a semistructured interview. A history of abuse in the parents' past was defined to include incidents of neglect as well as physical abuse. Current abuse in offspring was determined by searching the state registry for confirmed reports of abuse or neglect when the children were 1 year old. At the time of the initial assessment, 49 parents reported childhood histories of abuse or neglect. At follow-up, 10 babies in the study were identified as maltreated. Of these infants, 9 had parents with histories of abuse or neglect; however, 40 parents with comparable childhood histories were not detected for maltreatment. As only 9 of the 49 parents who initially reported childhood abuse were identified as maltreaters, the rate of intergenerational transmission reported in this investigation was 18%.

This study pointedly illustrates how variation in subjects (identified abusers versus a high-risk sample) and research design (retrospective versus prospective) affect the outcome of research findings. If this study had been conducted retrospectively, with only the parents who were identified as maltreaters, the link between a history of abuse and subsequent child maltreatment would have appeared deceptively strong, as 9 out of 10 of the abusive parents reported histories of abuse (90%). By employing a prospective research design, Hunter and Kilstrom demonstrated that the majority of parents who had been abused did not maltreat their children (82%).

The transmission rate provided by Hunter and Kilstrom is likely an underestimate of the true rate of transmission, however, because the follow-up extended for only one year, and agency reports were the only source of data used to determine current abuse status. Parents who developed parenting difficulties as their children got older, and parents who maltreated their children but were never reported for child abuse or neglect, would not have been identified as maltreaters in this study. Despite these caveats, this study clearly demonstrates the superiority of prospective longitudinal research designs and highlights the need to interpret cross-sectional retrospective studies that did not use comparison subjects with considerable caution.

Hunter and Kilstrom identified a number of protective factors that differentiated parents who repeated the cycle of abuse from those that did not. The nonrepeaters were found to have more extensive social supports, physically healthier babies, and fewer ambivalent feelings about their children's births than did the repeaters. In addition, parents who broke the cycle were more openly angry about their earlier abuse and better able to give detailed accounts of those experiences.

Nonrepeaters were also less likely to have been abused by both of their parents, and more apt to have reported a supportive relationship with one of their parents when growing up.

Egeland and Jacobvitz (1984) conducted the controlled study that produced the highest transmission rate (70%). They conducted a prospective longitudinal study of a sample of 160 high-risk, first-time pregnant, low-income, predominantly single mothers. The women were followed from their third trimester of pregnancy for approximately five years by the time of the report. Information to determine whether the women had histories of abuse in childhood was obtained through semistructured interviews conducted with the women when their children were approximately 4 to 5 years of age. Assessments of current child-rearing practices were made on multiple occasions—when the children were 7 and 10 days old, every three months for the first year of life, biannually the following year, and annually thereafter. Information from the case records of the county hospital, maternal and infant care clinics, and welfare and child protection agencies were also used to assign maltreatment status. Measures of stress, social isolation, and child characteristics were also obtained.

In this study, a history of abuse was restricted to incidents of severe physical punishment, including being thrown against a wall, hit repeatedly with an object, or intentionally burned. Current abusers were subdivided into three categories: a "physical abuse" group, made up of those who used severe physical punishment tactics; a "borderline abuse" group, comprising those who administered daily or weekly spankings that did not cause bruises or caused red marks that disappeared; and an "other" group, which included women whose children were being cared for by someone else (reasons for out-of-home care were not specified). The authors reported an intergenerational transmission rate of 70% for mothers with a history of severe physical abuse. This percentage, however, included mothers who physically abused their children (34%), mothers who fell into the borderline abuse category (30%), and mothers whose children were being reared away from the home (6%).

The findings of this study are confounded by the high-risk nature of Egeland and Jacobvitz's sample. The influence of a history of abuse upon subsequent parenting cannot be separated from the effects of poverty, stress, and social isolation. The results of this study actually reflect the interaction of multiple determinants of abuse (e.g., history of abuse, poverty, stress, isolation), and not the influence of a single determinant (e.g., history of abuse). It is important to keep in mind the simultaneous effects of these different variables when interpreting the findings of this study. Unless the independent effects of these variables are tested empirically, it is impossible to determine their separate influences on subsequent parenting.

The broad definition of *current abuse* used also affected the results. In general, the broader the definitional criteria employed, the greater the apparent link between a history of abuse and current abuse. As noted, Egeland and Jacobvitz included the borderline abuse category in their computation of the rate of intergenerational transmission. They found that 30% of the mothers who reported histories of abuse fell into this category, but an even larger percentage of mothers who reported emotionally supportive childhoods were categorized as borderline abusers (39%). Given the failure of the borderline abuse category to differentiate these two groups, the validity of this category, and the conclusion that aberrant childhood histories "caused" the borderline parenting, is questionable. In fact, a national survey of disciplinary practices reported that 97% of all children in the United States have been physically punished (Straus, 1983). In order that research results not be misinterpreted and misapplied, it is preferable to restrict the definitions of *current abuse* and *past abuse* used in research to the more severe manifestations of abuse, as most lay people and professionals usually think of serious forms of maltreatment that would require state intervention when thinking about the intergenerational hypothesis. (The originally reported transmission rate of 70% is revised to 40% by Dr. Byron Egeland in Chapter 12 of this volume. The mothers who fell into the borderline abuse category are no longer being included in the computation of the rate of intergenerational transmission of abuse.)

Despite these concerns, the study by Egeland and Jacobvitz was extremely well designed. It was conducted prospectively with a cohort of high-risk subjects; well-matched comparison subjects were utilized; subjects were followed from their third trimester of pregnancy until their children were approximately 5 years old; and multiple direct assessments were obtained and used together with agency record information to document current abuse. The rate of abuse reported in the mothers with a history of severe physical abuse provides a reasonable estimate of the rate of transmission in very high-risk, multiply stressed families (34%).

Egeland and Jacobvitz (1984; Egeland et al., 1988) also report a number of protective factors that differentiated the repeaters from the nonrepeaters in their study. They found that nonrepeaters were more likely to have one parent or foster parent who provided support and love during childhood, to be currently involved in a relationship with an emotionally supportive boyfriend or spouse, and to report fewer current stressful life events. They also were more likely to have participated in therapy at some point in their lives, to have greater awareness of their history of abuse, and to be consciously resolved not to repeat the pattern of abuse with their own children. These factors are highly similar to the factors reported by Hunter and Kilstrom (1979).

Deriving an Estimate of the
True Rate of Transmission

The studies reviewed above suggest that the best estimate for the rate of the intergenerational transmission of abuse is approximately 30% (Kaufman & Zigler, 1987, 1988, 1989). For the reasons previously discussed, we believe the estimate obtained by Hunter and Kilstrom (1979) is somewhat low. The finding by Egeland and Jacobvitz (1984) that only 34% of the severely abused mothers in their study physically abused their children provides the basis of the above estimate. Egeland and Jacobvitz used a sample at risk for abuse because of multiple factors. It is reasonable to assume that a somewhat smaller percentage of individuals with histories of abuse would be found to maltreat their children seriously if more representative, lower-risk populations were studied.

Mediating Factors
in the Transmission of Abuse

In response to a recent review of the literature on the intergenerational transmission of violent behavior (Widom, 1989), DiLalla and Gottesman (1991) note that most studies of family violence fail to consider the impact of biological and genetic factors. In this section, we briefly review the evidence supporting a biological and genetic component to aggressive behavior, discuss the relevance of this evidence to our understanding of the transmission of abuse, and highlight the importance of interaction models that consider the effects of both genetic and environmental factors.

In their review, DiLalla and Gottesman (1991) cite a number of works that address the salience of biological and genetic factors in the etiology of violent behavior, including adoption studies suggesting a genetic component for the expression of antisocial behavior (e.g., Cloninger, Sigvardsson, Bohman, & von Knorring, 1982; Crowe, 1974; Hutchings & Mednick, 1975), twin studies of antisocial probands corroborating the findings of the adoption studies (e.g., Cloninger & Gottesman, 1987), and physiological studies of aggressive behavior (e.g., Hare & Schalling 1978; Linnoila et al., 1983; Olweus, 1987).

Although there does appear to be evidence supporting the importance of genetic and biological factors in the etiology of antisocial and aggressive behavior, *antisocial behavior, aggression,* and *abusive parenting* are not synonymous terms. Abusive parenting is but one of several alternative symptoms required to meet the diagnosis of antisocial personality (ASP) disorder according to the *Diagnostic and Statistical Manual of Mental Disorders* (DSM-III-R; American Psychiatric Association, 1987). As not all individuals who meet the criteria for ASP abuse their children, and not all abusive parents meet criteria for ASP, it is unclear how relevant the adoption and twin studies suggesting the salience of genetic factors in the transmission of ASP are in explaining the transmission of child maltreatment. As increased rates of ASP have been reported in a sample of maltreating parents who were compared with a demographically matched control cohort (D. Cicchetti, personal communication, July 1991), the findings of the adoption and twin studies likely merit further consideration when researchers undertake future studies of factors associated with the transmission of abuse.

In their review, DiLalla and Gottesman (1991) highlight only the main effects of genetic and biological factors on the expression of violent behavior. Although genetic factors may put an individual at risk for the expression of antisocial and violent behavior, it is the interaction of genetic and environmental factors that results in the greatest risk. A number of studies have demonstrated the importance of interaction effects in the development of ASP (Cadoret & Cain, 1981; Cadoret, Cain, & Crowe, 1982; Cloninger et al., 1982), with some studies suggesting that the effects of genetic and environmental risks are multiplicative, not additive (e.g., Cloninger et al., 1982). One study highlighting this finding is described below.

Cloninger et al. (1982) studied a cohort of 862 Swedish men adopted at an early age by nonrelatives. The adoptees ranged from 23 to 43 years of age at the time of the study. In accordance with Swedish practice at that time, neither the adoptee nor the adoptive parents were informed about the identity or behavior of the genetic parents. Data about criminality, alcohol abuse, occupational status, and medical and social history were obtained for the adoptees and each genetic and adoptive parent from registers of child welfare offices, Temperance Boards, the State Criminal Board, and the national health care system, including local insurance agencies, hospitals, and clinics. Environmental risk was determined by considering the number of temporary placements experienced prior to adoption, the length of time with the genetic mother prior to placement, and indices of adversity in the adoptive family (e.g., divorce, psychopathology, low SES). *Genetic risk* was defined as evidence of antisocial behavior or alcoholism in the genetic parents.

Adoptees at low environmental and genetic risk had a base rate of criminality of 2.9%. Adoptees with high environmental and low genetic risk had a 6.7% rate; adoptees at low environmental and high genetic risk had a 12.1% rate; and those with both a high environmental and genetic risk had a 40% rate of criminality. Environmental factors alone were associated with a 2-fold increased risk, genetic factors alone with a 4-fold increased risk, and the combination of environmental and genetic factors with a 14-fold increased risk for criminality.

These findings are consistent with the model for the joint effects of genotype and environment proposed by Kendler and Eaves (1986) and others (e.g., Gottesman & Shields, 1973; Mather & Jinks, 1982). The model suggests that, for some conditions, genes' primary effects are on the extent to which an individual is sensitive to the risk-increasing or risk-reducing aspects of the environment. This type of a conceptualization is valuable in explaining why some individuals subjected to a given set of environmental circumstances are apt to experience negative sequelae (e.g., become violent, repeat the cycle of abuse) and others are not.

With regard to the different physiological abnormalities associated with aggressive behavior cited by DiLalla and Gottesman (1991), the association between impulsive behavior and low 5 hydroxyindole-acetic acid (5-HIAA) is one of the findings that has been most consistently reported in the literature (Brown, Goodwin, Ballenger, Goyer, & Major, 1979; Linnoila et al., 1983; Mann & Stanley, 1986). 5-HIAA is one of the metabolites of the neurotransmitter serotonin, and it is usually assayed in cerebrospinal fluid. Further evidence in support of the serotonin hypothesis of aggressive behavior has been obtained in studies showing aggressive individuals to have a diminished response to pharmacological probes that affect the serotonin system (Coccaro et al., 1989; Mann & Stanley, 1986).

The relevance of the physiological abnormalities associated with aggressive behavior cited by DiLalla and Gottesman in explaining abusive parenting cannot be evaluated, as no studies of maltreating parents have examined indices of serotonergic functioning, or other physiological abnormalities associated with aggressive behavior. If the above genotype-environment model is relevant for the expression of the physiological abnormalities associated with aggressivity, it is possible that individuals with a genetic predisposition toward aggressive behavior may be more likely to manifest serotonin deficiencies, or other physiological abnormalities, in response to pernicious environments than are others without the genetic predisposition. Likewise, individuals with the genetic predisposition who have a number of protective factors in their environment would not be expected to exhibit excessive aggressive behavior or the associated physiological abnormalities. Further consideration of the importance of genetic and biological factors that may mediate the transmission of abuse appears warranted, but only together with the examination of psychosocial factors.

The studies reviewed in the first section of this chapter highlight a number of protective factors that differentiate those individuals who repeat the cycle of abuse from those who do not. The nonrepeaters in the samples discussed were more likely to have healthier babies, to report histories that included a positive relationship with one parent or foster parent while growing up, to have participated in therapeutic interventions, to have awareness of their past abuse and to have resolved not to repeat the pattern, to be involved in relationships with emotionally supportive spouses or boyfriends, and to have more extensive social supports and/or fewer current stressful life events.

In order to learn about the manner in which genetic and environmental factors may interact to promote the intergenerational transmission of abuse, it is necessary to conduct multidisciplinary studies in which both biological and psychosocial factors are assessed. These studies should examine other outcomes too, as it is well documented that children with histories of abuse are at risk for a number of negative sequelae other than excessive aggressivity and poor parenting. Additional outcome measures that should be addressed include educational and occupational achievements (Martin & Elmer, 1992), the quality of current relationships (Sroufe & Fleeson, 1986), and the presence of depressive disorders (Kaufman, 1991) and other psychiatric problems (D. Cicchetti, personal communication, July 1991).

No matter how well designed any study is that attempts to examine the transmission of abuse, the accuracy of predictions concerning the likelihood of a given individual repeating the cycle of abuse will always be limited by a number of factors. Child abuse is a low-base-rate phenomenon, and it is difficult to make predictions of the occurrence of low-base-rate phenomena (Meehl & Rosen, 1973). The large number of risk and protective factors that influence the probability of abuse being transmitted across generations further decreases the likelihood of accurate prediction regarding individual cases. In addition, the effects of unexpected chance events that can alter the course of an individual's life further compromise the ability to predict whether a given abused child will or will not become an abusive parent (see Kaufman & Zigler, 1989, for further discussion).

Closing Remarks

In the past, uncritical acceptance of the intergenerational hypothesis has caused undue anxiety in many victims of abuse, led to biased responses by mental health workers, and influenced the outcome of court decisions. For example, we have heard the story of one women in her 70s who was badly abused as a child, who was advised by a mental health professional when she was in her 20s never to have children, because it would be inevitable that she would repeat the cycle of abuse. Wanting the abuse to go no further, the woman followed the professional's advice and never bore children. We were also informed of a woman who nearly lost custody of her children in a routine child custody case when it came up in her divorce trial that she had been badly abused as a child. Even though her own parenting practices were reportedly exemplar, the judge feared that at some point she would resort to abusing her children because she had been abused. Fortunately, the judge chose to seek consultation prior to denying the mother any custody rights. The judge was advised to evaluate the mother's capacity to parent based on her current child-rearing practices, and not on her childhood experiences. This advice resulted in the mother being awarded primary custody of her children.

It is time for the intergenerational hypothesis in its popularized form to be abandoned. The association between abuse in childhood and poor parenting in adulthood has been overstated. Most parents with histories of abuse do not maltreat their children. Although a transmission rate of approximately 30% is hardly inconsequential, it is a far cry from the 99% figure promulgated in the popular press. We concur with the conclusions of Dr. Egeland in Chapter 12 of this volume: It is time for practitioners and researchers to stop looking for evidence to support the intergenerational hypothesis and to focus instead on understanding the mechanisms involved in the transmission of abuse and the factors that decrease the likelihood of its occurrence. Undoubtedly, a history of abuse is a considerable risk factor associated with the etiology of child maltreatment, but the pathway to abusive parenting is far from inevitable and involves many complex interactions between genetic and environmental factors.

References

Altemeier, W., O'Connor, S., Vietze, P., Sandler, H., & Sherrod, K. (1982). Antecedents of child abuse. *Journal of Pediatrics, 100,* 823-829.

American Psychiatric Association. (1987). *Diagnostic and statistical manual of mental disorders* (3rd ed., rev.). Washington, DC: Author.

Bleiberg, N. (1965). The neglected child and the child health conference. *New York State Journal of Medicine, 65,* 1880-1885.

Blue, M. (1965). The battered child syndrome from a social work viewpoint. *Canadian Journal of Public Health, 56,* 197-198.

Brown, G., Goodwin, F., Ballenger, J., Goyer, P., & Major, L. (1979). Aggression in humans correlates with cerebrospinal fluid amine metabolites. *Psychiatry Research, 1,* 131-139.

Cadoret, R., & Cain, C. (1981). Environmental and genetic factors in predicting adolescent antisocial behavior in adoptees. *Psychiatric Journal of the University of Ottawa, 6,* 220-225.

Cadoret, R., Cain, C., & Crowe, R. (1982). Evidence for gene-environment interaction in the development of adolescent antisocial behavior. *Behavior Genetics, 13,* 301-310.

Cloninger, R., & Gottesman, I. (1987). Genetic and environmental factors in antisocial behavior disorders. In S. A. Mednick, T. E. Moffitt, & S. A. Stack (Eds.), *The causes of crime: New biological approaches* (pp. 92-109). Cambridge: Cambridge University Press.

Cloninger, R., Sigvardsson, S., Bohman, M., & von Knorring, A. (1982). Predisposition to petty criminality in Swedish adoptees: Cross-fostering analysis of gene-environment interaction. *Archives of General Psychiatry, 39,* 1242-1247.

Coccaro, E., Siever, L., Klar, H., Maurer, G., Cochrane, K., Cooper, T., Mohs, R., & Davis, K. (1989). Serotonergic studies in patients with affective and personality disorders. *Archives of General Psychiatry, 46,* 587-599.

Conger, R., Burgess, R., & Barrett, C. (1979). Child abuse related to life change and perceptions of illness: Some preliminary findings. *Family Coordinator, 58,* 73-77.

Corbett, J. (1964). A psychiatrist reviews the battered child syndrome and mandatory reporting legislation. *N.W. Medicine, 63,* 920-922.

Crowe, R. (1974). An adoption study of antisocial personality. *Archives of General Psychiatry, 39,* 1242-1249.

DiLalla, L. F., & Gottesman, I. (1991). Biological and genetic contributors to violence: Widom's untold tale. *Psychological Bulletin, 109,* 125-129.

Egeland, B., & Jacobvitz, D. (1984). *Intergenerational continuity of parental abuse: Causes and consequences.* Paper presented at the Conference on Biosocial Perspectives in Abuse and Neglect, York, ME.

Egeland, B., Jacobvitz, D., & Sroufe, L. A. (1988). Breaking the cycle of abuse. *Child Development, 59,* 1080-1088.

Elmer, E., & Gregg, G. (1967). Developmental characteristics of abused children. *Pediatrics, 40,* 596-602.

Fontana, V. (1968). Further reflections on maltreatment of children. *New York State Journal of Medicine, 68,* 2214-2215.

Gaines, R., Sandgrund, A., Green, A., & Powers, E. (1978). Etiological factors in child maltreatment: A multivariate study of abusing, neglecting, and normal mothers. *Journal of Abnormal Psychology, 87,* 531-540.

Galdston, J. (1965). Observations on children who have been physically abused and their parents. *American Journal of Psychiatry, 122,* 440-443.

Gottesman, I., & Shields, J. (1973). Genetic theorizing and schizophrenia. *British Journal of Psychiatry, 122,* 15-30.

Green, A., Gaines, R., & Sandgrund, A. (1974). Child abuse: Pathological syndrome of family interaction. *American Journal of Psychiatry, 131,* 882-886.

Hare, R., & Schalling, D. (Eds.). (1978). *Psychopathic behavior: Approaches to research.* New York: John Wiley.

Harper, F. (1963). The physician, the battered child, and the law. *Pediatrics, 31,* 899-902.

Herrenkohl, E. C., Herrenkohl, R. C., & Toedter, L. J. (1983). Perspectives on the intergenerational transmission of abuse. In D. Finkelhor, R. J. Gelles, G. T. Hotaling, & M. A. Straus (Eds.), *The dark side of families: Current family violence research* (pp. 305-316). Beverly Hills, CA: Sage.

Hunter, R. S., & Kilstrom, N. (1979). Breaking the cycle in abusive families. *American Journal of Psychiatry, 136,* 1320-1322.

Hutchings, B., & Mednick, S. (1975). Registered criminality in the adoptive and biological parents of registered male criminal adoptees. In R. R. Fieve, D. Rosenthal, & H. Brill (Eds.), *Genetic research in psychiatry* (pp. 105-116). Baltimore: Johns Hopkins University Press.

Kaufman, J. (1987, June 23). From abused child to good parent [Letter to the editor]. *New York Times,* p. A30.

Kaufman, J. (1991). Depressive disorders in maltreated children. *Journal of the American Academy of Child and Adolescent Psychiatry, 30,* 257-265.

Kaufman, J., & Zigler, E. (1987). Do abused children become abusive parents? *American Journal of Orthopsychiatry, 57,* 186-192.

Kaufman, J., & Zigler, E. (1988). Do abused children become abusive parents? In S. Chess & A. Thomas (Eds.), *Annual progress in child psychiatry and child development.* New York: Brunner/Mazel.

Kaufman, J., & Zigler, E. (1989). The intergenerational transmission of child abuse. In D. Cicchetti & V. Carlson (Eds.), *Child maltreatment: Theory and research on the causes and consequences of child abuse and neglect* (pp. 129-150). Cambridge: Cambridge University Press.

Kempe, C. (1973). A practical approach to the protection of the abused child and rehabilitation of the abusing parent. *Pediatrics, 51,* 804-812.

Kempe, C. H., Silverman, F. N., Steele, B. F., Droegemueller, W., & Silver, H. K. (1962). The battered-child syndrome. *Journal of the American Medical Association, 181,* 17-24.

Kendler, K., & Eaves, L. (1986). Models for the joint effect of genotype and environment on liability to psychiatric illness. *American Journal of Psychiatry, 143,* 279-289.

Linnoila, M., Virkunnen, M., Scheinin, M., Nuutila, A., Rimon, R., & Goodwin, F. K. (1983). Low cerebrospinal fluid 5-hydroxyindoleacetic acid concentration differentiates impulsive from nonimpulsive violent behavior. *Life Sciences, 33,* 2609-2614.

Mann, J. J., & Stanley, M. (Eds.). (1986). Psychobiology of suicidal behavior [Special issue]. *Annals of the New York Academy of Sciences, 487.*

Martin, J., & Elmer, E. (1992). Battered children grown up: A follow-up study of individuals severely maltreated as children. *Child Abuse and Neglect, 16,* 75-87.

Mather, K., & Jinks, J. (1982). *Biometrical genetics: The study of continuous variation.* London: Chapman & Hall.

McHenrey, T., Girdany, B., & Elmer, E. (1963). Unsuspected trauma with multiple skeletal injuries during infancy and childhood. *Pediatrics, 31,* 903-908.

Meehl, P., & Rosen, A. (1973). Antecedent probability and the efficiency of psychometric signs, patterns, or cutting scores. In P. Meehl (Ed.), *Psychodiagnosis: Selected papers* (pp. 32-62). New York: W. W. Norton.

Oliver, J., & Taylor, A. (1971). Five generations of ill-treated children in one family pedigree. *British Journal of Psychiatry, 119, 473-480.*

Olweus, D. (1987). Testosterone and adrenaline: Aggressive antisocial behavior in normal adolescent males. In S. A. Mednick, T. E. Moffitt, & S. A. Stack (Eds.), *The causes of crime: New biological approaches* (pp. 263-282). Cambridge: Cambridge University Press.

Paulson, M., & Blake, P. (1969). The physically abused child: A focus on prevention. *Child Welfare, 48,* 86-95.

Quinton, D., Rutter, M., & Liddle, C. (1984). Institutional rearing, parental difficulties and marital support. *Psychological Medicine, 14,* 107-124.

Silver, L., Dublin, C., & Lourie, R. (1969). Does violence breed violence? Contributions from a study of the child abuse syndrome. *American Journal of Psychiatry, 126,* 404-407.

Smith, S., & Hanson, R. (1975). Interpersonal relationships and childrearing practices in 214 parents of battered children. *British Journal of Psychiatry, 127,* 513-525.

Spinetta, J. (1978). Parental personality factors in child abuse. *Journal of Consulting and Clinical Psychology, 46,* 1409-1414.

Sroufe, L. A., & Fleeson, J. (1986). Attachment and the construction of relationships. In W. Hartup & Z. Rubin (Eds.), *Relationships and development* (pp. 51-72). New York: Cambridge University Press.

Steele, R., & Pollack, C. (1968). A psychiatric study of parents who abuse infants and small children. In R. E. Helfer & C. H. Kempe (Eds.), *The battered child* (pp. 89-133). Chicago: University of Chicago Press.

Straus, M. A. (1979). Family patterns and child abuse in a nationally representative sample. *International Journal of Child Abuse and Neglect, 3,* 213-225.

Straus, M. A. (1983). Ordinary violence, child abuse, and wife-beating: What do they have in common? In D. Finkelhor, R. J. Gelles, G. T. Hotaling, & M. A. Straus (Eds.), *The dark side of families: Current family violence research* (pp. 213-234). Beverly Hills, CA: Sage.

Wasserman, S. (1967). The abused parent of the abused child. *Children, 14,* 175-179.

Widom, C. S. (1989). Does violence beget violence? A critical examination of the literature. *Psychological Bulletin, 106,* 3-28.

CHAPTER 14

The Abused Elderly Are Dependent
Abuse Is Caused by the Perception of Stress Associated With Providing Care

Suzanne K. Steinmetz

Considerable research in the gerontology literature has documented the impact of stress associated with providing care to an elder. "Caught in the middle," "the sandwich generation" (E. Brody, 1966, 1970), and "generationally inverse families" (Steinmetz, 1988; Steinmetz & Amsden, 1983) are phrases used to describe middle-aged caregivers who are simultaneously providing some level of care for aging parents as well as caring for their own children. As the caregiving responsibility for an elderly family member increasingly takes over the life of the caregiver, it is not unrealistic to expect some negative consequences. The title selected for a book describing the difficulties faced by families caring for individuals with Alzheimer's disease, *The 36-Hour Day* (Mace, 1981), illustrates the feelings experienced by caregivers. A 55-year-old daughter who was providing care to both her 74-year-old mother and 89-year-old aunt described her feelings in a similar fashion:

> DON'T DO IT, DON'T EVER, EVER DO IT! Do whatever you can. You can give them so much more of yourself when you go to visit them if they are not living with you. It is so easy to be loving and to carry them to the doctor's office when they don't live with you. . . . I could give her more moral support and a lot more loving attention if I didn't have to physi-

AUTHOR'S NOTE: Support for this project was provided by Public Health Service grant D31AH65033.

cally care for her. . . . I could go get her and say "Oh your hair is so pretty and let's go here and let's go there." I don't feel like taking her to Longwood Gardens on Sunday when I've had her 6 days a week besides. . . . I would have a much better relationship, [if we were] separate. The way it is now, all I want to do is to get away from her. (quoted in Steinmetz, 1988, p. 137)

My challenge in this essay is to provide evidence that the stress, frustration, and feelings of burden experienced by caregivers who are caring for dependent elders can result in abusive and neglectful treatment. Karl Pillemer (Chapter 15, this volume) argues that it is the dependent family member who is abusing the caregiving elder.[1] Based on a growing number of studies, it is clear that both situations occur. Because the availability of resources to address this problem is limited, an attempt to evaluate the relative need of each group is needed. If the goal of an exercise such as this debate is to provide guidance for policymakers and social planners, then it is of critical importance to analyze the elder's risk of abuse by spouse, by adult caregiving child, and by dependent adult child.

Defining Elder Abuse

The label placed on a phenomenon greatly influences our perception of, and the attributes associated with, the phenomenon. The term *elder abuse* is ambiguous because the legal and social service definitions do not necessarily correspond to definitions used by researchers. Thus it is not surprising that noncomparable and often contradictory findings result. Although the generally accepted definition of *family violence,* "the intentional use of physical force on another person" (Steinmetz & Straus, 1974, p. 4), is suitable for designing academic studies of family violence, this definition is incongruent with legal definitions used by law enforcement, adult protective services (APS), and social service agencies. Such a definition would include not only acts of physical abuse, but also verbal abuse, emotional or psychological abuse (e.g., threats, insults), medical abuse (e.g., overmedicating, refusal to give medicine or to follow medical orders), resource or material abuse, and neglect. These categories of abuse and neglect are consistent with APS legislation as well as the basis for many studies (Block & Sinnott, 1979; Fulmer & O'Malley, 1987; Phillips, 1983; Steinmetz, 1988).

It is also important to consider the findings based on caregivers' self-reported fear of becoming violent (Pillemer & Suitor, 1992) or self-reported threats to commit violent acts (Steinmetz, 1988), as they provide indicators of situations that, without intervention, might easily develop into physical abuse. In fact, Pillemer and Suitor (1992) note that in their study of caregivers, "those who were only fearful of becoming violent differed little from those respondents who actually became violent" (p. S170).

Defining the Actors

In other forms of domestic violence, the dyad or participating members define the behavior. For example, child abuse is defined as neglect or physical, emotional, or sexual abuse or exploitation of a child by a parent or caretaker. Spouse, partner, or courtship violence is defined in terms of the participants and their relationship to one another. Elder abuse, on the other hand, is defined primarily by the age of the victim, an age that varies from state to state based on eligibility for services, rather than the relationship of victim to perpetrator. (For a discussion of differences in states' definitions of elder abuse and resultant rates of elder abuse and maltreatment, see American Public Welfare Association and National Association for State Units on Aging, 1986.) Spousal or partner violence has been documented to be the most prevalent form of family violence in national or regional random samples, regardless of the age of the spouses (Gelles & Straus, 1988; Pillemer & Finkelhor, 1989; Straus, Gelles, & Steinmetz, 1980).

This raises the issue of whether we are measuring elder abuse or simply relabeling behaviors when they occur among those over 60 or 65 years of age. In other words, is *elder abuse* a distinct category of family violence or is it simply an adjective denoting the age of the victim and modifying a variety of categories of family violence?

Unfortunately, when elder abuse is based on the age of the participants, one critical aspect, the dimension of dependency, is not considered. To determine if the 35-year-old child is dependent on the elderly parent, or providing care to the 65-year-old parent, requires an examination of the sociodemographic characteristics of the individuals and the roles they have assumed.

Defining the Act

Adult protective service agencies serve the needs of all adults over 18 years of age, not just individuals over 65 years of age. The focus is on identifying and protecting the adult experiencing abuse; the perpetrator or form of abuse is secondary. Furthermore, the relationship is not clearly defined and includes family, other informal caregivers, nursing home attendants, neighbors, and those committing consumer fraud who target the elderly.

One of the most comprehensive surveys of agency-based data was conducted by the American Public Welfare Association and National Association of State Units on Aging (1986). Data were compiled on reported, suspected, or alleged elder abuse for 1983 and 1984 from the state agencies mandated to collect these data. Although data were collected from all but 6 states, only 29 states had categorized their data by age, thus allowing for an examination of abuse or neglect occurring among individuals 65 years or older. Of these, 13 states included self-abuse/neglect as well as abuse and neglect perpetrated by informal caregivers and 7 states included institutional abuse as well as that perpetrated by informal caregivers and self-abuse/neglect, which made nationwide comparisons problematic.

Data based on APS statistics present a picture of dependent, frail elders, predominantly women, in their late 70s or early 80s, who are experiencing maltreatment at the hands of informal caregivers— primarily immediate family members. The argument could be made, of course, that APS statistics represent the most severe cases, those who have come to the attention of the authorities, therefore they underestimate the actual amount of elder abuse.

Although the research of Pillemer and his colleagues represents a major contribution to our understanding of physical violence against an individual over 65 years of age, the findings based on responses to the Conflict Tactic Scales (CTS; see Straus et al., 1980) bear little resemblance to the cases received by adult protective services. For example, Pillemer and Finkelhor (1989) note that individuals were categorized as experiencing physical abuse if they experienced any of the physical violence categories of the CTS. Yet, in another article discussing the use of the CTS for obtaining measures of verbal and physical abuse, Pillemer and Prescott (1989) state, "No claim is made here that the concept of elder abuse and neglect should be defined for the purpose of social policy in the same way as for this study" (p. 69). The classification of neglect was also problematic. On one hand, individuals could be classified as experiencing neglect if the elder "reported that a caregiver had failed to provide needed care 10 or more times in the preceding year," a very rigorous test for neglect and one that assumes that the elder must have a calendarlike mind with an unbelievable ability to recall events. However, elders could also be classified as experiencing neglect if they "termed the lack of care as 'somewhat' or 'very serious' " (Pillemer & Finkelhor, 1989, p. 182). It is not possible to determine which method of classification was used most frequently.

The Sample

As in all research, the sample selected and the questions posed define the results. For more than a dozen years we have debated the differences in findings from studies based on interviews with battered women and those from large representative samples of males and females. If one wants to study the characteristics of battered women, the circumstances leading up to the battering incident, or the processes involved in the decision to leave a relationship characterized by violence, in-depth interviews with women who have come to shelters for battered women is an appropriate way to do so. However, these findings will not be comparable to large, representative samples of males and females designed to produce incidence or prevalence rates of spousal violence. Similarly, data compiled from caseloads of APS agencies portray self-neglect and self-abuse as constituting the majority of elder abuse cases handled (American Public Welfare Association and National Association for State Units on Aging, 1986); yet this is not the picture portrayed in either Pillemer and Finkelhor's (1989) study or my own work (Steinmetz, 1988).

Three distinct characteristics distinguish the adult children and elders in Pillemer and Finkelhor's (1989) study and those in other studies of informal caregivers of elders (Brown, 1989; Fulmer & O'Malley, 1987; Pillemer & Suitor, 1992; Steinmetz, 1983, 1988; Steinmetz & Amsden, 1983). First, the dependent elders were considerably older in my sample (mean age = 82.0) (Steinmetz, 1988) than were the dependent elders in Pillemer and Finkelhor's random sample (mean age = 73.8). There is evidence that both dependency and conflict between younger caretakers and "elderly" parents increase with age. Therefore, one would expect that Pillemer and Finkelhor's sample, composed of younger and more independent elders, would not show the same patterns of dependency and abuse that are found in a study composed of caretakers 60 years of age or older who had the full-time responsibility of caring for an even older dependent parent.

In addition to their sample of adult children being fairly young, they also appear to have been experiencing problems such as physical or mental illness or alcoholism that rendered them unable to function as independent adults. One of Pillemer's (1985) cases illustrates this point: "The daughter of one victim moved in with her, and has never contributed in any way to her mother's support. 'I support her. She has epilepsy and is on disability. She's supposed to give me $50.00 a month but she never does' " (p. 153).

Second, 73% of the adult children in Pillemer and Finkelhor's study had never married, and nearly two-thirds of the children had never left home. Clearly, some of the conflict found could result from parental perceptions of children not fulfilling normative adult roles—growing up, moving out, and setting up their own households—as well as the adult children's resenting reminders that they have not yet obtained full independence.

In contrast, with few exceptions, the elders in my study resided in the adult child's household, and only in one family had the parent and child always lived together (Steinmetz, 1988). Therefore, it was the middle-aged (or older) child, and his or her family's lifestyle, that had to accommodate the elder. In these exceptions, the elderly parent had refused to move in with the adult child even though it was evident that the parent was no longer able to live independently. The solution, in these families, was for the child and his or her family to move into the elder's home. Unfortunately, conflicts over home ownership, which was considered to be synonymous with being the boss of the household, resulted.

For example, a 55-year-old daughter noted that she had almost always lived with her 74-year-old mother (the only case in my study). After marrying, she continued to live with her mother while her husband was in the service. Shortly after her husband returned, they moved into their own home. Her father was quite ill, and taking care of him was too difficult for the mother to do alone, so the younger couple had the mother and father move in with them. Having lived with her parents for several decades, she observed:

> I don't think that the burden would be great on me if we lived in a one story house. . . . This house requires a great deal of maintenance. . . . I see things that need doing and I do not have the time . . . or the money for them. I think it is feasible that we move, but it is not to mother. She has it in her mind that she is going to die in this house in that room. She will stay here come hell or high water, and I'm afraid it's hell and high water. It's her house, she owns it. I signed it over to her. I need my head examined, but we decided that it [was best] for tax purposes, it was tax free for her. (quoted in Steinmetz, 1988, pp. 146-147)

In another family, a 53-year-old daughter rented out her own home and moved her family into her father's home when the 91-year-old father, in failing health and no longer able to live alone, refused to move in with his daughter. The daughter noted:

Three generations in the house is just too much. . . . He has called the police to report a car parked in front of the house for no reason. . . . [He has stated] "you wish I were dead." He doesn't respect privacy . . . because this is *his* home. . . . He has a bad temper and he constantly said, "If you don't like it here, then move somewhere else." I would say "that I would like to." . . . we have lived here because he would not move into our house. . . . we still have ours down the street that we rented out. (quoted in Steinmetz, 1988, pp. 186-187)

Finally, the adult children in Pillemer and Finkelhor's study were fairly young, with a mean age of 38. For comparison, the mean age in my studies was 52, and in Pillemer and Suitor's (1992) study of Alzheimer's patients, it was 55 years of age.

Research Design

Comparability across studies is also hindered by differences in the types of samples (e.g., random, convenience, quota) and methods of data collection (e.g., observation, questionnaire, personal interview) as well as by differences in the instruments used. Elder abuse research has used third-party reporting by professionals, victimization data collected by law enforcement and APS agencies, and interviews with caretakers and elders (for a review of these studies, see Steinmetz, 1987, 1988). Given the range of methodologies for collecting the data, as well as the diversity of samples, it is not surprising that there is little congruence among the studies.

It is important to recognize that the criteria for selecting the individuals to be interviewed define the parameters of the findings. For example, Sengstock and Liang (1982) selected only verified cases of abuse; therefore, the high levels of physical abuse they report, when compared with other studies, are not unexpected. Pillemer and Finkelhor (1989) interviewed a random sample of individuals 65 years or older and found that the abusive family member was often dependent on the elder and in nearly 60% of the cases was a spouse. Their findings are inconsistent with those from other studies based on samples of informal caregivers that correlated increasing dependency to increasing stress (S. J. Brody, 1978; Kosberg, 1983) and abuse (Brown, 1989;

Cicirelli, 1983; Fulmer & O'Malley, 1987; Phillips, 1983; Pillemer & Suitor, 1992; Steinmetz, 1983, 1988; Steinmetz & Amsden, 1983). Pillemer and Finkelhor (1989) administered the CTS to individuals over 65 years of age by telephone and in person; the researchers note that they were not likely to tap those most vulnerable—the frail elderly with physical and mental impairments. Because the sampling procedure identified households headed by independent elders, when a 65-year-old or older individual was dependent, he or she was likely to be a spouse. It is not surprising, then, that in this study 58% of the perpetrators of abuse were spouses. Although in some families the spousal abuse represented lifelong abusive marital relationships, in other families both the elderly spouse's physical and emotional dependency on the caregiver and abusive behavior most likely resulted from Alzheimer's disease or other personality-altering illnesses, such as strokes. Pillemer (1985) provides examples of this problem:

A frail women . . . had a stable relationship with her husband. He developed Alzheimer's disease and needed constant supervision. "He would beat me pretty bad, choke me. He grabbed me and said 'I'll kill you.' " . . .
An elderly women was the primary caretaker for her wheelchair-bound husband. He was totally incontinent. In the preceding few months, he had become violent. He ripped his diapers off and would not let her change them. He threatened her with his walker and hit her when she tried to take care of him. (p. 154)

A problem faced by APS workers is how to ascertain the credibility of the information provided by the "abused" elder. This is accomplished by observing the elder and asking a series of questions to assess his or her cognitive functioning. Unfortunately, in a one-shot, relatively brief telephone interview it may not be possible to screen out adequately any elderly who might be suffering from paranoia or the early stages of dementia. The report of a 53-year-old daughter who had been caring for her 93-year-old mother for eight years illustrates this problem:

You don't know what I went through! She got on my nerves so bad that my niece came and got her. . . . she kept her for a while and got on her nerves so bad that I had to go down south and get Mamma and bring her back. . . . I put her in a foster home and had to go and get her . . . she didn't fit in. If I said "mamma, here's your dinner," she'd say "I don't want it." She broke her hip and told the doctor that I threw her down and broke her hip. (quoted in Steinmetz, 1988, p. 20)

If we had interviewed this elder, could we report with confidence that the adult child had thrown her mother down the stairs? Another caregiver, a 47-year-old daughter who had been caring for her 84-year-old mother for five months, described her mother's paranoia and inability to deal with reality:

> One day she called us up and said that she had been shot. Several times in the middle of the night she would come to our bedroom door and she would want to know . . . where her [dead] sister Helen was now. (quoted in Steinmetz, 1988, p. 20)

Without corroborating data, the validity of the responses, especially in view of the complexity of the CTS when administered by phone and the age of the elder, is problematic. Interviewing the caregiver should not be interpreted as a lack of sensitivity to the elder's perception of the situation. Caregivers often make it quite clear that their views of events probably differ from their parents' perceptions of the same events. Just as family therapists have long recognized that there is the wife's marriage, the husband's marriage, and the couple's marriage, there is the adult child caregiver's view of parent-child interaction as well as the elder's view. However, a symbolic interaction perspective suggests that the caregiver's perception of reality would strongly influence his or her behavior. I have found that if caregivers perceive caregiving to be stressful, they are more likely to resort to abuse, regardless of the actual degree of dependency of the elder on the caregiver (Steinmetz, 1988).

Examining the Findings on
Elder Dependency and Abuse by Caregivers

Pillemer, in Chapter 15 of this volume, notes that I am the leading proponent of the view that increased dependency is linked to abuse. He states that this view is not supported by his data. He suggests that we should refocus our research on the characteristics of the abuser, rather than the victim. Clearly, more scientific data are needed on all participants who play a role in elder abuse. However, focusing on one member of an interacting pair (caregiver-elder) and assuming that we can obtain an adequate picture of elder abuse and recommend appropriate prevention and/or interventions programs are not prudent approaches and do not reflect the complexity of the elder-caregiver relationship.

Many of the studies that have examined elders' dependency and the impact on the caregiving family, a rich body of literature covering more than three decades of research, carefully articulate the relationships among dependency, stress, and burden. More recently this literature has been linked to elder abuse.

In studies I have conducted, caregivers were asked how frequently they had to provide a series of modified activity of daily living (ADL) tasks for the elder and how much it bothered them to do so (Steinmetz, 1983, 1988; Steinmetz & Amsden, 1983). They were also asked questions to ascertain the problems and associated stress resulting from feeling totally responsible for the elder's well-being and sharing a residence with the elder. A moderate relationship between objective levels of elder's impairment or caregiver's need to provide dependency-related tasks and abuse of the elder was observed. However, a much stronger relationship was observed between the subjective feelings of stress and burden as a result of having to assist the elder and abuse of the elder.

Similar findings are provided by Fulmer and O'Malley (1987) in their analysis of 107 cases referred to an elder abuse assessment team with 147 cases of the same age group who were not referred to the abuse assessment team. They used a five-point Likert scale to rate a variety of forms of dependency (administration of medication, ambulation, continence, feeding, maintenance and hygiene, and management of finances). The elder's dependency on the caregiver was found to be an important predisposing factor for elder abuse and neglect. Fulmer and Ashley (1989) conducted a factor analysis on data generated from the Elder Assessment Instrument. They found that level of dependency on the care provider was an important variable in predicting elder abuse and neglect.

Phillips (1983) categorized families into "abusive" and "good relationships." This procedure was somewhat problematic because the nurses who interviewed the families were unable to assign 12 of the 63 families into one category or the other and independent judges made the final assignment. This may account for the lack of significant findings between physical functioning and abuse. However, the strongest direct relationship in Phillips's causal model was that between "family members in the house also available to help" and abuse. Based on her data, it is clear that the availability of others to assist with providing care, thus reducing the responsibility and dependency of the elder's care on a single caregiver, reduces the likelihood of abuse.

Brown (1989) interviewed one-third of the Native Americans over 60 years old residing at the Oljato Chapter of the Navajos in Arizona.

An additional close member of the family (spouse, child, grandchild) was also selected to be interviewed. This study found that dependency patterns provided an important abuse indicator. Caregivers who lived with an elder and had total responsibility for his or her care (clearly indicators of dependency) were more likely to be physically abusive. These findings were consistent when reported by either the elder or the other family member.

Finally, Pillemer and Suitor's (1992) research on caregivers of elders with Alzheimer's disease examined the effect of dependency on abuse. Using a combined measure of actual violence and fear of violence, they report that violent caregivers lived with the elders, provided care for more functionally impaired elders, and provided help with a greater number of activities. These findings are contrary to the large number of articles in which Pillemer and colleagues have adamantly stated that elder dependency as measured by functional impairment does *not* result in being abused by the caregiver (see Pillemer, Chapter 15, this volume). Given that Cicirelli (1983), Phillips (1983), and I (Steinmetz, 1988) used causal modeling to distinguish the relative impact of a variety of factors related to dependency that contributed to elder abuse, Pillemer and Suitor's (1992) statement that their findings "stand in contrast to the simplistic view propounded in the elder abuse literature that the dependency of the care recipient leads directly to violence" (p. S171) is most curious.

If one defines dependency in terms of ability to perform ADLs, then a relationship between dependency and abuse is limited. However, if one defines dependency in terms of the number of responsibilities that the caregiver has to fulfill and the inability to be relieved of these responsibilities (e.g., elder lives with the caregiver, or the lack of others to assist in this care), then a relationship between dependency and abuse is found. If the research findings are to be useful in preventing or ameliorating elder abuse, policymakers and social service providers would be advised to focus on the dynamics in these families rather than on a specific definition of dependency based exclusively on the elder's level of functional impairment.

An interesting example is provided by Greenberg, McKibben, and Raymond (1990) in their analysis of 204 abused elders and their adult children. Of this group, 51% of the elders were described as "frail" and 20% were "homebound." Therefore, 71% of this group of abused elders were substantially dependent on their adult children for care and assistance. However, 25% of the adult children were financially dependent on the elderly parents. In these families were the adult children abusive caregivers or abusive dependent adult children? The answer depends on the definition of dependency that is used. Although setting up a straw man with the goal of systematically knocking down the myths is a useful approach for presenting one's arguments, one needs to have a viable straw man. Pillemer's straw man is lacking. Although he expends considerable effort on presenting data to refute the simplistic notion that elders' level of impairment leads to abuse, none of the recent literature and few studies in the past have proposed this limited relationship between dependency defined as functional impairment and abuse.

Stone, Cafferata, and Sangl (1987), using data from the 1982 long-term care survey, found that primary caregivers of the elderly were most likely to be immediate family members. Adult daughters were caregivers in 29%, wives in 23%, and husbands in 13% of the families. As the number of frail elderly increases daily, we can expect the problem of elder abuse to increase also. It is important that high-quality, inexpensive, continuum-of-care facilities are available to meet the needs of this increasingly larger population of vulnerable elderly. With more women in the workforce (who are likely to continue working until age 70 unless they are experiencing serious medical problems), we need to ask, Who will care for our elderly parents? Given their own unfortunate experiences, many adults who have cared for an elderly parent have told their children that when they can no longer maintain their independence they want to be institutionalized. A 58-year-old daughter who had cared for her mother for eight years reported:

> I didn't have anyone to go to. . . . I was so deeply depressed. She [the 93-year-old mother] told me she didn't want to go into a home. What can I do? I told my son "If I get disabled I don't want you to hesitate. I don't want to be a burden on you. Put me in a home, I won't mind it. I've been through it. I know what it is." (quoted in Steinmetz, 1988, p. 227)

In a similar vein, a 66-year-old daughter who had been caring for her 86-year-old father for four years noted in a discussion with her daughter:

> I want you to promise me that when I get like this that you will please put me someplace. She said, "I couldn't do that." I said, "I want you to do it because I don't want to wreck someone's life, and that is exactly what it is. . . . Please put me someplace. Let me maintain my sense of dignity. I don't want to be in somebody's home and I don't want to feel

that I am a burden—that's what it is a burden. (quoted in Steinmetz, 1988, p. 176)

Intervention is necessary for elderly parents who are being abused by their dependent, often disabled, adult children for whom they are providing care. Deinstitutionalization has resulted in the burden of caring for emotionally, mentally, and chronically ill children being placed on the family. As the parents age, we can anticipate that this problem will continue to increase.

Likewise, spouses need assistance in caring for partners who have become abusive as the result of Alzheimer's disease or a stroke—or are simply continuing with patterns of spousal abuse established earlier in the marriage. With increasing life expectancy, higher costs of living, and inadequate social security and pensions, we can assume that the responsibility of caring for an elderly parent, for a large percentage of families, will ultimately fall on an adult child. Even if an elderly spouse had provided care for his or her dependent partner, it is still likely that he or she will also eventually require assistance from other family members.

Family members, especially adult children, will continue to be a major source of care for elderly parents as the cost of institutional care continues to rise. These informal caregivers, tackling an around-the-clock job with no training and limited resources, will increasingly be at risk of abusing elders unless we are able to provide education, resources, and home-based assistance.

It is important to identify the caregiving situations and characteristics of elders and caregivers that are likely to result in the use of abusive techniques to gain or maintain control. In my studies based on a sample of dependent elders, as well as those of other researchers, level of dependency (primarily emotional and mental health) was positively correlated with abuse. However, an even stronger predictor of abuse was the caregiver's perception of the stress associated with providing the care. Thus the expressed feeling of burden and stress from having to perform tasks for the elder provided a more accurate prediction of abuse than did the duration of caregiving or the level of care needed. This suggests that families and social service agents need to consider the caregiver's subjective feeling about providing care as well as the level of care that will need to be provided when an elder can no longer live independently and alternative arrangements need to be made.

Three distinct populations have been identified in which elders are at risk: An elder may be abused by adult children who are caring for him or her, by an elderly spouse, or by adult children who are physically, mentally, or emotionally disabled and are dependent on the elder. In a society as rich as ours, the issue should not be *which* population is in greatest need of limited resources, but rather how we can best meet the needs of all at-risk elders and their families.

Note

1. Academic debates such as those in this book are an important component in expanding our knowledge base. Although my challenge in this essay is to debate Karl Pillemer's position, I would like to note that I have the greatest respect for his research, which has contributed immensely to our knowledge of elder abuse.

References

American Public Welfare Association and National Association of State Units on Aging. (1986). *A comprehensive analysis of state policy and practice related to elder abuse: A focus on legislation, appropriations, incidence data, and special studies.* Washington, DC: Author.

Block, M., & Sinnott, J. (1979). *The battered elder syndrome: An exploratory study.* Baltimore: University of Maryland, Center on Aging.

Brody, E. (1966). The aging family. *Gerontologist, 6,* 201-206.

Brody, E. (1970). The etiquette of filial behavior. *Aging and Human Development, 1,* 87-94.

Brody, S. J. (1978). The family caring unit: A major consideration in the long-term support system. *Gerontologist, 18,* 556-561.

Brown, A. S. (1989). A survey on elder abuse at one Native American tribe. *Journal of Elder Abuse and Neglect, 1,* 17-37.

Cicirelli, V. G. (1983). Adult children's attachment and helping behavior to elderly parents: A path model. *Journal of Marriage and the Family, 45,* 815-825.

Fulmer, T., & Ashley, J. (1989). Clinical indicators which signal elder neglect. *Applied Nursing Research Journal, 2,* 161-167.

Fulmer, T., & O'Malley, T. (1987). *Inadequate care of the elderly: A health care perspective on abuse and neglect.* New York: Springer.

Gelles, R. J., & Straus, M. A. (1988). *Intimate violence: The causes and consequences of abuse in the American family.* New York: Simon & Schuster.

Greenberg, J. R., McKibben, M. & Raymond, J. A. (1990). Dependent adult children and elder abuse. *Journal of Elder Abuse and Neglect, 2,* 73-86.

Kosberg, J. I. (Ed.). (1983). *Abuse and maltreatment of the elderly: Causes and interventions.* Littleton, MA: John Wright, PSG.

Mace, N. L. (1981). *The 36-hour day: A family guide to caring for persons with Alzheimer's disease, related dementing illness, and memory loss in later life.* Baltimore: Johns Hopkins University Press.

Phillips, L. R. (1983). Abuse and neglect of the frail elderly at home: An exploration of theoretical relationships. *Journal of Advanced Nursing, 8,* 379-392.

Pillemer, K. (1985). The dangers of dependency: New findings on domestic violence against elderly. *Social Problems, 33,* 146-158.

Pillemer, K., & Finkelhor, D. (1989). Causes of elder abuse: Caregiver stress versus problem relatives. *American Journal of Orthopsychiatry, 59,* 179-187.

Pillemer, K., & Prescott, D. (1989). Psychological effects of elder abuse: A research note. *Journal of Elder Abuse and Neglect, 1,* 65-73.

Pillemer, K., & Suitor, J. J. (1992). Violence and violent feelings: What causes them among family caregivers. *Journal of Gerontology, 47,* S165-S172.

Sengstock, M. D., & Liang, J. (1982). *Identifying and characterizing elder abuse.* Detroit, MI: Wayne State University.

Steinmetz, S. K. (1983). Dependency, stress and violence between middle-aged caregivers and their elderly parents. In J. I. Kosberg (Ed.), *Abuse and maltreatment of the elderly: Causes and interventions* (pp. 134-139). Littleton, MA: John Wright, PSG.

Steinmetz, S. K. (1987). Family violence: Past, present and future. In M. B. Sussman & S. K. Steinmetz (Eds.), *Handbook of marriage and the family* (pp. 725-765). New York: Plenum.

Steinmetz, S. K. (1988). *Duty bound: Elder abuse and family care.* Newbury Park, CA: Sage.

Steinmetz, S. K., & Amsden, D. J. (1983). Dependent elders, family stress, and abuse. In T. H. Brubaker (Ed.), *Family relationships in later life* (pp. 173-192). Beverly Hills, CA: Sage.

Steinmetz, S. K., & Straus, M. A. (Eds.). (1974). *Violence in the family.* New York: Harper & Row.

Stone, R. G., Cafferata, G. L., & Sangl, J. (1987). Caregivers of the frail elderly: A national profile. *Gerontologist, 27,* 616-626.

Straus, M. A., Gelles, R. J., & Steinmetz, S. K. (1980). *Behind closed doors: Violence in the American family.* Garden City, NY: Anchor/Doubleday.

CHAPTER **15**

The Abused Offspring Are Dependent

Abuse Is Caused by the Deviance and Dependence of Abusive Caregivers

Karl Pillemer

Why do people abuse elderly family members? As with other forms of family violence, this question is as critically important to answer as it is difficult to do so. Some of the difficulties are methodological: Obtaining information on a hidden—and, for many people, shameful—topic is a daunting task at best. The search for risk factors has also been clouded by elder abuse's 15-year history as a social problem: Early assertions, founded on faulty data (or no data at all) have been repeated so frequently that they have come to be widely believed, despite the lack of evidence. Research has yet to move creatively beyond some of these mistaken assumptions about elder abuse.

In some ways, an examination of what has been written to date on elder abuse has a certain Alice in Wonderland feel to it. This is a field in which review articles outnumber actual research reports; in which most of the researchers use health and human service professionals, rather than victims and their families, as their subjects; and in which such basic research tools as random sample surveys and case-control studies are rarely used. State laws and intervention programs have

AUTHOR'S NOTE: This chapter was prepared with support from the Florence V. Burden Foundation and the Ittleson Foundation. I am grateful to Richard J. Gelles for helpful comments on an earlier version.

237

been founded on this shaky information, with little or no scientific evaluation.

An appropriate example of the problems in developing a body of knowledge about elder abuse is the issue of *dependency*. Since the earliest writings about maltreatment of the aged, dependency has been postulated as a major risk factor. Two views have been juxtaposed (see Fulmer, 1990): one that emphasizes the increased frailty and dependence of elders on caregivers and an alternative view that focuses on the deviance and dependence of abusive relatives on their victims. In Chapter 14 of this volume, Suzanne Steinmetz offers a thoughtful and cogent review of the former perspective.

In contrast, in this chapter I present an argument that deemphasizes the role of the dependency of the victim and highlights instead the pathology and dependency of the abuser. I do so based on an evaluation of the available scientific evidence. To be sure, in every case the empirical evidence is flawed to some degree. However, a review of the most reliable and valid studies conducted to date calls for a refocusing on characteristics of the abuser—rather than of the victim—as major risk factors for elder abuse.

What are the criteria by which we should evaluate the issue of dependency and elder abuse? There appear to me to be several crucial questions to be addressed. First, what are the origins of the view that the dependency of the victim leads to abuse? Second, is there evidence that abused elders are especially likely to be ill or impaired? Third, is there evidence that victims are especially dependent on the abusive relatives? Finally, what about the reverse proposition: Is there evidence that abusers are dependent on their victims?

In the remainder of this chapter, I will address these questions in turn. In keeping with the topic of the present volume, I focus my discussion on physical violence. However, it is impossible to restrict the analysis entirely to physical abuse, because many of the studies discussed below include victims of several types of maltreatment, such as physical, psychological, and material abuse (e.g., Bristowe & Collins, 1989; Phillips, 1983; Pillemer & Finkelhor, 1989).

"Pity the Perpetrator":
Victim Dependency as the Cause of Abuse

In Chapter 14, Steinmetz argues that few studies have "proposed [a] limited relationship between dependency defined as functional impairment and abuse." On this point, I would strongly disagree. In fact, if there can be a "traditional" view in a field that is little over a decade old, then the traditional view of elder abuse can be summed up in the following way. Elderly people, it is held, become sick, frail, dependent, and difficult to care for. They then cause stress for their caregivers; as a result of this stress, these otherwise responsible and well-meaning relatives lose control and become abusive toward the elders. In this view, elder abuse is seen as essentially a natural outgrowth of the aging process that leads to the need for family care.

This view has been described succinctly by Baumann (1989), who notes that, as with many social problems, "claims-makers" developed a view of the issue designed to bring it quickly to national attention and to garner resources to begin to treat it. In this case, advocates used analogies with child abuse to call attention to elder abuse. As Baumann notes, statements about the dependency of the elderly were a major way to justify allocating resources to elder abuse. Assertions that the elderly are abused because of their increased needs for care provided a rationale for assistance; our society is seen as morally obligated to provide for these elders, because they, like children, cannot fend for themselves.

Indeed, much early writing on elder abuse emphasized the dependency of the elder in precisely this way. For example, Hickey and Douglass (1981) claim, from their survey of professionals, "The sudden or unwanted dependency of parents is a key factor in understanding neglect and abuse. . . . To the extent that dependent individuals must rely on others for care, protection, and sustenance, they are at-risk of being hurt, unprotected, etc." (p. 174). Similarly, Davidson (1979), in an early report, tied abuse directly to the "crises" created by the needs of an elderly parent for care: "Yet just as the child is abused by his parent who resents the dependency of the child because the parent himself lacks satisfaction of needs, the adult child who must assume a caretaker role to his own parents may become abusive as a result of his parents' dependency and the lack of need satisfaction" (p. 49). Steinmetz (1988) was another early proponent of this view. She argued that families actually undergo "generational inversion," in which the elderly person becomes dependent upon his or her children. This places the caregiver under severe stress.

This view has been so pervasive that many have come to consider elder abuse exclusively a problem of family caregiving. In a number of articles, abusers are referred to as "caregivers," and abuse is defined as actions by caregivers. For example, O'Malley, O'Malley, Everitt, and Sarson (1986) suggest that all elder abuse be subsumed under the term *inadequate care*. As such, the definition of abuse they propose is "active intervention by a caretaker such that unmet needs are created with resultant physical, psychological, or financial injury" (p. 26). Many individuals have adopted this view in designing interventions, so much so that probably the most frequently recommended programs to reduce elder abuse are those that treat caregiver stress (see Douglass, 1988; Scoggin et al., 1989).

Baumann (1989) points out that there are several related themes in the literature on elder abuse that reinforce the notion that the victim's characteristics are the most important factors that lead to abuse. Old people are usually characterized as "frail" and "vulnerable." The abused elderly are frequently referred to as incompetent and unable to care for themselves. These characteristics both lead to additional family stress and are seen as leading to greater risk for the victims, who are assumed not to be able to seek help for abuse on their own. There is more than a trace of ageism in this view. The situation of elderly persons is equated with that of children, in that they are seen as being in need of protection simply because of their age status.

Victim Dependency:
The Research Evidence

To paraphrase the famous expression: Nothing is so sad as a wonderful theory punctured by a few facts. Indeed, it is difficult to find firm research results that support the claim that physical abuse results directly from the elder's ill health and dependency. The available evidence shows instead that the analogy between elder abuse and child abuse is a false one, and that the widely held view that elder dependency and the demands for care are the major cause of elder abuse is in fact a fallacy.

What is the contrary evidence? Let us begin with a simple point. It is clear from the gerontological literature that a large number of elderly persons are dependent on relatives for some degree of care (Rabin & Stockton, 1987). However, findings about the prevalence of elder abuse indicate that only a small minority of the elderly (approximately 3-4%) are abused. Because abuse occurs in only a small proportion of families, no direct correlation can be assumed between dependency of an elderly person and abuse. In fact, two recent studies that included only caregivers to Alzheimer's disease victims (a high-risk situation for caregiver stress) found that only a small percentage of these caregivers became abusive: 5% in one study (Pillemer & Suitor, 1992) and 12% in another (Joslin, Coyne, Johnson, Berbig, & Potenza, 1991).

In order to determine the importance of elder dependency, our best source of information is the few studies that have used case-control designs. Most studies of elder abuse have involved case studies of victims identified through service agencies, with no comparison group. For this reason, the generalizations made from these studies are necessarily suspect. In the present instance, we are examining the assertion that the abused elderly tend to be physically and/or mentally impaired. Many of the aged, however, suffer from chronic conditions, and a substantial proportion have some form of dementia, especially among those over the age of 85 (Evans et al., 1989). Without a comparison group, it is impossible to know if abuse victims are more or less impaired than other persons.

Over the past few years, several researchers have begun to use case-control designs to understand risk factors for elder abuse. Although these studies all have weaknesses (owing in part to the difficulty of the phenomenon under study), they have at least attempted to compare abuse victims with nonabused elders. I provide only a brief description of the methods here; readers are referred to the original studies for more information.

Bristowe and Collins (1989) wished to compare abusive families with families where appropriate care was being provided to elderly relatives. Four categories of maltreatment were included: passive neglect, active neglect, verbal abuse, and physical abuse. Most of the cases came from a homemaker agency, in which the staff identified clients as in either appropriate care or abusive situations. To augment the sample, requests were made in the media for additional cases of abuse.

In my own research, I obtained data on victims of physical abuse from the caseloads of three model projects on elder abuse (Pillemer, 1985, 1986). These persons were individually matched on gender and living arrangement with nonabused clients of the agencies that sponsored the projects. A comparison relative in each of the comparison group families was matched with the abuser.

Another study in which I was involved selected physical abuse cases drawn from a more recent evaluation of elder abuse intervention projects in New York, Wisconsin, California, and Hawaii (Pillemer & Wolf, 1991). Again, the abuse victims were individually matched on gender and living arrangement with clients from the agencies who had not been abused.

Homer and Gilleard (1990) studied clients who were receiving respite care or had been referred for respite care during a six-month period. Caregivers were asked about three types of maltreatment:

physical abuse, verbal abuse, and neglect. The studt compared the caregivers who reported that they had been abusive with those who did not.

Phillips (1983) selected respondents from social service agencies, who were then assigned to abuse and nonabuse groups by service providers. Phillips's study is unique in that she used a "blind" interview technique, in which the interviewers were not aware of whether the respondent was or was not an abuse victim.

In a study I conducted with David Finkelhor, a general population survey of persons 65 and older in the greater Boston area was conducted to determine the prevalence of elder abuse (Pillemer & Finkelhor, 1989). Victims of physical abuse, verbal aggression, and neglect were compared with nonabused control cases randomly selected from the larger sample.

Finally, data from a large-scale study of caregivers to Alzheimer's disease victims were used to examine violence in those relationships (Pillemer & Suitor, 1992). Cases in which the caregiver reported he or she had been violent were compared with those in which the caregiver had not reported violence. In addition, the fear of becoming violent toward the care recipient was examined.

None of these studies found support for the notion that elder abuse results from the excessive dependency of the victim. Instead, these studies uniformly failed to find important differences in health and functional status between victims and nonvictims. Three of the studies in fact found the abuse victims to be *less* impaired than the controls (Bristowe & Collins, 1989; Pillemer, 1985; Pillemer & Wolf, 1991). Abused elders were not found in any of these studies to have other characteristics that might point toward greater activity limitations, such as advanced age or cognitive impairment.

Regarding the 1992 article I cowrote with Suitor, Steinmetz's statement that we found that violent caregivers "provided care for more functionally impaired elders, and provided help with a greater number of activities" is simply incorrect. Differences between violent and nonviolent caregivers on the Activities of Daily Living Scale and on a helping scale were *not* statistically significant. Further, initial differences on these two variables between caregivers who feared becoming violent and those who did not disappeared in a multivariate analysis (see Pillemer & Suitor, 1992, Tables 2-3).

The unanimity of the results from these studies is striking in light of the divergent methods used. Several of the studies have included only caregivers (Homer & Gilleard, 1990; Phillips, 1983; Pillemer & Suitor, 1992), whereas others, such as that by Bristowe and Collins

(1989), included both caregivers and noncaregivers. The Pillemer and Finkelhor (1989) study compared abuse victims with the general population, and the Pillemer (1985, 1986) and Pillemer and Wolf (1991) studies compared identified cases with nonabused agency subsamples. Despite the divergence in methods, these comparison group studies provide *no evidence* that abuse victims are significantly more impaired than nonvictims.

In light of the findings from these studies, the predominance of the view that elder impairment in itself leads to abuse is somewhat remarkable. In a different context, Ethel Shanas (1979) likened a myth about old age to a "hydra-headed monster," referring to the legendary beast that grew two heads for each one that was cut off, and was thus impossible to kill (at least until Hercules came along). In using this image, Shanas wished to convey the persistence of the myth—regardless of the number of scientific studies to refute a popular view, it reappeared again and again in public opinion. A similar phenomenon appears to exist in this popular view of the causes of elder abuse. As I have asserted elsewhere, in the absence of new case-comparison evidence, the notion that physical abuse results from the health problems of the elder should be rejected and alternative hypotheses explored (Pillemer & Finkelhor, 1989).

Even if poor health is not a major risk factor for abuse, it is possible that abused elders are nevertheless more dependent on their relatives. In the few studies that have addressed this issue, however, no evidence has appeared that this is the case. In both the Pillemer (1985, 1986) and Pillemer and Wolf (1991) studies, the abuse victims were distinctly *unlikely* to rely on the abuser for assistance with activities of daily living. For example, in the first study, respondents were asked to identify their most likely helpers. Those in the abuse group were much less likely to name their abusers as the persons they would be most likely to rely upon for help (26% versus 63%; $p < .01$).

In the Pillemer and Wolf (1991) study, respondents were asked who the person was who would be most likely to help them if they became more sick or disabled; only 20% said that this person was the abuser. In the same study, caseworkers were asked to name the person whom each abuse victim could call in a crisis; in only 6% of the cases was this the abuser. Even in cases where the abuser lived with the victim, someone else was usually named as the person most depended upon.

As another measure of the dependency of the victim on the abuser, respondents in both of these studies were asked directly: "People depend on each other for many things. How much do you depend on [the abuser or a comparison relative] in each of the following areas?"

Respondents were asked to answer whether they were dependent or independent in six areas: housing, financial support, cooking or cleaning, household repair, companionship/social activities, and transportation.

In both the Pillemer (1985, 1986) and Pillemer and Wolf (1991) studies, abuse victims were not found to be more dependent in *any* of these areas. In the first study, no significant differences were found in five of the six areas. A difference was found in financial dependency, with the abuse group more likely to be independent than the comparison group. Pillemer and Wolf (1991) found that in five areas, the abuse group was significantly less dependent on the abuser than the nonvictims were on the comparison relatives; in the sixth, financial dependency, the abuse group was less dependent, but not significantly so.

In sum, the available research evidence does not support the notion that the illness or dependency of an elderly person places him or her at special risk of becoming an abuse victim. To be sure, additional replication studies are necessary to verify this statement further. However, in the absence of any comparison group data to the contrary, it seems misguided to continue to assert that elder dependency and caregiver stress lead to elder abuse. I now turn to the question of whether it is more appropriate to focus on characteristics of the *abuser* rather than of the victim in the search for causes of elder abuse.

Abuser Dependency:
The Research Evidence

Interestingly, findings were available early on indicating that elder abusers were themselves dependent individuals. In a study published in 1982, Wolf, Strugnell, and Godkin surveyed community agencies in Massachusetts regarding elder abuse cases they had encountered. The authors identified a "web of mutual dependency" between abuser and abused. In two-thirds of the cases in that study, the perpetrator was reported to be financially dependent on the victim. Another early study by Hwalek, Sengstock, and Lawrence (1984) also identified financial dependency of the abuser as a risk factor in abuse.

Several more recent studies have confirmed this profile of the abuser as dependent on the victim. In the Pillemer (1985, 1986) study, respondents were asked a dependency index (identical to that described above), with the questions reversed. That is, they were asked: "How much does [the abuser or comparison relative] depend on *you* in each of the following areas?" Abusers were found to be significantly more dependent on the elders in four areas: housing, household repair, financial assistance, and transportation. The more recent Pillemer and Wolf (1991) study inquired only about two forms of abuser dependency in two areas: finances and cooking and cleaning. A statistically significant difference was found for financial dependency, with abusers much more likely to be dependent.

In the Pillemer and Finkelhor (1989) analysis of cases from a random-sample survey, nearly identical results emerged. Abusers were significantly more likely to be dependent financially for household repairs, for transportation, for housing, and for cooking and cleaning than were the relatives of nonabused comparison cases. Other studies as well, although they did not include control groups, have found substantial percentages of financially dependent abusers (Anetzberger, 1987; Greenberg, McKibben, & Raymond, 1990).

The question then arises, Why are the abusers dependent? All studies that have addressed this issue have been unequivocal in their assessment: Elder abusers—rather than being healthy, stable, well-intentioned caregivers—tend to suffer from a variety of mental health, substance abuse, and stress-related problems. Overwhelmingly, the studies indicate that the abusers have a range of such problems that play a major role in the abuse situation.

It is interesting to note that these results occur both in studies of caregivers and in those that included all relatives. In the Pillemer and Finkelhor (1989) study, discriminant function analyses demonstrated that abuser deviance and dependence were the strongest predictors of abuse. Homer and Gilleard (1990) found greater alcohol consumption on the part of abusive caregivers to be related to physical abuse, whereas caregivers' depression and anxiety led to verbal abuse. Bristowe and Collins (1989) also found alcohol consumption by the abuser to be the major distinguishing factor between the abusive and nonabusive groups. Greenberg et al.'s (1990) recent analysis of predictors of dependency among abusive adult children found similar results: Substance abuse was the major factor. Qualitative data from the same study indicated that chronic psychological problems are characteristic of dependent abusers.

Further, all studies that have sought such information have found that abusers are overwhelmingly more likely to have been violent in other contexts, to have been arrested, or to have been hospitalized for psychiatric reasons (see Pillemer & Finkelhor, 1989; Pillemer & Wolf, 1991). It is impossible to contrast these findings with the Steinmetz study, because this type of question was simply not asked. Items relating to deviance and dependency on the part of the caregivers were not included in the study, so it was impossible to evaluate the relative strength of the abuser-dependency and victim-dependency hypotheses.

Discussion

Our knowledge about the problem of elder abuse may no longer be in its infancy, but it has certainly not progressed much beyond the toddler stage. It is interesting to note that there has been the most debate over the one issue on which we have the clearest data. Simply put, all of the more rigorous studies of elder abuse have failed to find dependency of the victim to be a primary characteristic of maltreatment situations. They have, on the other hand, found substantial evidence that elder abusers are often not primary caregivers at all, but are instead deeply troubled individuals who depend heavily on the persons they abuse.

I by no means intend to imply that this issue is entirely resolved. Readers familiar with research methods will have noted many flaws in the available research. Further, we are just now becoming aware of the complex, multifaceted nature of the problem we have labeled "elder abuse." For example, many of the studies did not differentiate among different types of abuse and neglect; it may be that the pattern described here holds more strongly for physical abuse and less so for other types of maltreatment (see Wolf & Pillemer, 1989, for preliminary data that support this possibility). Further, the samples in the studies cited above were almost exclusively white; the dynamics of abuse involving African Americans, Asian Americans, and Hispanics may differ from the findings presented here. Clearly, there is fertile ground here for additional research.

Based on existing studies, however, it seems we must conclude that the hypothesis that caregiver stress is a major cause of elder abuse is incorrect. One might then ask: Why is this an important issue? In fact, the question of who is depending on whom in families where elder abuse exists has several major implications.

Those who argue that elder abuse results from problematic characteristics of elderly people have—unintentionally, I believe—blamed the victim. In the same way that some writers held that "spoiled" children were more likely to be abused, or that nagging, demanding wives were more likely to be battered, the elderly themselves have been cited as the cause of abuse. Focusing on caregiver stress normalizes the problem; it relieves the abuser of much of the blame because, after all, the elderly are demanding, hard to care for, and sometimes even downright unpleasant.

The research data argue that we should refocus on the *abuser*. We must begin to examine how people come to depend on elderly relatives, and the ways in which that dependency sometimes results in abuse. Other explanations should not be excluded; as I have argued elsewhere (Pillemer, 1985), in some cases caregiver stress may play a role in elder abuse. But the dominance of the view that abusers are caregivers who are pushed to their limits has tended to keep researchers from focusing on a more promising explanation: the deviance and dependency of abusers.

Practice and policy can also benefit from this refocusing. Based on the hypothesis that dependency of victims leads to abuse, supportive services have been offered to caregivers, such as home care services, housekeeping, meal preparation, and support groups. Although such services may play some role in preventing or ameliorating elder abuse, the research findings summarized in this chapter point to a need for other services.[1]

A focus on the abuser suggests that either the rewards of dependency on the victim can be increased or the costs of abusing the victim can be heightened. To achieve the former goal, unhealthy dependence of a relative on an older person could be reduced through psychotherapy, employment counseling, and financial support for the abuser while he or she establishes an independent household. In some cases, the change in living situation may be nursing home placement for a dependent, abusive spouse.

The costs of abusing an elderly person can be raised in a variety of ways. One option is to offer victim assistance services to the abused elderly. For example, the battered women's movement has had great success with support groups for victims. Such groups convey to victims that they have a right to be free from abuse, and help them to develop strategies to resist it. Another possibility is the development of "safe houses" or emergency shelters for elder abuse victims. A shelter can help a victim to escape from abuse and then provide support so that the victim can make a decision about whether to live independently or return to the abuser, who now is aware that the victim will no longer tolerate being maltreated.

Another alternative that follows a refocusing on abusers is legal action. When elder abuse was conceived of as occurring because of caregiver strain, involving the police rarely seemed necessary. In the framework proposed here, elder abuse (and especially violence) is seen as having parallels with spouse abuse: relatively independent persons sharing a residence with physically stronger ones who victimize them. Using legal sanctions against abusers may deter future victimization. Let me conclude with an exhortation to do two things. First, let us continue to expand the research base on elder abuse, using more complex multivariate models of maltreatment, and resist relying on monocausal explanations such as caregiver stress. Second, as we await further research findings, let us begin to base our policy and practice on the knowledge that many abusers are not caregivers and many victims are not cared for (at least by their abusers). Such a view will allow new and creative solutions to the problem to emerge.

Note

1. The following discussion is adapted from Wolf and Pillemer (1989).

References

Anetzberger, G. J. (1987). *Etiology of elder abuse by adult offspring*. Springfield, IL: Charles C Thomas.
Baumann, E. A. (1989). Research rhetoric and the social construction of elder abuse. In J. Best (Ed.), *Images of issues: Typifying contemporary social problems*. New York: Aldine de Gruyter.
Bristowe, E., & Collins, J. (1989). Family mediated abuse of noninstitutionalized frail elderly men and women in British Columbia. *Journal of Elder Abuse and Neglect, 1*, 45-64.
Davidson, J. L. (1979). Elder abuse. In M. R. Block & J. D. Sinnott (Eds.), *The battered elder syndrome: An exploratory study* (pp. 49-55). College Park: University of Maryland, Center on Aging.
Douglass, R. L. (1988). *Domestic maltreatment of the elderly: Towards prevention*. Washington, DC: American Association of Retired Persons.
Evans, D., et al. (1989). Prevalence of Alzheimer's disease in a community population of older persons. *Journal of the American Medical Association, 262*, 2551-2554.
Fulmer, T. (1990). The debate over dependency as a relevant predisposing factor in elder abuse and neglect. *Journal of Elder Abuse and Neglect, 2*, 51-58.
Greenberg, J. R., McKibben, M., & Raymond, J. A. (1990). Dependent adult children and elder abuse. *Journal of Elder Abuse and Neglect, 2*, 73-86.
Hickey, T., & Douglass, R. (1981). Neglect and abuse of older family members: Professionals' perspectives and case experiences. *Gerontologist, 21*, 171-176.
Homer, A. C., & Gilleard, C. (1990). Abuse of elderly people by their carers. *British Medical Journal, 301*, 1359-1362.
Hwalek, M., Sengstock, M. C., & Lawrence, R. (1984, November). *Assessing the probability of abuse of the elderly*. Paper presented at the annual meeting of the Gerontological Society of America, Philadelphia.

Joslin, B. L., Coyne, A. C., Johnson, T. W., Berbig, L. J., & Potenza, M. (1991, November). *Dementia and elder abuse: Are the caregivers victims or villains?* Paper presented at the annual meeting of the Gerontological Society of America, San Francisco.

O'Malley, T., O'Malley, H. C., Everitt, D. E., & Sarson, D. (1986). Categories of family mediated abuse and neglect of elderly persons. *Journal of the American Geriatrics Society, 32,* 362-369.

Phillips, L. R. (1983). Abuse and neglect of the frail elderly at home: An exploration of theoretical relationships. *Journal of Advanced Nursing, 8,* 379-392.

Pillemer, K. (1985). The dangers of dependency: New findings on domestic violence against elderly. *Social Problems, 33,* 146-158.

Pillemer, K. (1986). Risk factors in elder abuse: Results from a case-control study. In K. Pillemer & R. S. Wolf (Eds.), *Elder abuse: Conflict in the family* (pp. 236-263). Dover, MA: Auburn House.

Pillemer, K., & Finkelhor, D. (1989). Causes of elder abuse: Caregiver stress versus problem relatives. *American Journal of Orthopsychiatry, 59,* 179-187.

Pillemer, K., & Suitor, J. J. (1992). Violence and violent feelings: What causes them among family caregivers. *Journal of Gerontology, 47,* S165-S172.

Pillemer, K., & Wolf, R. S. (1991, November). *Helping elderly victims: Results from the evaluation of four elder abuse model projects.* Paper presented at the annual meeting of the Gerontological Society of America, San Francisco.

Rabin, D. L., & Stockton, P. (1987). *Long-term care for the elderly: A factbook.* New York: Oxford.

Scoggin, F., Beall, C., Bynum, J., Stephens, G., Grote, N. P., Baumhover, L. A., & Bolland, J. M. (1989). Training for abusive caregivers: An unconventional approach to an intervention dilemma. *Journal of Elder Abuse and Neglect, 1*(4), 73-86.

Shanas, E. (1979). The family as a social support system in old age. *Gerontologist, 19,* 169-174.

Steinmetz, S. K. (1988). *Duty bound: Elder abuse and family care.* Newbury Park: CA: Sage.

Wolf, R. S., & Pillemer, K. (1989). *Helping elderly victims: The reality of elder abuse.* New York: Columbia.

Wolf, R. S., Strugnell, C. P., & Godkin, M. A. (1982). *Preliminary findings from three model projects on elder abuse.* Worcester: University of Massachusetts Medical Center, University Center on Aging.

PART IV

Issues in Social Intervention

This final section turns to controversies concerning social intervention: What should the public *do* about this violence? The three debates in Part IV all agree on an underlying plight: Although we do not know with certainty what "works," social intervention cannot wait until we settle these debates. Violence can and does have devastating consequences, so, in the face of uncertainty, we must proceed.

This section contains three debates about social interventions; two of these controversies concern doing something about violence against children. The first is about policies and procedures for reporting suspected child abuse and neglect to child protective agencies: Are current reporting laws and procedures effective, efficient, and fair? Douglas Besharov contends there are "twin" reporting problems: Too many deserving cases escape detection, but too many undeserving cases are nonetheless brought into the system. In contrast, David Finkelhor argues that our current laws and procedures result in too few critical cases reaching the attention of authorities. The second debate is about doing something to stop child sexual abuse. Although child sexual abuse prevention programs come in many forms, the controversy here centers primarily on sex abuse education programs for young children: Is such education effective and appropriate? Carol Plummer argues that although these education programs should not be the only effort to stop sexual abuse, they are appropriate, and she believes a claim about their effectiveness can be made. In their opposing chapter, N. Dickon Reppucci and Jeffrey Haugaard maintain there is *no* evidence that such programs are effective; further, they argue that such programs might be inappropriate. The third debate shifts attention to efforts to do something about wife abuse: Is it good public policy to encourage or even mandate that police arrest wife abusers? Richard Berk argues that although arrest is "no better" than other police interventions, it is "no worse," and hence mandating arrest is good public policy. In their opposing chapter, Eve Buzawa and Carl Buzawa argue that arrest is "no panacea" at best and a harmful policy at worst.

These final chapters offer a vivid illustration of the difficulties in evaluating the evidence supporting differing viewpoints. Some of the controversies involve disagreements about what constitutes evidence. For example, in the debate about whether or not a pro-arrest policy is desirable, Berk relies on what he terms "scientific evidence," whereas Buzawa and Buzawa explicitly challenge the assumption that "the complexity of human behavior is easily amenable to accurate measurement." The issue of what constitutes evidence also is apparent in the debate about the desirability and effectiveness of educating children to avoid sexual abuse. Plummer argues that scientific evidence about program effectiveness is all but impossible to obtain, but that available evidence, although sketchy, does indicate such effectiveness. Reppucci and Haugaard come to a different conclusion: They maintain that scientific evidence is obtainable and that the available evidence does not support a claim that programs are effective. Most clearly, these authors have differing visions of what does and what does not constitute evidence to support a position. These chapters also illustrate how there can be differences in interpretation even when spokespersons do agree on what constitutes evidence. What is and what is not "too high" a rate of unsubstantiated cases of child abuse? What numbers do and what numbers do not indicate the "efficiency" of the child abuse reporting system? In this instance, Finkelhor and Besharov rely on the same statistics, yet they have different interpretations of their meaning. These chapters therefore share with others in this volume disagreements about how to gather and interpret evidence.

The controversies addressed in this section also illustrate how, regardless of disagreements, spokespersons might well be working toward the same goal. For example, when controversies are about interventions for child victims, concern is with the well-being of children. Hence Besharov is troubled by the problem he sees of the overreporting of suspected cases of child abuse because inappropriate reporting "endangers abused children": He asserts that "children in real danger are getting lost in the press of inappropriate cases." Finkelhor's opposing argument that we need more reporting rather than less is nonetheless made to achieve the same end—the protection of children. He believes we need more reporting because "large numbers of seriously abused and neglected children are still not coming to the attention of child protective authorities." In the same way, Plummer supports child sexual abuse educational programs because they can help "make the world safer for children." Reppucci and Haugaard are not so certain and call for more research on effectiveness because "our children deserve no less." This similarity in goals despite disagreement holds when attention is on interventions designed to address wife abuse. Proponents on both sides of the controversy share the goal of effective police intervention. Berk argues that, on the average, it makes sense to arrest wife abusers because "we can do no better"; Buzawa and Buzawa believe that "victim support and offender rehabilitation" programs offer "far greater potential" than offender punishment. So, regardless of their disagreements, these authors all want to do something to stop family violence.

Although these authors might share general goals of intervention, they certainly do not share ideas about how to accomplish them. As with other controversies, each of these spokespersons sees negative consequences of supporting the "other side." Hence Besharov maintains that Finkelhor's plan to increase reporting is "unrealistic" and actually "harmful to children," whereas Finkelhor argues that Besharov's attention to reducing inappropriate cases disguises an underlying attitude that stopping child abuse is not worth the inefficiency and intrusions into personal life it might entail. Likewise, Reppucci and Haugaard believe that child sexual abuse education programs "may actually retard the development of other programs . . . that might be more effective." Plummer, on the other hand, believes that Reppucci and Haugaard's calls for "more research" are merely a disguise for attempts to "dismantle prevention as a force in ending sexual abuse." Finally, Buzawa and Buzawa argue that the pro-arrest policies supported by Berk require money and have led to a "tragic diversion of funds from rehabilitation programs and shelters," whereas Berk maintains that emphasis on rehabilitation is misguided because there is "not a shred of scientific evidence that we know how to rehabilitate violent offenders effectively." Basic agreements that something should be done can melt into controversies about *what* should be done and *how* it should be done.

Although the controversies discussed in this section have much in common with others in this volume, debates about social interventions differ from others in two ways. First, unlike some controversies for which "sides" were chosen long ago and where the evidence supporting the perspectives can now be quite dated, debates about social interventions tend to be more dynamic. Some of this fluidity comes from the fact that we know even less about what to do to stop violence than we know about its meaning or its causes—controversies are fueled when so little is known. Disagreements over social interventions are dynamic also because what we know constantly changes.

Given our lack of knowledge about "what works," new social interventions often are implemented primarily on the basis of good intentions and high hopes. Because new policies, procedures, and programs rarely work as well in practice as they do in theory, practical experiences with new procedures often raise new questions that lead to new research and possibly to new interpretations. Hence, as noted by Buzawa and Buzawa, Berk's earlier work was far more strident in arguing that pro-arrest was always good public policy; Berk's position here is informed by new evidence. Likewise, Plummer repeatedly mentions how child sexual abuse prevention programs have changed in response to practical experience and research findings. What such programs were a few years ago might not be what they are now. Although such changes mean that evaluation of viewpoints and evidence is—and should be—an ongoing process, the rapidity of change in knowledge is not always reflected by such speedy changes in public perceptions or social policies. So, as Plummer notes, public perceptions of the content of child sexual abuse programs do not reflect how such programs have changed; as Buzawa and Buzawa note, the now common policy of mandating arrest of wife abusers is based only on the earliest claims that arrest always works best.

These chapters differ from others in this volume in a second way: Because the topic here is social *intervention*, each directly illustrates how efforts to do something about family violence involve balancing the rights of individuals, families, and the public in general. As such, and more so than with other controversies, these particular debates raise a host of distinctly ethical questions. For example, in the controversy over whether or not arresting wife abusers should be simple social policy, the trade-off is between public responsibility to "do something" and individual rights and desires. Buzawa and Buzawa maintain that good policy must be "based on a compassionate awareness of victim needs and preferences." They are attempting to maximize the rights of individuals, but Berk argues that policy, by definition, can be oriented only to the "typical" case. According to Berk, any difference between individual characteristics or needs and the "typical" case served by public policy is merely an "unfortunate fact." This balancing of rights also is obvious in the debate between Finkelhor and Besharov on child abuse reporting. Here the question is about balancing the rights of families and the rights of children in families. Besharov argues that even the current number of unsubstantiated cases is too high, because investigations are "inherently a breach of parental and family privacy." Finkelhor, conversely, believes that "serious intrusion into the privacy and freedom of individuals" is morally justifiable because increased reporting would lead to more truly needy cases receiving attention.

Problems of balancing individual and family rights against the very real needs of victims and the need for social change are even more perplexing when intrusive policies in practice primarily serve to reduce the privacy and rights of already stigmatized portions of the population. As Richard Gelles noted in previous chapters, service providers such as physicians, social workers, and police tend to diagnose a pathology such as family violence on the basis of characteristics having little to do with behaviors and everything to do with class and race. Buzawa and Buzawa make the same point in this section: Although violence occurs across economic classes and races, it is primarily the urban poor who come to police attention. In brief, social interventions do not affect all members of society in the same way.

Within the condition that these debates about social interventions are constantly changing, within the condition that we know painfully little about what works, readers once again are asked to judge the value of these opposing viewpoints. Because money for intervention is limited, we must choose which interventions to develop, support, fund, and implement. And that is the dilemma: Regardless of our intentions, to promote one method of intervention is to discourage attention to other things we might be doing. The chapters in this section raise another perplexing problem: Doing something to stop violence often involves trade-offs in balancing the rights of the public, individuals, and families. There are many things we *could* do to stop violence, but what *should* we do?

CHAPTER **16**

Overreporting and Underreporting Are Twin Problems

Douglas J. Besharov

Child protective agencies are plagued simultaneously by the twin problems of under- and overreporting of child abuse and neglect. On one hand, many abused and neglected children go unreported because they are afraid to come forward on their own or they are overlooked by informed professionals. The price is great: Failure to report exposes children to serious injury and even death. On the other hand, a large proportion of reports are dismissed after investigations find insufficient evidence upon which to proceed. These cases, variously called "unfounded," "unsubstantiated," or "not indicated," divert resources from already understaffed agencies, thus limiting their ability to protect children in real danger. In addition, such reports trigger what may be deeply traumatic experiences for all members of the families involved.

These two problems are linked and must be addressed together before real progress can be made in combating child abuse and neglect. In this chapter, I argue that, to reduce both problems, public child protective agencies should take two parallel steps: They should enhance the public and professional education they provide, and they should upgrade their ability to screen inappropriate reports.

The policy framework adopted in this chapter is based on *Child Abuse and Neglect Reporting and Investigation: Policy Guidelines for Decision Making*, a report issued by a national group of 38 child protective professionals from 19 states (Besharov, 1988, chap. 13). Meeting for three days in 1987 at Airlie House in Warrenton, Virginia, under the auspices of the American Bar Association's National Legal Resource Center for Child Advocacy and Protection in association with the American Public Welfare Association (APWA) and the American

Enterprise Institute, the "Airlie House group," as it has come to be called, developed policy guidelines for reporting and investigative decisions. (I was the "rapporteur" for the effort.)

Past Progress

Reporting begins the process of protection. Adults who are attacked or otherwise wronged can go to the authorities for protection and redress of their grievances. But the victims of child abuse and neglect are usually too young or too frightened to obtain protection for themselves; they can be protected only if concerned individuals recognize the danger and report to the proper authorities. Thus all states now have child abuse reporting laws. Initially, reporting laws mandated only that physicians report "serious physical injuries" or "nonaccidental injuries." In the ensuing years, however, these laws were expanded so that almost all states now require any form of suspected child maltreatment to be reported, including physical abuse, sexual abuse and exploitation, physical neglect, and emotional maltreatment.

The categories of persons required to report have also been broadened. All states now mandate reports from a wide array of professionals—including physicians, nurses, dentists, mental health professionals, social workers, teachers (and other school officials), child-care workers, and law enforcement personnel. About 20 states require *all* citizens to report, regardless of their professional status or relationship to the child. All states *allow* any person to report.

These reporting laws, and associated public awareness campaigns, have been strikingly effective. In 1963, about 150,000 children came to the attention of public authorities because of suspected abuse or neglect (U.S. Children's Bureau, 1966, p. 13). By 1976, an estimated 669,000 children were reported annually. In 1987, almost 2.2 million children were reported, more than 14 times the number reported in 1963 (data for 1987 are from Robin Alsop, American Association for Protecting Children, personal communication, July 7, 1989; data for 1986 are from John Fluke, American Association for Protecting Children, a division of the American Humane Association, personal communication, July 8, 1988; see also American Association for Protecting Children, 1987, p. 1). (See Table 16.1.)

Many people ask whether this vastly increased reporting signals a rise in the incidence of child maltreatment. Although some observers believe that deteriorating economic and social conditions have contributed to a rise in the level of abuse and neglect, it is impossible to tell for sure. So many maltreated children previously went unreported that

TABLE 16.1 Child Abuse and Neglect Reporting, 1976-1987

Year	Number of Children Reported
1976	669,000
1977	838,000
1978	836,000
1979	988,000
1980	1,154,000
1981	1,225,000
1982	1,262,000
1983	1,477,000
1984	1,727,000
1985	1,928,000
1986	2,100,000
1987	2,178,000

NOTE: These statistics are estimates based on information supplied by the states to the American Humane Association. They include "unfounded" reports, which now make up an estimated 55-65% of all reports.

earlier reporting statistics do not provide a reliable baseline against which to make comparisons. One thing is clear, however; the great bulk of reports now received by child protective agencies would not be made but for the passage of mandatory reporting laws and the media campaigns that accompanied them.

Although child protective programs still have major problems, the results of this 20-year effort to upgrade child protective programs have been unquestionably impressive. All states now have specialized child protective agencies to receive and investigate reports, and treatment services for maltreated children and their parents have been expanded substantially.

As a result, many thousands of children have been saved from death and serious injury. The best estimate is that over the past 20 years, child abuse and neglect deaths have fallen from more than 3,000 a year—and perhaps as many as 5,000—to about 1,100 a year (Sedlak, 1989, p. 2).[1] I do not mean to minimize the remaining problem; even at this level, maltreatment is the sixth largest cause of death for children under 14.[2]

Unreported Cases

Despite this progress, large numbers of obviously endangered children still are not reported to the authorities. Although all statistics concerning what happens in the privacy of the home must be approached with great care, the extent of nonreporting can be appreciated with the help of the National Study of the Incidence and Severity of Child Abuse and Neglect (conducted for the federal government by Westat, Inc.). This study estimated that, in 1986, selected professionals saw about 300,000 physically abused children, another 140,000 sexually abused children, and 700,000 who were neglected or otherwise maltreated (Sedlak, 1987). According to the study, the surveyed professionals reported only about half of these children. (The study methodology did not allow Westat to estimate the number of children seen by nonprofessionals, let alone their reporting rates.)

The surveyed professionals failed to report almost 40% of the sexually abused children they saw. They did not report nearly 30% of fatal or serious physical abuse cases (defined as life-threatening or requiring professional treatment to prevent long-term impairment) or almost 50% of moderate physical abuse cases (defined by bruises, depression, emotional distress, or other symptoms lasting more than 48 hours). The situation was even worse in neglect cases: About 70% of fatal or serious physical neglect cases went unreported, as did about three-quarters of the moderate physical neglect cases. This means that in 1986, at least 50,000 sexually abused children, at least 60,000 children with observable physical injuries severe enough to require hospitalization, and almost 184,000 children with moderate physical injuries were not reported to child welfare agencies (Sedlak, 1989, pp. 3-19).

Failure to report can be fatal to children. A study in Texas revealed that, during one three-year period, more than 40% of the approximately 270 children who died as a result of child maltreatment had not been reported to the authorities—even though they were being seen by public or private agencies, such as hospitals, at the time of death, or had been seen within the past year (Region VI Center on Child Abuse, 1981, p. 26). Sometimes two or three children in the same family are killed before someone makes a report. An analysis of child fatalities in one state described how, "in two of the cases, siblings of the victims had died previously. . . . In one family, two siblings had died mysterious deaths that were undiagnosed. In another family, a twin had died previously of abuse" (confidential material held by author).

Unfounded Reports

At the same time that many seriously abused children go unreported, an equally serious problem further undercuts efforts to prevent child maltreatment: The nation's child protective agencies are being inundated by "unfounded" reports. Although rules, procedures, and even terminology vary—some states use the term *unfounded*, others *unsubstantiated* or *not indicated*—an "unfounded" report, in essence, is one that is dismissed after an investigation finds insufficient evidence upon which to proceed.

A few advocates, in a misguided effort to shield child protective programs from criticism, have sought to quarrel with estimates that I and others have made that the national unfounded rate is between 60% and 65% (Finkelhor, 1990, pp. 22-29). They have grasped at various inconsistencies in the data collected by different organizations to claim either that the problem is not so bad or that it has always been this bad—take your choice. To help settle this dispute, the American Public Welfare Association conducted a special survey of child welfare agencies in 1989. The APWA researchers found that, between fiscal year 1986 and fiscal year 1988, the weighted average for the substantiation rates in 31 states declined 6.7%—from 41.8% in fiscal year 1986 to 39% in fiscal year 1988 (American Public Welfare Association, 1990, pp. 17-21). As Table 16.2 indicates, some states do not have substantial problems with unfounded reports—but most do.

The director of the APWA study, Toshio Tatara, explained the sources of some of the discrepancies among the various estimates of unfounded reporting rates:

AAPC [the American Association for the Protection of Children] (which uses the same basic formula as the one used in this report) suggests that the average substantiation rate for child abuse and neglect has been, almost consistently, about 40 to 42 percent, nationwide. On the other hand, the recent study of national incidence and prevalence of child abuse and neglect conducted by Westat found that the nation's child abuse and neglect substantiation rate is much higher (i.e., 53 percent in 1986). However, it is believed that the difference between these two rates can be explained by three important facts. First, Westat used the "count of reports accepted for investigation" as the "denominator" to generate the rates. Because the "count of reports accepted for investigation" is much smaller than the "number of reports received," the value generated from this formula is much larger than one that is obtained through the use of AAPC's formula. Second, the data that Westat analyzed were "unduplicated" counts of reports. On the other hand, AAPC used the "counts of reports" that were provided by the states, and these counts are generally "duplicated" and are larger than "unduplicated" counts in numbers. Third, Westat also counted as substantiated those reports which it labelled as "indicated." But these "indicated" cases were, in fact, only cases whose investigations were still pending. The actual percentage of

TABLE 16.2 Child Abuse/Neglect Substantiation Rates in 31 States

States	FY 1986	FY 1987	FY 1988
Alaska	0.154	0.179	0.204
Arizona	0.268	0.262	0.235
Arkansas	0.340	0.360	0.371
Colorado	0.417	0.416	0.400
Delaware	0.500	0.496	0.450
District of Columbia	0.350	0.285	0.322
Florida	0.367	0.354	0.355
Georgia	0.528	0.530	0.474
Hawaii	0.563	0.528	0.567
Illinois	0.485	0.427	0.434
Iowa	0.296	0.294	0.295
Kentucky	0.475	0.479	0.459
Maryland	0.396	0.396	0.395
Massachusetts	0.371	0.333	0.309
Mississippi	0.492	0.523	0.488
Montana	0.531	0.674	0.772
Nebraska[a]	0.588	0.558	0.542
Nevada	0.505	0.505	0.479
New Jersey	0.349	0.357	0.360
New York	0.344	0.358	0.322
North Carolina	0.360	0.353	0.340
Oregon	0.349	0.351	0.344
Pennsylvania	0.345	0.355	0.355
Rhode Island	0.461	0.471	0.462
South Carolina	0.286	0.267	0.276
South Dakota	0.456	0.429	0.407
Texas	0.536	0.529	0.430
Utah	0.281	0.281	0.436
Vermont	0.571	0.587	0.543
Virginia	0.242	0.231	0.226
Wisconsin	0.361	0.379	0.371
Mean average of rates:	0.405	0.405	0.401
Weighted average using raw state data	0.418	0.414	0.390

SOURCE: American Public Welfare Association (1990).

a. The count of "investigations" was used as the denominator for this state. In addition, the figures of some states were adjusted, as appropriate.

"founded" cases was 26 percent; 43 percent were "unfounded"; and 26 percent were still pending. (American Public Welfare Association, 1990, p. 20)

These data from APWA suggest that the unfounded rate is even higher than my estimate of 65%, at least in the bigger states.

The experience of New York State indicates what these statistics mean in practice. Between 1979 and 1983, as the number of reports received by the state's Department of Social Services increased by about 50% (from 51,836 to 74,120), the proportion of substantiated reports fell about 16% (from 42.8% to 35.8%). In fact, the unduplicated number of substantiated cases—a number of children were reported more than once—actually fell by about 100, from 17,633 to 17,552. Thus almost 23,000 additional families were investigated, whereas fewer children received child protective help (Root, 1984).

In Chapter 17 of this volume, David Finkelhor also claims that the substantiation rate is increasing. In support of this proposition, he cites the National Study of the Incidence and Severity of Child Abuse and Neglect to the effect that the substantiation rate rose from 43% in 1980 to 53% in 1986. But, as Tatara explains above: In 1986, "Westat also counted as substantiated those reports which it labelled as 'indicated.' But these 'indicated' cases were, in fact, only cases whose investigations were still pending. The actual percentage of 'founded' cases was 26 percent; 43 percent were 'unfounded'; and 26 percent were still pending."

Few unfounded reports are made maliciously. Studies of sexual abuse reports, for example, suggest that, at most, 4-10% are knowingly false (Berliner, 1988; Jones & McGraw, 1987; Pearson & Thoennes, 1988, pp. 91, 93).[3] Instead, many unfounded reports involve situations in which the person reporting, in a well-intentioned effort to protect a child, overreacts to a vague and often misleading possibility that the child may be maltreated. Others involve situations of poor child care that, though of legitimate concern, simply do not amount to child abuse or neglect. In fact, a substantial proportion of unfounded cases are referred to other agencies for the latter to provide needed services to the family.

Moreover, an unfounded report does not necessarily mean that the child was not actually abused or neglected. Evidence of child maltreatment is hard to obtain and may not be uncovered when agencies lack the time and resources to complete a thorough investigation or when inaccurate information is given to the investigator. Other cases are labeled "unfounded" when no services are available to help the family. And some cases must be closed because the child or family cannot be located. A certain proportion of unfounded reports, therefore, is an inherent—and legitimate—aspect of reporting suspected child maltreatment and is necessary to ensure adequate child protection. Hundreds of thousands of strangers report their suspicions; they cannot all be right.

Unfounded rates of the current magnitude, however, go beyond anything reasonably needed. The determination that a report is unfounded can be made only after an unavoidably traumatic investigation that is, inherently, a breach of parental and family privacy. To determine whether a particular child is in danger, caseworkers must inquire into the most intimate personal and family matters. Often, it is necessary to question friends, relatives, and neighbors, as well as schoolteachers, day-care personnel, doctors, clergy, and others who know the family.

Richard Wexler (1985), when he was a reporter in Rochester, New York, told what happened to Kathy and Alan Heath (not their real names):

> Three times in as many years, someone—they suspect an "unstable" neighbor—has called in anonymous accusations of child abuse against them. All three times, those reports were determined to be "unfounded," but only after painful investigations by workers. . . . The first time the family was accused, Mrs. Heath says, the worker "spent almost two hours in my house going over the allegations over and over again. . . . She went through everything from a strap to an iron, to everything that could cause bruises, asking me if I did those things. [After she left] I sat on the floor and cried my eyes out. I couldn't believe that anybody could do that to me." Two more such investigations followed.
>
> The Heaths say that even after they were "proven innocent" three times, the county did nothing to help them restore their reputation among friends and neighbors who had been told, as potential "witnesses," that the Heaths were suspected of child abuse. (pp. 19, 20-22)

Laws against child abuse are an implicit recognition that family privacy must give way to the need to protect helpless children. But in seeking to protect children, it is all too easy to ignore the legitimate rights of parents. Each year, about 700,000 families are put through investigations of unfounded reports. This is a massive and unjustified violation of parental rights.

In response, a national group of parents and professionals formed to represent those falsely accused of abusing their children. Calling itself VOCAL, for Victims of Child Abuse Laws, the group has thousands of members in chapters across the country. In Minnesota, VOCAL members collected 2,000 signatures on a petition asking the governor to remove Scott County Prosecutor Kathleen Morris from office because of her alleged misconduct in bringing charges, subsequently dismissed, against 24 adults in Jordan, Minnesota. In Arizona, VOCAL members were able to sidetrack temporarily a $5.4 million budget supplement that would have added 77 investigators to local child protective agencies.

Inappropriate Reporting
Endangers Abused Children

Besides being unfair to the children and parents involved, such high rates of unfounded reports endanger children who really are abused. For fear of missing even one abused child, workers perform extensive investigations of vague and apparently unsupported reports. Even when a home visit of an anonymous report turns up no evidence of maltreatment, workers usually interview neighbors, schoolteachers, and day-care personnel to make sure that the child is not abused. And, as illustrated by what happened to the Heaths, even repeated anonymous and unfounded reports do not prevent further investigation.

All this takes time. As a result, children in real danger are getting lost in the press of inappropriate cases. Forced to allocate a substantial portion of their limited resources to unfounded reports, child protective agencies are less able to respond promptly and effectively when children are in serious danger. Some reports are left uninvestigated for a week or even two weeks after they are received. Investigations often miss key facts as workers rush to clear cases, and dangerous home situations receive inadequate supervision as workers ignore pending cases to investigate the new reports that arrive daily on their desks. Decision making also suffers. With so many cases of insubstantial or unproven risk to children, caseworkers are desensitized to the obvious warning signals of immediate and serious danger.

These nationwide conditions help explain why 25-50% of child abuse deaths involve children previously known to the authorities (Besharov, 1988, chap. 9). Tens of thousands of other children suffer serious injuries short of death while under child protective agency supervision. In one Iowa case, for example, the noncustodial father reported to the local department of social services that his 34-month-old daughter had bruises on her buttocks; he also told the agency that he believed that the bruises were caused by the mother's live-in boyfriend. The agency investigated and substantiated the abuse. (The boyfriend was not interviewed, however.) At an agency staff meeting the next day (two days after the initial report), a decision was made against removing the child from the mother's custody, and, instead, to make follow-up visits coupled with day care, counseling, and other appropriate services. *But no follow-up visit was made.* Eight days later, the child was hospitalized in a comatose state, with bruises, both old and new, over most of her body. The child died after three days of unsuccessful treatment. The boyfriend was convicted of second-degree murder. The father's lawsuit against the agency for its negligent handling of his report was settled for $82,500.[4]

Ironically, by weakening the system's ability to respond, unfounded reports actually discourage appropriate ones. The sad fact is that many responsible individuals are not reporting endangered children because they feel that the system's response will be so weak that reporting will do no good or possibly even make things worse. In 1984, a study of the impediments to reporting conducted by Jose Alfaro, then coordinator of the New York City Mayor's Task Force on Child Abuse and Neglect, concluded, "Professionals who emphasize their professional judgment have experienced problems in dealing with the child protective agency, and are more likely to doubt the efficacy of protective service intervention and are more likely not to report in some situations, especially when they believe they can do a better job helping the family" (p. 66).

Enhanced Public
and Professional Education

Few people fail to report because they don't care about an endangered child. Instead, they may be unaware of the danger the child faces or of the protective procedures that are available. A study of nonreporting among teachers, for example, blamed their "lack of knowledge for detecting symptoms of child abuse and neglect" (Levin, 1983, p. 14). Likewise, few inappropriate or unfounded reports are deliberately false statements. Most involve an honest desire to protect children coupled with confusion about what conditions are reportable.

Thus the best way to encourage more complete and more appropriate reporting is through increased public and professional understanding. Recognizing this, almost half of the states have specific statutes mandating professional training and public awareness efforts (see, for example, State of Florida, 1985). Of course, legislation is not required for a state to provide public and professional education, and most states lacking specific statutes offer such training.

These efforts need much better focus, however. Confusion about reporting is largely caused by the vagueness of reporting laws, aggravated by the failure of child protective agencies to provide realistic guidance about deciding to report. As the Airlie House group concluded, "Better public and professional materials are needed to obtain more appropriate reporting" (Besharov, 1988, p. 346). The group specifically recommended that "educational materials and programs should: (1) clarify the legal definitions of child abuse and neglect, (2) give general descriptions of reportable situations (including specific examples), and (3) explain what to expect when a report is made. Brochures and other materials for laypersons, including public service announcements, should give specific information about what to report—and what not to report" (p. 346).

To fulfill this recommendation, educational materials must explain, clearly and with practical examples, the legal concept of "reasonable cause to suspect" child maltreatment. Unfortunately, the few attempts to do so have foundered on the fear that an overstrict definition will leave some children unprotected. That an overly broad definition might do the same is often overlooked.

"Reasonable Suspicions"

Child maltreatment usually occurs in the privacy of the home. Unless the child is old enough—and not too frightened—to speak out, or unless a family member steps forward, it can be impossible to know what really happened. Thus the decision to report is often based on incomplete and potentially misleading information—as important facts are concealed or go undiscovered.

This is why reporting laws do not require potential reporters to be sure that a child is being abused or neglected or to have absolute proof of maltreatment. In all states, reports are to be made when there is "reasonable cause to suspect" or "reasonable cause to believe" that a child is abused or neglected.[5] Reporters do not have to prove, on the phone, that a child has been abused or neglected. They need only show a reasonable basis for their suspicions. A formal legal opinion from Iowa's attorney general explains the rationale for this broader approach to reporting: "We will never know if a report of child abuse is valid or not until the appropriate investigation is made" (Iowa Attorney General, 1978; cited in *Family Law Reporter*, 1978, vol. 5, p. 2015).

Too often, however, this practical wisdom is taken to unreasonable lengths. Potential reporters are frequently told to "take no chances" and to report any child for whom they have the slightest concern. There is a recent tendency to tell people to report children whose behavior suggests that they may have been abused—even in the absence of any other evidence of maltreatment. These "behavioral indicators" include, for example, a child's being unusually withdrawn or shy as well as a child's being unusually friendly toward strangers. However, only a small minority of children who exhibit such behaviors have actually been maltreated. Twenty years ago, when professionals were construing their reporting obligations narrowly to avoid taking action to protect endangered children, this approach may have been needed. Now, however, all it does is ensure that child abuse telephone hot lines will be flooded with inappropriate and unfounded reports.

The legal injunction to report suspected maltreatment is not an open-ended invitation to call in the slightest suspicion or "gut feeling." A vague, amorphous, or unarticulable concern over a child's welfare is not a sufficient reason to report. Sufficient objective evidence of possible abuse or neglect must exist to justify a report. Such evidence may be either "direct"—firsthand accounts or observations of seriously harmful parental behavior—or "circumstantial"—concrete facts, such as the child's physical condition, suggesting that the child has been abused or neglected. Educational materials for public and professional audiences as well as materials for agency staff should use such specific examples to illustrate when there may be evidence of suspected child abuse or neglect.

Upgraded Screening Capacity

No matter how well *reasonable cause to suspect* is defined and incorporated into public and professional education, there will always be a tendency for persons to report cases that should not be investigated. In fact, we want people to err on the side of caution in deciding whether to call child protective agencies. But what should be phoned in to an agency is not necessarily what should be investigated. Thus educational efforts, if they are going to work, must be backed up with clear—and firm—intake policies.

Many hot lines, however, accept reports even when the caller cannot give a reason for suspecting that the child's condition is a result of the parent's behavior. I observed one hot-line worker accept a report involving a 17-year-old boy who was found in a drunken stupor. When asked whether there was reason to suspect the parents were in any way responsible for the child's condition, the caller said no. I don't dispute that the boy, and perhaps his family, might benefit from counseling, but that hardly justifies the initiation of an involuntary child protective investigation.

Hot-line workers receive calls from tens of thousands of strangers; they must screen reports. Investigating all reports, regardless of their validity, would immobilize agencies, violate family rights, and invite lawsuits. As the Airlie House experts noted, "Agencies that carefully screen calls have lower rates of unsubstantiated reports and expend fewer resources investigating inappropriate calls" (Besharov, 1988, p. 347).

Until recently, most states did not have formal policies and procedures for determining whether to accept a call for investigation. For example, the American Humane Association (1983) found that in 1982 only a little more than half the states allowed their hot-line workers to reject reports, and that even those that did usually limited screening to cases that were "clearly" inappropriate. Many are now developing general intake policies, and, as Table 16.3 illustrates, it is possible to state them with some precision.

The difficulty comes in implementation. First, there are always political pressures to accept reports from influential agencies or individuals concerned about a child's welfare or eager to obtain social services for a family. There is also the very real fear that a report that should be accepted will be rejected.

Hardest to assess are reports that appear to be falsely—and maliciously—made by an estranged spouse, by quarrelsome relatives, by feuding neighbors, or even by an angry or distressed child. As a general rule, unless there are clear and convincing grounds for concluding that the report is being made in bad faith, any report that falls within the agency's legal mandate must be investigated. Reports from questionable sources are not necessarily invalid; many anonymous reports are substantiated following an investigation.

Even a history of past unsubstantiated reports is not a sufficient basis, on its own, for automatically rejecting a report. There may be a legitimate explanation why previous investigations did not substantiate the reporter's claims. Therefore, a subsequent report containing enough facts to bring the case within statutory definitions must be investigated—unless there is clear and convincing evidence of its malicious or untrue nature. The key, in such situations, is to insist that the person reporting provide the specific information that aroused the suspicion. If the agency determines that the report was made maliciously, consideration should be given to referring the case for criminal prosecution or to notifying the parents so that they can take appropriate action.

Many reports that do not amount to child abuse or child neglect nonetheless involve serious individual and family problems. (That such situations have not resulted in actual child maltreatment does not reduce the family's need for assistance.) In such cases, child protective

TABLE 16.3 Reports That Should Be Rejected

■ Reports in which the allegations clearly fall outside the agency's definitions of *child abuse* and *child neglect*, as established by state law (prime examples include children beyond the specified age, alleged perpetrators falling outside the legal definition, and family problems not amounting to child maltreatment).

■ Reports in which the caller can give no credible reason for suspecting that the child has been abused or neglected. (Although actual proof of the maltreatment is not required, some evidence is.)

■ Reports whose unfounded or malicious nature is established by specific evidence. (Anonymous reports, reports from estranged spouses, and even previous unfounded reports from the same source should not be rejected automatically, but need to be evaluated carefully.)

■ Reports in which insufficient information is given to identify or locate the child. (This is not technically a rejection; moreover, the information may be kept for later use, should a subsequent report be made about the same child.)

SOURCE: Besharov (1985, p. 60).

NOTE: In questionable circumstances, the agency should recontact the caller before deciding to reject a report. When appropriate, rejected reports should be referred to other agencies that can provide services needed by the family.

service (CPS) intake workers should be equipped to refer callers to other, more appropriate, social service agencies. All hot lines and agencies should possess this capability. Therefore, before making a referral, CPS intake staff should have some assurance that these other agencies will provide the necessary services. Unfortunately, such referrals frequently are made without notifying the other agencies of the practice and without checking to make sure that they can help the persons referred.

The keys to successful implementation of a rigorous intake policy are the quality of intake staff and the degree of support they receive from agency administrators when exercising their professional judgment in screening cases. In many places, unfortunately, reporting hot lines are staffed by clerical personnel who record basic information about situations and assign cases for subsequent investigation by caseworkers. However, the kind of sophisticated intake decision making described above cannot be performed by clerks, nor by untrained caseworkers.

Intake staff should be experienced and highly trained personnel with the ability to understand complex situations quickly and the authority to make decisions. They should be able to advise potential reporters about the law and child protective procedures generally; to assist in diagnosis and evaluation; to consult about the necessity of photographs, X rays, and protective custody; to help reporters deal with distressed or violent parents; to refer inappropriate reports to other agencies better suited to deal with a family's problems; and to provide information and assistance to parents seeking help on their own.

We need to do a much better job at identifying suspected child abuse. Children are dying because they are not being reported to the authorities. At the same time, we need to reduce inappropriate reporting. Child protective agencies do not have the resources to investigate an unlimited number of reports—and they never will.

To call for more careful reporting of child abuse is not to be coldly indifferent to the plight of endangered children. Rather, it is to be realistic about the limits of our ability to operate child protective systems and to recognize that inappropriate reporting is also harmful to children. If child protective agencies are to function effectively, we must address both these problems. The challenge is to strike the proper balance. The effort will be politically controversial and technically difficult, but we owe it to the children to try.

Notes

1. Compare Sedlak's estimate of 1,100 with that found in National Committee for Prevention of Child Abuse (n.d.).
2. This figure is based on comparison data from the U.S. Department of Health and Human Services (1980).
3. Jones and McGraw (1987, Table 2) estimate that 8% of sexual abuse reports are falsely made—2% by children and 6% by adults.
4. See *Buege v. Iowa* (1980); see also Jury Research, Inc. (1982), and *State v. Hilleshein* (1981), a criminal prosecution in the same case.
5. Although there is a small technical difference between the two phrases, most legal authorities have concluded that they are fundamentally equivalent and have the same impact on reporting decisions. See, for example, Illinois Attorney General (1977) and Massachusetts Attorney General (1975). Because *reasonable cause to suspect* is the more common phraseology, it is adopted in this chapter.

References

Alfaro, J. (1984). *Impediments to mandated reporting of suspected child abuse and neglect in New York City.* New York: Mayor's Task Force on Child Abuse and Neglect.
American Association for Protecting Children. (1987). *Highlights of official child abuse and neglect reports: 1985.* Denver: American Humane Association.
American Humane Association. (1983). National substantiation and screening practices. *National Child Protective Services Newsletter, 7, 3,* 10.

American Public Welfare Association. (1990). *Children of substance abusing/alcoholic parents referred to the public child welfare system: Summaries of key statistical data obtained from states.* Washington, DC: Author.

Berliner, L. (1988). Deciding whether a child has been sexually abused. In B. Nicholson (Ed.), *Sexual abuse allegations in custody and visitation cases* (pp. 48-69). Washington, DC: American Bar Association.

Besharov, D. J. (1985). *The vulnerable social worker: Liability for serving children and families.* Washington, DC: National Association of Social Workers.

Besharov, D. J. (Ed.). (1988). *Protecting children from abuse and neglect: Policy and practice.* Springfield, IL: Charles C Thomas.

Buege v. Iowa, No. 20521 (Allamakee, Iowa, July 30, 1980).

Finkelhor, D. (1990). Is child abuse overreported? *Public Welfare, 48,* 23-29.

Illinois Attorney General. (1977, October 6). Opinion No. S-1298.

Iowa Attorney General. (1978, September 28). Opinion No. 78-9-12.

Jones, D., & McGraw, J. M. (1987). Reliable and fictitious accounts of sexual abuse in children. *Journal of Interpersonal Violence, 2,* 27-45.

Jury Research, Inc. (1982). Case summary (Solon, Ohio, March 3, 1982).

Levin, P. G. (1983). Teachers' perceptions, attitudes, and reporting of child abuse/ neglect. *Child Welfare, 62,* 14-20.

Massachusetts Attorney General. (1975, June 16). Opinion No. 74/75-66.

National Committee for Prevention of Child Abuse. (n.d.). *Child abuse and neglect fatalities: A review of the problem and strategies for reform.* Chicago: Author.

Pearson J., & Thoennes, N. (1988). Difficult dilemma: Responding to sexual abuse allegations in custody and visitation disputes. In D. Besharov (Ed.), *Protecting children from abuse and neglect: Policy and practice* (pp. 91-112). Springfield, IL: Charles C Thomas.

Region VI Resource Center on Child Abuse. (1981). *Child abuse deaths in Texas.* Austin: University of Texas, Graduate School of Social Work.

Root, C. (1984, September 14). [Memorandum to Sandy Berman from Charles Root, New York State Department of Social Services].

Sedlak, A. (1987). *Study of national incidence and prevalence of child abuse and neglect.* Rockville, MD: Westat.

Sedlak, A. (1989). *Supplementary analyses of data on the national incidence of child abuse and neglect.* Rockville, MD: Westat.

State of Florida. (1985). Statutes, Annotated, Section 415.509(2).

State v. Hilleshein, 305 N.W.2d 710 (Iowa 1981).

U.S. Children's Bureau. (1966). *Juvenile court statistics.* Washington, DC: U.S. Department of Health, Education and Welfare.

U.S. Department of Health and Human Services. (1980). *Vital statistics of the United States for 1980: Advance report of final mortality statistics.* Washington, DC: Government Printing Office.

CHAPTER 17

The Main Problem Is Still Underreporting, Not Overreporting

David Finkelhor

No, child abuse is not overreported. The evidence suggests that large numbers of seriously abused and neglected children are still not coming to the attention of child protective authorities. To remedy this, more professionals and members of the public need to be sensitized to recognizing and reporting child abuse. If, in concert with these increased reports, child protective authorities improve their investigatory skills and expand their treatment services, we may get closer to identifying and helping all the children at risk.

When the mandatory reporting system was first established in the United States, few people fully envisioned the results. Between 1976 and 1987, reports of suspected child abuse and neglect rose nationally from an estimated 669,000 to 2,163,000, an average increase of more than 10% per year. Although some see in this trend a contemporary epidemic of abuse, most authorities think that what primarily happened is that many kinds of widespread and serious abuse that went undetected in the past are now being reported because professionals and ordinary citizens have a greater awareness about the problem (Gelles & Straus, 1988; Sedlak, 1991a). A substantial amount of research backs up this idea (Finkelhor, Hotaling, Lewis, & Smith, 1990; Peters, Wyatt, & Finkelhor, 1986; Russell, 1986).

In spite of this dramatic increase in reporting, however, most researchers and clinicians believe that a large quantity of abuse is still not being counted in these statistics. This is also the conclusion of the best national study of child abuse reporting that we have to date—the National Incidence Study (NIS) (Sedlak, 1991a). One of the main functions of the NIS was to look at how much child abuse known to professionals still was not recognized by official state child protective services (CPS) agencies. The NIS researchers established an extensive data collection apparatus to find out about such cases directly from the professionals in the community and compare them to what was known to the official reporting agencies—evaluating these cases according to strict criteria to judge their seriousness. The results show the majority of serious abuse known to professionals was not recognized by state CPS agencies. Fully 65% of all maltreatment and 60% of the most serious cases known to professionals (these were children who had fatal or serious injuries or impairments as a result of abuse and neglect) were still not being recognized by CPS, that is, not getting into the child protection system (Sedlak, 1991b). This included 53% of all the physically abused and 35% of the sexually abused. The NIS shows an enormous reservoir of serious child abuse that CPS is still not fully aware of in spite of increased reporting.

But even these figures underestimate the amount of unreported child abuse and neglect, because the study's statistics are based only on what professionals know. A certain quantity of child abuse does not come to the attention of any professional. Although it is virtually impossible to count something so hidden, most experts believe this quantity is also vast. One way to make a crude guess about its size is to compare the percentage of adults who admit ever having been abused as children with the number of children actually being reported. For example, if 15% of women and 5% of men say they were sexually abused (low estimates based on surveys of adults), this would imply between 300,000 and 400,000 new child victims per year, numbers that are two to three times higher than those currently reported (Finkelhor, 1984; Finkelhor et al., 1990). All of this suggests a major problem of underreporting.

Recently, however, a view has been advanced that the large and increasing number of reports is not necessarily progress toward revealing the full extent of the problem, but rather evidence of an *overreaction* by professionals. In this view the level of current reporting is "unreasonably high," "unwarranted," "demonstrably harmful to the children and families involved" (Besharov, 1988b). The answer in this view is a new policy that would define child abuse more narrowly, apply stringent harm requirements before a report is made, and discourage reports by nonprofessionals.

Although this analysis has challenged policymakers to evaluate current practices, it is nonetheless misguided. *Child abuse is not overreported.* Aggressive reporting is crucial to our ability to identify serious child abuse and is supported by the public. Moreover, the proposed reforms would inevitably result in the weakening of our ability to identify abused children. The myths of the overreporting argument can be broken down into four claims, which I will take up and critique in order:

1. that a large and increasing proportion of what is reported as child abuse is not serious and not really child maltreatment
2. that a large and increasing percentage of child abuse reports are unfounded, an indication of overzealous reporting[1]
3. that when a report is unfounded or not substantiated it involves "an unavoidably traumatic investigation which is, inherently, a breach of parental and family privacy" (Besharov, 1992)
4. that the current level of unfounded cases is patently "unreasonable," and necessitates a radical revision in current practice

Nonserious Reports

One tenet of the "overreporting" argument is that much of what is now being identified, reported, and treated as child abuse consists of "minor situations that simply do not amount to child maltreatment" (Besharov, 1988b, p. 83). According to this argument, in their zeal, child abuse professionals and the public have gone beyond their mandate and now started to search for minor kinds of bad parenting or cases of simple poverty to try to rectify through the child welfare system (Christensen, 1989a).

In an article in the *Wall Street Journal*, Douglas Besharov (1988a) dismissed 80% of all substantiated cases as "excessive corporal punishment, minor physical neglect, educational neglect or emotional maltreatment," saying that they "pose no serious physical danger." Another critic claims that only one in every hundred reports turns out to involve the sort of problem that the public generally thinks of as child abuse (Wexler, 1985).

But these are rhetorical minimizations of the problem that would be rejected by most observers. For example, in the 80% rejected category, the critic would lump all emotional abuse, which can include such things as children locked for weeks or months in their rooms and children threatened with death. It also excludes any physical neglect where no serious physical injury occurs, for example, the mother who abandons her 3-month-old child in an alley or the mother who regularly leaves three unsupervised children under 6 years old for the day in a squalid, rat-infested tenement—as long as these children are rescued before any actual physical injury occurs. It would rule out nine-tenths of all physical abuse victims because they did not suffer injuries severe enough to require professional care; for example, a child who had been shot at by his father, as long as the father missed.

However, one of the major reasons for a child abuse reporting system is to discover abusive situations *before* serious injury occurs. Thus the presence of injury is not the proper criterion of what should be reported. Under such a criterion, the child protective system loses much of its protective function.

Claims such as these, that most substantiated child abuse is "minor," are based on distorted inferences from the National Incidence Study, our most comprehensive study of child abuse to date. In fact, the findings of the study, as indicated above, actually support the conclusion that child abuse is serious and underreported. For example, the type of abuse for which reports and cases have been growing fastest in recent years is sexual abuse. Sexual abuse cases constituted only 7% of all cases in the late 1970s, but by 1986 they constituted almost 16%. According to the National Incidence Study (Sedlak, 1991a), while all known abuse cases were increasing 57% between 1980 and 1986, sexual abuse cases were more than tripling. Sexual abuse is hardly a minor type of abuse whose increased reporting has resulted from an unwarranted expansion in the definition of child abuse. So here is one major increase that is hardly unwarranted.

Nor is it true that an increasing portion of child protection work is monopolized by so-called minor cases. Here again evidence from the NIS data (Sedlak, 1989) is clear. Between 1980 and 1986, the proportion of CPS cases at the lowest level of severity did not increase significantly. In fact, in 1986 only 16% of children known to community agencies whose maltreatment was categorized by the study as "low priority" were investigated by CPS. According to the NIS director, "very little of CPS time and resources are being expended on the low priority, but . . . more than half of the very serious cases of child maltreatment still fail to come to the official attention of CPS" (Sedlak, n.d.).

The study also refuted charges that much child neglect is simply poverty being remedied through the child welfare system. The researchers evaluated all cases in the study to exclude any situation where the family problem was simply lack of resources. A case of neglect required an abdication of caretaker responsibility, not simply a child deprived of necessities (Sedlak, McFarland, & Rust, 1987). Even with this screening, there were an estimated half million cases of neglect in 1986. Of course, poverty certainly is a contributory factor in many such situations, but the implication that such cases need only economic and not child welfare intervention is wrong. The overall portrait one gets from the available data is not of a system that is casting an increasingly large net by diluting the meaning of child abuse. Rather, the picture is of a large reservoir of serious child abuse that families and abusers have managed in past years to hide successfully from detection, and that now is finally being discovered by professionals and community members who have been sensitized to the problem. Many of these serious cases are still, for one reason or another, not getting into or being rejected by the CPS system. The big overload of new cases does indeed make it difficult for CPS to work efficiently. However, to deal with these problems, the system needs to be expanded, not cut back.

A Decreasing Rate of Substantiation?

A second focus of the argument about overreporting concerns the so-called substantiation rate for child abuse reports. Critics argue that the percentage of unsubstantiated cases has been rising—because of overzealous reporting—and poses an intolerable threat to family privacy, not to mention civil liberties. But the critics do not have good evidence. Although some states have seen a decline in the substantiation rate, the national rate (to the extent we can follow it) has not declined. Our best study to date in fact suggests that nationally the rate is *increasing*. And the indications of decreasing rates in some states and localities may be entirely the result of statistical artifacts.

The most rigorous evaluation of the national trend in substantiation rates, at least for a recent time period, comes again from the second National Incidence Study of Child Abuse and Neglect (Sedlak, 1991a). In this study, researchers picked a random sample of counties in 1980 and 1986 and monitored all reports to CPS agencies, using a standardized set of definitions and data collection procedures. This methodology was the best way to control for the inconsistencies and changes in state child abuse counting systems. The NIS actually found an *increase* in the substantiation rate, up from 43% in 1980 to 53% in 1986. Because this is the only data set using completely equivalent definitions and sampling procedures at two points in time, this is the most reliable indicator we have. It contradicts the overreporting thesis.

A variety of other sources have tried to marshal data about trends in reporting rates (see Finkelhor, 1990), but none has been as systematic as the NIS. Some individual states have seen changes, but it is hard to rule out statistical artifacts as the major cause.[2] Some declines in the rate may even be the result of implementation of the kinds of improved screening systems recommended by the critics. So, currently, the most generous evaluation of the critics' argument is that we do not know entirely what is happening to substantiation rates nationally, although perhaps some localities have noticed trends. However, the best evidence points to either no dramatic change or even some increase.

The "Unavoidable" Trauma

There is a great deal of confusion about what is involved when a child welfare agency declares a case "unsubstantiated" or "unfounded." The overreporting argument rests in part on a claim that "unsubstantiated" cases generally involve "unavoidably traumatic investigation[s]" that are, "inherently, a breach of parental and family privacy" and constitute "massive and unjustified violation of parental rights" (Besharov, Chapter 16, this volume)—reasons to rein in the child welfare system and to discourage child abuse reporting. The true situation is unfortunately not clear, but the available evidence does not support this claim.

A first rebuttal of the "unavoidably traumatic" argument is the fact that for many child abuse reports that are classified as "unsubstantiated" the family is never contacted, let alone invaded. According to the first National Incidence Study, in 11% of unsubstantiated cases, no investigation at all was conducted (U.S. Department of Health and Human Services, 1981). A more recent study in 12 counties in five states found that 32% of all reports of maltreatment were "screened out" (unsubstantiated) without any investigation at all, many because no injury was reported or the allegation was vague, some because the event happened too long ago or the perpetrator was not a caretaker, others because the child was no longer at risk (e.g., was living somewhere else), and still others because the family could not be located or had left the CPS jurisdiction (Wells, 1989). So one cannot make the claim that an unfounded report means a family is investigated. It is unfortunate that many people continue to equate an "unsubstantiated" case with a "false allegation" (Christensen, 1989b; Wexler, 1985). In reality, unsubstantiated cases frequently are cases in which, for reasons of time or jurisdiction, no investigation was made at all.

But even when some contact with the family is made, this contact is not necessarily "unavoidably traumatic." According to child protection officials, in the typical unsubstantiated investigation, a worker goes out to visit a family, talks with the parent about the incident, talks with the child about the incident, and, on the basis of the explanation given (say, for a bruise or injury) and the demeanor of the child, decides that the report has no basis. There are, of course, horror stories and terrible miscarriages of the investigatory process, but there is no evidence that these are widespread.

The generally benign quality of child protection investigations is supported by a recent study conducted by researchers at the C. Henry Kempe Center (Fryer, Bross, Krugman, Benson, & Baird, 1990). The center completed a "consumer satisfaction"-type survey on a sample of 176 Iowa families who had been the objects of both substantiated and unsubstantiated child welfare investigations. Among many reassuring findings, 74% of the respondents rated the quality of the services as excellent or good and 72% said the intervention changed their family life for the better; only 11% rated the intervention as poor. Although a low response rate to this mailed survey means the responses are not necessarily representative of all CPS-investigated families, it is nonetheless interesting that satisfaction levels were the same for those with both substantiated and unsubstantiated outcomes. Considering that virtually nobody wants to be the object of an investigation, these levels of satisfaction with CPS investigations are remarkable and belie the characterization of them as "unavoidably traumatic."

An important issue clouded by the argument that investigations are a "breach of . . . *family* privacy" (Besharov, 1988b) is that the family is not the proper unit of analysis. Children and parents have different interests at stake in these matters. What may be *intrusion* for parents may be *rescue* for a child. Even in cases where abuse is not substantiated, the investigation may result in an improvement in conditions for a child by alerting parents to the potential for intervention or by informing parents about the availability of services.

Another problem with the alarmist argument about unsubstantiated cases is that it assumes that the parties involved in all unsubstantiated investigations are innocent and therefore any intrusion is unjust. But this also is not the case. In many unsubstantiated investigations, workers were simply unable to make a determination. Some of these children were being abused and will later be reported again. Accor14ding to one study, approximately 25% of unsubstantiated cases will be reported again within a four-year period (Wells, cited in Eckenrode, 1986).[3]

In other situations, a case is labeled unsubstantiated as part of a negotiated settlement with the child protection authorities in the same way that a criminal conviction may be plea-bargained. In some agencies, if parents admit to the maltreatment and agree to a course of action, workers may declare the case unsubstantiated in return (Eckenrode, 1986). Although child protective investigations should be as unintrusive as possible, one cannot simply judge all the intrusion that occurs in unsubstantiated cases as gross violations of the rights of innocent people.

So the strongest argument that can honestly be made at the present is that the intrusiveness of child abuse investigations is currently unknown and that isolated violative incidents have been reported. (Incidentally, most of the most highly touted complaints about child abuse investigations, the ones cited by spokespersons for the organization Victims of Child Abuse Laws [VOCAL], concern not situations in which a report was unsubstantiated, but situations in which reports were substantiated and CPS initiated actions to remove children from parents that were later found to be inappropriate; see Speigel, 1985.) But empirical data and also readily available information from CPS agencies refute the claim that investigations are "unavoidably traumatic." There is even evidence that some families later have positive feelings about their treatment by child abuse investigators.

Unwarranted Intervention

Aside from the controversies about whether unsubstantiated reports are traumatic and increasing, however, there is no question that they are numerous. Even if the rate is as low as 40% of all reports, we are discussing perhaps more than a million such unconfirmed reports annually. Is this evidence of inefficiency, at least, if not overreporting? Not really. If these numbers are considered from a larger perspective, the child abuse detection process actually seems relatively efficient. Like any other social enterprise, child abuse detection is a fallible process. The question is whether the costs of the failures are somehow disproportional to the social value of the successes.

One of the best and most direct standards against which to compare the child abuse detection system is the criminal justice system. Although there are important differences, there are also many similarities. Both are trying to detect antisocial behavior, both receive reports directly from the public, both deal with acts that are not always clearly defined, both have procedures for differentiating "substantiated" ("guilty") from "unsubstantiated" ("not guilty") cases, both have unpleasant sanctions in store for those whose deviance is substantiated, and involvement in both is considered stigmatizing to some degree for both substantiated and unsubstantiated offenders.

The criminal justice system is not a very efficient system at any level. Take, for example, the number of crime reports to the police that result in arrests. In 1986, only 19% of all crimes reported or known to the police resulted in arrests (Flanagan & Jamieson, 1988). This number has been declining steadily over the past 10 years and is down 33% since 1977. The number of crimes known to police that result in *convictions* is even lower. Of course, this involves many crimes, such as burglaries, in which the police do not have any idea who the criminals might be. Although a lot of police time may go into these investigations, no one is necessarily stigmatized by them.

To look at the efficiency of the most stigmatizing portion of the criminal justice system, we should examine the arrest-to-conviction component. Being arrested but not convicted is somewhat parallel to being reported but not "substantiated" for child abuse. The numbers are revealing. For example, of all persons arrested on rape charges, only 50% are convicted (of rape or any lesser charge). For persons arrested on assault charges, the rate of conviction (for that or any charge) is 51% (Flanagan & Jamieson, 1988, Table 5.1). The rate for all violent offenses is about 55%. This is about the same as the rate for substantiation of child abuse, according to the NIS (53% in 1986). So the child protection system is no more "unreasonably" inefficient than the criminal justice system.

But arrest and prosecution are far more intrusive events than a child abuse investigation. The defendant's name gets in the newspaper. Family and friends are likely to know. People lose jobs simply by virtue of having been arrested. They must hire attorneys, at considerable expense, and lose time from work in order to defend themselves. They may be incarcerated for a short time. And this is no small number of people. More than 650,000 people were arrested for violent crimes in 1986; at a conviction rate of 55%, this means almost 300,000 arrested and not convicted. Almost 2 million more were arrested for property crimes, of which 670,000 would not be convicted. Adding violent and property crimes together, this is almost a million arrests without conviction.

How can American society tolerate this enormous inefficiency in crime control and its wholesale intrusion into people's lives? According to public opinion polls, drugs and crime are the second- and third-greatest concerns Americans have about their communities (after unemployment) (Flanagan & Jamieson, 1988, p. 119). Americans want more people arrested, not fewer. They want more aggressive control of crime (Flanagan & Jamieson, 1988, p. 142), and are willing to tolerate inefficiency and intrusion if these are the costs.

According to American legal theory, all individuals arrested are presumed innocent until convicted. The idea that almost a million innocent people are arrested and not convicted in the United States each year would presumably be intolerable if this were seen as unwarranted state intrusion into the privacy of innocent people. But popular stereotypes about the legal system provide rationalizations for this inefficiency and intrusion. In spite of the constitutional presumption, most people generally believe that a person who has been arrested has probably done something wrong. Moreover, to the extent that people know that large numbers of arrested people are not ultimately convicted (i.e., their crimes are not substantiated), they have assuaging explanations. For example, people are apt to believe that criminals are cagey and hire good defense attorneys to get them off. They also are told repeatedly that requirements for conviction under our constitution are very stringent, so that the evidence against offenders has to be overwhelming. They know that criminals get off on technicalities. To some extent they also know that prosecutors are overworked and simply cannot afford to prosecute vigorously everyone who should be prosecuted.

Interestingly, the inefficiencies in the child protection system could be described in much the same terms and with substantial truth. Why do so many child abuse investigations end in unfounded cases? In this line of reasoning, abusers are cagey, resist investigation, and have good alibis. Standards for substantiation are very stringent. And investigators are overworked and cannot afford to investigate vigorously every child abuse report that should be investigated. These are all true.

Very few people interpret the operation of the criminal justice system in the same way the overreporting critics interpret the operation of the child welfare system. If one applied their analysis to the criminal justice system and its large number of reported crimes without arrests and arrested criminals without convictions, one might say that overzealous law enforcement officials, without clear definitions of what constitute crimes, encourage too many people to report crimes and arrest too many people on insufficient evidence, and end up wasting time on minor offenses while the serious crimes are not attended to. This is a point of view that has its evidence as well.

The point here is not that one view of the criminal justice system is true and the other is false. There is some truth to both. Rather, the point is that a degree of inefficiency and serious intrusion into the privacy and freedom of individuals seem perfectly rational and justifiable if the goal is important enough. The issue is balancing individual rights with the need to protect innocent victims.

Two other examples are relevant. Every year the Internal Revenue Service audits more than a million tax returns. In many of these cases the intrusion into people's private lives is severe, and no wrongdoing is found. In fact, every three years the IRS randomly selects 50,000 returns for what *Consumer Reports* describes as the "most grueling tax audit imaginable . . . every line on your tax return will be scrutinized" and citizens are required to bring in canceled checks and receipts to justify everything ("The Worst Audit of All," 1989). This is an enormous random invasion of people's financial and personal privacy for no reason other than research on how people fill out their tax returns.

Another example: Millions of people are frisked every day and have their baggage opened and examined in the airports of this country. Almost nobody is found to be carrying a weapon. This is an invasion of privacy people would have had a hard time imagining a generation ago, yet few people complain. No one wants to be the victim of an airline hijacking.

Policymakers are willing to implement and the public is willing to tolerate very inefficient systems of deviance detection that sometimes entail serious invasions of privacy *when the objective is important enough.* People are frightened about crime; they don't want their neighbors and fellow citizens cheating on their tax returns; and they are afraid of airline hijackings.

By comparison, the child welfare system is certainly more efficient at rooting out problematic behavior than the criminal justice system and the airline security system, and probably the tax audit system as well. It is also arguably less invasive under most conditions for those unfairly targeted. But the key issue highlighted by this comparison is that the degree of inefficiency and intrusion tolerated is a function of the importance of the objective. Ultimately, the overreporting argument appears to be that addressing child abuse is not worth it. Child abuse detection and the cases that are uncovered are not important enough for us to tolerate a million unsubstantiated cases a year.

In this, I think the critics are clearly out of step with the American public. The public has again and again (and increasingly) in national public opinion surveys urged that more be done about the problem of child abuse. In one recent national survey, respondents specifically endorsed the idea that "public child welfare agencies should investigate all reports of child abuse regardless of the seriousness of the charge" (67%) over a proposal consistent with aims of the overreporting critics, "Parents should be reported as child abusers only when there is clear evidence of serious harm or injury to a child" (30%) (Schulman, Ronca & Bucuvalas, Inc., 1988). This suggests that there is strong public support for the current level of increased reporting.

Conclusion

The goals of making the child protection system more efficient, effective, and fair are laudable ones. The system has many problems and many faults. The premise that child abuse is overreported is wrong, but the idea that the system could devote a greater portion of its effort to identifying and treating the most serious cases is a good one. Many people inside and outside the system believe that reports could be much better prioritized, so that investigators' time is spent on the most serious cases that are most likely to need and to benefit from intervention. There is hope that certain kinds of risk assessment instruments can direct attention to the most threatened children. But prioritizing is a far cry from cutting back on reports.

Nonetheless, some critics want to increase this efficiency—detecting more serious abuse and at the same time excluding less serious cases or unsubstantiated reports—by eliminating or severely limiting reports by nonprofessionals (Besharov, 1988b). In spite of claims, there is no evidence that reports by lay persons (or nonprofessionals) are made lightly. And there is no evidence that restricting reports from lay persons would greatly increase efficiency. A situation that would be easy for a relatively well-informed lay person to exclude would also be easy for a CPS investigator to exclude at the time of the initial phone call. Meanwhile, it is likely that many serious cases would also never get reported. It makes much more sense to improve the way that the investigators triage the reports than to limit the choices available to them. If the research shows that lay reporters are less reliable, then risk assessments can take the sources of reports into account. But this is far different from discouraging lay persons from reporting altogether.

It is very misleading to say that overreporting and underreporting are "equally serious" problems. The consequences are vastly different. Once a case is reported, we can always choose to take no action, even to investigate. But without a report at all, there is no possibility of any help.

Other suggestions from the overreporting critics do have some merit. For example, there is broad support for the idea of defining *child abuse* more clearly, particularly in areas such as emotional abuse (Baily

& Baily, 1986; Garbarino, Guttman, & Wilson, 1986), so that workers can decide which reports warrant intervention. Of course, as emotional maltreatment is better defined, it may spark more rather than fewer reports. States also are moving toward procedures that give more rights and options to families that are subjected to child abuse investigations. The system for collecting and analyzing statistics on child abuse needs to be refined; for example, the use of the term *substantiation* does lead to confusion, as does the use of the total number of "reports" (substantiated and unsubstantiated) as an indicator of the size of the child abuse problem.

But these reforms are tinkering around the edges compared with the major restructuring that many people, including the recent U.S. Advisory Board on Child Abuse and Neglect (1990), believe is required. First, the system needs more trained staff to respond to reports, conduct investigations, and provide services to families. By almost everyone's analysis, the increase in serious child abuse cases coming to CPS attention has not been matched by commensurate increases in staffs and budgets to deal with these cases (Daro & Mitchel, 1989; Salovitz & Keys, 1988). This lack of trained staff has been one of the primary obstacles to effective action.

Second, the child protective system needs a better-trained, better-paid, and more professionalized workforce to improve decision making and public and professional confidence and esteem. Child welfare work needs to be honored, welcomed, and rewarded. The public clearly wants to combat child abuse, and people need to be educated that this means accepting increased social and financial costs, including a modest level of outside scrutiny into the affairs of families. They also need to recognize that this sometimes entails difficult moral choices between family, neighborhood, and professional loyalties on the one hand and the welfare of children on the other. Public and professional esteem for the child welfare system will certainly make it easier and more efficient to identify and confirm child abuse.

But perhaps most important, the child welfare system needs to do a far better job, not just of detecting child abuse, but of protecting the children who are discovered to be at risk.[4] This means providing support services for parents, respite care, good foster homes, counseling for parents and children, financial aid, and social work assistance to deal with the crises that put families on the brink of abuse and neglect. If we have nothing to offer when abuse is reported, it is silly to argue about whether we are reporting too little or too much. And if we are truly offering help, rather than stigma, blame, and punishment, what would there be to complain about?

Notes

1. In child protection parlance the synonymous terms *unfounded* and *unsubstantiated* do not mean "false" or "scurrilous," as they do in colloquial usage. Rather, they mean "not founded" or "not substantiated," where *founded* and *substantiated* have technical administrative implications. *Not founded* may simply mean "not investigated."

2. Such statistical artifacts include changes in what is counted as a report, how duplicate reports are handled, and the quality of the records kept about contacts to reporting authorities. For example, some states count every call as a report, others count only cases accepted for investigation, and still others have changed from one method to another. This is why data provided by states themselves, as in the APWA study cited by Besharov (Chapter 16, this volume), are not a reliable measure of substantiation rates. They should also not be used to make comparisons between states. The NIS is the only study so far to have gotten around these problems.

3. Some 11% of substantiated cases of sexual abuse in day care had been previously investigated and deemed unsubstantiated (Finkelhor & Williams, 1988).

4. Many of the children who die from child abuse and neglect are already known to CPS authorities, as indicated by Besharov (Chapter 16, this volume), but overreporting has little to do with these deaths. Insufficient services have been a chronic problem from the very beginning of the child protection system. Not infrequently, agencies fail to intervene in these cases because they are being overly cautious about the breach of parental rights. Thus unwarranted attacks on the system for violating families are arguably a more immediate contributor to child fatalities than are unsubstantiated reports.

References

Baily, T., & Baily, W. (1986). *Operational definitions of child emotional maltreatment* (Final report). Augusta, ME: Bureau of Social Services.

Besharov, D. (1988a, August 4). The child-abuse numbers game. *Wall Street Journal.*

Besharov, D. (1988b). The need to narrow the grounds for state intervention. In D. Besharov (Ed.), *Protecting children from abuse and neglect: Policy and practice* (pp. 47-90). Springfield, IL: Charles C Thomas.

Besharov, D. (1992). A balanced approach to reporting child abuse. *Child, Youth and Family Services Quarterly, 15*(1), 5-6.

Christensen, B. J. (1989a, February). The child abuse "crisis": Forgotten facts and hidden agendas. *The Family in America*, pp. 1-8.

Christensen, B. J. (1989b, March 11). Child abuse is exaggerated. *Pittsburgh Post-Gazette.*

Daro, D., & Mitchel, L. (1989). *Child abuse fatalities continue to rise: The results of the 1988 annual fifty state survey.* Chicago: National Committee for Prevention of Child Abuse.

Eckenrode, J. (1986, June). *The substantiation of child abuse and neglect reports.* Summary of proceedings of a research conference sponsored by the National Center on Child Abuse and Neglect, Washington, DC.

Finkelhor, D. (1984). *Child sexual abuse: New theory and research.* New York: Free Press.

Finkelhor, D. (1990). Is child abuse overreported? *Public Welfare, 69*, 23-29.

Finkelhor, D., Hotaling, G. T., Lewis, I. A., & Smith, C. (1990). Sexual abuse in a national survey of adult men and women: Prevalence, characteristics and risk factors. *Child Abuse and Neglect, 14,* 19-28.

Finkelhor, D., & Williams, L. (1988). *Nursery crimes: Sexual abuse in day care.* Newbury Park, CA: Sage.

Flanagan, T., & Jamieson, K. (Eds.). (1988). *Sourcebook of criminal justice statistics: 1987.* Washington, DC: Government Printing Office.

Fryer, G. E., Bross, D. C., Krugman, R. D., Benson, D. B., & Baird, D. (1990). Good news for CPS workers. *Public Welfare, 69,* 38-41

Garbarino, J., Guttman, E., & Wilson, J. (1986). *The psychologically battered child.* San Francisco, CA: Jossey-Bass.

Gelles, R. J., & Straus, M. A. (1988). *Intimate violence: The causes and consequences of abuse in the American family.* New York: Simon & Schuster.

Peters, S., Wyatt, G., & Finkelhor, D. (1986). Prevalence. In D. Finkelhor & Associates (Eds.), *A sourcebook on child sexual abuse pp. 15-59).* Beverly Hills, CA: Sage.

Russell, D. (1986). *The secret trauma: Incest in the lives of girls and women.* New York: Basic Books.

Salovitz, B., & Keys, D. (1988, Fall). Is child protective services still a service? *Protecting Children,* pp. 17-23.

Schulman, Ronca & Bucuvalas, Inc. (1988). *Public attitudes and actions regarding child abuse and its prevention: 1988.* Chicago: National Committee for Prevention of Child Abuse.

Sedlak, A. (1991a). *Study findings: Study of national incidence and prevalence of child abuse and neglect: 1988.* Washington, DC: U.S. Department of Health and Human Services.

Sedlak, A. (1991b). *Supplementary analyses of data on the national incidence of child abuse and neglect.* Rockville, MD: Westat.

Sedlak, A. (1989, April). *National incidence of child abuse and neglect.* Paper presented at the Biennial Meeting of the Society for Research in Child Development, Kansas City, MO.

Sedlak, A. (n.d.). *Relation between type and severity of maltreatment, recognition of maltreated children, and CPS awareness of recognized children.* Rockville, MD: Westat.

Sedlak, A., McFarland, J., & Rust, K. (1987). *Report on data processing and analysis.* Rockville, MD: Westat.

Speigel, L. D. (1985). *A question of innocence.* Parsippany, NJ: Unicorn.

U.S. Advisory Board on Child Abuse and Neglect. (1990). *Child abuse and neglect: Critical first steps in response to a national emergency.* Washington, DC: Government Printing Office.

U.S. Department of Health and Human Services. (1981). *Study findings: National study of the incidence and severity of child abuse and neglect.* Washington, DC: Author.

Wells, S. J. (1989). *Screening and prioritization in child protective services intake.* Grant status report, Grant No. 90-CA-1265 from the National Legal Resource Center for Child Advocacy and Protection.

Wexler, R. (1985, September). Invasion of the child savers. *The Progressive,* pp. 19-22.

The worst audit of all. (1989). *Consumer Reports, 54*(3), 173, 175.

CHAPTER 18

Prevention Is Appropriate, Prevention Is Successful

Carol A. Plummer

Sexual abuse is an old phenomenon, but neither the public nor the professional community had significant awareness of it until the 1970s. Prior to then, sexual abuse was vastly underreported, misunderstood, or minimized in the professional literature. As survivors of sexual abuse began to speak out in the media about their childhood suffering, the public listened, believed, and felt the agony. As researchers and therapists documented the extent of the problem, the true scope of sexual abuse was recognized. Yet, recognition was not the final goal. Soon both professionals and the public rallied to respond to the pain resulting from abuse, attempted to identify abuse more readily in the present generation of children, and sought ways to end or prevent the problem.

The History of
Child Sexual Abuse Prevention

Forward-looking mental health practitioners and rape crisis workers were not content simply to bandage the wounded after sexual abuse; they wanted to find ways to prevent this problem. Prevention already flourished in fields concerned with such problems as drug abuse, suicide, and unwanted pregnancy, but preventing sexual abuse necessitated a distinctive strategy. Two considerations were paramount in developing sexual abuse prevention techniques. First, in order to keep abuse from occurring, it was imperative to determine what caused it, or, at least, what factors contributed to it. Second, the pattern of abuse dynamics (how children were selected, coerced, sworn to secrecy, and plagued with silencing guilt) needed to be carefully studied to determine how best to intervene.

To be certain, prevention of *anything* is a tricky business. By definition, primary prevention needs to occur prior to the problem in order to prevent it. Consequently, proving that intervention prevented an event (that it did not occur) is impossible, because the event may not have occurred anyway. This problem has plagued all primary prevention programs and made them scientifically suspect. Likewise, it is nearly impossible to prove that preventive intervention *did not* prevent the unwanted outcome if it does not occur. Proving prevention's *effectiveness* is a difficult task; proving its *ineffectiveness* is equally problematic.

To evaluate the usefulness of sexual abuse prevention, a historical perspective is helpful. By the early 1980s, social service systems were being overwhelmed by disclosures of past and present abuse. As parents became aware of the scope of abuse in their communities, they were concerned with keeping their own children safe from abuse. Thus pressures to attempt prevention came strongly from both increased public concern and the foresight of nearly burned-out treatment professionals. It is significant that sexual abuse prevention grew out of demand.

By 1980, the National Center on Child Abuse and Neglect encouraged and legitimated prevention efforts through prevention grants to six diverse community settings. Others, most notably the Child Assault Prevention Program, began with no federal funding and expanded quickly because of requests from schools. At times, because of the perceived threat of abuse and hopes for guarantees from prevention, there was a rush for implementation. As with other newly discovered social issues, public demand sometimes pushed practice ahead of theory. However, as the leaders of these programs set the national tone, there was a demand from the start to have an emerging theory to justify each intervention. Although the programs, aimed in part at educating children, were experimental, they were not haphazard in design or implementation. Experts were consulted on topics of child development, community values and norms, and cultural sensitivity.

Programs grew based on community need, and largely from concerns of parents and treatment professionals. Development included input from education, law enforcement, social services, and child development experts, as well as ongoing feedback from parents and students (Kent, 1982). Although critics may disagree with the choices made for programs, decisions were made with the input of specialists, and were not dependent solely on the developers' "best guesses."

Despite budget and expertise limitations, significant energy was spent on program evaluations in the earliest years. Formative and summative evaluations were consistently undertaken and programs improved as a result, although funding and staff limitations of small programs restricted most from conducting elaborate large-scale research. Few of these earliest evaluation studies were ever documented or submitted for publication. However, concern about and encouragement of research have been hallmarks of prevention from the beginning. Therefore, some of the harsher criticisms of prevention programs, including that they are well intentioned but naive, may have to do with critics' lack of knowledge of prevention's history and process (Plummer, 1986).

What Is "Prevention"?

A major consideration when looking at the effectiveness of "prevention programs" is a definition of terms. The prevailing theories regarding prevention approaches reflect the unique components operating when sexual abuse occurs. As Finkelhor (1984) shows in his "four preconditions" model, for abuse to occur there must be a proclivity to abuse in the offender, inadequate internal and external controls of that behavior, and access to children. Given that all preconditions must be present for abuse to occur, intervention in *any* of the four arenas could prevent abuse. Unfortunately, sexual abuse is often shielded by secrecy and/or threats, with usually only the offender and victim aware of the behavior. Some children do not even know the behavior is "inappropriate." As a result, unlike cases of physical abuse or neglect, which are more likely to be discovered by a concerned adult, with sexual abuse it is more important to lower the children's risk of abuse by educating them. However, teaching of children should be the last line of defense (Plummer, 1986), not the only prevention strategy utilized. Were it possible to keep children innocent, if adults could always detect possible abuse situations and be ever present to prevent abuse, children may never have been included in prevention efforts.[1]

A comprehensive sexual abuse prevention program has numerous essential components: community awareness, parent education, teacher training, age-appropriate and culturally sensitive programming for children, a multidisciplinary community-based task force, ongoing evaluation, and necessary updates (Plummer, 1986). Optimally, all parts will be strong. They will be aimed at strengthening behavioral controls of offenders, restricting access to victims, or, less often, altering the societal factors that "create" offenders. These components were evident from the inception of all major sexual abuse prevention programs, regardless of ideology or location (Cooper, 1991; Crisci, 1983; Kent, 1979; Plummer, 1984a; Tobin & Levinson Farley, 1990). Yet, from the beginning, the news media were most intrigued by the idea of children being told about abuse or "sex" or "saying no" to adults. This was the "glamorous" or unusual aspect of the program, the one filmed and reported on and (even) heralded. In the end, this focus neither did prevention programs justice nor informed people (professionals included) of the breadth and depth of prevention's scope. Prevention was reduced to "Say no and tell someone" in the eyes of the casual observer, despite what programs really accomplished in their totality. Prevention of sexual abuse was never conceptualized or implemented by program developers as entirely or even primarily aimed at making children responsible for keeping themselves safe. As I have noted in earlier work: "If we inform children about sexual abuse and ways to prevent it we adults believe children can be empowered to HELP avoid or interrupt their own victimization SOMETIMES. This limitation must be acknowledged. We cannot always prevent sexual abuse or exploitation of children by giving them information or skills" (Plummer, 1986, p. 4).

Although good prevention programs have always balanced discussion of positive touch with information about negative touch experiences, in recent years prevention has expanded to include healthy images of sexuality (considering not only what we are working against, but what we are aiming *for*). Some, such as Gail Ryan (1992) of the C. Henry Kempe National Center for the Prevention and Treatment of Child Abuse and Neglect (Denver), have also challenged us to include juvenile sex offender prevention, rather than only education of potential victims. The Ounce of Prevention's "Heart to Heart" program teaches teen parents how to protect their children from potential abuse. Of course, even programs that mainly seek to educate parents or train professionals on the topic also are legitimately "prevention programs."

Sexual abuse prevention is multifaceted and aims to achieve long-term societal change. Perhaps that is ultimately the issue most disturbing to some critics. It will take more than simply watching children more carefully to stop sexual abuse. It necessitates changing attitudes in a society where often children are seen as property, women as sex objects, pornography as harmless, sexual crimes as uncontrollable, the effects of abuse as negligible, the extent of abuse as insignificant, and unwanted touch as a normal part of life. Prevention of sexual abuse will call into question many of our unexamined values and would truly make the world a different place, a job that will not be completed overnight.

Preventing Prevention:
The Critics Speak

Criticisms of sexual abuse prevention have fallen into two categories. Some have raised welcome questions regarding the efficacy of programs in order to challenge improvement. Others seem motivated more by a desire to hamper prevention efforts, even despite their own research results (Berrick & Gilbert, 1991). The criticisms of sexual abuse prevention have focused on numerous concerns. Some focus on the characteristics of leaders in prevention efforts. Others challenge the ideological and political agenda of sexual abuse prevention programs. Still others target the content of programming for children, developmental appropriateness, and unintended consequences. Some question the methodological rigor of research claiming effectiveness.

Although it is reasonable to expect some objections to prevention programs, it is shocking to see both the extent and the intensity of the opposition to sexual abuse prevention. Prevention was briefly the darling of the media in the early 1980s, but by 1990 there were numerous serious critics of prevention programs. This was inordinately reflected in the media and powerfully influenced the general public's view of sexual abuse prevention. It coincided with media stories chastising overzealous child protective interventions and warning of outbursts of false allegations. Ralph Underwager, a psychologist frequently hired to defend accused offenders, was one of the oft-quoted proponents of these beliefs. Sunday magazine covers depicted drawings of large children looming over small fathers who were supposedly being ruined by their own children's fabrications.

In this context, sexual abuse prevention work has been judged more harshly than other types of prevention programs. Drug and alcohol abuse prevention programs were not discontinued because some were arguably ineffective, scary, or even harmful. The idea promoted was that better programs would survive and weak programs should be improved. Even sexual abuse treatment and intervention, which often have less than successful track records, are not subject to such scrutiny. There have not been calls for treatment programs to be decimated because they didn't get everything right on the first try. Some attacks on sexual abuse prevention may be related to questions of its perceived effectiveness, reflected in a predictable backlash caused by its challenging some core values of our particular present culture. Sexual abuse prevention, more than treatment, intervention, or research, is undeniably about social change: altering the conditions that allow sexual abuse to occur.

In *Protecting Young Children From Sexual Abuse: Does Preschool Training Work?* (Gilbert, Berrick, LeProhn, & Nyman, 1989) and *With the Best of Intentions: The Child Sexual Abuse Prevention Movement* (Berrick & Gilbert, 1991), the authors make various claims about prevention advocates in arguing against prevention. According to them, prevention proponents are "overwhelmingly female," "include many sexual abuse victims," and are linked by a common "feminist" ideology (Berrick & Gilbert, 1991, p. 9). These assertions reveal a great deal more about the biases of the writers than about those critiqued, but, more important, such personalistic and ideological dismissals leave the reader with inaccurate impressions. Although some prevention proponents do operate out of a feminist perspective, many do not. Some have placed their prevention efforts in the "child safety" or "child protection" camps (Crisci, 1983). Others have advocated for "children's rights" (Tobin & Levinson Farley, 1990). Many have based their programs on the fact that secrecy about this issue has been the primary force of perpetuation and have argued to "break the silence." The "feminist baiting" currently popular, however, is appalling to most who work to prevent sexual abuse. Why does belief in equality between the sexes, being a survivor, or even being female make a prevention advocate suspect? These authors seem to have an issue with feminism, which they assume negates the professionalism and legitimacy of this "movement." They call prevention work "more of a social movement than an institutionalized network of professional services" (Berrick & Gilbert, 1991, p. 9) when further questioning prevention's motives. By calling prevention advocates "opportunistic" (p. 20) and arguing that such advocates seek to "gain public funds" for their work in the "feminist cause" (Berrick & Gilbert, 1991, p. 18), these authors use prejudicial buzzwords that are both unfair and untrue. Like any group concerned with a social problem, sexual abuse professionals sought to inform the public and used the media when it began to spotlight this issue. The use of "public funds" was short-lived, and prevention was never adequately funded through such sources. They do not provide the primary financing for the majority of programs. Furthermore, although critics claim prevention professionals are "opportunistic," such persons have traditionally earned about half as much as treatment or research professionals, and have always been allocated much smaller budgets by private and public agencies. Prevention leaders have simply been a group of lay and professional people, including sexual abuse survivors, trying their best to prevent sexual abuse.

Although Berrick and Gilbert view programs as suspect, owing to their "feminist" agenda, it is curious that such critics are not explicit about their own theoretical underpinnings. Their "agenda" is not merely objective professional excellence, as they would purport. They seem to be dedicated to dismantling prevention as a force in ending sexual abuse. Their attacks sometimes defy their own results, and their arguments lack professional objectivity. Acting more like lawyers in a courtroom trying to tear down the credibility of a witness than like social scientists, these critics flail in all directions against prevention's aims, methods, "failures," and even successes. For example, Berrick and Gilbert (1991) disregard the significant findings with which they disagree, highlight "important" findings that are not statistically significant, and make vast generalizations not supported by the research, including their own. Most of the questions they raise are old ones that have been grappled with for more than a decade: not adapting adult programs for children, the use of terminology, the appropriateness of educating preschoolers, the potential for being insensitive to cultural diversity, and testing/measurement issues. The criticisms, such as those found in *With the Best of Intentions*, may dubiously be offered with the best of intentions, but mostly show how little the authors know about child sexual abuse prevention—its development, implementation, and current controversies.

Prevention professionals must listen carefully to legitimate concerns about the value of and problems with current prevention efforts. Although there are those who prefer not to institute societal changes that may reduce child sexual abuse, there are many sincere questions that demand the attention of prevention advocates. In Chapter 19 of this volume, for example, Reppucci and Haugaard demonstrate a more reasoned approach and some legitimate points. Certainly, prevention advocates agree that there is a need to conduct more research, improve weak programs, focus on more than children, and examine possible negative effects, and with the fact that knowledge gain does not necessarily translate to skill usage. Yet the flaw in Reppucci and Haugaard's argument stems from their basing their analysis on information or premises gathered from Berrick and Gilbert's faulty conclusions. Because their arguments appear more reasoned, and are thus more likely to be taken seriously, the basis of their statements must be challenged. As mentioned earlier, positively proving the effectiveness of prevention is an impossible task. However, prevention proponents must ask of our critics: Is your criticism about the specifics of our programs (theory, language, approach, appropriate target)? Or is your criticism about the concept of prevention itself? This philosophical difference is crucial, and understanding it can help us to sort out valid and invalid criticisms.

Program Effectiveness

To determine if sexual abuse prevention is "working," definitions must be clear, because programs are not identical. Programs range in duration from one day to several weeks. They are presented by teachers or outside instructors and may or may not have follow-up. Should *effectiveness* be defined as programs doing what they claim (educating children about sexual abuse), or as children implementing what they learn (using skills to avoid abuse)? Are prevention programs effective only if there is a decrease in reported abuse (supposedly owing to a decrease in its occurrence)? Or are prevention programs effective if they increase reports, as both adults and children identify abuse and take action more quickly, with less shame or confusion?

The goals of most prevention programs include the following:

1. to raise the awareness of the general public
2. to educate parents about abuse, its prevention, and early intervention
3. to train professionals to understand abuse dynamics, symptoms, and reporting responsibilities (in some cases, to train teachers to present prevention programs to their students)
4. to teach children factual information about sexual abuse
5. to develop skills in children that may help them to avoid sexual abuse
6. to work toward ending child sexual abuse in our communities

Effectiveness has been measured for specific populations, in specific settings at specific times with specific programs implemented in specific manners. Yet effectiveness changes if even one variable (such as age or place) is altered. Further, comparing programs with different ideologies or outcome goals is often unfair and irresponsible (Nibert, Cooper, Ford, Fitch, & Robinson, 1989). In addition, finding that a few programs are not immediately and completely "effective" does not mean that all prevention is ineffective or even harmful. Nancy Reagan's "Just Say No" efforts were simplistic, gave false hope to the nation, and did not work, but that does not mean that all efforts to curb drug abuse are ineffective.

To examine prevention's effectiveness seriously means several things. If there is a real desire to know if prevention can be effective, the programs studied must be adequately funded and based on the best research available at the time. The studies must consider all components of a sexual abuse prevention program, not only the training for children. Children were never meant to accomplish prevention singlehanded. Longitudinal studies will be necessary, because most advocates suggest a graduated training, with reinforcements and more sophisticated concepts as the child matures. Finally, consideration must be given to what constitutes effectiveness in training for children: knowledge or attitude change, increased assertiveness, skill acquisition, increased reporting, more immediate reporting, and so on. Acceptable standards of effectiveness need to be determined. Granted that all children do not need to have significant gains, but is only 25% sufficient? What if the children learn only 50% of the concepts taught? These outcomes should send us back to the drawing board to create programs more universally beneficial. Unfortunately, some persons questioning prevention seem to advocate stopping programs, rather than examining how improvements could be made and should be supported.

Sexual abuse prevention programs were developed, implemented, and underfunded in a context. This context, not incidentally, resulted in prevention's acceptance and progress in the late 1970s and early 1980s. By the time the Reagan budget had undermined social service programs and civil rights, prevention was under scrutiny. Granted, some of the challenges are warranted; sexual abuse prevention programs need to be held accountable. They need to be researched, improved, and (in certain cases) even stopped. However, it must be acknowledged that most programs live on a shoestring, doing what they can despite the knowledge that optimally they need to do more. The "multimillion-dollar industry of prevention" that some critics mention has been propagated by businesses hoping to sell books, films, and educational materials (see, e.g., deYoung, 1988). It is *not* of benefit to prevention proponents, who are often appalled by the marketing of inferior products. Prevention additionally has suffered because it has often been considered an extra, "fluff," and is typically the first department to be cut in mental health, social service, and rape crisis programs. Prevention employees are often very low paid, resulting in frequent turnover. Often they are allotted no time to keep abreast of research or updates on prevention. And, in the push for voluntarism, prevention programs have most often been staffed by volunteers. All these realities about prevention must be considered in serious studies, or the results will inevitably be dismal, despite the possibility that the lack of both national and institutional commitments to prevention is what set it up for failure.

Prevention Efforts With Adults

The results of prevention efforts in adult education have been overwhelmingly successful in the short time they have existed. Popularity is not a good measure of success, but it could indicate both a "face validity" by the discerning public and positive outcomes that have not yet been documented because research has been so sparse. Berrick and Gilbert (1991, p. 121) assert that overall community awareness of the problem is undeniably in large part the result of prevention's efforts in local communities. Parents have indisputably gained new information and skills and likewise give high ratings to the programs designed for their children (Nibert, Cooper, & Ford, 1989). Professionals, from social workers to educators, have gained more information about the problem, improved their ability to detect possible abuse, and refined their skills in dealing with prevention presentations and disclosures. Despite some claims that this overwhelming support and success must be because parents or teachers are not "informed," there is no documentation offered as grounds for dismissing these positive program outcomes.

Should Children Be Educated About Child Sexual Abuse?

The targets of most of the criticism of prevention have been the content, format, aims, and outcomes of programs discussing sexual abuse prevention with children. However, even the most vocal critics do not deny that most children learn some of the information presented without suffering any ill effects. No fewer than 30 studies (with sample sizes ranging from 24 to 3,500) have documented that elementary, junior high, and high school students learn the main concepts taught in prevention programs. Although there has been some problem with the "ceiling effect" in evaluations, this may indicate that children have gained information about prevention from sources other than class-room presentations. This, too, could point to prevention's success in community awareness efforts and its "trickle down" to youth—from television, comic or coloring books, or parent or teacher instruction. Information regarding what sexual abuse is and what should be done to prevent it are the messages most easily learned by children (Borkin & Frank, 1986; Finkelhor & Strapko, 1992). The older the child and the more concrete the information, the more learning occurs (Lutter & Weisman, 1985). Comparative research has found, not surprisingly, that programs actively involving children resulted in greater under-standing of concepts (Wurtele, 1987; Woods & Dean, 1985). Generally, the programs that last longer and provide follow-up or "booster ses-sions" also show stronger information retention (Ray, 1984; Wurtele, Saslawsky, Miller, Marrs, & Britcher, 1986). However, certain attitudes based on societal myths or beliefs, such as that offenders are usually strangers or that victims are partially at fault, have been found to be more difficult to alter. Even in these areas, however, significant changes have often been found (Plummer, 1984b).

Increased knowledge and attitude change do not translate automat-ically to skills acquisition and, more critically, to skills usage in a potentially dangerous situation. Some testing designed to examine skills acquisition through role plays or responses to video situations have shown that children can learn to tell what they will do. Arguably, this still does not establish what they actually would do in a practical situation. Yet, simulation studies have shown that children who receive prevention messages are less likely to go with strangers (Fryer, Kraizer, & Miyoshi, 1987; Poche, Brouer, & Swearingen, 1981). These findings are encouraging, but there are ethical issues inherent in pretending that children are being potentially abducted. Many prevention profession-als are not enthusiastic about replicating these studies, or about trying ones involving simulated approaches by persons known to the chil-dren (a more common problem). Given the particular challenges in the field of child sexual abuse, clear and convincing evidence of children's ability and willingness to use prevention skills in real situations may not be possible. Not many adults, even those with self-defense training and assertiveness skills, can be certain how they would respond during an attempted rape. To focus only on this measure will frustrate practi-tioners by continually circling us around to unanswerable questions: Will these skills be used? And, if so, will that use be effective? The answers, almost assuredly, are yes, sometimes, and yes, sometimes. Likewise, sometimes children will have gained information or skills from other sources, or figured them out for themselves.

For this reason, prevention advocates often suggest a blanket approach: less concern with where the information comes from or which intervention prevented the assault as long as a combination of efforts achieves the goal of keeping children safe. This suggests an approach along the lines of the movement to reduce cigarette usage: package warnings, school programs, smoke-outs, TV spots, doctors' advice, and so on. To be certain, researchers need to be much more exacting. It is hoped that they will eventually find the methods and measures to give feedback so that the most effective interventions can be identified and the use of different interventions prioritized.

How Should Children Be Educated About Sexual Abuse?

For some, rethinking prevention efforts has less to do with *whether* children should be informed than it does with *how* they should be informed. Trudell and Whatley (1988) and Sanford (1980) have argued that programs should not inadvertently insinuate that children should/must use prevention skills or that children are partially to blame for abuse. Debate continues regarding the use of formal anatomical terms versus "private parts" or other vague references to genitalia or sexual abuse (Anderson, 1991).[2] Research has documented the need for more interactive teaching, practice sessions for children, and at least yearly repetitions at the elementary level. Kolko (1988) makes an argument for not limiting discussion to touch discrimination, but including personal safety, assertiveness, and problem solving, as many programs already do. Finkelhor and Strapko (1992) point out that sexual abuse prevention may be a child's first introduction to the topic of sexuality, so care must be taken not to present sex negatively. Wurtele (1987) encourages more attention to developmental issues, regarding both content and approach. Others debate the "trust your feelings" message, and some programs are opting for a rule-based message, or a combination of the two (Ray-Keil, 1989). The teaching of self-defense methods as part of prevention continues to be controversial. It may build self-esteem and assist some children in escaping some abuse, but it also has the potential of escalating the offender's violence or making the child overly confident of his or her power to escape. These questions are being answered differently in different programs, but it is encouraging to see that they are being both asked and addressed.

Outcome data on preschool sexual abuse prevention programs show the least definitive results and are the most controversial. Critics have stated that certain concepts, such as that good/liked people can do bad/disliked behaviors, are incomprehensible to the youngest preschoolers (deYoung, 1988). Most prevention advocates have long argued that preschoolers should not bear the burden of protecting themselves, but that adults must supervise and protect them (Plummer, 1986). Prevention programs for these populations have added emphasis on adult responsibility and should include considerations such as selecting baby-sitters, screening day-care providers, facility design issues, policy changes in day care, teaching parents about symptoms of abuse, and training for religious leaders. Undeniably, many programs need to enhance the adult-focused components of their prevention programs for preschoolers. Still, given the risk for abuse between ages 3 and 6, it could be argued that some preschoolers *can* learn the concepts and skills and that to withhold this information is to rob them of their last defensive option against abuse. Withholding information raises ethical issues as much as does the concern about increasing a child's "fear," which is actually caution.[3]

Past research shows a wide variation in learning by preschool children. At least eight studies have shown that children can learn basic prevention concepts, even if they do not learn all of the messages taught (Borkin & Frank, 1986; Cooper, 1991; Finkelhor & Strapko, 1992; Gilbert et al., 1989; Nibert, Cooper, Ford, et al., 1989; Poche et al., 1989; Wurtele, Gillespie, Currier, & Franklin, 1992). If only 50% of the children learn, there is a strong argument that this is effective, especially when children's abilities vary so widely among 3- to 5-year-olds. Were negative outcomes shown to be a major risk, perhaps prevention education could wait until first grade. However, because some studies show 30%-50% of sexual abuse victims are under the age of 7 (Wurtele & Miller-Perrin, 1992), the discomfort of *adults* with the loss of children's "innocence" should not weigh more heavily than actual risk to the youngest victims. Overall, expanding adult involvement and creating developmentally appropriate programs are important challenges. Research does justify a continuation of educating preschoolers as part of the broader program. Positive outcomes far outweigh the question of prevention ineffectiveness, which remains totally unproven.

Unanticipated Outcomes

It is one thing to question whether or not a program accomplishes what it claims to do, but it is equally important, especially with the sensitive matter of sexual abuse, to consider what may unintentionally result. Unintentional outcomes could be either positive or negative, depending on their nature and the perspective of the examiner. To date, most studies have found no negative impact of prevention programs on most children. Indeed, at least three studies have shown that children report less fear and more confidence as a result of certain programs (Binder & McNiel, 1986; Lutter & Weisman, 1985; Plummer, 1984b). Studies asking parents about the negative effects of programs on their children have also found overwhelming acceptance and few or no negative consequences such as fear, nightmares, anxiety, or bed-wetting (Nibert, Cooper, & Ford, 1989; Wurtele & Miller-Perrin, 1987). A few studies have shown an increase in anxiety, but these can be interpreted in several ways. Nonclinical judgments of "anxiety" could indicate heightened awareness and realism, and thus readiness to ward off attacks. As Finkelhor and Strapko (1992) report, the research on fearfulness and anxiety is "fairly reassuring." Of course, even a small number of children negatively affected cannot be ignored; this area deserves further study.

Methodological Issues in Prevention

Prevention effectiveness can never be proven definitively. However, by increasing and improving research methods, it is possible to learn much more about it. Several constraints have kept this from occurring rapidly and thoroughly. Whether there will be research monies and who will receive them are preliminary concerns. Both research academicians and prevention practitioners should participate in framing the questions and seeking relevant answers. Currently there are fewer dollars allocated for such research and, at the same time, a cry for more "proof."

Given the sensitive topic, the issue of access to children, the age of the subjects, and ethical considerations, studies will be difficult, even with adequate funding and cooperation between researchers and practitioners. Probably the major question, rarely addressed in the literature, is whether or not we will have programs to evaluate—programs with the quality and longevity needed to make possible a fair evaluation of prevention. The fact is, both the quality and quantity of programs have decreased. In California alone, in the past few years there has been a decrease from 85 to only 10 programs. In Michigan, the "Michigan model" for comprehensive health proposed a watered-down sexual abuse prevention program that discouraged the use of other prevention materials and programs. Now it appears this model may be further compromised or dismantled completely. Of course, the need for valid and reliable testing instruments, control groups, and longitudinal data collection are challenges needing creative study and attention.

Methodological issues will continue to pose a challenge for researchers of prevention programs. As all persons in this field seem to agree, providing the best possible prevention interventions requires continuing examination of program approaches, with more and better research funded to determine prevention's direction. However, pointing to research and shouting, "Inadequate!" should not be a substitute for preventive efforts to protect children from a real and present danger. It is easier to criticize than to create, but children need and deserve our creativity.

Prevention: The Success Story

While advocating for better research on prevention with children, we must also base our definitions of effectiveness on other criteria. Sexual abuse prevention has been effective already, even without the jury in on all counts. Success can be claimed because we have accomplished several objectives on the way to the ultimate goal of reducing or ending sexual abuse. Although reaching that goal will take decades of commitment and action, these accomplishments justify our continued striving:

1. Prevention efforts have educated millions about sexual abuse and various ways it can be prevented. This may have a general deterrent effect on offenders.

2. Prevention programs have successfully educated millions of children about sexual abuse prevention, breaking the silence and eroding the ignorance that makes abuse more possible. Knowledge *can be* power.

3. Parents have become better protectors of their children as a result of their education and training regarding sexual abuse prevention.

4. There has been no clear indication of negative consequences of prevention education for children, and there is reason to believe that "unanticipated outcomes" have been more positive than negative.

5. Some studies have shown the ability of some children to utilize prevention skills in order to avoid potentially dangerous situations.

6. Prevention programs have often resulted in increased reporting of abuse, perhaps stopping abuse more readily than if no information had been given to children.

7. Teachers and other professionals who come into contact with children frequently have been trained to create more protective environments and to respond more helpfully if abuse is suspected.

8. Prevention programs have addressed the special needs of children of a variety of ages, ability levels, and cultural groups to prevent abuse more adequately.

Although none of these areas is completely effective and none has been adequately researched, preliminary results are promising. Programs aiming for prevention of sexual abuse have made significant strides in only 15 years. These efforts have not been perfect and have been much easier to criticize than to create, but prevention has proven itself in each category of its endeavors. Despite political opposition, financial onslaughts, and even programmatic imperfections, prevention is desired by the public and supported by research; it deserves a chance to get the work done to make the world safer for children.

Notes

1. Grant applications for the National Center on Child Abuse and Neglect mandated prevention education of children for all prevention programs funded by that agency in 1980.

2. It is revealing that the critics who state that young children cannot assimilate abstract or nonspecific information are the same persons who instruct us *not* to impart concrete information because it will frighten or force value judgments on children. The message is that there is no way to say what abuse is or how to prevent it, so don't say it. As well, the idea that children must be able to label clearly what is and what is not abuse is ludicrous. Most programs instruct children to take action based on their feelings in a situation *and* a rule to talk to a grown-up about questionable touches. Children are not asked to decide what is legally sexual abuse.

3. The "finding" that programs make children more negative about touch in general comes from a study in which preschoolers simply reported less positive responses to tickling and bathing activities after a prevention program. An alternative interpretation of this is that the children may have been able to recognize that they did not always like tickling or bathing. Also, they may have felt freer to say how they truly felt about such activities because the program explicitly gave them permission to speak about such matters.

References

Anderson, C. (1991, October). *Healthy sexuality as prevention.* Paper presented at the Midwest Conference on Incest and Child Sexual Abuse, Madison, WI.

Berrick, J. D., & Gilbert, N. (1991). *With the best of intentions: The child sexual abuse prevention movement.* New York: Guilford.

Binder, R., & McNiel, D. (1986). *Evaluation of a school-based sexual abuse prevention program: Cognitive and emotional effects.* Paper presented at the annual meeting of the American Psychiatric Association, Washington, DC. (Available from R. Binder, 401 Parnassus Ave., San Francisco, CA 94040)

Borkin, J., & Frank, L. (1986). Sexual abuse prevention for preschoolers: A pilot program. *Child Welfare, 65,* 75-83.

Cooper, S. (1991). *New strategies for free children: Child abuse prevention for elementary school children.* Columbus, OH: National Assault Prevention Center.

Crisci, G. (1983). *Personal safety curriculum.* (Available from the Franklin/Hampshire Community Mental Health Center, 76 Pleasant St., Northampton, MA 01060)

deYoung, M. (1988). The good touch/bad touch dilemma. *Child Welfare, 67,* 60-68.

Finkelhor, D. (1984). *Child sexual abuse: New theory and research.* New York: Free Press.

Finkelhor, D., & Strapko, N. (1992). Sexual abuse prevention education: A review of evaluation studies. In D. J. Willis, E. Holden, & M. Rosenberg (Eds.), *Prevention of child maltreatment: Developmental and ecological perspectives* (pp. 150-167). New York: John Wiley.

Fryer, G., Kraizer, S., & Miyoshi, T. (1987). Measuring actual reduction of risk to child abuse. *Child Abuse and Neglect, 11,* 173-185.

Gilbert, N., Berrick, J., LeProhn, N., & Nyman, N. (1989). *Protecting young children from sexual abuse: Does preschool training work?* Lexington, MA: Lexington.

Kent, C. A. (1979). *Child sexual abuse project: An educational program for children.* Minneapolis, MN: Hennepin County Attorney's Office of Sexual Assault Services.

Kent, C. A. (1982). *Illusion theater impact study: Phases in developing a child sexual abuse prevention education program.* (Available from Illusion Theater, 28 Hennepin Ave., Minneapolis, MN 55403)

Kolko, D. (1988). Educational programs to promote awareness and prevention of child sexual victimization: A review and methodological critique. *Clinical Psychology Review, 8,* 195-209.

Lutter, Y., & Weisman, A. (1985). *Sexual victimization prevention project.* Final Report to the National Institute of Mental Health, Grant R18MH39549.

Nibert, D., Cooper, S., & Ford, J. (1989). Parents' observations of the effect of a sexual abuse prevention program on preschool children. *Child Welfare, 68,* 539-546.

Nibert, D., Cooper, S., Ford, J., Fitch, L. K., & Robinson, J. (1989). The ability of young children to learn abuse prevention. *Response to the Victimization of Women and Children, 12*(4), 14-21.

Plummer, C. (1984a). *Preventing sexual abuse: Activities and strategies for those working with children and adolescents.* Holmes Beach, FL: Learning Publications.

Plummer, C. (1984b). *Preventing sexual abuse: What in-school programs teach children.* National Conference for Family Violence Researchers. (Available from C. Plummer, P.O. Box 421, Kalamazoo, MI 49005-0421)

Plummer, C. (1986). Prevention education in perspective. In M. Nelson & K. Clark (Eds.), *The educator's guide to preventing child sexual abuse* (pp. 1-5, 69-79). Santa Cruz, CA: Network.

Poche, C., Brouer, R., & Swearingen, M. (1981). Teaching self-protection to young children. *Journal of Applied Behavioral Analysis, 14,* 169-176.

Ray, J. (1984). *Evaluation of the child sex abuse prevention project.* Spokane, WA: Rape Crisis Network.

Ray-Keil, A. (1989). Prevention for preschoolers: Good, bad or confusing? *Connections in the Prevention of Child Exploitation* [Newsletter of the Committee for Children, Seattle, WA].

Ryan, G. (1992). Stopping the cycle of sexual abuse before it develops. *Association for Sexual Abuse Prevention Newsletter, 5*(1).

Sanford, L. T. (1980). *The silent children: A parent's guide to the prevention of child sexual abuse.* Garden City, NY: Doubleday.

Tobin, P., & Levinson Farley, S. (1990). *Keeping kids safe: A child sexual abuse prevention manual.* Holmes Beach, Fl · Learning Publications.

Trudell, B., & Whatley, M. (1988). School sexual abuse prevention: Unintended consequences and dilemmas. *Child Abuse and Neglect, 12,* 103-113.

Woods, S., & Dean, K. (1985). *Evaluating sexual abuse prevention strategies.* Paper presented at the 7th National Conference on Child Abuse and Neglect. (Available from S. Woods, Child and Family Services of Knox County, 2602 E. Fifth Ave., Knoxville, TN 37914)

Wurtele, S. K. (1987). School-based sexual abuse prevention programs: A review. *Child Abuse and Neglect, 11,* 483-495.

Wurtele, S. K., Gillespie, E., Currier, L., & Franklin, C. (1992). A comparison of teachers versus parents as instructors of a personal safety program for preschoolers. *Child Abuse and Neglect, 16,* 127-137.

Wurtele, S. K., & Miller-Perrin, C. L. (1987). An evaluation of side effects associated with participation in a child sexual abuse prevention program. *Journal of School Health, 57,* 228-231.

Wurtele, S. K., & Miller-Perrin, C. L. (1992). *Preventing child sexual abuse: Sharing the responsibility.* Lincoln: University of Nebraska Press.

Wurtele, S. K., Saslawsky, D., Miller, C., Marrs, S., & Britcher, J. (1986). Teaching personal safety skills for potential prevention of sexual abuse: A comparison of treatments. *Journal of Consulting and Clinical Psychology, 54,* 688-692.

CHAPTER 19

Problems With Child Sexual Abuse Prevention Programs

N. Dickon Reppucci
Jeffrey J. Haugaard

In the 1970s, child advocates and feminist groups helped make the general public and professionals aware of the prevalence of child sexual abuse (Finkelhor, 1986). Even the most conservative estimates suggested that 10% of America's female children were subjected to some form of child sexual abuse (Haugaard & Reppucci, 1988). The problem was brought to center stage in the media with the sensational 1984 McMartin Day Care Center case in Los Angeles, in which the center's owner and six teachers were accused of systematically abusing hundreds of children over 10 years. The publicity from front-page headlines and evening newscasts from this case and others that followed, as well as cover stories in *Newsweek* and *Life* and television reports on *60 Minutes* and *Nightline,* resulted in "something of a national obsession" (Note, 1985, p. 429). The ongoing efforts to create child sexual abuse prevention programs received added emphasis through this surge in public awareness. Millions of children have now been exposed to these programs.

The widespread documented incidence of child sexual abuse (Haugaard & Reppucci, 1988), especially the disturbing data that 25-30% of all sexually abused children are under the age of 7 (Finkelhor, 1986; Nibert, Cooper, Ford, Fitch, & Robinson, 1989) and that the modal age for such abuse is 10 years (Melton, 1992), has highlighted the pressing need for effective prevention programs. To date, the vast majority of programs have modeled themselves on sexual assault programs for women (Berrick & Gilbert, 1991) and have focused on empowering elementary school and younger children by teaching them concepts for understanding and repelling sexual abuse. Although laudatory, this goal may be an inappropriate placement of responsibility (Melton, 1992), because most children exposed to these programs may not have the cognitive, emotional, or physical capabilities to protect themselves.

In Chapter 18 of this volume, Plummer concludes that "sexual abuse prevention has been effective already" while simultaneously concluding that "none" of the areas of progress that she cites "has been adequately researched." As scientists, we agree with her latter conclusion, and therefore cannot agree with her former one. We believe that most of her conclusions are based on hope and conjecture. We would like to share that hope, but we believe that the current empirical data base is too fragile to sustain claims of effectiveness. Thus we argue that the available evidence suggests that we do not know whether or not the programs are effective. We believe, however, that the targeting of children as their own protectors may be misguided, and that advocates' faith in these programs may actually retard the development of other programs targeting parents, other adults, and the community that might be more effective.

In order to clarify our position, we first describe briefly the concepts, goals, and research requirements of prevention programs in general. We then turn to the issue of developmental readiness and raise concerns that typical child sexual abuse prevention programs may not be well attuned to the developmental levels of the children receiving them, as the programs may require cognitive capabilities and emotional maturity that many young children do not possess. Next, we summarize the general findings from several evaluations of typical prevention programs and point out the flawed nature of the research designs. Finally, we examine six critical assumptions upon which the programs are based and conclude that caution is warranted regarding widespread use of these programs. We argue that the major research action goal of the 1990s should be the development of new and better programs that include the systematic evaluation of both positive and negative effects.

Prevention Programs and Evaluation

Three types of prevention—primary, secondary, and tertiary—are generally identified in analyses of preventive practice. Primary prevention consists of interventions to prevent a specified problem, such as child sexual abuse, from ever happening; secondary prevention usually suggests early identification and early intervention to stop the problem from continuing; and tertiary prevention aims to reduce the severity and effects of the problem after it has occurred by means of some sort of treatment and rehabilitation. Primary prevention has been the goal of public health practice for the past 200 years, and several successes have been recorded, including the development of vaccines to eliminate several infectious diseases, fluoridation of drinking water to combat tooth decay, and numerous technological advances such as public sanitation and sewage disposal facilities to eliminate the spread of diseases. However, the focus on preventing psychological, behavioral, and social disorders began in earnest only with the emergence of the community mental health movement in the 1960s. Moreover, documented successes of such endeavors have appeared only recently (Price, Cowen, Lorion, & Ramos-McKay, 1988), and conclusive documentation of effectiveness remains elusive.

Reasons for this state of affairs include the complexity of what these programs are trying to accomplish and of the research designs that are necessary in order to provide the documentation, the lengthy time periods needed to demonstrate primary prevention, and the enormous costs involved in evaluating such projects. Nevertheless, it does not lead us to Plummer's conclusion that "positively proving the effectiveness of prevention is an impossible task."

Recently, Muehrer and Koretz (1992) provided a list of seven fundamental methodological issues that must be addressed in order for the impact of preventive interventions to be accurately determined:

> (a) adverse outcomes to be prevented and desirable outcomes to be promoted, both short- and long-term, must be specified; (b) a theoretical framework for intervention design, with particular emphasis on how specific intervention components are to modify known risk and protective factors, must be articulated; (c) process measures to ensure that the intervention was implemented as planned and to facilitate replication must be included; (d) target populations must be identified and sample selection procedures justified; (e) pilot data must be used to determine whether the proposed sample size will be large enough to detect an intervention effect (i.e., statistical power calculations are needed); (f) an experimental research design should be used to examine potential causal relationships between the risk and protective factors and the outcomes (i.e., to rule out alternative explanations for the findings); and (g) participants need to be followed longitudinally to determine whether the intervention has lasting impact. (pp. 109-110)

To date, no evaluation of any child sexual abuse prevention program has accounted for more than a few of these concerns.

Why Question the Effectiveness of Sexual Abuse Prevention?

Given the importance of preventing child sexual abuse, why would anyone want to question the use of prevention programs? As a way of answering, we turn to the field of medicine. Say that someone claimed to have discovered a vaccine that would prevent the spread of AIDS. If the vaccine worked, it would reduce the incidence of AIDS. If, however, the vaccine was ineffective and only appeared to work, and if it was accepted by the medical community as being effective, then it could result in the increased spread of AIDS. This would occur if those who took the vaccine believed that it would work and stopped using sexual practices that are inconvenient but known to be effective in stopping the transmission of AIDS.

The same concern is appropriate for all types of prevention programs. If adults assume that child sexual abuse programs are effective, they may believe that their children are protected from abuse by participating in the programs. The adults may then become less protective themselves. This tendency may be greatest when the programs are presented in schools that have effectively taught children other skills, such as reading, arithmetic, and health practices. If the prevention programs are not effective, then the children may be put at greater risk for being abused than if the program had not been presented at all, because it will be assumed that they are protected. Consequently, we believe that if a program called "child sexual abuse prevention" is presented, it needs to *prevent* child sexual abuse.

Why Evaluate?

Program evaluation can be complex, time-consuming, and costly. In a social environment in which the need for sexual abuse prevention is clear, but only limited funds are available, it is tempting to use all of the funds to provide the prevention programs so that more children can be reached. Despite the costs, however, evaluation should be a critical component of any program. The goal of evaluation is seldom to determine that a program is or is not useful. Most any program that has been constructed carefully has some value. A good evaluation will help to show which parts of a program are achieving their goals and which are not. Evaluation can also show with which audience a program is most effective. Given that there are limited funds for abuse prevention, evaluation is needed to show which prevention programs work best with which children. The short-term costs of evaluating a program must be compared with the long-term costs of presenting ineffective programs. Because we are looking for long-term protection for our children, we must commit to undertaking the short-term costs.

The Complexity of Sexual Abuse Prevention

The complexity of the process that a child must engage in either to repel an abusive approach or to report an occurrence of abuse can be highlighted by separating it into three parts: First, a child must recognize that he or she is in an abusive situation; then, the child must believe that he or she can and should take some sort of action; finally, the child must possess and use specific self-protective skills. To be effective, prevention programs must focus on all of these three parts. Providing a child with skills in only one or two is likely to reduce the effectiveness of the program drastically.

Prevention programs must first inform children about what sexual abuse is. Most have done this by trying to teach the concept of good, bad, and confusing touches. However, young children are very poor at making fine distinctions between such abstract entities, so teaching these concepts may be very difficult (Berrick & Gilbert, 1991; Haugaard & Reppucci, 1988). Moreover, even adults are not clear about what is and is not sexual abuse (Melton, 1992). Although most adults may agree that certain acts always entail sexual abuse (e.g., a parent having intercourse with a child), considerable disagreement exists about other acts (e.g., whether a 7-year-old is being sexually abused by a parent who cleans the child's genitals each night during a bath). Therefore, more concrete teaching about what acts are sexual abuse may also be problematic.

Assuming that a child is able to label a certain experience as sexual abuse, the child must then understand that he or she should report or repel it. Many programs attempt to teach children that they do not have to allow other people to touch them (under most circumstances), and that they have the right to say no to anyone who tries to touch them in an unacceptable fashion. However, children at different cognitive levels often find it difficult to decide when an action should or should not be taken. For example, young children are much better at following broad and general rules (e.g., "Do not let anyone touch your private parts") than they are at following rules that require making distinctions (e.g., "Doctors or nurses can touch your private parts, and your parents can touch you if they are helping you clean yourself or if you are hurt there, but no one, not even your parents, can touch you there at other times"). Such rules may be incomprehensible to many children, who may simplify them so that anyone who is caring for them can touch them in certain places, or that no one can touch them or make them do anything they don't want to do.

If a child understands that a certain act is sexual abuse and that something should be done to stop it, then the child must feel empowered and competent to implement a plan of action. The typical plan that is taught is that the child should not keep the abuse a secret, should tell an adult until someone believes the child, and should run away if possible. However, such a strategy may not give the child enough information, especially if the child is fearful of threatened or imagined punishments that might occur. Most adults have been in situations where they know that something should be done, but if they are unprepared or afraid, they prefer to do nothing in order to avoid a wrong or ineffective action. It seems unreasonable to expect that children, who usually are not as cognitively or emotionally competent or as powerful as adults, will be able to engage in these complex behaviors in emotionally delicate and sometimes frightening situations.

Most existing prevention programs seem to be based on the idea that they can teach children at various developmental levels enough information in a very short time span to enable them *both* to understand the issues and to act to protect themselves. Given both the cognitive complexity of the issues and the emotionally charged situation that probably exists in most abusive encounters, it seems highly unlikely that most young children could learn enough to be effective in preventing their own abuse. We now turn to an examination of extant programs and their evaluation.

Prevention Programs for Schoolchildren

Although a few programs have been designed for use with junior and senior high school students, most target preschool and elementary school children and are implemented in schools or day-care centers. Classroom programs involving lectures and discussions are most widespread, partly because of intimacy and convenience; children participate in small groups in a situation that usually allows time for questions (Berrick & Gilbert, 1991). In the majority of cases, empowerment is the guiding conceptual framework (Tharinger et al., 1988). Two very different goals are usually emphasized: *primary prevention* and *detection*. Neither of these goals has been investigated systematically.

Programs for children generally address the following topics: educating children about what sexual abuse is; broadening their awareness of possible abusers to include people they know and like; teaching that each child has the right to control access to his or her body; describing a variety of "touches" that a child can experience; stressing actions that a child can take in a potentially abusive situation, such as saying no or running away; teaching that some secrets should not be kept and that a child is never at fault for sexual abuse; and stressing that the child should tell a trusted adult if touched in an inappropriate manner until something is done to protect the child (Conte, 1988; Finkelhor, 1986). However, in order to avoid controversy and increase the number of schools willing to accept the programs, most child sexual abuse prevention is approached from a protective, rather than sexual, standpoint. For example, discussions of bullies or relatives who forcefully try to kiss a child are frequently used to illustrate good and bad touching. More intimate or long-term types of sexual abuse, specific discussions of molestation by parents, and information that some "bad" touches can actually feel good tend to be ignored. Our concern is that modifications of content in order to increase schools' acceptance of the programs may reduce their preventive influence because of the information that they fail to convey.

Many prevention programs involve only one or two presentations, whereas a much smaller number have involved 25 to 30 short sessions. A few sessions may be enough for detection, because some abused children will identify themselves after even brief exposure, such as after viewing a 30-second public service announcement on television. However, little justification exists to suggest that primary prevention can be accomplished with very few sessions.

Prevention educators generally agree that the instructors of the programs should be authority figures such as teachers or specially trained volunteers or mental health professionals. The various program formats should be entertaining, of high interest, and nonthreatening. Movies, slides, videotapes, plays, discussions, and role-play situations, as well as printed materials such as coloring books or comic books, are used. Unfortunately, neither the validity nor the efficacy of the formats or instructors is known (Roberts, Alexander, & Fanurik, 1990).

Although most programs emphasize that parental involvement is critical, low participation rates are the norm (Berrick, 1988). Prevention educators lament this lack of participation, but tend to accept it rather than to develop innovative programs that target parents.

Outcome Research[1]

The most common and consistent finding among the few programs that have been evaluated is a statistically significant, yet often slight (e.g., a two-point gain on a 20-item questionnaire), increase in knowledge about sexual abuse following participation in a prevention program (Berrick & Gilbert, 1991; Conte, Rosen, Saperstein, & Shermack, 1985; Harvey, Forehand, Brown, & Holmes, 1988; Ray & Dietzel, 1984; Saslawsky & Wurtele, 1986). Moreover, many children answer a high percentage of the questions accurately even before they participate in a prevention program (Berrick & Gilbert, 1991; Swan, Press, & Briggs, 1985), which suggests that either the children know more than prevention educators think they do or better assessment instruments are needed in order to demonstrate the value of the programs. For example, the limited-item questionnaires may not represent the children's full increase in knowledge (Conte, 1984; Hazzard & Angert, 1986; Kleemeier & Webb, 1986). In one of the few longitudinal studies, Plummer (1984) found that although a majority of concepts were retained in an eight-month follow-up of 69 fifth graders, three crucial questions concerned with breaking promises, whether molesters were often people whom the child knew, and who was to blame if the child was touched in a sexual way were answered incorrectly significantly more often at the eight-month follow-up than immediately after the program was completed. Differences in knowledge retained between school-age and preschool children, not surprisingly, indicated that older children learned more (Borkin & Frank, 1986; Conte et al., 1985). Given the small increase in knowledge typically found, the more meager results with preschool children raise questions about even minimal usefulness of prevention programs for this group.

In the most extensive set of studies to date, and arguably among the most objective, because the investigators were not studying their own programs, Gilbert, Berrick, LeProhn, and Nyman (1989) and Berrick and Gilbert (1991) evaluated several representative curricula (e.g., Child Assault Prevention [CAP]; Talking about Touching) for preschool, first-grade, and third-grade children. The programs ranged in duration from a single 15- to 30-minute session to 27 short sessions over a three- to six-week period. They found that the average number of concepts presented was 18 for preschoolers, 24 for first graders, and

23 for third graders; the average length of classroom instruction was 28 minutes for preschoolers, 67 minutes for first graders, and 83 minutes for third graders. Clearly, very little time was allocated per concept taught, and, surprisingly, the youngest children received the least amount of time.

These investigators found the usual small but statistically significant knowledge gains for the first and third graders, but little evidence of positive gains for preschoolers. They question the developmental readiness of preschoolers to absorb the most basic concepts being taught. For example, the preschoolers appeared unable to comprehend the concept of a mixed-up or confusing touch and found it difficult to distinguish how touches or feelings about touches can change and to differentiate between types of secrets. Preschoolers also were more likely to interpret pictures of activities such as tickling and bathing as negative after participation in prevention programs. (For a study of preschoolers that found more positive results, see Nibert et al., 1989; for a critique of Nibert et al., see Reppucci & Herman, 1991.)

Another study that warrants attention is that of Kraizer, Witte, and Fryer (1989). These investigators measured behavioral skills associated with prevention of sexual, physical, and emotional victimization before and after children ages 3 through 10 had participated in the Safe Personal Safety Training Program. This standardized, scripted videotape curriculum provides training for parents and teachers as well as for children in five age-appropriate segments. It teaches basic concepts and role-playing techniques and then develops mastery of skills through role playing and discussion in the classroom. Program evaluation was completed with 670 children from rural, suburban, and urban schools in three states. The researchers conducted pre- and post-testing of both participants and matched control children. Behavioral change attributable to the program was measured through role plays, and these results were correlated with measures of knowledge and self-esteem in order to assess a child's ability to resist victimization successfully.

The scripted role play measured the child's ability and willingness to terminate unwanted touch effectively and appropriately in the face of flattery, emotional coercion, rejection, bribery, and secrecy, all behaviors that research has shown to be used by sexual offenders (Conte, Wolf, & Smith, 1989). Although many of the participants had previously been exposed to more typical child abuse prevention programs, no skill differences were revealed by the pretesting between these children and the others who had not been in such programs. The participants showed a significant increase in skills associated with the reduction of risk for child abuse, whereas the control children did not. These results suggest that children's active participation rather than the more typical passive observing or reading techniques may be a critical element in programming. This investigation is noteworthy for its use of a behavioral versus questionnaire measure of change, and its relatively positive results are promising. However, the increase in role-play responses from 31% to 59% correct, although significant, was not particularly large, and the measures were taken within one week after completion of the program.

In summary, prevention programs that have any sort of systematic evaluation deserve praise because so few have made any attempt to evaluate their effectiveness. However, the evaluations conducted so far all have had basic design flaws, and none has come close to meeting the seven basic methodological criteria for evaluating prevention programs spelled out by Muehrer and Koretz (1992). Although a few have used nontreatment control groups matched for such variables as age, gender, and socioeconomic status, and a repeated measures design, most have not. Therefore, there is no way to determine whether the programs caused any changes that might have occurred. Other design problems include small samples, lack of attention to the reliability and validity of the measuring instruments, no pretesting to establish a baseline of knowledge, and short-term follow-up assessments, usually after less than two months. (For more comprehensive reviews of evaluation studies that have arrived at similar conclusions, see Berrick & Gilbert, 1991; Melton, 1992; Reppucci & Herman, 1991; for a differing perspective, see Finkelhor & Strapko, 1992.)

Critical Assumptions

Most child sexual abuse prevention programs are developed from anecdotal clinical information (Conte, 1984) and are based on six critical assumptions, discussed in turn below.

Assumption 1: Children are the appropriate target of intervention, and their empowerment will prevent sexual abuse. Berrick and Gilbert (1991) convincingly demonstrate that the roots of this assumption lie in feminist theory and programs for women to combat rape that focus on awareness and self-defense techniques. The first Child Assault Prevention program, now widely used nationwide, was developed by Women Against Rape, and this philosophy is explicit in the CAP program manual:

The sexual abuse of children, particularly the abuse of female children by adult males, demands that we extend our critique of rape prevention one step further. . . . The CAP Project stems from the same feminist critique of rape prevention, applied to the condition of children. . . . While precautions are often necessary, we do not advocate the restriction of children's activities. Rather we encourage children to solve problems using their own resources. This approach is considerably different than most child abuse programs which focus on community education, adult intervention, and parental responsibility. (quoted in Berrick & Gilbert, 1991, p. 11)

The issue is whether this faith in promoting self-defense and the psychological empowerment of children is justified. Based on the concerns regarding the issue of developmental readiness raised earlier in this chapter and a wealth of evidence to support these concerns from developmental research (see e.g., Berrick & Gilbert, 1991; Elkind, 1987; Piaget & Inhelder, 1969), as well as findings on offenders' behavior that suggest that neither self-defense techniques nor a child's saying no would be a powerful deterrent to an offender (Conte et al., 1989), targeting children appears unlikely to be an effective strategy for preventing child sexual abuse. No evidence exists to suggest that what may be appropriate for adult women is equally appropriate for children. Moreover, as Melton (1992) states, "The primary focus on changing behavior of potential victims of sexual abuse is not only unfair but also unrealistic. Telling children that they have control over their bodies makes them no more powerful, a fact to which all children—most American children—who have been corporally punished can attest" (p. 181).

Assumption 2: A link between children's knowledge and their behavior exists such that increasing their knowledge about sexual abuse will increase their ability to prevent abuse. Although prevention educators, parents, and others would like to believe in this assumption, no empirical evidence exists to support it (Reppucci & Haugaard, 1989). As Wald and Cohen (1986) put it: "We want to stress that there is not, as of yet, an adequate basis for concluding that such programs are either good or bad or both. Yet, . . . they are based on an unproven assumption that knowledge enables children to protect themselves" (p. 296).

Assumption 3: Prevention educators know what types of skills will make a child less susceptible to sexual abuse, and these skills are being taught. Sexual abuse comes in many different forms. Skills useful for preventing one type of abuse might not be useful for preventing another very different type, and some skills may be useful for children of one age but not for children of another. Although this would suggest that developmentally sensitive curricula are imperative, current sexual abuse prevention programs "generally have failed to consider cognitive-developmental factors" and "look remarkably similar across age groups" (Melton, 1992, p. 182). Clarity as to specific skills and behaviors that prevention programs should teach is needed in order to allow researchers to develop means of measuring their acquisition. Kraizer et al.'s (1989) program, based on what actually happens in abusive situations, is a step in the right direction. However, *in vivo* assessment situations are very difficult to construct because of various ethical problems, not the least of which is that subjecting children to actual sexual abuse situations in order to assess what prevention behaviors they exhibit is not acceptable. In addition, of course, there is no fail-safe method for predicting what sort of skills would enable a child to defend against any and all abusers. Moreover, studies of offenders suggest that they tend to fear only detection (Burdin & Johnson, 1989; Conte et al., 1989), thus teaching young children strategies such as when to say no, fight, yell, or run is relatively useless because of the superior knowledge, strength, and skill of the adult perpetrator. Such actions by children may even put them in more jeopardy; yet these are, in large part, the standard skills being taught.

Assumption 4: Prevention programs have no negative effects, or possible negative effects are so minor that they are insignificant when compared with the positive outcomes. Although a few investigators have found no evidence of increases in fears or other anxieties among participants in prevention programs (Binder & McNiel, 1987; Hazzard, Webb, & Kleemeier, 1988; Miltenberger & Thiesse-Duffy, 1988; Wurtele & Miller-Perrin, 1987), others have found evidence that some small proportion, usually about 5-10%, may suffer from nightmares, upset stomachs, or other anxieties after being exposed to these programs (Garbarino, 1987; Gilbert et al., 1989; Kleemeier & Webb, 1986; Swan et al., 1985; Wurtele, Kast, Miller-Perrin, & Kondrick, 1989). Kleemeier and Webb (1986) summarize their results as showing "few negative reactions," even though the children's parents reported that 33% of the children displayed emotional reactions such as irritability and anxiety and 20% exhibited negative behavioral responses. These results, in conjunction with numerous anecdotes about temporary negative reactions—for instance, some preschool children being afraid to ride home from school with anyone but their parents (Conte, 1988)—and the fact that no long-term or subtle effects, such as possible negative effects on nonsexual physical contact with parents and other significant adults, exploratory sexual play with peers, and/or attitudes toward sexuality in general, have been investigated, suggest, at most, a cautionary acceptance of the assumption of little or no adverse impact from the programs. Evaluation studies can provide important information for reducing any negative consequences. For example, studies might show that only certain components of the programs are associated with negative outcomes, and these components could be altered or eliminated.

Assumption 5: Primary prevention is an achievable goal of the existing prevention programs. No evidence exists that primary prevention has ever been achieved by the existing prevention programs. Although we recognize that demonstrating effectiveness of primary prevention programs with convincing empirical data is a time-consuming and expensive affair, the fact that there is not even a published case study of a child using what he or she was taught to prevent an incident of abuse is troubling, especially because there are reports that children who had been participants in prevention programs still became victims of abusers (Reppucci & Herman, 1991). Moreover, the hope that these programs may deter potential abusers because of their fear of detection has not been supported by any sort of evidence.

Assumption 6: Detection of ongoing abuse has been achieved. This assumption appears to be on a solid foundation in that many individual cases of ongoing or past abuse have been discovered as a result of these interventions. Unfortunately, no systematic information is available regarding what percentage of children are likely to disclose abuse or how many of the disclosures are confirmed. Nevertheless, Finkelhor and Strapko (1992) claim that detection is the "most important and unambiguous finding" of the prevention programs, and even suggest renaming them "disclosure" programs. This suggestion may have considerable merit if the programs are primarily useful for detection rather than prevention. It also suggests that the search for alternative means of preventing child sexual abuse takes on even more urgency.

Conclusions

More definitive information about the six critical assumptions and more thorough evaluations of ongoing prevention programs are necessary if we are to determine their influence on children. Extensive investigations of the full range of prevention programs must be undertaken. Because the safety of children is the ultimate goal, we need to know much more about which programs work to teach which skills to which children. We need more sophisticated research regarding the process that a child must go through to repel or report abuse and determine how this process is experienced by children at various levels of cognitive and emotional development and in various ecological contexts. Furthermore, innovative forms of prevention programs must be developed that focus on parents. The low participation rates by parents in the current school-based programs are cause for alarm. Educators and mental health professionals should try providing programs targeting parents and other adults through places of employment, churches, and community service groups, such as the Lions Club and Kiwanis, and through small discussion groups in local homes. Although all of these approaches would be time-consuming, they would undoubtedly increase parental involvement and heighten awareness of the problem among all adults. Moreover, such programs would reach more males, the major perpetrators and the parents least likely to attend a typical school-sponsored evening session. Two major benefits could be that some potential abusers might be discouraged if they believed that children might actually tell someone of an approach (Finkelhor, 1986), and the inappropriate burden of children's being responsible for preventing their own sexual exploitation could be removed.

Even though child sexual abuse prevention programs focusing on environmental and social change have not yet been developed, attention should be paid to such approaches. As Melton (1992) points out, the history of public health strongly suggests that prevention programs designed to change the risky behavior of individuals are not very successful. Eliminating or reducing the opportunities for risky behaviors has produced greater increases in safety in other areas than teaching or persuading people to avoid risky behaviors themselves. For example, childproof caps and lead-free paints are much more effective at reducing poisonings than are programs aimed at increasing parents' vigilance and children's avoidance behaviors, and legal regulation of the marketplace has had more impact on teenagers' smoking and alcohol consumption than has health education. In other words, we need to consider alternative approaches to sex abuse prevention that do not target the child and may prove to be more effective.

In this chapter, we have not meant to be unduly critical regarding efforts to empower young children to become able to recognize and cope with the dangers of sexual abuse. However, we do feel that it is reasonable to question whether this relatively exclusive focus on children as their own protectors is appropriate, to emphasize that children's developmental capacities must be considered, and to encourage more rigorous evaluations of both positive and negative effects of every prevention program. Moreover, by questioning these past and current efforts, we do not denigrate them. They are important first steps toward the goal of preventing child sexual abuse, and some of them have shown promise. Nevertheless, our current state of knowledge regarding the best paths toward prevention requires a questioning stance so that we do not become complacent because we want to believe that we have found an effective solution. Advocates of current approaches must recognize that only by questioning these interventions can we sharpen them and develop new and more effective ones. As children grow to maturity, they experience various ecological contexts, including family, school, peer group, neighborhood, and society as a whole; each influences them and may be the appropriate context for intervention. It is crucial that educators and researchers be open to these contexts as foci for intervention and supportive of rigorous evaluation. Given the enormity of the problem and the large numbers of youth affected, innovative programs must be developed, implemented, and evaluated. Our children deserve no less!

Note

1. Our discussion of outcome research has been necessarily truncated at the request of the editors because of space limitations. However, because Plummer believes that we have based our analysis "on information or premises gathered from Berrick and Gilbert's faulty conclusions," it is important to point out that our analysis is based on a thorough examination of existing primary sources, not a single source (see, for example, our previous work: Haugaard & Reppucci, 1988; Reppucci & Haugaard, 1989; Reppucci & Herman, 1991).

References

Berrick, J. D. (1988). Parental involvement in child abuse prevention training: What do they learn? *Child Abuse and Neglect, 12*, 543-553.

Berrick, J. D., & Gilbert, N. (1991). *With the best of intentions: The child sexual abuse prevention movement.* New York: Guilford.

Binder, R. L., & McNiel, D. E. (1987). Evaluation of a school-based sexual abuse prevention program: Cognitive and emotional effects. *Child Abuse and Neglect, 11,* 497-506.

Durkin, J., & Frank, L. (1986). Sexual abuse prevention for preschoolers: A pilot program. *Child Welfare, 6,* 75-83.

Burdin, L. E., & Johnson, C. F. (1989). Sex abuse prevention programs: Offenders' attitudes about their efficacy. *Child Abuse and Neglect, 13,* 77-87.

Conte, J. R. (1984, August). *Research on the prevention of sexual abuse of children.* Paper presented at the Second National Conference for Family Violence Researchers, Durham, NH.

Conte, J. R. (1988). Research on the prevention of sexual abuse of children. In G. T. Hotaling, D. Finkelhor, J. T. Kirkpatrick, & M. A. Straus (Eds.), *Coping with family violence* (pp. 300-309). Newbury Park, CA: Sage.

Conte, J. R., Rosen, C., Saperstein, L., & Shermack, R. (1985). An evaluation of a program to prevent the sexual victimization of young children. *Child Abuse and Neglect, 9,* 319-328.

Conte, J. R., Wolfe, S., & Smith, T. (1989). What sexual offenders tell us about prevention strategies. *Child Abuse and Neglect, 13,* 293-301.

Elkind, D. (1987). *Miseducation: Preschoolers at risk.* New York: Knopf.

Finkelhor, D. (1986). Prevention: A review of programs and research. In D. Finkelhor & Associates (Eds.), *A sourcebook on child sexual abuse* (pp. 224-254). Beverly Hills, CA: Sage.

Finkelhor, D., & Strapko, N. (1992). Sexual abuse prevention education: A review of evaluation studies. In D. J. Willis, E. Holden, & M. Rosenberg (Eds.), *Prevention of child maltreatment: Developmental and ecological perspectives* (pp. 150-167). New York: John Wiley.

Garbarino, J. (1987). Children's response to a sexual abuse prevention program: A study of the *Spiderman* comic. *Child Abuse and Neglect, 11,* 143-148.

Gilbert, N., Berrick, J., LeProhn, N., & Nyman, N. (1989). *Protecting young children from sexual abuse: Does preschool training work?* Lexington, MA: Lexington.

Harvey, P., Forehand, R., Brown, C., & Holmes, T. (1988). The prevention of sexual abuse: Examination of the effectiveness of a program with kindergarten-age children. *Behavior Therapy, 19,* 429-435.

Haugaard, J. J., & Reppucci, N. D. (1988). *The sexual abuse of children: A comprehensive guide to current knowledge and intervention strategies.* San Francisco: Jossey-Bass.

Hazzard, A. P., & Angert, L. (1986, August). *Child sexual abuse prevention: Previous research and future directions.* Paper presented at the annual meeting of the American Psychological Association, Washington, DC.

Hazzard, A. P., Webb, C., & Kleemeier, C. (1988). *Child sexual assault prevention programs: Helpful or harmful?* Unpublished manuscript, Emery University School of Medicine.

Kleemeier, C., & Webb, C. (1986, August). *Evaluation of a school-based prevention program.* Paper presented at the annual meeting of the American Psychological Association, Washington, DC.

Kraizer, S., Witte, S. S., & Fryer, G. E., Jr. (1989, September-October). Child sexual abuse prevention programs: What makes them effective in protecting children? *Children Today,* pp. 23-27.

Melton, G. (1992). The improbability of prevention of sexual abuse. In D. J. Willis, E. Holden, & M. Rosenberg (Eds.), *Prevention of child maltreatment: Developmental and ecological perspectives* (pp. 168-189). New York: John Wiley.

Miltenberger, R. G., & Thiesse-Duffy, E. (1988). Evaluation of home-based programs for teaching personal safety skills to children. *Journal of Applied Behavior Analysis, 21,* 81-87.

Muehrer, P., & Koretz, D. S. (1992). Issues in preventive intervention research. *Current Directions in Psychological Science, 1,* 109-112.

Nibert, D., Cooper, S., Ford, J., Fitch, L. K., & Robinson, J. (1989). The ability of young children to learn abuse prevention. *Response to the Victimization of Women and Children, 12*(4), 14-21.

Note. (1985). The unreliability of expert testimony on the typical characteristics of sexual abuse victims. *Georgetown Law Journal, 74,* 429-456.

Piaget, J., & Inhelder, B. (1969). *The psychology of the child.* New York: Basic Books.

Plummer, C. (1984, August). *Preventing sexual abuse: What in-school programs teach children.* Second National Conference for Family Violence Researchers. (Available from C. Plummer, P.O. Box 421, Kalamazoo, MI 49005-0421)

Price, R., Cowen, E., Lorion, R., & Ramos-McKay, J. (Eds.). (1988). *Fourteen ounces of prevention: A casebook for practitioners.* Washington, DC: American Psychological Association.

Ray, J., & Dietzel, M. (1984). *Teaching child sexual abuse prevention.* Unpublished manuscript.

Reppucci, N. D., & Haugaard, J. J. (1989). Prevention of child sexual abuse: Myth or reality? *American Psychologist, 44,* 266-275.

Reppucci, N. D., & Herman, J. (1991). Sexuality education and child sexual abuse prevention programs in the schools. In G. Grant (Ed.), *Review of research in education* (pp. 127-166). Washington, DC: American Educational Research Association.

Roberts, M. C., Alexander, K., & Fanurik, D. (1990). Evaluation of commercially available materials to prevent child sexual abuse and abduction. *American Psychologist, 45,* 782-783.

Saslawsky, D. A., & Wurtele, S. K. (1986). Educating children about sexual abuse: Implications for pediatric intervention and possible prevention. *Journal of Pediatric Psychology, 11,* 235-245.

Swan, H. L., Press, A. N., & Briggs, S. L. (1985). Child sexual abuse prevention: Does it work? *Child Welfare, 64,* 667-674.

Tharinger, D., Krivacska, J., Laye-Donough, M., Jamison, L., Vincent, G., & Hedlund, A. (1988). Prevention of child sexual abuse: An analysis of issues, educational programs, and research findings. *School Psychology Review, 17,* 614-634.

Wald, M. S., & Cohen, S. (1986). Preventing child abuse: What will it take? *Family Law Quarterly, 20,* 281-302.

Wurtele, S. K., Kast, L., Miller-Perrin, C., & Kondrick, P. (1989). Comparison of programs for teaching personal safety skills to preschoolers. *Journal of Consulting and Clinical Psychology, 57,* 505-511.

Wurtele, S. K., & Miller-Perrin, C. L. (1987). An evaluation of side effects associated with participation in a child sexual abuse prevention program. *Journal of School Health, 57,* 228-231.

CHAPTER 20

What the Scientific Evidence Shows
On the Average, We Can Do No Better Than Arrest

Richard A. Berk

The policy decision to make arrest the mandatory or presumptive response in incidents of spousal violence must be considered along at least four dimensions: what the law allows, morality and ethics, practical limitations of what law enforcement can do, and the weight of scientific evidence. An example of the first is the role of probable cause in misdemeanor compared with felony wife battery.[1] An example of the second is whether violence committed against a stranger should be treated differently from violence committed against a loved one. An example of the third is whether police officers are able to determine at the scene if a restraining order has been violated. An example of the fourth is whether an arrest deters more effectively than an emergency order of protection.[2]

All four dimensions are important for an informed policy decision, and all four should be evaluated as a package. In this chapter, however, I will address only the weight of scientific evidence. I am not a legal scholar, an ethicist, or a police administrator, and even my strongly held opinions on the matters considered by these kinds of specialists carry no particular weight. It would be presumptuous of me, perhaps even dishonest, to use the cover of my scientific training to legitimate views I might express on nonscientific questions. Rather, my job is to convey in an evenhanded fashion what scientific evidence shows.[3] I will be concerned with where the weight of scientific evidence lies with respect to the deterrent value of arrest. Of particular importance will be specific deterrence: whether a person once arrested for spousal violence is less likely to commit new acts of spousal violence in the future.[4]

I will not address general deterrence (whether *other* prospective offenders will be deterred) here, although it is a subject of substantial interest and relevance. Basically, there is no scientific evidence on the matter one way or the other. The same holds for a host of other possible outcomes one might like to examine. For example, insofar as violence within families is transmitted across generations (i.e., children seeing violence at home will be more inclined to use violence as adults), one could ask about the impact an arrest might have on the next generation. Or one could consider the impact of an arrest on the economic viability of the household. As with general deterrence, there is insufficient scientific evidence on these matters to warrant further discussion here.

How to Think About the Scientific Evidence

Before considering the scientific evidence, it may be productive to take a brief detour into the nature of causal inference in science. If one is to evaluate the products of the scientific "game," a brief overview of the rules of that game seems necessary (see, for example, Berk, 1988; Berk & Rossi, 1990). These rules apply not only to the research I will later review, but to the empirical assertions made by Eve Buzawa and Carl Buzawa in Chapter 21 of this volume.

To begin, one needs a definition of a *causal effect*; if the goal is to evaluate the evidence for or against a causal effect of arrest, one needs to be clear about what a causal effect is. To take first a medical illustration, one might be interested to know whether an elderly person catches the flu depending on whether or not that person earlier is given a "flu shot." In this chapter, the issue is whether an offender commits a new act of spousal violence depending on whether or not that offender has earlier been arrested for a previous spousal violence incident. More abstractly, it is common to define a causal effect as the difference between the outcome under one "condition" and the outcome under another "condition." Sometimes the condition of interest is called the *treatment condition* (e.g., a flu shot) and the baseline condition is called the *control condition* (e.g., no flu shot).[5] When there is more than one condition of interest, each is called a (different) treatment condition.[6]

There is certainly nothing surprising about such a definition, in part because it corresponds so well to common sense. But at least two critical implications follow. First, causal effects are *always* comparative;

an outcome under one condition is *compared* with an outcome under another condition. Consider again our medical example. The impact of a flu shot is compared with the impact of the absence of a flu shot.

In addition, proper interpretation always requires that one be clear not only about the content of the treatment condition (i.e., what is actually being delivered), but the content of the control condition as well. Here, the absence of a flu shot is not nothing, but "business as usual." Business as usual for the elderly person in question might include regular sleep and a balanced diet. For this individual, therefore, the likelihood of catching the flu may well be low with or without the flu shot, and hence the flu shot may not prove to be more effective than the control condition. In contrast, business as usual for another elderly individual may include little sleep and poor nutrition. Compared with this control condition, the flu shot may prove to be very effective. In other words, the causal effect of the flu shot in these two instances may differ because of the control condition *with which the flu shot's outcome is compared.*

In studies of the causal effect of arrest in spousal violence incidents, an arrest can be most simply compared with "doing nothing." But again, "nothing" is *not* nothing, but normal police practice. "Nothing" may include trying to mediate the dispute, offering some form of crisis counseling, transporting the victim to a shelter for battered women, or ordering the offender from the premises for eight hours. One of the advances of recent research on the impact of arrest in spousal violence incidents is to "unpack" police business as usual and explicitly determine the causal effects of the components with respect to one another. For example, arrest may be compared with crisis counseling delivered by mental health professionals. Yet, the key point is that the effectiveness of arrest will depend upon with what it is compared. All causal effects are actually *relative* causal effects.

Second, it is impossible to implement literally the definition of a causal effect. One cannot, for example, both give a flu shot to an elderly person and at the same time not give that flu shot. Likewise, one cannot at the same time both arrest and not arrest a spousal violence offender. This leads to what is called the "fundamental problem of causal inference." One cannot directly observe causal effects; rather, they must be *inferred.*

In practice, this leads to a second use of comparisons. One may try to infer (instead of directly observe) the existence of a causal effect by comparing the outcome before the introduction of the treatment condition with the outcome after the treatment condition has been introduced. In our flu shot illustration, the elderly person might be left to his or her own devices during one flu season and given the flu vaccine before the next flu season. The causal effect of the flu shot would be *inferred* through a comparison of the health experiences of the person across the two flu seasons. Alternatively, one might, before a given flu season, give a flu shot to one elderly person but not give a flu shot to *another* elderly person. The causal effect of the flu shot would then be *inferred* through a comparison of the health experiences of two individuals. In other words, in the first case one is comparing the outcomes for the same individual over two time periods, and in the second case one is comparing the outcomes for two individuals over the same time period. A similar logic can be applied to estimating the causal effect of an arrest. For example, one offender might be arrested and another offender might be counseled. Or an offender might be counseled after one violent incident and arrested after another.

However, whether the concern is with flu shots or arrests, this second use of comparisons (across time or across subjects) is a risky undertaking. For the over-time comparison, one must be convinced that the two time periods are in every relevant way the same. Likewise, for the over-subject comparison, one must be convinced that the two subjects are in every relevant way the same. For example, it would probably be misleading to infer the causal effect of a flu vaccine over two different flu seasons if the virulence of the flu strains differed. If, for example, the flu strain were more virulent in the flu season when the vaccine was tested, the comparison would be biased against finding the vaccine effective. In a similar fashion, it would be potentially misleading to give the flu vaccine to an elderly person with a long history of health problems and not give the flu vaccine to an elderly person with excellent health history (although sensible on ethical grounds). Again, the bias would be against finding the vaccine effective.

Analogous problems surface for research on the impact of arrest. Imagine how one might be misled when trying to infer the causal effect of arrest by comparing an arrested first offender with a counseled habitual offender. Clearly, the comparison is biased toward finding that arrest is more effective. For over-time comparisons, the offender's life circumstances (e.g., employment) might change. Thus a counseling intervention might be introduced at "Time 1," when the offender had a job, and an arrest intervention might be introduced at "Time 2," when the offender did not. The bias in this comparison would perhaps favor counseling.

For the kinds of empirical questions raised in this chapter, the strategy of responding to the fundamental problem of causal inference by making comparisons over two time periods for a single individual, or over two individuals for a single time period, is doomed. For the treatment conditions we are considering, the comparisons are very unlikely to be fair; in effect, the deck will be stacked before the cards are dealt.

But there is a solution. Although it may be impossible to find two individuals who are truly comparable, one can *construct groups* that are comparable. Imagine setting up a special kind of lottery for spousal violence offenders. In this lottery, half would "win" the prize of an arrest and half would "win" the prize of counseling. Which prize went to which offenders would be determined by a random mechanism much like those used in state lotteries across the country. In fair state lotteries, each lottery ticket has effectively the same chance of winning. In our offender lottery, each offender would have the same chance of either being arrested or being counseled. Because each offender would have the same chance of being among those arrested or among those counseled, the arrested *group* and the counseling *group* would be approximately comparable.[7]

Then, fair comparisons could be made, not between pairs of individuals, but between the *averages* of the two groups (because it is the groups, not the individuals, that are comparable). For example, one could compare the *proportion* of offenders in the arrested group who committed new offenses with the *proportion* of offenders in the counseled group who committed new offenses. The difference between these proportions would be one kind of estimate of the average causal effect of arrest, compared with counseling. Thus if 20% of the arrested group "failed" and 30% of the counseled group "failed," the difference of 10% is the average causal effect. In this illustration, the "failure rate" would be 10% higher for counseling than for arrest.

The sorts of group comparisons just described, based on a fair lottery mechanism, are the foundation of "randomized trials" in medicine and "randomized field experiments" in the social sciences (which are really the same thing) and a number of the natural sciences (e.g., ecology). The basic idea is to assign subjects "at random" to the various treatment conditions. The result is that, on the average, the subjects assigned to both conditions are comparable *before the treatment conditions are applied.* Any later differences, therefore, may be attributed to the treatments delivered. Fair comparisons between the *groups* naturally follow.

Randomized experiments are widely accepted as the "gold standard" in empirical scientific research (Marini & Singer, 1988). Although not without their problems (e.g., Smith, 1990), they are the best that science can do when causal inference is a high priority. The nearest approximations, based on multivariate statistical adjustments, are typically a very distant second and typically have much lower credibility (Berk, 1988; Freedman, 1991; Holland, 1988).[8]

Unfortunately, the advantages of randomized experiments and group comparisons have a considerable price. The focus on *average* causal effects does not imply that the causal effects for all individuals are the same. Going back to our medical example, a vaccine would be considered a great success if only 5% of the people vaccinated got the flu, compared with 50% of the people who were not vaccinated. But 5% of the vaccinated individuals got sick; for them, the vaccine failed. And 50% of the individuals not vaccinated remained healthy; they did not need the vaccine. Moreover, with almost any vaccine, there will likely be side effects. For example, perhaps 3% of the people vaccinated developed allergic reactions. In short, a vaccine that is a great success on the average will almost certainly fail (or worse) for some individuals.

How does public policy respond to situations in which on the average the public good is served, but not without individual exceptions? There are three common responses. One option is simply to proceed, acknowledging that a few individuals will necessarily bear the costs for a greater public good. This is often the case for vaccination campaigns to prevent large-scale epidemics (e.g., measles). A more expensive option is to compensate the individuals who bear the costs. For example, individuals who have side effects from a measles vaccine may have their medical costs covered. Finally, if the individuals who will bear the costs can be found in advance, they may be spared the intervention, and/or the impact of the intervention can sometimes be mitigated. Thus individuals allergic to one kind of measles vaccine may not be allergic to another.

The same issues arise in experiments on the causal effect of arrest. Even if arrest has greater deterrent value than a variety of other interventions, it does not mean that it will work for all offenders. And for some offenders, arrest may even backfire; more violence follows, rather than less. It may still be sensible to institute a policy favoring arrest. The fact that an arrest will sometimes make an offender more violent may be seen as a necessary (though unfortunate) price to pay. To deny this as an option is to deny the overall beneficial effects of virtually all medical and technological advances over the past 200 years. However, it may also be possible to compensate victims when arrest backfires. For example, a victim may be given access to free legal counsel should she wish to seek a restraining order, a divorce, or some other legal remedy. And finally, if it is possible to determine in advance the offenders for whom arrest will likely fail or backfire, other options can be considered. For example, one might automatically deny bail for offenders who, because of a long history of spousal violence, would perhaps not be deterred by arrest, or if there is ample historical evidence that arrests have failed to deter the offender in the past.

To summarize, on the question of whether or not arrest "works," the best that science can do is provide unbiased estimates of the average causal effect of arrest compared with other kinds of interventions. Even under the best of circumstances, the average causal effect will neglect individual experiences that depart markedly from what is typical. This is an unfortunate fact of scientific life and an unfortunate fact of public policy. It does not follow that doing "nothing" is preferable. As noted above, "nothing" is always something. And it may be a "something" with no scientific justification and/or with a far worse benefit-to-cost ratio. But at a deeper level, if one requires that all public policy be free of risk, there can be no public policy at all.

The Scientific Evidence

In 1981, the Minneapolis Police Department conducted a randomized field experiment on how the police should respond to incidents of misdemeanor domestic violence.[9] Three competing practices were tested: arresting the offender, ordering the offender from the premises for 24 hours, and trying to restore order (only). The overall conclusion, published in some of the very best scientific journals after extensive review (e.g., the *Journal of the American Statistical Association*), was that arresting the offender was the most effective means of reducing the likelihood of new violence, compared with either of the other two treatments (Berk & Sherman, 1984, 1988; Berk, Smyth, & Sherman, 1988; Sherman & Berk, 1984). Very sophisticated and independent reanalyses of the data have since confirmed the overall conclusions reported (Lowery, 1985; Tauchen, Tauchen, & Witte, 1986).[10]

Despite the many caveats found in accounts of the experiment (e.g., Berk & Sherman, 1988, p. 76) and critiques stressing the limitations of a single study (Lempert, 1989), the results of the Minneapolis experiment soon became criminal justice gospel (Sherman & Cohn, 1989).[11] The finding that arrest "worked" became part of the rhetoric linked to a series of major reforms in how domestic violence incidents were handled by the criminal justice system. Under the banner of "deterrence," for example, many police departments adopted a policy of presumptive arrest in spouse abuse cases, and some departments made arrest mandatory.

The scientific community also responded. The key issue was whether the findings could be generalized to other areas of the country, and the National Institute of Justice funded six replications in six new sites.[12] Most of these studies have yet to publish all their results, but it is already clear that findings of "no difference" will dominate. For example, Dunford, Huizinga, and Elliott (1989) report that on the average in Omaha, Nebraska, arresting the offender proved no more effective than any of the other interventions tried. Similar conclusions are reached by Sherman, Smith, Schmidt, and Rogan (1992) in their analysis of the experiment conducted in Milwaukee, Wisconsin; by Hirschel, Hutchinson, Dean, Kelley, and Pesackis (1990) in their analysis of the experiment conducted in Charlotte, North Carolina; and Berk, Campbell, Klap, and Western (1990) in an analysis of the experiment conducted in Colorado Springs, Colorado.

As an illustration, consider the experiment in Colorado Springs. There were four treatment conditions: an emergency order of protection and arresting the offender, an emergency order of protection and immediate crisis counseling for the offender, an emergency order of protection only, and "simply" trying to restore order (which was the "business-as-usual" treatment). All the treatment conditions that included an emergency order of protection performed a little better than trying to restore order alone, but arrest did not stand out as most effective.

The findings of "no difference" in the six sites are striking because of local variation in content of the treatments, the mix of offenders studied, and the kinds of misdemeanor spouse abuse incidents included in the experiments.[13] In other words, the finding that arrest does not dominate a variety of other interventions seems to generalize to six rather heterogeneous sites. At the same time, it is important to stress that no intervention at any site proved to be better than arrest. Consequently, if on legal or ethical grounds arrest is the preferred response, one is not depriving the community of a superior criminal justice intervention. Put another way, *one can do no better than by arresting the offender.*

There is much more to the story, however. In a very recent paper based on a randomized field experiment undertaken in Milwaukee, Sherman and his colleagues (1992) considered potentially important *differential* effects. These researchers argue that arrest will deter individuals with strong attachments to their local communities. That is, individuals with strong local ties, perhaps through job, friends, or family, will respond well to arrest. For example, they may be shamed after being arrested. However, it follows that individuals with little "stake in conformity" will not be deterred. Moreover, there may well be a subset of individuals not subject to informal controls, who see confrontations with police as a challenge through which self-worth may be enhanced. These individuals, therefore, could become *more* violent in response to arrest. Empirical support for both hypotheses is reported. Among the important implications is that a consistently applied policy of mandatory arrest may actually place some victims at greater risk; there is an identifiable group of offenders for whom arrest may serve to motivate a new assault.

A second paper published in the same journal basically confirms the findings of Sherman and his colleagues and shows that they held across the four experimental sites for which the necessary data are available (Berk, Campbell, Klap, & Western, 1992). But that confirmation was interpreted far more cautiously. In particular, the differential effects found by Sherman and his colleagues were measured by whether or not the offender was employed and whether or not the offender was married. Employed offenders were apparently deterred by arrest, but unemployed offender were not. Indeed, unemployed offenders may have been made more violent. In a similar fashion, married offenders were deterred by arrest, but unmarried offenders were not. And also in a similar fashion, unmarried offenders may have been made more violent.

However, it cannot be overemphasized that whether or not an offender is employed and whether or not an offender is married were *not* randomly assigned. This means that when the impact of arrest was estimated separately for employed and unemployed offenders, the two groups (i.e., employed and unemployed) were not on the average comparable. For example, the employed offenders may have had less violent histories or less stressful relations at home. The same holds for estimates of the impact of arrest estimated separately for married and unmarried offenders. Married and unmarried offenders will differ on the average. For example, unmarried individuals may be younger on the average and perhaps more attached to life on the street. In short, although there is probably something going on, it is not at all clear at this point what that something is.

Second, when there are differential effects, the idea of a single average effect gets complicated. At a site with a preponderance of "good-risk" offenders, arrest will on the average perhaps show beneficial effects. At a site with a preponderance of "bad-risk" offenders, arrest will on the average perhaps show harmful effects. In other words, the estimate of average effect confounds the impact of arrest with *a site's mix of offenders*.[14]

A number of implications follow. To begin, this makes generalizing the "no difference" findings described earlier very difficult. Sites with mixes of good-risk and bad-risk offenders that differ from the mixes at the six experimental sites will likely have different average results. Many of these could well show beneficial (or harmful) effects for arrest on the average. In short, there is no scientific evidence for Buzawa and Buzawa's (Chapter 21, this volume) claim that, on the average, arrest does not work. The proper summary is that "it depends."

In addition, any statements about average differences in the impacts of arrest between employed and unemployed offenders or between married and unmarried offenders must be considered highly suspect. These average effects for offender subgroups also risk confounding the impact of arrest with the mix of offenders. So, in fact, one cannot be confident that arrest is beneficial for employed or married offenders and or that it is perhaps even dangerous for the victims of unemployed or unmarried offenders.

Finally, and on a more optimistic note, the findings suggesting that differential effects may exist perhaps open the door to greater use of a variety of criminal justice interventions and to greater use of informed police discretion. If there is even anecdotal evidence that arrest works better for some kinds of offenders than others, rigorous tests should be implemented. In the meantime, it might make sense to act on the available evidence in situations where the consequences for faulty policies may not be too serious (e.g., first offenders in misdemeanor domestic violence incidents).

Conclusions and Recommendations

The current balance of scientific evidence *from the particular sites studied* suggests that although arrest is not superior to a variety of other criminal justice interventions, one can on the average do no better. Consequently, unless there are legal, ethical, or practical reasons to prefer some other intervention, arrest remains a viable option.

However, there is also some new evidence that arrest can have differential effects, depending on the background of the offender. Although the relevant background characteristics are not fully clear and the underlying mechanisms are downright obscure, the door is now open to a bit more flexibility in how criminal justice interventions are implemented in different communities and even in how police respond to particular incidents within a given community. The balance of evidence suggests that there are good risks and bad risks for arrest.

Communities that believe they have a "better class of offender" may with more confidence implement a policy favoring arrest. Communities that believe they have a "worse class of offender" may decide to make arrest a less common option. Similar processes could be allowed to operate at the level of the police officer on patrol.[15]

However, there may be some practical complications for the differential application of arrest in spousal violence cases, and these would apply to many of the otherwise interesting suggestions that Eve Buzawa and Carl Buzawa make in Chapter 21. In effect, a criminal justice sanction would be applied, depending in part on characteristics of the offender and the crime that have no formal relevance to the seriousness of the crime or the culpability of the offender. For example, how reasonable is it to arrest a batterer who threatens his lover, but not to arrest a batterer who threatens his wife? Is it fair? Is it even legal?[16] Perhaps a better strategy is to focus on the high-risk offender, defined, insofar as possible, by prior record and the seriousness of the immediate offense. For such individuals, arrest could be *coupled* with interventions that would help to protect the victims. For example, a high-risk offender would perhaps be held in jail until a bail hearing and then perhaps denied bail. Restraining orders could perhaps be automatically signed. And victims could be strongly encouraged to make use of shelters.

Finally, analysis of data from the six new experimental sites is far from complete. Over the next year, more findings will no doubt appear, and the data sets will become available for others to analyze. The book is never closed on any important scientific question, and in the case of police responses to spousal violence, we are still working through the early chapters.

Where, then, do I disagree with the Professors Buzawa? Perhaps most important, I think there is a fundamental difference in purpose. I am trying as best I can to evaluate the scientific evidence in an evenhanded manner. Buzawa and Buzawa are essentially advocates for a particular point of view. They believe they know the right answers, and as a result, they selectively marshal evidence to support their position. For example, they are critical of the scientific method when I use it, but cite Sherman's new work, which is based on the exact same research design, favorably. To take another example, they criticize the Minneapolis experiment as but a single study from which no general conclusions can be drawn, yet they draw general conclusions from the Milwaukee experiment, also a single study, apparently because the results fit better with their preconceptions. To take a final example, there is not a shred of scientific evidence that we know how to rehabilitate violent offenders effectively, as desirable as that goal may be. Indeed, all of the rehabilitation strategies tried in the replications of the Minneapolis Domestic Violence Experiment did *not* prove superior to arrest! To make rehabilitation the focal point of any policy response to wife battery is to act on little more than wishful thinking. If Eve and Carl Buzawa were trying to be evenhanded, they would be as consciously skeptical of their pet interventions as they are of arrest.

Notes

1. It is common in a felony incident for police to be able to make an arrest on probable cause. For a misdemeanor incident, police often must either witness the incident or have a victim or witness ready to file a complaint.

2. One could easily add a fifth dimension: cost. As a practical matter, criminal justice interventions are expensive in dollars and in opportunity costs (i.e., resources used for one task cannot be used for another). The problem with introducing cost considerations is that it makes any overall assessment too difficult. We can certainly determine the costs of various allocations of police resources. However, there is no consensus about how to weigh the costs of crimes committed or deterred, especially over the long term. How much is it worth, for example, to deter one beating?

3. There is an important distinction between being objective and being evenhanded. Even if pure objectivity were desirable, it is impossible to achieve. But it *is* possible to look at any particular scientific question from many different and competing points of view. That is what I mean by being evenhanded.

4. There is also an underlying theme. Any assertion I make, or that Eve Buzawa and Carl Buzawa make, should be backed up by evidence. Readers should ask, How do they know that? What is the evidence? How credible is the evidence? Readers should not take on faith that because a college professor says something, it is true. College professors have a strong need to profess, and many will profess on most any topic, irrespective of what they may really know.

5. This assumes that one can reasonably expect a relevant outcome under each of the conditions for each of the units being studied. For example, if an arrest leads to a long prison term, one could not observe even the medium term, whether an arrest deterred or not.

6. Although I am using flu as an illustration, there is nothing about the scientific method or its underlying rationale that is in any sense "medical." The scientific method has been successfully applied to agriculture, quality control within factories, global warming, education, economic development, and a host of other topics. It can even be applied to historical accounts such as those offered by Buzawa and Buzawa. The scientific method is nothing more than a means, imperfect to be sure, of fostering a rigorous and evenhanded evaluation of evidence.

7. How close the approximation is would depend substantially on the number of offenders assigned to one or the other group. The larger the number, the closer the

approximation. In the studies I will later review, the number of offenders is in each case large enough to make the approximation very close.

8. This is not the place to argue the point. Skeptical readers are encouraged to take on the last three references. Of course, the superiority of randomized experiments assumes that they are implemented largely as designed. Typically they are, although there have been some very embarrassing exceptions.

9. The first six paragraphs of this section draw heavily from Berk et al. (1992).

10. This is not the place to get into technical details, but the Binder and Meeker (1988) "critique" lauded by Buzawa and Buzawa is fundamentally uninformed and has carried little weight with the scientific community. Many of the methodological concerns expressed were initially raised by the authors of the Minneapolis study themselves as inherent limitations of *any* single research project. Others are just plain wrong. And criticisms of how the Minneapolis study was used in the policy arena were aired far more thoroughly and thoughtfully by Lempert (1989). Citations to Binder and Meeker are little more than an indicator that the author in question has read the literature.

11. At the time, the Minneapolis experiment provided the best information available and *should*, therefore, have played a key role in questions of what "worked." The quarrel is with a failure by policymakers to appreciate the provisional nature of findings from any single experiment.

12. In contrast to what Professors Eve Buzawa and Carl Buzawa claim in Chapter 21, the research methods were lifted almost intact from the Minneapolis experiment, and it now seems that some of the minor changes made have actually weakened the results. I know because I was present at the gatherings at which the new studies were designed and have reanalyzed data from a number of the sites.

13. For example, sites differed in the kinds of counseling offered to offenders and the criminal justice consequences that followed arrest.

14. This may explain why arrest worked best in Minneapolis. But it may also have been true that the treatments with which arrest was compared were weaker than in the six new sites. That is, the "baseline" got stronger. For example, in Minneapolis, arrest was compared with separating the victim and offender for a period of time or a brief effort to restore order. In Colorado Springs, the comparison conditions included crisis counseling by professional therapists. Arrest could well have had an equal impact in the two sites, but the *difference* in impact between arrest and the control conditions could have been smaller in Colorado Springs because the "competitors" were stronger. Recall that causal effects are inherently comparative.

15. But if there are really important differential effects for different kinds of offenders, it makes any general statement about "what works" pure nonsense. What works "on the average" depends on the mix of offenders included in the study and at the study site more generally. A study or site with a large proportion of "good risks" will show that, on the average, arrest is a very powerful deterrent. A study site with a small proportion of "good risks" will show that, on the average, arrest does not deter and may even make things worse.

16. There are a number of practical problems as well. If what the police do depends on some biographical characteristic of the offender, it must be something that the police can quickly and accurately determine at the scene. Yet, anyone who has ever looked closely at offense or arrest reports knows that in the confusion, tension, and risk that often accompany spousal violence incidents, police frequently get many of the recorded details wrong.

References

Berk, R. A. (1988). Causal inference for sociological data. In N. Smelser (Ed.), *The handbook of sociology* (pp. 155-174). Newbury Park, CA: Sage.

Berk, R. A., Campbell, A., Klap, R., & Western, B. (1990). A Bayesian analysis of the Colorado Springs spouse abuse experiment. *Criminal Law and Criminology, 83,* 170-200.

Berk, R. A., Campbell, A., Klap, R., & Western, B. (1992). The differential deterrent effects of an arrest in incidents of domestic violence: A Bayesian analysis of three randomized field experiments. *American Sociological Review, 57,* 698-708.

Berk, R. A., & Rossi, P. H. (1990). *Thinking about program evaluation.* Newbury Park, CA: Sage.

Berk, R. A., & Sherman, L. W. (1988). Police responses to family violence incidents. *Journal of the American Statistical Association, 83,* 70-76.

Berk, R. A., Smyth, G. K., & Sherman, L. W. (1988). When random assignment fails: Some lessons form the Minneapolis spouse abuse experiment. *Journal of Quantitative Criminology, 4,* 209-223.

Binder, A., & Meeker, J. (1988). Experiments as reforms. *Journal of Criminal Justice, 16,* 347-358.

Dunford, F. W., Huizinga, D., & Elliott, D. S. (1989). *The Omaha domestic violence police experiments* (Technical report, final report to the National Institute of Justice). Washington, DC: Government Printing Office.

Freedman, D. A. (1991). Statistical models and shoe leather. In P. V. Marsden (Ed.), *Sociological methodology* (Vol. 21, pp. 291-314). Oxford: Basil Blackwell.

Hirschel, J. D., Hutchinson, I. W., III, Dean, C. W., Kelley, J. J., & Pesackis, C. E. (1990). *Charlotte Spouse Assault Replication Project: Final report.* Unpublished manuscript, National Institute of Justice.

Holland, P. W. (1988). Causal inference and path analysis. In C. C. Clogg (Ed.), *Sociological methodology* (Vol. 18, pp. 449-484). Washington, DC: American Sociological Association.

Lempert, R. (1989). Humility is a virtue: On the publicization of policy-relevant research. *Law and Society Review, 23,* 145-161.

Lowery, J. (1985). *The impact of arrest: A discrete failure time analysis of crime.* Unpublished doctoral dissertation, University of California, Santa Barbara.

Marini, M. M., & Singer, B. (1988). Causality in the social sciences. In C. C. Clogg (Ed.), *Sociological methodology* (Vol. 18, pp. 347-410). Washington, DC: American Sociological Association.

Sherman, L. W., & Berk, R. A. (1984). The specific deterrent effects of arrest for domestic assault. *American Sociological Review, 49,* 261-271.

Sherman, L. W., & Cohn, E. G. (1989). The impact of research on legal policy: The Minneapolis domestic violence experiment. *Law and Society Review, 23,* 117-144.

Sherman, L. W., Smith, D. A., Schmidt, J. D., & Rogan, D. P. (1992). Crime, punishment and stake in conformity: Legal and extralegal control of domestic violence. *American Sociological Review, 57,* 680-690.

Smith, H. L. (1990). Specification problems in experimental and nonexperimental social research. In C. C. Clogg (Ed.), *Sociological methodology* (Vol. 20, pp. 59-91). Oxford: Basil Blackwell.

Tauchen, G., Tauchen, H., & Witte, A. D. (1986). *The dynamics of domestic violence: A reanalysis of the Minneapolis experiment.* Working paper, Department of Economics, Wellesley College.

CHAPTER **21**

The Scientific Evidence
Is Not Conclusive
Arrest Is No Panacea

Eve S. Buzawa
Carl G. Buzawa

There has been a clear and profound increase in the use of arrest by police as a response to domestic violence. Official policies, which in the past denigrated the role of arrest, in many jurisdictions now promote arrest as the preferred method of handling assaultive behavior. In fact, one recent report stated that by 1989, mandatory or preferred arrest policies were in place (if not fully enforced) by 84% of urban police agencies. Fifteen states and the District of Columbia had policies that "mandated" arrest in cases where there was probable cause to believe that domestic violence had occurred (Sherman, 1992b). To some extent, this is a natural, perhaps even inevitable, reaction to practices of the past, when police and the entire criminal justice establishment inappropriately denigrated the criminality and harm of "domestic violence." It is also the by-product of an unusual confluence of political pressure and arguments made by some social scientists who view arrest as a "magic bullet," an inexpensive way to solve (or at least contain) the epidemic of interpersonal violence. For reasons described below, we believe this analogy is unjustified.

In Chapter 20 of this volume, Richard Berk, an early advocate of "scientific" research on the effects of arrest, uses medical models of research to conclude that although arrest is not superior to other criminal justice interventions, "one can on the average do no better." We welcome the implicit new hint of doubt that arrest is the preferred outcome of police action. We, of course, might wish that such doubts had been initially expressed by proponents of arrest, including Professor Berk. In contrast, and along with many others, we have continually expressed concern about the utter confidence that has been placed in the results of experimental research and the implicit assumption that the complexity of human behavior is easily amenable to accurate measurement and "scientific" regulation, often without regard for the merit of alternative strategies. If so, we might have been spared the feverish media campaign of the 1980s that resulted in the widespread imposition of policy nostrums such as mandatory arrest. Although Professors Sherman and Berk were initially quite careful in reporting the results of their research, subsequent extensive media campaigns and huge funding given to the five replications of the Minneapolis Domestic Violence Experiment gave tacit support to its very preliminary "findings." Alternative research methodologies not employing classical experimental designs and proposals to pursue alternative policy responses such as treatment were not well supported by funding agencies such as the National Institute of Justice.

In any event, arrest should be used judiciously as an appropriate, even essential, tool for certain, but not all, applications now being adopted in official policies. For purposes of this chapter, we will review the historical context of police intervention in domestic violence, explore why it has changed, and, finally, take the position that the mandatory or "automatic" use of arrest is improper for a variety of reasons.

Historical Context

There can be little argument with the basic premise that until relatively recently, virtually all U.S. jurisdictions systematically minimized the role of arrest in handling domestic violence cases. In fact, the "classic" police response to domestic violence could be characterized as one of virtual nonfeasance, the development of procedures by which the police evaded their responsibility to protect victims of crimes within families. This was done through a number of mechanisms. In many jurisdictions, "domestic" cases were diverted by dispatchers attempting to dissuade callers from requesting police response. In such manner, many cases would be "solved" without dispatch (Bannon, 1974; Martin, 1979). When a caller could not be deterred, the call would be characterized as "family trouble" and assigned a very low priority; response was subject to the availability of personnel. As a result, only a relatively small percentage of cases ever received any police response, let alone arrest.

When police actually responded to calls, the likely police reaction, absent a breach of public peace, would be simply to separate and calm down the parties, and then exit as quickly as possible. The reasons for such an apathetic response are varied. As a practical matter, until recently, police lacked legal authority to make arrests for misdemeanor violence unless witnessed or unless the victim pressed charges (Buzawa & Buzawa, 1979). Police in large departments lacked information systems to alert them to chronic abusers (Pierce & Deutsch, in press); training was minimal, resulting in profound ignorance in handling domestic violence (Loving & Quirk, 1982); and these calls were clustered on nights and weekends, when other urgent calls competed (Bannon, 1974).

Police attitudes reinforced such barriers. Officers already predisposed toward "real law enforcement" became quite cynical about "domestic" calls, where they perceived little was accomplished. After all, the observable outcome of a "good" interaction, cessation of violence, hardly compared with the excitement or adrenaline rush (and the very real rewards) of apprehending the perpetrator of a "real" crime. The psychological and organizational rewards of a "good pinch" (Van Maanen, 1974) were not accorded to an arrest in a family assault (Stanko, 1989). Finally, answering such calls was incorrectly viewed as being very dangerous. As a result of these factors, officers were told to extract themselves from potential danger as soon as possible (Garner & Clemmer, 1986; Uchida, Brooks, & Koper, 1987).

The Bias Against Arrest

Under these circumstances, it is not surprising that arrest was not a favored, or usual, outcome of police action. Despite general public beliefs to the contrary, police do not arrest lightly, and there is inconclusive evidence to indicate whether or not domestic violence results in fewer arrests than other assaults. In a recent review of many different studies of domestic assaults, we reported that estimates of arrests as a proportion of police-citizen encounters varied between 3% and 21%, depending on department characteristics and the research instruments used (Buzawa & Buzawa, 1990).

Domestic violence arrests historically were also not closely related to the formal legal criteria that might justify such action. For example, some studies have shown little correlation between injury to the victim and arrests (Buzawa & Buzawa, 1990). Instead, several legally extraneous factors were important to arrest decisions. These centered on how the offender and victim related to the police. Roughly summarized, if the offender showed disrespect to the police and/or continued an assault while in the officer's presence, chance of arrest dramatically increased. In contrast, if the offender did not challenge the police, and the victim was perceived to be aggressive/confrontational, arrest was unlikely. Moreover, police officers superimposed their own value systems on victims. Hence, if the victim "caused" the violence by being unfaithful or still cohabiting with the abuser, arrests were far less frequent (Buzawa, Austin, Bannon, & Jackson, 1992). Finally, many departments considered victim preference for arrest a requirement. After all, she was in the best position to know the severity of injury and efficacy of available alternatives. Also, in practice, a successful prosecution was unlikely without her cooperation.

Although the above demonstrates the existence of many different arrest practices, it is clear that arrest has never been a customary outcome of a domestic call. This cannot be viewed as simply accidental, because there is a known victim and a specific offender, and, in many cases, injury is present or the violence acknowledged. Hence the bias against arrest must be conceded.

The real issue is, What does this bias signify? Does it simply validate that the police do not care about victims of domestic violence? Does it mean we must force them to adopt ever-stricter requirements demonstrating commitment to victims that is primarily measured by willingness to make arrests? Must a police department adopt a policy of mandatory arrest?

These questions are worthy of study, given the troubled history of police in this area. However, the answers may not be as clear-cut as arrest advocates would presume. To evaluate these questions, we should review the history of the push to increase arrest, describe the costs and benefits of arrest, and consider available alternatives within the larger context of evolving police practices.

The Push for More Arrest

The drive to increase arrest has been the result of an unusual confluence of political pressure to break with past practices, a series of lawsuits, widely publicized research allegedly demonstrating the deterrent value of arrest, and, less obviously, an overall shift to more punitive sanctions to "solve" social problems.

Political pressure to have the police make more arrests in domestic violence cases has arisen primarily from the efforts of feminists and battered women's advocates. For many years, they have urged legislatures to enact comprehensive solutions. Although efforts to develop and fund battered women's shelters were the immediate goal, it soon became apparent that systemic change in the delivery of victim services was essential. The entire system was seen as indifferent, but early efforts focused on the police. The failure of the police to make arrests was seen as a graphic demonstration to both offender and victim that her injury was not important to society. It was stated that the offender might even infer that further battering was somehow condoned (Edwards, 1989; Ferraro, 1989; Stanko, 1989).

This political pressure resulted in the passage of reform legislation throughout the country. This legislation virtually always included provisions removing impediments to arrest by eliminating the requirement that a police officer witness a misdemeanor assault prior to arrest. Other provisions often encouraged and even, in later statutes, mandated arrest when an officer found a domestic assault or a violation of the terms of a protective order.

Conceptually, this political effort might be viewed as part of a struggle to force society and its representative agents to redefine intimate violence in a manner that naturally led to criminalization and hence arrest. When battering was defined as a "domestic disturbance" (a common police category), the image was for the police to "quell" or stop the breach of peace and separate the mutual combatants (Saunders, 1988). Conversely, if police respond to situations of "wife abuse," the suggested image is one of stopping a crime, validating the rights of the battered woman victim to be free of violence, and punishing the offender. This image is obviously far more conducive to making arrests (Loseke, 1991; Saunders, 1988) and, in this context, the police failure to arrest is unjustifiable (Schechter, 1982; Smith, 1988).

Although this may seem mere imagery, the effect, perhaps intentional, of efforts to portray the conduct as one of battering women versus "domestic disturbances" or even domestic violence (the generic term we usually use) has been to increase the probability of formal criminal justice sanctions against the offender and, concomitantly, the use of arrests. In a similar manner, the recategorization of violence against minors from the generic category of "family troubles" to "child abuse" greatly contributed to criminal justice involvement by focusing on the criminal aspects of the conduct (Nelson, 1984). A similar effort to redefine and emphasize the criminal content of drunk driving has led to an emphasis on arrests and imposition of much tougher sentences in recent years.

Of equal importance in changing police practices has been a series of lawsuits filed against police departments since the late 1970s. Plaintiffs in several class action suits demanded and received consent orders decreeing that police would treat domestic assault as they would violence by a stranger. In addition, and perhaps equally important in encouraging change, a wave of individual lawsuits claimed that police performance failures harmed individual plaintiffs and constituted negligence and/or violated women's rights of equal protection. The multimillion-dollar verdict and later press and television coverage of the Tracey Thurman case (in which a woman was partially paralyzed as the result of a beating by her estranged husband, despite repeated calls to the Torrington, Connecticut, police department) did more to focus attention on the police than any political pressure group. Many departments were simply told by their administrators and municipal insurance companies to change past practices (Pleck, 1989). As a result, a clear and enforced policy demanding arrest became the preferred outcome.

Publicized research has been the final factor making arrest the de facto standard measuring police conduct. The 1981 Minneapolis Police Department study, published in 1984 by Lawrence Sherman and Richard Berk (as discussed more fully by Berk in Chapter 20 of this volume) "proved," at least in the popular literature, and for many federal, state, and local policymakers, that making an arrest was far more effective in deterring the future violence of an offender than mere separation or attempts by the police department to mediate conflict. This study, although labeled by the authors as tentative in nature, became the subject of an extraordinarily well-planned publicity campaign emphasizing arrest.

The Case Against Mandatory Arrest

Does Arrest Deter?

In the face of the mounting publicity, why are we troubled by the growing prominence of arrest as "the preferred or mandated response"? Professor Berk bases part of his argument on the deterrent value of arrest and concludes that we currently know that no other policy is a better deterrent than arrest. We acknowledge that research supports the theory that in some circumstances arrest deters certain specific offenders. The theory is simple, and compelling in its simplicity. Once an offender is punished by arrest or other sanction, the implicit threat of future punishment will be more credible, thus inhibiting further violence.

The rationale assumes the following: An arrest imposes punishment distinct from the formal sanctions imposed through sentencing (Williams & Hawkins, 1989); an offender understands the certainty of punishment; his conduct is not spontaneous (or irrational) so as to be amenable to deterrence; and he picks powerless victims, so that if a potential victim obtains "protection," violence will cease.

Unfortunately, empirical data fail to show much deterrent value for arrest. Review of the literature of general and specific deterrence for both adult and juvenile offenders is still unclear. Studies in the areas of drunk driving, burglary, traffic offenses, drug offenses, and corporate crime have all failed to link arrest with deterrence (Manning, 1993).

The domestic violence literature is also inconclusive as to the deterrent value of arrest. The original Minneapolis study did show a decline in repeat violence as measured by six-month recidivism data. However, the methodology and the validity of this admittedly "pilot" study have been severely, and we believe accurately, critiqued (Binder & Meeker, 1988).

Berk's statement in Chapter 20 that independent reanalyses of the Minneapolis data have confirmed the overall conclusions reported in Sherman and Berk (1984), and his accompanying note characterizing the Binder and Meeker "critique" as fundamentally uninformed and carrying "little weight with the scientific community" is highly questionable. First, Berk fails to cite any references substantiating that reanalyses of the original data have been published, or that these reanalyses support the original conclusions. Indeed, Binder and Meeker (1988) present a limited reanalysis based on the published data in Sherman and Berk's 1984 *American Sociological Review* article that argues that the original analysis did not support the conclusions made.

Second, we strongly disagree with Berk over the reception of the Binder and Meeker critique in "the scientific community." Binder and Meeker's (1988) work, along with a later article by Lempert (1989), is routinely cited as critiquing the Minneapolis experiment for validity problems owing to inadequate sample size, few officers generating most of the data, poor control over delivered treatments, and lack of generalizability of the findings (see Dutton, Hart, Kennedy, & Williams, 1992, p. 112; Hirschel & Hutchinson, 1992; Hirschel, Hutchinson, & Dean, 1992). Binder and Meeker (1988) have also been cited for pointing out that the Minneapolis experiment was promoted in ways unjustified by its limited results (see Goldstein, 1990, p. 172). Binder and Meeker's research concerns are shared by Sheptycki (1991a, 1991b), who notes three *major* deficiencies. First, 28% of the cases that make up the experimental sample came from three police officers. His conclusion is that the "effects" of arrest may be more the result of the unique distribution of arrest and the implicit inability to enforce experimental protocols than of any innate characteristics of the response. Second, the service community was far from representative. In Minneapolis, ethnic minorities constituted 43% of the victims and 55% of the suspects. The 60% unemployment rate for the experiment's suspects is compared with an unemployment rate of 5% in the general work force. As Sheptycki (1991a) observes, "This experiment seems to have targeted the underclass" (p. 120). Third, the Minneapolis study failed to standardize the other "treatments." Some officers may have attempted extensive mediation; others may have simply threatened the parties. Such divergent forms of mediation would naturally produce differential effects. Thus the construct validity of the experiment is questionable, because "the deterrence value of arrest is only relative to the deterrence value of the other treatments" (Sheptycki, 1991a, p. 120).

Others have cited Binder and Meeker (1988) and their analytic criticism of Sherman and Berk to justify their particular analytic strategies (see Dunford, 1992; Sherman et al., 1992, p. 153, n. 52). In fact, even Sherman, Berk's coauthor, routinely cites Binder and Meeker (1988) as critics of the Minneapolis experiment, along with Lempert (1989) (see Sherman, 1992a, 1992b, chap. 5; Sherman, Schmidt, Rogan, Gartin, & Cohn, 1991, p. 828, n. 2).

In response to methodological criticism, and as part of a campaign to promote "experimental research in social sciences," the National Institute of Justice improved the methodology and funded replication of the Minneapolis experiment in six additional jurisdictions (Atlanta, Georgia; Charlotte, North Carolina; Colorado Springs, Colorado; Metro Dade County [Miami], Florida; Omaha, Nebraska; and Milwaukee, Wisconsin). As Berk admits in his chapter, results from the replication studies simply do not broadly confirm the deterrent value of arrest.

The Omaha study did not initially report any significant differences between arrested and nonarrested offenders (Dunford, Huizinga, & Elliott, 1990). However, when a one-year follow-up of the victims was conducted, the frequency of repeat violence increased to approximately 25% of those arrested, compared with 5% of those who were not. Although differences were not statistically significant, researchers who conducted the replication study in Charlotte report that "advise and separate" as a police strategy appeared to correlate with less recidivism than either arrest or mediation (Hirschel, Hutchinson, Dean, Kelley, & Pesackis, 1990). Sherman (1992a) confirms that, in the separate Milwaukee replication study, arrest (at least when followed by relatively rapid release) resulted in *enhanced* violence. In fact, other studies have confirmed that any deterrent value of arrest alone was only short-term in nature (Dutton, 1987). Sherman (1992a) theorizes that this might occur among susceptible offenders as the result of anger engendered by arrest. In time, this may overpower the residual deterrent value of arrest, especially among those in the unemployed, urban population who might have little to lose by arrest. Sherman warns us, with perhaps some exaggeration, that such policies may disproportionally place inner-city black women in increased danger.

In any event, we believe that long-term counseling and other rehabilitation measures may ultimately prove more effective than arrest in deterring future violence. In stating this, we expressly disagree with Berk's conclusion that "all of the rehabilitation strategies tried in the replications of the Minneapolis Domestic Violence Experiment did *not* prove superior to arrest" (Chapter 20, this volume). First, when we refer to "treatment," we are not referring to 30-minute on-the-scene counseling by a patrol officer, but rather batterer treatment programs administered by trained counselors, psychologists, and social workers. Second, in Dade County, the one site where there was follow-up counseling by a trained "safe streets" unit, arrest *with* follow-up by the safe streets unit for rehabilitation was found to be more effective than other strategies. This may mean that arrest *itself* may not be effective but should be part of a coordinated intervention. If, in fact, treatment could be applied without the potentially negative consequences of arrest, then this ought to be explored. Finally, Berk's implicit standard that an alternative outcome must be *superior* to arrest or else arrest should be used does not strike us as appropriate.

In fact, although treatment is not always effective, it may still be appropriate for many offenders. The majority of offenders in the Minneapolis and replication studies had previous criminal histories; they are really not representative of all abusers. Further, many systems today, in incurring the costs of arrest, tend to ignore the victim's needs for counseling, protection, and support services and the offender's needs for rehabilitation. Naturally, an "ideal" would be a "budgetary feast" (Bardach, 1980) allowing all alternatives to be adopted at all times, but such conditions are unlikely as demands for police services continue to escalate despite declining budgets.

In any event, we believe that deterrence should not be the center-piece for a strategy of containing domestic violence. For many offend-ers, the violent outburst is an impulsive act, not controllable. In these cases, it is merely the continuation of a cycle of predictable events, starting with a basic propensity for violence, coupled with a limited repertoire of nonviolent communication skills, an often pathological relationship between victim and offender, and a particular catalyst sparking a violent eruption.

It is difficult to believe that the remote possibility of arrest will break this cycle. In virtually any realistic scenario, there is only a small possibility of arrest. The police are rarely called or dispatched; Kaufman Kantor and Straus (1990) estimate that only 6-7% of husband-wife assaults are even reported to the police. There is also an as-sumption that mandating a particular police response will result in compliance, but evidence demonstrates that many officers success-fully circumvent such policies (Ferraro, 1989; Stanko, 1989). Finally, the victim does not always prefer to press charges, and an officer (even in good faith) may not be able to make an arrest. The remote prospect of arrest may simply prove insufficient to prevent impulsive conduct.

Even if we assume that in certain cases rational "economic" calcula-tions may deter irrational behavior, it is unclear whether the most violent group of offenders would be affected. It may be a critical problem that hard-core abusers and those who have previously been arrested may not be deterred by the prospect of arrest (Ferraro, 1989). One must critically examine the "typical profile" of the service popu-lation of police. Research demonstrates that domestic violence occurs across economic classes, races, and rural and suburban areas as well as in our largest cities. However, most of these groups never call the police. Instead, the police are disproportionally called to scenes of violence among the urban poor. Many within this population have had exposure to the criminal justice system and/or have great antipathy toward the police. In earlier writings we have expressed concern that in communities known for poor police-community relations, it may be the case that we are not measuring the deterrent value of arrest but rather the policy's deterrence of calls to police by victims. Similar concerns have been expressed by Sheptycki (1991a, 1991b).

In a more cynical vein, Mama (1989) observes that special domestic violence units in England staffed by women police officers are re-stricted to high-minority areas that are already heavily policed. She suggests that such units may be more concerned with convicting black males than with addressing the needs of victimized women.

In any event, the replication studies suggest that groups who have been previously arrested may be those for whom arrest is least likely to be a deterrent and *most* likely to lead to increased future violence. For this reason, paradoxically, the deterrent value of arrest is likely to be most effective among those who need it the least—the situational deviant who batters only under extraordinary stress. Unfortunately, this is the type of individual for whom research indicates that *any* intervention would work—that is, treatment or even just police responding to a call and then leaving (Ford & Regoli, 1992). This type of individual may not be likely to batter again, if, when the police have been called, the victim has the *power* to have him arrested and the police are shown to follow victim arrest preference.

Troubling as well is the emphasis on deterrence for determining social policy. If a person has violent tendencies, that individual should be punished for crimes committed and then either rehabilitated or incapacitated via incarceration. Of these concepts, rehabilitation is clearly the most relevant long-term goal. If there is deterrence without rehabilitation, the offender may simply assault another victim. Rotation of victims is not a sound compelling basis for social policy.

Alternatively, we have seen no compelling argument that merely arresting, without long-term treatment, causes rehabilitation. An arrest, although temporarily incapacitating an offender, is typically followed by fast release. We grant that it is entirely appropriate that the criminal justice system promote rehabilitation when judges impose mandatory counseling as a sentence. However, an arrest does not necessarily mean that criminal prosecution will be successful or, if successful, result in imposition of a rehabilitation program. In fact, there is some doubt about the long-term success of court-mandated rehabilitation programs for batterers.

In any event, we are disturbed that the overemphasis upon deterrence as the justification for arrest may cause results unintended and unwanted, even by its proponents. Prior to the Minneapolis study, funding for "crisis intervention" efforts in police departments and shelters for victims of domestic violence had grown rapidly. Victims of domestic violence were often provided with services from state and local agencies. The funding for crisis intervention efforts had already crested prior to the Minneapolis study in response to political pressure, and funding for shelters began a substantial decrease thereafter. One can, of course, deride any likelihood of a causal relationship between these trends. They are, after all, not susceptible to rigorous "medical model" research. The changes may, in fact, be purely coincidental. In any event, empirical research is unlikely to reveal that policymakers consciously chose to starve domestic violence shelters to encourage arrests. Despite this, police administrators, in an atmosphere of scarce municipal and state funds, clearly justify their role in domestic violence (and implicitly divert money that might otherwise go to shelters) largely on the basis of the "fact" that arrests deter the violence prior to the need for shelter. Bardach (1980) calls this bureaucratic game "up for grabs," wherein any sudden influx of funds leads to political competition among agencies. The Minneapolis study, the news and entertainment media, and the federal government's campaign for deterrence merely gave the police the weaponry to fight such "turf wars" with social service agencies that might otherwise have been the natural recipients of the funds. In fact, Gelles (1993) suggests that there was a sudden shift in the steady increase of shelter funding following the release of reports on the Minneapolis Domestic Violence Experiment in 1984. Since that time, there has been a continual decrease in shelter support. This certainly is suggestive of the possibility that once arrest was seen as an "answer" to the problem of domestic violence, support of other options became expendable.

Finally, we believe that, legally and morally, it is not the role of the police to inflict punishment. Although here it might be for a "politically correct" cause—deterrence—this use of police sets a very dangerous precedent that may later be used to justify other "informal" police punishments—such as beating people stopped for traffic offenses who have verbally accosted an officer.

Victim Preferences Should Be the Preferred Response

The preferred feminist image is that the victim wants her rights validated and the offender punished. This process starts with a dramatic event: an arrest. The corollary is that the primary obstacle to this vision is the obstinate failure of the police to perform their sworn duty. Reality, however, is not as clearly defined. Studies have shown that many victims of domestic violence do not want arrest. (Black, 1980, estimates that only one in four desire arrest; Smith & Klein, 1984, estimate only one in five.)

In contrast, the desires of victimized women may be complex. Some desire only cessation of the violence—any other action is unwanted interference. Others desire that the police, as agents of the state, recognize their victimization. This does not necessarily equate to desire for arrest, but may mean only that they expect officers to demonstrate disapproval—perhaps by speaking sternly, making clear the victim's option to arrest, ensuring her safety, and threatening arrest upon reoccurrence. Still others desire that the police assist change in the balance of power in a relationship away from a crude measure of physical strength and violence to an emphasis on acceptable societal norms of conflict resolution. For that purpose, a warning may be sufficient. Finally, other victims may, despite violence, desire that the police act merely as mediators. For many of these scenarios, the victim may believe that arrest is inappropriate.

Treating all victimized women as a common group denigrates the real distinctions in this diverse group as well as commits the conceptual error of assuming that all batterers respond similarly to a given approach. This prevents the victim from using the criminal justice process to ensure her safety. In short, automatically assuming arrest as the preferred option forecloses an opportunity to empower victims by giving them control over the outcome of the police intervention.

We recognize that arguments have been proposed to justify the exclusion of victim preferences. When a bank is robbed or a person murdered, the criminal justice system attaches little weight to the victim's beliefs or relation to the offender. The crime itself is an acknowledged harm to society as well as to the particular victim. In addition, many advocates of battered women believe that battering may so traumatize a victim that she may be incapable of understanding her long-term interests or of judging the reality of the situation. If one believes that most victims fall into this category, mandatory arrest and other policies that expressly discount the decision-making role of the victim are justified (Lerman, 1981; Martin, 1978). Finally, some arrest advocates note that past poor performance by the police may have led victims to despair, realistically, that the police can ever effectively intervene. The use of mandatory arrest in this context might rest on a concept similar to that behind affirmative action: It is seen as a policy necessary to right previous wrongs perpetrated by the legal system.

Despite the cogency of the arguments presented by advocates of mandatory arrest, we believe that victim preference should be honored in the decision to arrest. Despite good intentions, a policy mandating arrest is ultimately very patronizing toward battered women. The premise is that we, a highly educated, politically liberal/radical elite, can best assess the interests of disempowered victims unable to judge their own needs accurately. Conceptually, this position is as offensive as the old "patriarchy," where legal rights were all given to the male, who, by virtue of his superior intellect and logic, knew what was best for "his" women. Even assuming that we believe this elitism to be proper, where do we draw the line? If a person's living arrangements are self-destructive, or include substance abuse, should society automatically intervene? The complete enforcement of legal rights for an individual who does not want to assert those rights and prefers a nonlegal alternative is an improper use of the legal system.

Second, mandatory arrest advocates ignore the complexity of why women may choose not to request arrest. A woman's experience may tell her that arrest is ineffective and that violence increases when the offender is freed. Although this may seem illogical, the recent replication studies suggest this *may* occur, especially in "high-risk" poor neighborhoods. Whether further research bears this out or not, we simply cannot discount that in many situations, a woman may legitimately believe that she is *more* at risk after arrest.

Furthermore, a victim may have many other collateral reasons for not desiring arrest. An arrest may affect her family financially by leading to loss of family income or by triggering parole or probation revocation. Such a policy may also discourage women from middle or upper social classes from seeking police assistance because of the social stigma of arrest. Many small communities publish arrest reports in the local newspapers, perhaps harming victims and their children more than the batterers.

In any event, there can also be little dispute that arrest does not, on balance, strengthen the relationship of the couple involved. We find it troubling that many victims' advocates presume to state categorically that this is unimportant because such a relationship is "obviously pathological." Many other societal programs are, after all, designed to salvage such relationships, by minimizing the pathology and rehabilitating the offending parties.

Past poor performance by the police may have effectively discouraged many women from seeking assistance. However, our experience in interviewing many battered women suggests that in most urban areas, few are now discouraged from calling the police because of poor police performance. In addition, the effect of previous years of not-so-benign neglect might be ameliorated by policies that emphasize law enforcement without necessarily stressing arrest.

It is of concern that the emphasis on arrest may not necessarily have sensitized police to victim needs. Instead, official policies favoring arrest may merely change overt manifestations of behavior for pragmatic organizational reasons. In the past, avoidance may have reflected organizational realities—fear of injury, dislike of social work, lack of organizational incentives, and so on. Pro-arrest policies may now be dictated by fear of liability, political pressure, or, unfortunately, overly publicized or politicized preliminary research. Although one may state that the reasons motivating an arrest are insignificant because only behavior is relevant, this ignores the reality of policing. Despite the existence of policies limiting officer discretion, rank-and-file officers have a long, if not proud, heritage of not following the "spirit" of laws and departmental edicts the goals of which they do not share. In this case, officers may not receive departmental orders, may simply not respond quickly, may refuse to find "probable cause" to make an arrest, or, alternatively, may arrest *both* victim and offender, as both may technically fit the requirements for mandatory arrest. The last of these may appear an unlikely exaggeration, but a review of the research reveals a disturbing increase in "dual arrests" in mandatory arrest jurisdictions, especially where a very high percentage of the women arrested had previously been classified as "victims." One can easily imagine an unsympathetic officer threatening to "run both parties in" unless a victim stops demanding an arrest. The police literature has consistently found that organizational and extralegal factors, rather than a desire to serve the public, in this case the victim, predominate in the decision to arrest.

Sheptycki's (1991b) analysis of innovations in the policing of domestic violence in London substantiates the fact that police often are more concerned with their own organizational needs and, in many cases, are no better at considering the needs of victims than they were when they carried out the traditional response. This is reiterated by Radford and Stanko (1991), who believe that the current response has completely negated feminist definitions, politics, research, and provision of support services in a way that may be appealing to white, middle-class women but really does not address the concerns of domestic violence victims.

The Costs of Arrest

The foregoing analysis naturally leads to the question of what the *unintended* costs of arrest might be; that is, what is the cost-benefit of the policy preferred by Berk? An effort to answer this question would be far beyond the scope of this chapter. However, we are concerned with the costs of arrest for victims in terms of disruption to them and their families in an economic and social unit (after all, arrest is not typically conducive to continued family life) and the potential for increased danger to the victim without appropriate and needed changes by the rest of the criminal justice system.

Victim preferences should be paramount, but the effect of a large number of domestic violence arrests upon the system should also be examined. Direct costs of a rigorously enforced arrest policy have not yet been estimated, but are likely to be very high. Sherman (1992b) estimates that, in the United States, police encounter 4 million acts of domestic violence annually (and, as previously explained, this is but a small fraction of the total number of such assaults). If the rate of arrest were to increase by 40-50%, significant police costs and human resources would need to be reallocated. It is precisely for this reason that many other cases that are not related to domestic violence do not result in arrest, despite the existence of probable cause.

In fact, some research has suggested that the rate of arrests in stranger assaults approximates that of "domestics" (Sherman, 1992a). There has yet to appear a single pro-arrest research monograph or advocacy paper that delineates the current police tasks that should be curtailed to make such an effort possible. In the light of shrinking police budgets, departments need to know how they can at the same time expend greater resources.

Indirect costs to the criminal justice system are also likely to occur. The emphasis in modern policing is the service-oriented "community policing" model. This term is generic, but its core is that the police should enlist the active support of their service community by being seen in "helping" roles, not focusing upon arrest. This is designed to rebuild trust between the poor and minority groups who often have had confrontations with the police. Instituting policies of wholesale arrests of these people, especially without victim support, contradicts this philosophy and obviously may set back police-community relations. Further, community policing has involved a policy of attempting to "demarket 911." Citizens are encouraged to call other agencies for a variety of nonemergency problems, in part for financial reasons. A massive effort to increase calls for misdemeanor domestic assault obviously gives the public a mixed message.

Supplements to Arrest

Given the costs of excessive use of arrest and its problematic value as a deterrent, perhaps we should consider alternatives. As noted earlier, the methodological conceit of deterrence researchers may have indirectly promoted the tragic diversion of funds from rehabilitation programs and shelters that otherwise might have dealt more effectively with the causes and effects of violence for many types of offenders.

Instead, many such alternatives have scarcely been tried in the rush to make arrest the cornerstone of policy. In this context, education and training should better sensitize criminal justice professionals to the varied needs of victims and their preferences. Such training should increase the likelihood that organizational guidelines could be developed and individual decisions be based on a compassionate awareness of victim needs and preferences, rather than dogmatic organizational and legal constraints. Thus training and education could be harnessed in an attempt to internalize norms and attain greater compliance with the goal of assisting the victim (Manning, 1993). This is certainly not an untried or undocumented suggestion. To date, police research examining interdepartmental variations has noted the role of a variety of organizational variables, including how changes in training and education, policies, organizational commitment, and political climate affect arrest practices independent of the proper use of arrest. (For a particularly insightful discussion of police organizational responses to domestic violence, see Manning, 1993.)

Second, we should try to follow the European approach of focusing on services for victims and offenders rather than giving primary attention to mechanistic enforcement of victims' "rights" (Maguire & Shapland, 1990). A growing trend in Europe is the "institutionalization of victim support" (van Dijk, 1988), whereby funding for volunteer services comes from the central government. Maguire and Shapland (1990) report that in 1986, Great Britain gave £9 million over a three-year period for victim support services; this "transformed the organization from top to bottom." Third, well-planned and properly funded rehabilitation programs (including substance abuse) may dramatically decrease the need for arrests.

We recognize that there is nothing inherently incompatible between an arrest focus and these alternative measures; however, the fact is that, typically, funding and training are maintained for only one effort. To the extent that our country pursues offender punishment beginning with a mechanistic use of arrest in cases where victims do not request arrest, we will detract from developing victim support and offender rehabilitation programs with far greater potential.

References

Bannon, J. (1974). *Social conflict assaults: Detroit, Michigan.* Unpublished report for the Detroit Police Department and the Police Foundation.

Bardach, E. (1980). *The implementation game: What happens after a bill becomes a law.* Cambridge: MIT Press.

Binder, A., & Meeker, J. (1988). Experiments as reforms. *Journal of Criminal Justice, 16,* 347-358.

Black, D. (1980). *The manners and customs of the police*. New York: Academic Press.

Buzawa, E. S., Austin, T., Bannon, J., & Jackson, J. (1992). The role of victim preference in determining police response to victims of domestic violence. In E. S. Buzawa & C. G. Buzawa (Eds.), *Domestic violence: The changing criminal justice response* (pp. 255-270). Westport, CT: Greenwood.

Buzawa, E. S., & Buzawa, C. G. (1979). Legislative responses to the problem of domestic violence in Michigan. *Wayne Law Review, 25*, 859-881.

Buzawa, E. S., & Buzawa, C. G. (1990). *Domestic violence: The criminal justice response*. Newbury Park, CA: Sage.

Dunford, F. W. (1992). The measurement of recidivism in cases of spouse assault. *Journal of Criminal Law and Criminology, 85*, 120-136.

Dunford, F. W., Huizinga, D., & Elliott, D. S. (1990). The role of arrest in domestic assault: The Omaha Police Experiment. *Criminology, 28*, 183-206.

Dutton, D. G. (1987). *The prediction of recidivism in a population of wife assaulters*. Paper presented at the Third International Family Violence Conference, Durham, NH.

Dutton, D. G., Hart, S. D., Kennedy, L. W., & Williams, K. R. (1992). Arrest and the reduction of repeat wife assault. In E. S. Buzawa & C. G. Buzawa (Eds.), *Domestic violence: The changing criminal justice response* (pp. 111-127). Westport, CT: Greenwood.

Edwards, S. (1989). *Policing domestic violence: Women, the law and the state*. London: Sage.

Ferraro, K. (1989). Policing women battering. *Social Problems, 36*, 61-74.

Ford, D., & Regoli, M. J. (1992). The preventive impacts of policies for prosecuting wife batterers. In E. S. Buzawa & C. G. Buzawa (Eds.), *Domestic violence: The changing criminal justice response* (pp. 181-208). Westport, CT: Greenwood.

Garner, J., & Clemmer, E. (1986). *Danger to police in domestic disturbances: A new look*. Washington, DC: U.S. Department of Justice, National Institute of Justice.

Gelles, R. J. (1993). Constraints against family violence: How well do they work? *American Behavioral Scientist, 36*, 575-586.

Goldstein, H. (1990). *Problem oriented policing*. Philadelphia: Temple University Press.

Hirschel, J. D., & Hutchinson, I. W., III. (1992). Female spouse abuse and the police response: The Charlotte, North Carolina experiment. *Journal of Criminal Law and Criminology, 83*, 73-119.

Hirschel, J. D., Hutchinson, I. W., III, & Dean, C. W. (1992). The failure of arrest to deter spouse abuse. *Journal of Research in Crime and Delinquency, 29*, 7-33.

Hirschel, J. D., Hutchinson, I. W., III, Dean, C. W., Kelley, J. J., & Pesackis, C. E. (1990). *Charlotte Spouse Assault Replication Project: Final report*. Unpublished manuscript, National Institute of Justice.

Kaufman Kantor, G., & Straus, M. A. (1990). Response of victims and the police to assaults on wives. In M. A. Straus & R. J. Gelles (Eds.), *Physical violence in American families: Risk factors and adaptations to violence in 8,145 families* (pp. 473-486). New Brunswick, NJ: Transaction.

Lempert, R. (1989). Humility is a virtue: On the publicization of policy-relevant research. *Law and Society Review, 23*, 145-161.

Lerman, L. (1981). *Prosecution of spouse abuse: Innovations in criminal justice response*. Washington, DC: Center for Women Policy Studies.

Loseke, D. R. (1991). Changing the boundaries of crime: The battered women's social movement and the definition of wife abuse as criminal activity. *Criminal Justice Review, 16*, 249-262.

Loving, N., & Quirk, M. (1982). Spouse abuse: The need for new law enforcement responses. *FBI Law Enforcement Bulletin, 51*(12), 10-16.

Maguire, M., & Shapland, J. (1990). The victim movement in Europe. In A. Lurigio, W. Skogan, & R. Davis (Eds.), *Victims of crime: Problems, policies, and programs* (pp. 205-225). Newbury Park, CA: Sage.

Mama, A. (1989). *The hidden struggle: Statutory and voluntary sector responses to violence against black women in the home.* London: London Race and Housing Research Group.

Manning, P. K. (1993). The preventive conceit: The black box in market context. *American Behavioral Scientist, 36,* 639-650.

Martin, D. (1978). Battered women: Society's problem. In J. R. Chapman & M. Gates (Eds.), *The victimization of women* (pp. 111-141). Beverly Hills, CA: Sage.

Martin, D. (1979). What keeps a woman captive in a violent relationship? The social context of battering. In D. M. Moore (Ed.), *Battered women* (pp. 33-57). Beverly Hills, CA: Sage.

Nelson, B. (1984). *Making an issue of child abuse: Political agenda setting for social problems.* Chicago: University of Chicago Press.

Pierce, G., & Deutsch, S. (in press). Do police actions and responses to domestic violence calls make a difference? A quasi-experimental analysis. *Journal of Quantitative Criminology.*

Pleck, E. (1989). Criminal approaches to family violence 1640-1980. In L. Ohlin & M. Tonry (Eds.), *Family violence* (pp. 19-58). Chicago: University of Chicago Press.

Radford, J., & Stanko, E. A. (1991). Violence against women and children: The contradictions of crime control under patriarchy. In K. Stenson & D. Cowell (Eds.), *The politics of crime control* (pp. 188-202). London: Sage.

Saunders, D. G. (1988). Wife abuse, husband abuse, or mutual combat? A feminist perspective on empirical findings. In K. Yllö & M. Bograd (Eds.), *Feminist perspectives on wife abuse* (pp. 90-113). Newbury Park, CA: Sage.

Schechter, S. (1982). *Women and male violence: The visions and struggles of the battered women's movement.* Boston: South End.

Sheptycki, J. W. E. (1991a). Innovations in the policing of domestic violence in London, England. *Policing and Society, 2,* 117-137.

Sheptycki, J. W. E. (1991b). Using the state to change society: The example of "domestic violence." *Journal of Human Justice, 3,* 47-66.

Sherman, L. W. (1992a). The influence of criminality on criminal law: Evaluating arrests for misdemeanor domestic violence. *Journal of Criminal Law and Criminology, 85,* 901-945.

Sherman, L. W. (1992b). *Policing domestic violence: Experiments and dilemmas.* New York: Free Press.

Sherman, L. W., & Berk, R. (1984). The specific deterrent effects of arrest for domestic assault. *American Sociological Review, 49,* 261-272.

Sherman, L. W., Schmidt, J., Rogan, D., Gartin, P., & Cohn, E. (1991). From initial deterrence to long-term escalation: Short custody for poverty ghetto domestic violence. *Criminology, 29,* 821-850.

Sherman, L. W., Schmidt, J., Rogan, D., Gartin, P., Cohn, E., Collins, D., & Bacich, A. (1992). The variable effects of arrest on criminal careers: The Milwaukee Domestic Violence Experiment. *Journal of Criminal Law and Criminology, 85,* 137-169.

Smith, B. (1988). Victims who know their assailants: Their satisfaction with the criminal court's response. In G. T. Hotaling, D. Finkelhor, J. Kirkpatrick, & M. A. Straus (Eds.), *Coping with family violence: Research and policy perspectives* (pp. 183-192). Beverly Hills, CA: Sage.

Smith, D., & Klein, J. (1984). Police control of interpersonal disputes. *Social Problems, 31,* 468-481.

Stanko, E. A. (1989). Missing the mark? Police battering. In J. Hanmer, J. Radford, & E. A. Stanko (Eds.), *Judge, lawyer, victim, thief: Women, gender roles and criminal justice* (pp. 46-69). Boston: Northeastern University Press.

Uchida, C., Brooks, L., & Koper, C. (1987). Danger to police during domestic encounters: Assaults on Baltimore County Police, 1984-86. *Criminal Justice Policy Review, 2,* 357-371.

van Dijk, J. J. (1988). Ideological trends within the victim movement: An international perspective. In M. Maguire & J. Pointing (Eds.), *Victims of crime: A new deal?* Milton Keynes: Open University Press.

Van Maanen, J. (1974). Working the street: A developmental view of police behavior. In H. Jacob (Ed.), *The potential for reform of criminal justice* (pp. 83-130). Beverly Hills, CA: Sage.

Williams, K., & Hawkins, R. (1989). The meaning of arrest for wife assault. *Criminology, 27,* 163-181.

CHAPTER 22

Conclusion
Social Problems, Social Policy, and Controversies on Family Violence

This volume has considered a few of the many controversies surrounding the behaviors we call family violence. Although we asked the contributors to highlight their disagreements, it is clear that the authors of these chapters nonetheless share basic key values: None of them argues that violence is a moral good, and each of them defines family violence—or whatever they call it—as an appropriate topic of public concern. Yet to emphasize agreements is to conjure an image of these contributors as one united group, a "family of family violence experts," so to speak, where members are engaged in a common enterprise and where mutual goals are shared. That image is misleading. The chapters in this volume have only touched upon the many conflicts among these persons, disagreements that often are deep, long-lasting, and resistant to change.

In our introduction, we argued that such controversies stem from the newness and complexity of our topic, from our divergent perspectives and agendas, from the practical consequences of what we say, from the moral dimension of our work, and from the combination of rationality and passion associated with our concerns. In this conclusion we will sort these general elements of controversy in a different way. Here we will offer speculations that three general disputes lead to multiple specific controversies such as those contained in this volume. First, there are conflicts arising from the dual definition of family violence as an academic problem to be studied and as a social problem to be eliminated. Second, members of the family of family violence experts approach our work from different theoretical and methodological perspectives that lead to specific controversies about preferred theoretical frameworks and appropriate methods of gathering and evaluating data. Third, we approach our work with different and often incompatible moral evaluations of what specific behaviors are unacceptable, which specific victims deserve our attention and concern, and what we should be willing to sacrifice in order to do something to stop violence and to help victims.

First, what type of a problem is family violence? Is it first and foremost an academic problem to be studied, or is it first and foremost a social problem to be resolved? A commonsense answer might well be that it is both. Academic study, after all, depends in part on social problem sensibilities: Why would we study these things that make up what we call family violence if they were not practically important? Indeed, there was no academic attention to or research on this topic until these behaviors emerged on the political scene, where social activists were defining them as unacceptable characteristics of family life. Funds for, and interest in, research would be reduced or perhaps eliminated if family violence were to disappear from the list of things Americans worry about. Just as certainly, efforts to do something about a social problem such as family violence must be based on knowledge: We cannot do anything about changing a condition unless we know how common it is, who is affected by it, and what its causes and consequences are. How would we know what we were trying to change unless we went out into the world and did research of some kind? How would we know the extent to which our social interventions are effective if we do not study them? Hence it makes good sense to argue that academic problems and social problems, science and practical action, must go together.

Many persons have argued that there is no inherent contradiction between research to study and efforts to lead social change. Indeed, many of the contributors to this volume use scientific research to support social change agendas. This blending of science and social action is characteristic of this topic, where it is common for academic research to serve as evidence in public social policy hearings, where it is common for academic researchers to talk with journalists and to appear on popular television programs. Yet it remains that it often is difficult to combine science and social action, because academic research and social problem advocacy can involve incompatible logic and goals.

Consider first the traditional image of science. The scientific world is one where researchers ask complex questions in order to understand complex realities; it is of a world of dispassionate, objective inquiry, where the "truth" of a finding does not depend on researchers' personal beliefs. Within the traditional image of the scientific world, the standards for evaluating the worth of studies are found in traditional rules of logic, scientific method, and data analysis. Although critics long have noted that science in practice is far different from science in theory, the underlying image of science is of dispassionate inquiry in the search of objective truth about how the world "is"—whether we personally agree with what we find or not.

Consider now the world of social problems advocacy. In everyday life, to label something a social problem is to take a moral and political stand: It is to argue that a given condition is morally intolerable and that it is the public's responsibility to do something about it. It is not easy to convince the public that family violence should be morally condemned and eliminated, because, whether one personally agrees with it or not, Americans have a tendency to tolerate some forms of violence by some people on some occasions. We have a tendency to be unsympathetic to all but the purest victims of violence; we are especially suspect of social interventions when they involve invading the sanctity of the American home, or when they threaten to disrupt traditional power relationships between parents and children, between men and women in general, or between husbands and wives in particular. Circumventing or transforming typical American attitudes about the acceptability of some violence by some people on some occasions can require more than logic and reason; encouraging the public to define violence as morally intolerable can require something other than the unemotional and impersonal language of science. This social problems world is not about "dispassionate inquiry," it is about passionate belief in the need for social change. The social problems world is not about the objective search for the "truth," it is about convincing a disbelieving public that change is necessary; it is about transforming the world that "is" into a world we would "like it to be."

It should not be surprising that although many of the authors in this volume attempt to merge scientific and social change agendas, the results are not always satisfying when viewed from the "opposing side." These chapters illustrate how some members of the family of family violence experts hold scientific rules and logic as the best, the final, and perhaps the only arbiters of the "truth." Such authors here talk about the importance of "further scientific studies"; they criticize counter views by saying that the evidence for those views rests on "biased samples," on "hope" rather than on "research," or on "advocacy research" rather than "scientific research." At the same time, others in this volume criticize the scientific rules and their negative consequences for efforts to encourage social change. Some authors complain that the "scientific skepticism" of an opposing side serves to "promote fear in public life"; others believe that calls for more scientific research serve to discredit efforts at social change. We see the relevancies of social action opposing those of science in the several complaints that the ways violence is measured "scientifically" obscure and hence misrepresent the meaning and complexity of violence in lived reality, and in opinions that the methods of science are insufficient or even inappropriate for examining violence and social interventions. Herein lies the seed of controversy: When the goals and methods of science are incompatible with those of social action, which do we privilege? The members of the family of family violence experts do not agree.

The first great divide among family violence experts stems from the dual definition of this violence as something to be studied and something to be changed. Although this controversy is often subtle in these chapters, the second divide is more explicit and apparent: Regardless of whether we are first and foremost interested in violence as an academic problem or as a social problem, we approach our work from different perspectives that are further fuel for specific controversies. Such differences sometimes are theoretical: Do we use the vocabulary, concepts, and questions closely associated with psychology, sociology, or feminism? Each theoretical framework is a lens that brings only some characteristics of the social world, and only some people, into the foreground; each necessarily relegates other characteristics and people to the blurry background. Which theoretical lens should we use? Should we add violence by women to our list of social problems, or is the only true social problem violence by men? Should we concern ourselves with the battered woman's syndrome or with women's social and political entrapment? Does alcohol directly affect our behavior, or is it our ideas about alcohol that affect behavior? The answers to such questions depend, in part, on which theoretical framework is used. Which theoretical lens should we use? Family violence experts do not agree.

Just as different theoretical frameworks lead us to ask different kinds of questions, different methodological perspectives lead to dissimilar ways of gathering and interpreting evidence. The methodological disagreements woven throughout these chapters illustrate that we do not agree on the best route to producing or evaluating evidence. The present state of knowledge about a particular problem is uncritically accepted by one side, while at the same time the other side criticizes this knowledge for its limitations or errors. At times, one side focuses on the importance of "scientific rigor" and the opposing side questions the presence or even the applicability of such rigor. A given set of statistics can be presented as demonstrating pure facts, but the same statistics can be condemned as an arbitrarily constructed fantasy. Indeed, what constitutes evidence for some does not constitute evidence for others. What methodology is best? As the chapters in this volume illustrate, experts do not agree.

The dual nature of our topic matter and our theoretical and methodological differences are the first two divisions creating controversies. The third divide is more complex and subtle, and it often escapes notice. Choosing a specific focus for concern, study, and social intervention involves moral evaluations, three of which are illustrated in these chapters. First, which specific behaviors should be the center of our study and concern? Clearly and most certainly, none of these authors says that we need more violence in our world, none argues that any use of violence is preferable to no violence. Yet it remains that these spokespersons offer very different answers to questions about how we should define the behaviors of interest. Such decisions are inherently moral because by attending to some types of violence we leave others unexamined. Are we interested in "all" violence or only "extreme" violence? What specific behaviors should we condemn as those of "rape"? What specific behaviors are those of "elder abuse"? Are "psychologically unavailable" mothers guilty of child abuse? Our choices might well be consequential in the world of practical action, where the public tends to accept—or at least to tolerate—some forms of violence. If we focus only on studying and morally condemning extreme cases of violence, do we unintentionally condone violence that is not so extreme? Does attention only to extreme violence allow Americans to ignore how the routine and tolerated violence in our daily lives might well serve as a foundation for the extreme violence we deplore? Perhaps then we should focus on all violence in all forms. But if we do this, will we unintentionally undermine the seriousness of extreme cases of violence? If we define violence broadly to include behaviors that are statistically common and often defined as "tolerable," do we unintentionally lose public support? On what types of violence should we focus? We do not agree.

There is a second moral decision: Which specific people deserve our attention and concern? Are we interested in the behaviors of violence regardless of who does them and to whom? Or do we narrow our attention to particular classes of victims who are typically the most vulnerable to violence? And how do we define a "victim" of violence—by the experience itself, by the consequences, or by the victim's understanding and labeling of the experience? Such decisions are moral because when we choose to focus on some people, we are necessarily leaving the experiences of others unexamined. Who needs our attention? As this volume clearly illustrates, family violence experts do not agree.

The chapters concerning controversies on social interventions show a third type of moral decision: How much intrusive intervention into American homes is justified in order to stop violence and help victims? What is the proper balance among the rights of individuals, families, victims, and the public in general? What should we be willing to sacrifice in order to stop violence? The answers to such questions might—and should—include objective assessments of the costs and benefits to more or less intervention, to more or fewer rights of particular kinds. But the answers to such questions also will—and should—reflect our moral judgments about the power and the purposes of government authorities, the value of privacy in the home, and the proper balance of individual, family, and social rights. What rights should we expand, which should we preserve, which should we be willing to reduce in order to do something about this violence? Family violence experts do not agree.

Such are a few of the many general seeds of specific controversies. We offer them to stimulate reflection, but it also should be clear that we have offered them in a particular way. Our discussion has followed the rules of academic discourse: We have tried to be logical and evenhanded; we have not declared any one viewpoint as the "best." As such, our editors' comments throughout this volume have lacked a critical element of these controversies—passion. Furthermore, we will now admit to our readers that we did editorial work of a particular sort on some of the chapters in this volume. Through our editing, we sanitized some chapters, stripping them of caustic, scathing, libelous, sarcastic, and personalistic criticisms. In so doing, we removed the moral rage that illustrates the passion that can accompany controversy.

True, we wanted to encourage debate by showing readers some of the disagreements surrounding family violence. True, in our introduction to this volume we called these controversies "professional dirty laundry" because they show what professional groups of all types do not want their publics to know: We do not always agree. Nonetheless, we chose to wash the dirtiest of this laundry before we hung it in these pages for family outsiders to see. We will end our discussion with an apology about the consequences of our editorial decisions as well as our justification for them.

Without our editing, or with different editing, some of these chapters would have contained much stronger language about why the "other side" should not be supported, why the proponents of an opposing view are simply ignorant, or how proponents of an opposing side should not be trusted because what they say in these pages disguises an underlying and evil intent. Such language would have better illustrated the passion associated with this topic. Our apology is that where our editing erased the impassioned and intense objections to opposing sides, we implicitly promoted the value of scientific objectivity while we implicitly denied the prevalence and importance of passionate belief. Yet, most clearly, such sanitizing denies a common connection between beliefs: To the extent that we have strong feelings that our side is morally right, we have equally strong feelings about the extent to which the other side is morally wrong. Controversies can be more than a dispassionate disagreement about facts.

Although we apologize for privileging the dispassionate discourses of science at the expense of the passionate discourses of social problem advocacy, we would like to note that we did so for two practical reasons. The first concerns the consequences of extreme controversy for the possibility of producing new knowledge. As several of our contributors note, we know woefully little about the causes of violence, and we know even less about what works to stop it. We need to learn more, and caustic, irrational, and personalistic attacks lead us to ignore one another. Whenever we approach our work with the a priori attitude that another set of arguments need not be seriously considered, whenever we glibly dismiss others' viewpoints, we do not debate and we do not learn. In such instances, we stand on our own moral mountains and fling epithets at those standing on their moral mountains; we ignore others because they are "merely politically correct," or because they are "politically incorrect"; we dismiss others' work as "not science" or as "blinker-eyed empiricism." Nothing comes of this. When there is too much controversy, when controversy becomes attached to people rather than to ideas, we run the risk of insulating ourselves from others concerned with similar issues. In the end, we are alone in our small groups of like-minded others. Although these others might give us support and encouragement, we can learn little, because we speak only to ourselves. Too much controversy hinders the chance of increasing our knowledge; we cannot afford this when so little is known about so important a topic.

There is a second reason extreme controversy is destructive rather than constructive. Regardless of whether individual spokespersons identify themselves as scientists or social activists, regardless of theoretical or methodological perspectives, regardless of particular moral reasoning, family violence is a political problem. Whatever we say about this particular topic can be—and often is— politicized; regardless of our intentions, our comments enter public debate. We chose to sanitize some of the debates in this volume because we personally believe that when controversies are informed primarily by emotion, to the exclusion of logic, and when they become personalistic attacks, they hinder the chances of achievement of social action goals.

The arguments in this volume have demonstrated that disagreements often are subtle and most often are complex; the reasoned, detailed, and comprehensive debates presented here allow readers to make their own informed decisions. Yet the world of practical action does not often encourage or even allow attention to subtlety, complexity, or detail. Furthermore, although there is much upon which the authors of these chapters agree, agreements are ignored in the public sphere and disagreements are emphasized and often amplified. Within this public world, where social members expect "experts" to present a united front of agreement, too much controversy can reduce public trust. Why should members of the public trust what we say if we are so adamant about not trusting one another? If we present ourselves as zealots for one or another side, or if we challenge the moral character rather than the reasoning of the proponents of the other side, public trust will erode further. Hence, because family violence is a political problem, too much controversy can lead to insulation from the public. In such cases, others will be more powerful in effecting the shape of social change—or perhaps social change simply will not happen. Too much controversy, too much moral zeal, can be destructive to our shared goal of effecting social change.

These concluding comments have focused on how too *much* controversy can lead to too *little* controversy as opposing camps insulate themselves from opposing views. Too much controversy therefore is destructive rather than constructive; it can be counterproductive to achieving agendas for research and social change. It is important here to note that such disagreements among professional groups are common. Whenever a professional group is composed of persons who seek to study and persons who seek to change, whenever a group draws attention from a wide variety of professional interests, whenever the topic is political, there will be these tendencies for high controversy that spills out into the public; there will be tendencies toward professional fragmentation and insulation. We could, therefore, just as easily make similar comments about the family of experts on homelessness, the family of experts on education, the family of experts on drug abuse, crime, gun control, and so on. Although it is important to understand that extreme disagreements characterize many, if not most, professional groups and that the causes of controversy are social rather than individual, that does not reduce the negative consequences of too much moral zeal.

Do we believe that members of the family of family violence experts can become one big happy family characterized by solidarity, assistance, and trust? We think it unlikely. Do we believe that our simple call here to "talk about it" will resolve controversies? No. The complexity of the topic and the number and depth of controversies make it improbable that we will cooperatively reach a shared vision of the best theoretical perspectives, definition of the problems, understanding of causes, and routes to social change. Nonetheless, we must encourage discussion because it is better to engage in debate than to have controversies resolved on the basis of which side can muster the most political power. We must encourage discussion, because the alternatives of divisiveness, animosity, and isolation lead to no political, moral, or social good.

We have no choice but to examine and attempt to resolve controversies such as those aired in this volume, for it is not possible to make a simple intellectual claim that all the chapters in this book are correct, because each speaks to different aspects of a complex and multidimensional reality of violence. Some perspectives and some agendas for social change are simply incompatible. Nor is it feasible to make a claim that we should take seriously all forms of violence by all persons and that we should give our attention and support to all possible social interventions. At least in the foreseeable future, such conclusions are doomed to remain in the musty pages of academic journals and in the limited confines of professional discourse. Although we might like it to be otherwise, we live in a world of limited attention and resources. We cannot and will not do it all. As several of the contributors to this volume note, when one side "wins" it typically does not win an addition to existing public sympathy or resources. Most commonly, when one side wins, another loses, as resources and sympathy are transferred from one group to another, from one social intervention to another. In the future some—and only some—research will be funded; some—and only some—social interventions will find support. In the future, some sides will win, others will lose. Our choice is whether this will happen through debate or through the exercise of sheer political power.

We again thank the contributors to this volume for showing that debate is possible, and we hope our comments and speculations will encourage readers to examine further how particular controversies might be surrogates for underlying, often vaguely articulated, disagreements. Yet, although we have called for debate, we also believe that it will be difficult to resolve such underlying disagreements, because they are mirrors of general controversies within the modern-day United States. That is, it should not be surprising that family violence experts do not agree on what types of violence warrant attention and concern, because Americans in general do not agree. It should be expected that these experts would disagree about who should be the focus of attention and concern, because these varying viewpoints are shared by members of the public. Given that Americans in general do not agree about the compromises we should make in order to do something about violence—or any other social problem—it is not surprising that these experts likewise disagree. Such professional disputes, in other words, echo cultural controversies. As such, the debates in this volume are seeded by the features of our society. They are about Americans' failures to agree about the characteristics of the United States as it is; they are about Americans' failures to agree on what a good society should be.

Author Index

Subject Index

Abuse:
definitions of, 188-190
measuring, 190-191
Abused children, xii
as alcoholic adults
inappropriate reporting as danger to,
265-266
Abused elderly, xii
as dependent on caregivers, 222-235
distinct populations of, 234-235
intervention for, 234
with Alzheimer's disease, 234
Ackerman Institute, 57
Acquaintance rape:
definition of, 105
Advocacy research:
and overstatement of incidence of
date rape, 120-131
dysfunctional consequences of, 129-
131
implications for women, 130
into sexual aggression, 115
Alcohol use:
and arguments against disinhibition
theory and violence, 183-186
and timing of abusive events, 176
as associated with violence, 182-194
as causal agent of violence, 171-179
as destructive to individual growth
and family structure, 177, 178
as disinhibitor of social control, 177,
178
as instigator of violence, 177-178
as rationalization for violence, 177,
178
associated with child abuse, 175, 176,
177
associated with incest, 176
associated with physical abuse, 176

associated with spouse battering, 175
definition of, 191-192
in alteration of brain functioning, 177,
178
American Bar Association, National
Legal Resource Center for Child
Advocacy and Protection of, 257
American Enterprise Institute, 257-271
American Medical Association, 8
American Public Welfare Association
(APWA), 257
American Psychiatric Association, 11, 18,
137
Antisocial personality disorder, 215
Arrest, mandatory:
and spousal violence, 323-334
as deterrent, 342-348
as "magic bullet," 337
bias against, 339-340
case against, 342-352
costs of, 351-352
historical context of, 338-339
inconclusive scientific evidence on
spousal violence and, 337-353
Milwaukee Police Department experiment on, 330, 333, 345
Minneapolis Domestic Violence
experiment on, 329, 333, 334, 338,
342, 343, 344, 345, 347, 348
push for more, 340-342
scientific evidence on spousal violence and, 324-332
supplements to, 352-353
Tracey Thurman case and, 342
victim preference for or against, 348-
351
Assault:
context and meaning of, 78
definition of, 68

378

About the Authors

Richard A. Berk is a Professor in the Department of Sociology at the University of California, Los Angeles, in UCLA's Interdivisional Program in Statistics. He is also Director of the UCLA Center for the Study of the Environment and Society. His interests include applied social research and applied statistics, and his recent work includes research projects on the role of chance in death penalty cases, the use of community service as a part of probation sentence, factors affecting water conservation in households, and public perceptions of global warming. He is a former member of the Board of Directors of the Social Science Research Council, former Chair of the Methodology Section of the American Sociological Association, and an elected Fellow of the American Association for the Advancement of Science.

Douglas J. Besharov, a lawyer and a resident scholar at the American Enterprise Institute for Public Policy Research in Washington, D.C., was the first Director of the U.S. National Center on Child Abuse and Neglect, from 1975 to 1979. He is an Adjunct Professor at Georgetown University Law School and a Visiting Professor at the University of Maryland's School of Public Affairs. His most recent book is *Recognizing Child Abuse: A Guide for the Concerned.*

Lee H. Bowker is a sociologist and criminologist whose specialties include the victimization of women, prisoner subcultures, and the predatory personalities that typify members of certain groups of men. His approach to research problems fuses elements of feminism, humanism, and quantitative analysis. He is the author of 16 books and monographs, including *Women, Crime and the Criminal Justice System, Beating Wife-Beating, Ending the Violence,* and *Women and Crime in America.* He is currently Professor of Sociology and Dean of the College of Behavioral and Social Sciences at Humboldt State University, a unit of the California State University System.

He also serves as an expert witness in child custody, assault, and homicide cases that have grown out of situations involving woman battering.

Carl G. Buzawa is an Adjunct Professor of Criminal Justice at the University of Massachusetts—Lowell and an attorney in private practice. He received his B.A. from the University of Rochester, his M.A. from the University of Michigan, and his J.D. from Harvard Law School. He is the coauthor of two books and numerous chapters and articles in the area of the criminal justice response to domestic violence.

Eve S. Buzawa is Professor of Criminal Justice at the University of Massachusetts—Lowell. She is coauthor of two books on the criminal justice response to domestic violence and numerous chapters and articles. She is Past President of the Northeast Association of Criminal Justice Sciences and a current board member for the Academy of Criminal Justice Sciences. Currently, she is serving as series editor for the forthcoming Sage book series Gender and Crime, for which she is authoring a volume titled *Women as Victims*.

Sarah L. Cook is a doctoral candidate in community psychology at the University of Virginia in Charlottesville. Her involvement in campus antirape activities, including prevention and education programming, dates to her undergraduate years. She has organized a group of graduate students who are working cooperatively to accomplish dissertation research on the subject of sexual assault.

Byron Egeland is the Irving B. Harris Professor of Child Development at the University of Minnesota. He is the Principal Investigator of the Mother-Child Project, a 17-year longitudinal study of high-risk children and their families, and Project STEEP, an intervention program for high-risk mothers and their infants. He is a Fellow in the American Psychological Association and the American Psychological Society and has served on a number of national committees in the area of child abuse.

David Finkelhor is Co-Director of the Family Research Laboratory and the Family Violence Research Program at the University of New Hampshire. His latest publications include *Sourcebook on Child Sexual Abuse* (Sage, 1986), a widely used compilation of research on the subject of sexual abuse, and *Nursery Crimes* (Sage, 1988) a study of sexual abuse in day care. He has been studying the problem of family violence since 1977, and has published three other books—*Stopping Family Violence* (Sage, 1988), *License to Rape* (Free Press, 1984), and *Child Sexual Abuse: New Theory and Research* (Free Press, 1984)—and more than two dozen articles on the subject. He is coeditor of *The Dark Side of Families: Current Family Violence Research* (Sage, 1983), *Coping With Family Violence: New Research* (Sage, 1988), and *New Directions in Family Violence and Abuse Research* (Sage, 1988) and the recipient of grants from the National Institute of Mental Health and the National Center on Child Abuse and Neglect.

Jerry P. Flanzer (D.S.W., University of Southern California, 1973) is known for his work on alcoholism and family conflict as a clinician, program consultant, and researcher. He has published extensively and served as a Professor of Social Work at the University of Wisconsin, University of Arkansas, Catholic University of America, and Virginia Commonwealth University before opening Recovery and Family Treatment, Inc., providing individual, group, and family services and professional training in Alexandria, Virginia.

Richard J. Gelles is Professor of Sociology and Psychology and the Director of the Family Violence Research Program at the University of Rhode Island. He received his A.B. degree from Bates College (1968), an M.A. in sociology from the University of Rochester (1971), and a Ph.D. in sociology from the University of New Hampshire (1973). He is the author or coauthor of 16 books and more than 100 articles and chapters on family violence. His most recent books are *Physical Violence in American Families: Risk Factors and Adaptations in 8,145 Families* (Transaction, 1990), *Intimate Violence in Families* (Sage, 1990), and *Sociology: An Introduction* (4th edition, McGraw-Hill, 1991). He received the Outstanding Contributions to Teaching Award from the American Sociological Association, Section on Undergraduate Education, in 1979.

Neil Gilbert is Chernin Professor of Social Welfare at the University of California at Berkeley and Co-Director of the Family Welfare Research Group. He has served twice as a Fulbright Fellow studying European social policy and was awarded the University of Pittsburgh Bicentennial Medallion of Distinction. His numerous publications include 14 books and many articles that have appeared in the *Wall Street Journal, The Public Interest, Society,* and leading academic journals.

Jeffrey J. Haugaard is Assistant Professor in the Department of Human Development and Family Studies at Cornell University. A 1990 University of Virginia Ph.D. in clinical psychology, he is Chair of the Working Group on Implications for Education and Training of Child Abuse and Neglect Issues of the American Psychological Association, author of several professional articles and papers on child maltreatment, and coauthor, with N. Dickon Reppucci, of *The Sexual Abuse of Children: A Comprehensive Guide to Current Knowledge and Intervention Strategies* (Jossey-Bass, 1988).

Joan Kaufman, Ph.D., is Assistant Professor at the University of Pittsburgh. Her research interests focus on conducting multidisciplinary studies of the sequelae and intergenerational transmission of abuse. She is currently funded by the National Institute of Mental Health to study depressive disorders in maltreated children. The aim of this study is to determine if depressed children with histories of abuse form a distinct subgroup of childhood depressives with unique clinical, familial, and psychological correlates.

Mary P. Koss is Professor of Family and Community Medicine, Psychiatry and Psychology at the University of Arizona in Tucson. A national survey of college students she conducted is the subject of the 1988 book by Robin Warshaw, *I Never Called It Rape.* She is coauthor, with Dr. Mary Harvey, of *The Rape Victim: Clinical and Community Interventions.* She has testified on the measurement of rape prevalence before the U.S. Senate Committee on the Judiciary and on treatment of rape victims before the U.S. Senate Committee on Veteran's Affairs. She is Co-Chair of the American Psychological Association's Task Force on Violence Against Women, and a member of the National Institute of Mental Health Working Group on Violence. She is the recipient of the 1989 Stephen Schaafer Award for Outstanding Research Contributions to the Victim's Assistance Field given by the National Organization for Victim's Assistance and of the 1992 Safe Schools Coalition Award for Outstanding Empirical Contributions.

Demie Kurz is Co-Director of Women's Studies and has an appointment in the Sociology Department at the University of Pennsylvania. She writes on issues of gender and the family, including issues of domestic violence. She has been a member of the Philadelphia Task Force on Domestic Violence and other commissions working to increase the responsiveness of major institutions to domestic violence, particularly the health care system.

Donileen R. Loseke received her Ph.D. from the University of California, Santa Barbara. She is currently an Associate Professor of Sociology and a member of the Women's Studies teaching faculty at Skidmore College in Saratoga Springs, New York. Her published works focusing on social services for battered woman have appeared in *Social Problems, Journal of Contemporary Ethnography,* and *Symbolic Interaction.* She is the author of *The Battered Woman and Shelters: The Social Construction of Wife Abuse* (State University of New York Press).

K. Daniel O'Leary is Distinguished Professor of Psychology at the University at Stony Brook. He has received the Distinguished Scientist Award from the Clinical Psychology Division of the American Psychological Association, and he holds a National Institute of Mental Health training grant for pre- and postdoctoral fellows who study spouse abuse.

Karl Pillemer is Associate Professor of Human Development and Family Studies at Cornell University. His major research interests lie in the family relationships of the elderly, with a particular focus on the topic of troubled family relations and their effects on the older persons. Among his current research projects are a federally funded longitudinal study of family caregivers to Alzheimer's disease victims and a national evaluation of model elder abuse intervention projects.

Carol A. Plummer, M.S.W., C.S.W., was one of the earliest proponents of child sexual abuse prevention, beginning her prevention work in 1979. She is co-founder and a board member of the Association for Sexual Abuse Prevention, a membership organization of those committed to prevention work. She is author of *Preventing Sexual Abuse: Activities and Strategies for Those Working With Children and Adolescents* (Learning Publications, 1984) as well as numerous articles on sexual abuse prevention. She has trained nationally and internationally on sexual abuse and strategies for prevention, and has helped to organize three national conferences on sexual abuse prevention. She is also a therapist in private practice in Michigan and serves frequently as an expert witness in abuse cases. She is currently working on a second edition of her book.

N. Dickon Reppucci is Professor and Director of Graduate Studies in the Psychology Department at the University of Virginia, Charlottesville. A 1968 Harvard Ph.D. in clinical psychology, he is a Fellow of the American Psychological Association and the American Psychological Society, Associate Editor of *Law and Human Behavior*, Past President of APA's Division 27 (Community Psychology), and the author of more than 100 books, professional articles, and book chapters. He is coauthor, with Jeffrey J. Haugaard, of *The Sexual Abuse of Children: A Comprehensive Guide to Current Knowledge and Intervention Strategies* (Jossey-Bass, 1988).

Suzanne K. Steinmetz, Ph.D., is Professor and Chair of Sociology and Director of the Family Research Institute at Indiana University, Indianapolis. She received her doctorate in sociology at Case Western Reserve University in 1975 and is currently pursuing clinical training through a master's degree in social work. She is the author of *Cycle of Violence: Assertive, Aggressive and Abusive Family Interaction* (1977) and *Duty Bound: Elder Abuse and Family Care* (1988); coauthor of *Marriage and Family Realities* (1990); coeditor of *Violence in the Family* (1974), *Handbook of Marriage and the Family* (1987), *Sourcebook of Family Theories and Methods: A Contextual Approach* (1993), and *Family and Support Systems Throughout the Life Span* (1988); and author or coauthor of more than 70 additional publications. She is currently working on a volume titled *Handbook of Families at Risk*. Her research has focused on all aspects of family violence; most recently, she has focused her concern on adolescents at risk.

Murray A. Straus is Professor of Sociology and Co-Director of the Family Research Laboratory at the University of New Hampshire. He has served as President of the National Council on Family Relations (1972-73), the Society for the Study of Social Problems (1988-89), and the Eastern Sociological Society (1990-91). He was given the Ernest W. Burgess Award of the National Council on Family Relations for outstanding research on the family in 1977. He is the author or coauthor of more than 150 articles and 15 books, including the *Handbook of Family Measurement Techniques* (3rd edition, 1990), *Four Theories of Rape in the American Society* (1989), and *Physical Violence in American Families* (with Richard J. Gelles, 1990).

Lenore E. A. Walker, Ed.D., is a licensed psychologist in independent practice with Walker & Associates in Denver, Colorado, and Executive Director of the Domestic Violence Institute. A diplomate in clinical psychology from the American Board of Professional Psychology, she has pioneered the introduction of expert witness testimony on "battered woman self-defense" in U.S. courts. Her research on the psychological effects of battering on women and the dynamics of the battering relationship began in the 1970s with research funded by the National Institute of Mental Health. She is an international lecturer who provides training at the invitation of governments, private groups, and worldwide health organizations. Her psychology interests have concentrated on women's mental health issues and on stopping all forms of violence against women and children. She has published more than 50 articles and book chapters on these topics, as well as nine books, including *The Battered Woman* (1979), *Women and Mental Health Policy* (1984), *The Battered Woman Syndrome* (1984), *Feminist Psychotherapies* (with M. A. Dutton, 1988), *Handbook on Sexually Abused Children* (1988), and *Terrifying Love: Why Battered Women Kill and How Society Responds* (1989).

Kersti A. Yllö is Professor of Sociology at Wheaton College, where she is also Coordinator of Women's Studies. She received her Ph.D. from the University of New Hampshire. She has held Research Fellowships at the University of New Hampshire's Family Violence Research Program and at the Family Development Clinic at Boston Children's Hospital. Her publications on domestic violence include *License to Rape* (with D. Finkelhor) and *Feminist Perspectives on Wife Abuse* (with M. Bograd).

Edward Zigler is Sterling Professor of Psychology, Head of the Psychology Section of the Child Study Center, and Director of the Bush Center in Child Development and Social Policy at Yale University. He is author, coauthor, or editor of numerous scholarly publications and has conducted extensive investigations on topics related to normal child development as well as psychopathology and mental retardation. He is also well known for his role in the shaping of national policies for children and families. He regularly testifies as an expert witness before congressional committees, and has served as a consultant to a number of cabinet-rank officers. He was one of the planners of Project Head Start. Between 1970 and 1972, he served as the first director of the Office of Child Development (now the Administration for Children, Youth and Families) and as chief of the U.S. Children's Bureau. His many honors include awards from the Department of Health, Education and Welfare, the American Academy of Pediatrics, the Society for Research in Child Development, the American Academy of Child and Adolescent Psychiatry, and the American Academy on Mental Retardation.